Additional Praise for
*Analyzing Intelligence: National Security
Practitioners' Perspectives, Second Edition*

"An indispensable guide to one of the most critical issues affecting intelligence and policymaking in the twenty-first century, successfully combining the lessons to be drawn from both first-hand experience and academic research."

—**Christopher Andrew**, faculty of history, Corpus Christi College, University of Cambridge, and author of *Defend the Realm: The Authorized History of MI5*

"Roger George and James Bruce have produced, in this new edition of their classic volume, the best source for wisdom on modern intelligence analysis. With important contributions from superstars in the US profession, this new edition is a landmark signifying professionalization of the intelligence enterprise. It deserves a place on every serious student and practitioner's bookshelf."

—**Jennifer Sims**, senior fellow at the Chicago Council on Global Affairs, former deputy assistant secretary of state for intelligence coordination, and coeditor of *Vaults, Mirrors, and Masks: Rediscovering US Counterintelligence*

Praise for the first edition of *Analyzing Intelligence*

"*Analyzing Intelligence* is the most comprehensive book on the subject to date—a really valuable treatment for those anticipating becoming an intelligence analyst, as well as for those who already are."

—*Studies in Intelligence*

"[A] practical and wide-ranging study of intelligence analysis. The editors have done a superb job of seamlessly editing the work of a number of the world's recognized experts of intelligence gathering and analysis. Of special interest to readers should be those chapters related to the relationship between analysts and national-level security and policymakers. This book will be an invaluable resource for future analysts and those professionals currently involved in overcoming the enduring challenges associated with the role of intelligence in a free society."

—*Parameters*

"Law and policy recognize that intelligence is the strategic pivot of the current fight [against terrorism], so readers of *Proceedings* who seek a deeper understanding of how we might wage war more effectively should put *Analyzing Intelligence* at the top of their reading list."

—Naval Institute *Proceedings*

"The editors, Roger George and James Bruce, themselves respected career intelligence analysis, have assembled a compendium of essays by leading lights of the US intelligence community, essays that examine the history, efficacy, pitfalls, and achievements of US intelligence analysis roughly from World War II to the present. They also make a number of recommendations for improving analysis, thereby reducing the likelihood of 'intelligence failures' that have so frequently been in the media spotlight over the past several years. . . . Call it Ivory Tower meets James Bond . . . [it is] worth the read for those concerned with effectively 'connecting the dots' ahead of the next crisis on the horizon."

—*Naval War College Review*

Analyzing
Intelligence

Analyzing Intelligence

National Security Practitioners' Perspectives

SECOND EDITION

Roger Z. George and
James B. Bruce, Editors

*In Cooperation with the Center for Security Studies,
with support from the George T. Kalaris Fund for Intelligence Studies,
Edmund A. Walsh School of Foreign Service, Georgetown University*

Georgetown University Press
Washington, DC

Library of Congress Cataloging-in-Publication Data

Analyzing intelligence : national security practitioners' perspectives / Roger Z. George, James B. Bruce, editors ; in Cooperation with the Center for Security Studies, Edmund A. Walsh School of Foreign Service, Georgetown University. —Second edition.
    pages   cm
    "In Cooperation with the Center for Security Studies Edmund A. Walsh School of Foreign Service Georgetown University."
    Includes bibliographical references and index.
    ISBN 978-1-62616-025-5 (pbk. : alk. paper)
    1. Intelligence service—United States—Methodology.   2. Military intelligence—United States.   3. National security—United States.   I. George, Roger Z., 1949–   II. Bruce, James B.
JK468.16A843   2014
327.1273—dc23
                                                                                    2013016839

♾ This book is printed on acid-free paper meeting the requirements of the American National Standard for Permanence in Paper for Printed Library Materials.

15   14   9   8   7   6   5   4   3   2   First printing

Printed in the United States of America

To three pathfinders for the profession of intelligence analysis

Sherman Kent
Richards J. Heuer, Jr.
Jack Davis

CONTENTS

PREFACE

Just like the original publication of *Analyzing Intelligence*, this second edition presents practitioners' views of US intelligence analysis. In 2007, we found that producing our first edition was a process of discovery. We identified important themes and topics, and then recruited the best authors to address them. As we said then, a single author could not have written on such a broad range of topics as authoritatively or completely. We sought a book of diverse contributors where the whole would be greater than the sum of the parts. We believe we succeeded then, and we think we have met that goal even better in this second edition. Moreover, we believe the result is an even more integrated work, with important analytic themes woven throughout. While the book has many authors, we hope the reader will experience its coherence and interconnectedness, along with the distinct contributions of the individual chapters.

The first edition was our effort to explore both historical and current dimensions of intelligence analysis beyond the available literature and to contribute fresh ideas. Virtually all the authors had substantial experience in actually conducting, managing, or evaluating analysis. The second edition follows this logic, relying on the contributors' combined experiences, which the editors knew from having collaborated with many of them during their careers in analysis.

The editors' collaboration has been more than cooperation toward a common goal. For this project it has been a career-long sharing of ideas on how to make intelligence analysis a true discipline and encourage its practitioners as true professionals. In a sense it took two decades of contact between us to produce the first edition, as we frequently crossed paths in our professional lives. Both of us studied international relations theory and political science before joining the intelligence community. Our analytic careers both began at the National Intelligence Council and converged again at the Directorate of Intelligence at the Central Intelligence Agency (CIA). In these different organizations we became well acquainted with how intelligence analysis is conducted at both the intelligence community and agency levels. Here we were first exposed to the talents of such phenomenal analysts as Hal Ford, a vice chairman of the National Intelligence Council and mentor of national intelligence estimates drafters like ourselves. And we also encountered Jack Davis, at the time a national intelligence officer and later a legendary developer and teacher of tradecraft. Later we were again privileged to serve at the National Intelligence Council, drafting and managing national intelligence estimates, where we were able to see the impressive skills of some of the best analysts in the US government—and some of the frailties of the estimating process.

In these assignments and others, we observed how intelligence analysis works in practice and how it might be made to work better. Seasoned by firsthand contact with analysis at both its best and worst, we could not avoid developing ideas regarding how to improve it. These combined experiences have taught us to be humble but also to be more demanding of intelligence. We came to believe that "lessons learned" must be vigorously sought and rigorously developed, then shared with others; otherwise improvements in analytic habits will not occur. But we could not hope to provide a complete set of important lessons. Thus the other contributors to this book have multiplied our own practitioners' perspectives on how intelligence analysis can become a more recognized discipline and stronger profession.

Such ideas were also nurtured by our working on analytic tradecraft issues while serving in different parts of CIA. One of us worked on preparing some of the early alternative analysis instructional materials for CIA analysts. The other became a student of denial and deception as a factor degrading US intelligence and later served as a senior staff member on the President's Commission on the Capabilities of US Intelligence Regarding Weapons of Mass Destruction (the Silberman-Robb WMD Commission). Also, we had spent time together at the Sherman Kent School for Intelligence Analysis, where we were deeply involved in preparing new tradecraft primers and monographs to help overcome some of the cognitive biases and other tradecraft errors that played such a destructive role in the intelligence failure concerning Iraqi weapons of mass destruction. It was at the Kent School that the initial idea of this book was born in an excited discussion about wide variations in the quality of analysis.

We discovered in the six years since we published the first edition that both substantial change and progress has occurred in advancing the discipline of intelligence analysis. Those familiar with the first edition will recall that we cautiously suggested that intelligence analysis could become a more recognized profession than it was then, depending on how much progress could be made in a number of areas. This second volume, in fact, helps to document that progress, which has been both in the right direction and more rapid than we anticipated. Indeed, the new chapters highlight advances in the intelligence community in applying more analytic rigor to national, domestic, and even tactical intelligence analysis, along with expertise-building, training, and professional certification. We are quick to agree that progress remains uneven, but we are pleased that the profession has come this far in so few years. Readers of both editions will be pleased to learn of these changes in both the new as well as the updated chapters contained here. This is an exciting time to be an intelligence analyst or even to observe the evolving world in which they work.

This edition differs in another respect as well. The first volume was an initial effort to capture the enduring aspects of intelligence analysis; the question of its degree of professionalism was only a subtheme. This edition focuses more specifically on how to advance the profession, making it both more prominent and accepted. We consciously selected topics and authors to help us examine this issue and determine where progress has been made and where more still needs to be done.

The popularity of the first volume made us more aware of the need to keep our standards high, so we reached out to a number of practitioner colleagues and scholars to ask their advice on how to improve on what we started in 2007. We are particularly indebted to the critical reviews provided by Keith Fennell, Stephen Marrin, Lloyd Hoffmann, and an anonymous reviewer. Intelligence instructors at the National Intelligence University—John Botzenhart, William Colligan, John Griffiths, and Julian Meade—were especially thoughtful in their critiques of the first edition and suggested a number of new topics and different perspectives that were needed to make this edition more comprehensive, timely, and keenly focused on the themes most central to professionalization. Individually, the editors also sought the advice of former colleagues on specific topics, and their assistance was indispensable. In particular, we want to thank Charlie Allen, Douglas MacEachin, Ken Knight, William Nolte, and Paul Pillar for their perceptive advice and insights on various aspects of analysis and professionalization.

Both of us owe a debt of gratitude to a number of institutions that helped encourage our interest in preparing a book of this nature for future analysts. Georgetown University's Security Studies Program, where we teach as adjunct professors, has been a leader in graduate-level intelligence studies, both as a source of eager and challenging students and an ideal incubator for ideas found in this book. Likewise, the National War College, where each of us has taught at separate times, sets a high standard for professional education—a part of the Joint Professional Military Education model, which we argue is a suitable model for how the intelligence community should build its own integrated professional analysis program. Finally, the RAND Corporation was generous in allowing one editor/author time to work on this volume amid other research projects under way.

This book would not have been possible without the generous support of Georgetown University's Center for Security Studies, the research arm of its Security Studies Program. Its director, Bruce Hoffman, like Daniel Byman before him, has supported our efforts throughout our project. Don Jacobs of Georgetown University Press has been especially helpful in providing guidance throughout the revision process. We also appreciate CIA's Publication Review Board's timely review of our manuscript, as well as its excellent guidance.

Our wives, Cindy and Penny, have been in-house counselors when their husbands have been frustrated with slow progress or writing blocks. They now know what a book conversation between Jim and Roger means and have graciously supported us by brainstorming ideas, debating approaches, and reconciling views. They too were collaborators in getting this second edition completed.

Finally, the effort could not have been completed in a timely fashion and in a professional manner without the research and production assistance of Georgetown University graduate student Greg Wyatt, who ably supported this project, as did Matthew Larson for the earlier edition. It is for Greg and Matt that we hope books like this will be useful. Indeed, a major reason for producing both editions is to encourage members of their generation to make intelligence analysis their chosen profession—and to continue to help improve it.

CHAPTER I

Intelligence Analysis

What Is It—and What Does It Take?

JAMES B. BRUCE AND ROGER Z. GEORGE

[The takedown of Osama bin Laden was] a perfect fusion of intelligence collection, intelligence analysis, and military operations.

—Robert M. Gates, *Sixty Minutes*, May 15, 2011

In that often hidden nexus between collecting intelligence and conducting operations, *analysis*, as former analyst, CIA director, and defense secretary Gates reminds us, plays a vital role. When analysis is good, it improves the chances that operations or policy will succeed. When analysis is not good, it degrades the chances of successful operational or policy outcomes. If your job is to produce intelligence analysis, you have powerful incentives to get it right. This book is about getting it right.

Producing good analysis is hard. There are plenty of obstacles in its path. Good analysts often overcome them. Empowered by solid training, education, and experience, and perhaps seasoned with previous analytic failures and other "teaching moments" on their path to professionalization, they understand how to improve the odds favoring good analysis. The contributors to this book have all trod that path.

What Is Analysis?

Analysis, good or bad, is about producing judgments, forecasts, and insights. A word about each:

Judgment. Analysis, as explained in a recent authoritative study, is "an exercise in judgment under conditions of uncertainty."[1] A judgment is a conclusion or inference based on analysis of incomplete and uncertain information, with some generally bounded probability (never really known and not always stated) of being correct, but also with some chance of being wrong. Analytic judgments can be expressed with some degree of probability ("there is a 70 percent chance that . . .") or a statement of confidence ("we have moderate confidence that X is . . ."). Analytic judgments are typically expressed without accompanying statements of probability or confidence.

Intelligence analysts who concluded that the obscure compound in Abbottabad, Pakistan, housed Osama bin Laden, and who also forecast that he would be there during the time of the planned takedown, were exercising judgment under uncertainty. No one had conclusive proof or "smoking gun evidence" that the compound was his or that he would actually be there when the raid was conducted. These were judgments. The process that produced them was analysis. This analysis was based in part on good intelligence collection, the reliability of which was also critical to the successful takedown operation. In examples discussed later in this chapter, we examine two specific judgments under uncertainty: the state of the Soviet nuclear missile launch readiness during the 1962 Cuban Missile Crisis and whether weapons of mass destruction (WMDs) were present in Iraq in 2002.[2] In the first instance, analysis was good; in the second, it was poor. Throughout this book, the authors seek to explain how to achieve the good and avert the poor.

Forecast. A forecast is a judgment about the future. Warning intelligence is composed principally of forecasts, which are not "predictions." Customers of intelligence— policymakers and military leaders—care especially about what *will* happen and less about what has happened already, which is too late to influence. Through their policy initiatives and military operations, they are trying to accomplish something that will reduce threats or otherwise enhance US national security. Thus they need better understanding about what is coming, rather than about what has happened. Intelligence analysis that produces good forecasts helps them achieve that. Good forecasting is hard and the record is mixed. For example, if policymakers do not know that a staunch ally in the Middle East is about to be overthrown by virulent anti-American forces, then they cannot take actions to prevent it or even mitigate its effects, as happened in Iran in 1979. Some aspects of the Arab Spring of 2011 were reliably forecast, and some were not. Still, policymakers are often successfully warned in advance, such as in the 1967 Arab-Israeli War, outbreaks of military tensions between India and Pakistan, and the breakup of Yugoslavia—all cases where analysts provided sound forecasts that were helpful to policymakers. Analysts are often more successful when forecasting multiple scenarios, with indicators expected to accompany each. These also help policymakers anticipate alternative outcomes and hypothesize how different policy options might influence different outcomes.

Insight. When customers of intelligence receive analysis that offers a fresh, new perspective, or when it causes them to think about a hard problem in a new way—even if it does not present any new information—they appreciate the insight that analysis has brought them. Analytic insights are less about facts than they are about contextualizing them. For example, it is insightful for policymakers and military commanders to learn when a conventional war is metamorphosing into a counterinsurgency war, as happened in Iraq in 2003. The earlier they can get this kind of insight, the better they can adjust to a changing situation. This particular insight about counterinsurgency in Iraq came late in the game for policymakers and military planners. That it was provided much sooner than it was acted upon illustrates a separate problem for analysis: Policymakers do not *have* to use intelligence. They make their decisions for lots of reasons, and sometimes intelligence—even when at its best—makes no difference at all. Subsequently, we explain this complex intelligence–policy relationship in greater depth.[3] It affects the use that intelligence customers make—or don't make—of the judgments, forecasts, and insights that analysts provide them.

Analysis: The Cognitive Part of Intelligence

Slightly more than half a century ago, the American scholar and pioneering intelligence analyst Sherman Kent lamented that the US intelligence community (IC) lacked a professional literature.[4] Serving as the head of the Central Intelligence Agency's (CIA's) Office of National Estimates, Kent hoped to define and develop a professional intelligence analysis discipline, noting that academic professions could not operate without an understanding of the field or a comparable body of knowledge. Today, though there is a large body of writing on intelligence generally, critiques to advance analysis still seem in short supply. To be sure, many critical writers have concentrated on the past and current failings of intelligence or seek to expose sensational operations to excite or infuriate the public, while former intelligence officers and policy officials are often tempted to put the record "straight" as they see it. However, both approaches have typically neglected assessing the discipline of "intelligence analysis" or adding to the collective knowledge of what constitutes sound analytic principles and practices.

Is there even a professional discipline known as "intelligence analysis?" Considerable effort has been devoted to defining what is meant by the general term "intelligence," which surely encompasses analysis as one part of a multifaceted process of gaining specific, often secret information for government use.[5] Analysis is the thinking part of the intelligence process, or as the former career analyst and senior official Douglas MacEachin has phrased it, "intelligence is a profession of cognition."[6] It is all about monitoring important countries, trends, people, events, and other phenomena, and identifying patterns or anomalies in behavior and cause–effect relationships among key factors that explain past outcomes and might point to future developments with policy implications for the United States. Another key founder of CIA analytic practices and principles has phrased it succinctly: "The mission of intelligence analysts is to apply in-depth substantive expertise, all-source information, and tough-minded tradecraft to produce assessments that provide distinctive value-added to policy clients' efforts to protect and advance U.S. security interests."[7]

Analysis is just one part but, ultimately in our view, the decisive part of the intelligence process that produces "decision advantage" for policymakers.[8] The typical diagram of the intelligence cycle found in figure 1.1 exemplifies how many see the intelligence process. It starts with identifying what the customer needs (requirements) and ends with delivering the intelligence (dissemination) to satisfy those needs.[9] Despite its simplification of what is a very complex process, this conceptualization does underline the analyst's pivotal role in transforming information provided by various collection systems into

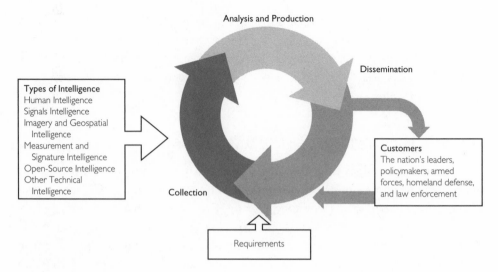

Figure 1.1   Intelligence Cycle

Source: Adapted from a briefing. *The Intelligence Community,* available at the director of national intelligence website (www.dni.gov).

judgments, forecasts, and insights for the policy customer. Whether that information is good, bad, or somewhere in between, the analyst must transform it into value-added information that is relevant and useful for the policymaker in a way that provides him or her with decision-making advantages not otherwise available.

This analysis comes in a variety of forms. Traditionally one thinks of products—"finished intelligence" analyses—that are printed and distributed to select government users. This definition of analysis conveys, however, a mechanistic and also somewhat linear process, which figure 1.1 represents. The "production line" metaphor conjures up an image of analysts writing, reviewing, editing, and publishing an assessment, and then moving onto the next question or task. While this is true at a basic level, the process is vastly more complex. In reality, the cognitive part of analysis is more akin to a computer model that has been collecting and interpreting incoming data and constantly reassessing how new data might change not only the findings but also the computer model being used to organize and interpret the data. The forms that analysis can take, then, are not limited to the printed or electronic word or graphic. As often, "analysis" occurs when analysts interact with policymakers over the telephone, through e-mail, during a videoconference, or at a meeting. This form of intelligence support has been referred to as "analytic transactions." Though impossible to quantify, perhaps tens of thousands of such transactions occur yearly.[10] Moreover, the sharing of data, hypotheses, interpretations, and questions among analysts and other nongovernment experts is possibly where the most insightful cognition is occurring, rather than on the page of a finished assessment or a PowerPoint slide.

The Professional Analyst—What It Takes

The analytic process, then, must be understood as demanding more than just a well-educated individual who can write concisely. The complete intelligence analyst must combine the skills of historian, journalist, research methodologist, collection manager, and skeptic. *He or she must synthesize the skills of a subject-matter expert (SME) with those of an expert in intelligence itself.* At a minimum, the fully qualified analyst must demonstrate a very unique skill set combined from the two groups below:

Skills of a university-trained SME:

- Substantive mastery of specific subject-matter content and good understanding of its relevance and implications for US national security policies.
- Skills in the use of social science research methods to organize and evaluate open-source data and information, including open-source intelligence (OSINT) research skills.
- Research imagination and scientific rigor to generate and test hypotheses, most often with qualitative data.

Skills of an expert in the conduct of intelligence:

- Collection. An understanding of three of the four clandestine collection disciplines most important to one's analytic portfolio: human intelligence (HUMINT), signals intelligence (SIGINT), geospatial intelligence (GEOINT), and measurement and signatures intelligence (MASINT).
- Cognition and tradecraft. An understanding of the cognitive processes inherent in conducting analysis, how the cognitive function may affect the analytic process itself, and how structured analytic tradecraft can mitigate cognitive error, including why openness to contrary opinion and "alternative" analysis also improve analytic outcomes.
- Foreign denial and deception (D&D). An understanding of how US adversaries and "intelligence targets" develop countermeasures to collection efforts in order to deny the information sought or to manipulate that information for deception purposes, and the analytic implications of successful D&D countermeasures.
- Learning from practice. The capacity to admit error and especially to learn from it, including "best practices" that will give valid and reliable results over the long haul.
- Collaboration. The ability to work successfully in collaborative environments, both virtually and directly, with intelligence professionals from diverse agencies and with customers of analysis.

Thus what distinguishes an intelligence analyst from a subject-matter expert outside the intelligence community are not the first three characteristics, which are shared with many international affairs specialists, although these attributes are required in intelligence. Indeed, the IC needs to further develop these important skills in its analysts.

SMEs are expected to be well versed in the history, politics, culture, and language of many countries or be technical experts in a wide variety of areas. They may also be plugged into US policy deliberations and even involved in advising government officials on the optimal policies to adopt. And many foreign affairs specialists have methodological expertise.

Where the intelligence analyst distinguishes himself or herself is not only in having these characteristics but also in having the other five. Fully professional analysts must be experts on how to use intelligence-collection capabilities and know their limitations, and be both imaginative and rigorous in considering explanations for missing, ambiguous, and often contradictory or deceptive data. At the same time, they need to be skilled in methodologically reliable analytic tradecraft and be able to be self-critics of their own biases and expectations of what the data show. And, most important, they must be open to changing their minds, learning from experience, and consciously asking the question "If I'm wrong, how might I need to modify the way I am analyzing the problem?" Professional growth requires the ability to learn from both errors and successes—one's own as well as others'—and mastering best practices that will improve the odds of successful analysis.

Finally, the increased use of group-based structured analytic techniques, and the new IC environment emerging after the Intelligence Reform and Terrorism Prevention Act of 2004 (IRTPA) that created the Office of the Director of National Intelligence (ODNI), increased the importance of collaboration among analysts within their agencies and among then. Analysis today is a highly collaborative activity, and good skills in analytic collaboration will enhance the odds of success.

A Growing Analysis Literature

As of 2014—nearly fifty years after Kent's lament—the body of scholarly writing on intelligence analysis remains surprisingly thin but growing. It is true that academics and intelligence professionals have seen a fast-growing literature on intelligence in recent years. Yet very few have exclusively addressed intelligence *analysis*, and fewer still have treated it comprehensively. This is surprising given the importance of the subject and the thousands of professionals who practice the craft daily throughout the sixteen agencies in the US intelligence community. Yet a survey of the literature on US intelligence analysis over the past several decades yields only a few scholars and practitioners who have addressed the pitfalls in analysis and paths to improve it.

In his *Psychology of Intelligence Analysis*, practitioner Richards Heuer has made a seminal contribution to improving analysis by incorporating knowledge and insights from the field of cognitive psychology.[11] Foundational to later advances in structured analytic tradecraft, this work is complemented by an ethnographic study of analysis by Rob Johnston. After Heuer, Johnston's data-rich *Analytic Culture in the U.S. Intelligence Community* identified numerous problems in the conduct of analysis IC-wide and proposed social science–based ways to improve it.[12] Former CIA analyst Stephen

Marrin, a uniquely qualified scholar-practitioner, has studied intelligence analysis as a potential profession and, with emphasis on training and education, has written widely and persuasively about how to professionalize it.[13] Addressing methods, Heuer and his colleague Randolph Pherson collaborated on an authoritative compendium of structured analytic techniques (SATs) that will serve as the baseline reference work on analytic tradecraft for years to come.[14] Robert Clark has successfully placed the collection target at the center of a modeling approach in *Intelligence Analysis: A Target-Centric Approach*.[15] Other practitioners have critiqued analysis and shown ways to improve it. The legendary CIA estimator and mentor of analysts Hal Ford has greatly illuminated the national intelligence estimates process, as has Cynthia Grabo with warning intelligence.[16]

Professors Richard Betts and Robert Jervis have both explored the perils of providing analysis to policymakers, sometimes when those officials were less than receptive to unwanted information; their work stands out as among the most thoughtful by scholars who, through consulting with analytic agencies, have gained a deep appreciation for the pitfalls of the intelligence-policy relationship.[17] Professor Joshua Rovner has likewise written on the intelligence-policy relationship but with a focus on the dangers and degrees of "politicization" that can occur when intelligence runs up against "high politics" and strong-willed policymakers.[18] His work, along with that of former CIA analyst Paul Pillar, ranks among the most complete treatments of the how intelligence and policy are often poorly matched.[19]

Former chairman of the National Intelligence Council and assistant DNI for analysis Thomas Fingar captures the personal side of providing analysis to policymakers in his insightful book *Reducing Uncertainty*. He correctly notes that analysts are not striving to predict the future, but importantly to "reduce uncertainty" faced by policymakers.[20] Reflecting earlier periods, Robert Gates and Russell Jack Smith, two former CIA deputy directors for intelligence, have also written insightful memoirs that explain the perspective of the most senior analysts in the business dealing routinely with the most senior policymakers.[21]

In recent years the intelligence literature also has been expanded by multiple investigations into the US intelligence community's failure to warn of the September 11 attacks and the failed estimate on Iraq's nonexistent weapons of mass destruction (WMDs). Unfortunately, these reviews have provided us with a rather incomplete picture on how to improve intelligence analysis. *The 9/11 Commission Report* provides a brilliant recounting of the hijackers' plot and copious recommendations on how to improve intragovernmental information sharing and defensive measures against global terrorism. However, scant attention has been devoted to understanding how analysis might have been better and to laying out any game plan for improving intelligence analysis on terrorism. The sound bites that the US intelligence community "lacked imagination" or "failed to connect the dots" are hardly sufficient insight on why US experts were unable to grasp the audacious nature of the threat.[22] Sadly, professionals learn little from this well-written report other than to acknowledge that agencies should have done better at information sharing, should have been writing more national estimates, and should have been thinking more imaginatively.

The record is better in the reviews conducted on US analysis covering Iraq's WMD programs. In addition to faulting collection efforts, fragmented intelligence community operations, management, and other aspects of the intelligence system, the Silberman-Robb WMD Commission was explicit in critiquing the analytic record, as well as the analytic process. The commission's critique was based on an in-depth examination of the analytic process involved in producing both current reporting and estimative intelligence on Iraq's suspected WMD programs and on other cases, including Libya, Afghanistan, Iran, North Korea, and terrorism. Overall, from these cases the report found a "lack of rigorous analysis." In particular it found "finished intelligence that was loosely reasoned, ill-supported, and poorly communicated" and "too many analytical products that obscured how little the intelligence community actually *knew* about an issue and how much their conclusions rested on inferences and assumptions."[23]

Although the WMD Commission noted several analytic successes, such as with some intelligence on Libya and the A. Q. Khan nuclear proliferation network, it also found a preponderance of "serious analytical shortcomings." These included

> inadequate Intelligence Community collaboration and cooperation, analysts who do not understand collection, too much focus on current intelligence, inadequate systematic use of outside experts and open source information, . . . and poor capabilities to exploit fully the available data. Perhaps most troubling, we found an Intelligence Community in which analysts had a difficult time stating their assumptions up front, explicitly explaining their logic, and, in the end, identifying unambiguously for policymakers what they *do not know*. In sum, we found that many of the most basic processes and functions for producing accurate and reliable intelligence are broken and underutilized.[24]

The WMD Commission's major recommendations on analysis focused on improvements in

- management of analysts;
- utilization of nontraditional sources, including open sources;
- understanding of how foreign denial and deception can have an impact on collection and analysis;
- long-term research and strategic thinking; and particularly
- tradecraft (or methodology) through much improved training, especially to produce analysis that is more rigorous and transparent.[25]

We intend to give particular attention to these issues and to others as well, including those identified in a recent authoritative study by the National Academy of Sciences. This study argued that much-improved analysis would result if analysts would "consider new information against previous analyses, interpret and evaluate evidence, imagine hypotheses, identify anomalies, and communicate their findings to decision makers in ways that help them to fulfill their missions."[26]

Putting Analysis into a Policy Context

To understand analysis and how to improve it, one must understand how it fits into the actual policymaking process. Certain realities must be recognized so that analysis can be better understood. First, policymakers live in an information-rich environment. Second, intelligence provides an important part of the information used to make decisions: Analysis tries to bound the uncertainty inherent in complex international developments and tailor understanding to fit specific government needs. And third, since analysts and policymakers are trying to accomplish different things, it is especially important to ensure the best possible communications between these very different mind-sets.

An Information-Rich Policy Environment

When US national security decision makers deliberate over significant policy issues, information that bears on those decisions is always important and often vital. Whether deciding to negotiate with or coerce another country, deciding to intercede in an ethnic conflict to halt genocide, or deciding how to stem an insurgency using a mixture of policy tools, the policymaker is relying on a multitude of information sources to determine the best course of action the government should take. National security policymakers enjoy access to a broad range of information to help them deliberate such issues and support their decisions. Some of that information will be reliable, some not. Some is biased, calculated to influence the outcome. Some is irrelevant or useless. Often it can be controversial. Some is secret or highly sensitive. But much of it comes from open sources such as newspapers, media outlets, the internet, and scholarly articles and books. Some originates in opinion pieces in magazines and newspapers, most written in Washington and New York. Still other information comes from personal and professional contacts, other interested US policymakers and stakeholder government agencies, policy advocates, and opponents—or even from select foreign officials or foreign plotters and power seekers, and additional knowledgeable parties who may be interested or disinterested and whose involvement may never be publicly known. And some information for policy decision making comes from the intelligence community.

Using Intelligence Analysis to Bound Uncertainty

Intelligence officials cannot control which sources of information policymakers will use or how they will use them—that is the sole prerogative of policymakers. But compared with those in the policy world, intelligence officers do have a unique vantage point to weigh and assess the relative reliability and accuracy of many sources of information available to decision makers. Notably, what intelligence officials *can* control is the quality and quantity of the intelligence information that will be provided to government officials. The better the quality and relevance of the information, the higher the policy impact— or so intelligence officers hope.

The lion's share of intelligence for these policymakers often comes in the form of analysis.[27] Such analytic products are referred to as "finished" intelligence because analysts have synthesized raw information collected from multiple sources and have interpreted the meaning of such information in the context of the policymakers' needs. That is analysis. These analytic products are almost always classified "secret" or "top secret" to protect intelligence sources and methods. They can be as short as a paragraph-length article found in the *President's Daily Brief* or as long as hundred-page estimative or forecasting studies such as national intelligence estimates (NIEs). These analyses can also fall somewhere in the middle in the form of periodic updates or specific "warning" documents designed to alert officials to emerging situations that may require their urgent attention and action. Many times these products are the result of analysts' judgment that an issue needs to be brought to the attention of a policymaker. However, senior policymakers will often request "tailored" analysis for a particular issue, typically quick but sometimes in depth, to help inform their decisions or actions. These results of the analytic process are typically aimed at explaining the facts of a situation, identifying key uncertainties, and projecting a range of possible outcomes based on a rigorous review of the facts, as well as the knowable unknowns.

Communicating with Policymakers

Since policymakers and intelligence analysts live in different trenches and seem to speak different languages—or "tribal tongues," as Mark Lowenthal has explained[28]—and the consequences of miscommunication could be consequential, analysts must redouble their efforts to ensure the clearest possible communications with their customers. A recent study that addressed this issue suggested three promising areas for improvement and for further study: the need for standard protocols for communicating the confidence placed in analytic judgments; the efficacy of policymakers requesting analysis in terms of how clearly their requests convey their intentions to analysts; and the impact of internal review processes on analytic products before they are released, and on how well the resulting reports actually convey analysts' intended meaning.[29] The two case studies that follow, and others in later chapters, illustrate some of these issues.

Why Intelligence Matters: The Cuban Missile Crisis Example

Why should senior policymakers pay attention to intelligence? Given their extremely tight schedules, long hours, and heavy workloads, decision makers have to be quite selective in what they read and whom they see. For their part, intelligence analysts can never assume access to senior policymakers or that their written products will even be read by the customer(s) for whom they were expressly prepared.

The simple reason that policymakers bother with intelligence is that intelligence, particularly the analytic products and the on-call expertise of the analysts who produce them, brings "value added" to the national security policymaking process. Most policy officials appreciate this. This is more true after September 11, 2001, when skeptical policymakers began to grasp the idea that US intelligence reporting, for all its shortfalls, was often as good as or better than the competition's. In general, the value added that intelligence brings to decision making is this: intelligence collection, analytic expertise, objectivity, and timeliness. We examine these four aspects found in the 1962 Cuban Missile Crisis as an illustration of how intelligence provides policymakers with decision advantage.

Collection

Compared with researchers working exclusively with open sources, intelligence analysts enjoy a special advantage: access to information provided by classified intelligence collection programs that is unavailable elsewhere. This global and unique resource of the US intelligence community costs taxpayers billions of dollars yearly. It includes technical collection means and human sources that are tasked to penetrate adversary governments and organizations such as terrorist groups.[30] Information collected by HUMINT or technical espionage can be a priceless resource for analysts and decision makers. This key attribute of intelligence—the collection of secret information by secret means—brings a major value added to policy support.

The analysis of such information can make the difference in a complex decision. For example, overhead photography collected by U-2 aircraft revealed offensive nuclear-capable missiles covertly deployed by the Soviet Union in Cuba in 1962. Sensitive documents such as the highly classified Soviet SS-4 missile manual provided to CIA by the spy Oleg Penkovskiy enabled analysis that probably extended the decision-making time available to President John F. Kennedy and his national security team during the heat of crisis. Together these extraordinary collection successes made a decisive difference in President Kennedy's ability to successfully manage the only direct nuclear confrontation between the United States and the Soviet Union during the Cold War.[31] Had the US government not discovered the secret missile emplacements—and discovered them before they became operational—it would have faced a significant new strategic disadvantage in the nuclear deterrence equation that had provided bipolar stability since the development of nuclear weapons. Defusing a crisis that brought the superpowers to the nuclear brink shows how intelligence provided uniquely valuable information from special collection sources to US analysts, information that policymakers could not have gotten from any other information provider.

Analysis and Judgment

US intelligence analysts are often regarded as the most authoritative experts in government on many specialized subjects, including particular countries and regions of interest to the United States. Intelligence agencies recruit from top graduate schools in most sub-ject areas, and the prevalence of graduate degrees among analysts at "all-source" agencies such as CIA, the Defense Intelligence Agency, and the State Department's Intelligence and Research Bureau is probably the equivalent of most universities and think tanks. Significantly, in-depth expertise in the analytic ranks is also focused on issues and prob-lems of direct interest to policymakers, rather than on historical or other academically interesting subjects of only tangential relevance to US national security.

Just as the Cuban Missile Crisis illustrates the impact of special collection capabili-ties that revealed the hidden Soviet missiles, it also demonstrates the power of analysis. This important success came on the heels of a failed national intelligence estimate issued just three weeks earlier that wrongly concluded the Soviets would not covertly emplace nuclear ballistic missiles in Cuba. This major failure was revealed when the missiles were actually discovered.[32]

The stunning information delivered by the U-2 aircraft from Cuban airspace was not just pictures of land below. It was raw imagery that revealed intelligence to the trained imagery analysts looking for telltale "signatures" uncovering the presence of offensive missiles with sufficient range to deliver nuclear warheads to targeted cities in the United States. But only the highest-quality analysis could have answered the most pressing ques-tion when the missiles were revealed: How much time would the decision makers have to act before the missiles would become operational and able to attack US targets? This high-stakes question required accurate interpretation of the U-2 imagery and in-depth analysis of the HUMINT provided by Penkovskiy. It was through a remarkable exploi-tation of Soviet classified materials (referred to as the Ironbark documents) he provided clandestinely that highly trained technical analysts were able to estimate—accurately, it turned out—how long it would take to complete the installation. On October 19, 1962, only five days after the missiles were discovered, analysts concluded that they would be operational by October 27, only thirteen days from their initial discovery—and what turned out to be the final day of the crisis when the Soviets backed down.[33] This sig-nificant finding not only bound the president's time frame—it probably extended it by as much as three days, permitting more precious time to manage the crisis before the Soviets would have been able to unleash a nuclear strike at American cities.[34] The role of intelligence in helping policymakers manage this dangerous crisis illustrated both collec-tion and analysis at its very best.[35] The tense crisis ended as the Soviets agreed to remove the missiles under close US monitoring. President Kennedy almost certainly could not have enjoyed the same successful outcome without the extraordinary level of intelligence support he received.

Objectivity

A key attribute of intelligence analysis is maintaining policy relevance while assidu-ously avoiding policy advocacy. This heritage of *policy neutrality* traces directly to Sher-man Kent and is nearly hardwired in the culture of analysis.[36] Analysts strive to work problems and issues of high salience to policymakers, but they seldom construct their analytic path in a way that easily suggests a preferred policy outcome. More typically, they seek to enlighten and inform policymakers and to reduce uncertainty about complex and evolving situations but to avert policy prescriptions. They find their satisfaction in helping the policymaker to think through complex issues without specifying what to do about them. Being information providers perhaps to a fault, intelligence analysts are happy to leave the policy choices to the officials responsible for making them.

Again the Cuban Missile Crisis makes the point: As the president and his executive committee worked their way through myriad policy options—ranging from doing nothing and accepting a Soviet fait accompli to launching "surgical" nuclear strikes against the missiles under construction—intelligence analysts played a vital but highly restrictive role in the decision-making process. Their place was to provide information and analysis that could illuminate policy choices and possible consequences but not to advocate or oppose any particular course of action. A particularly significant analytic contribution to the crisis-management process was analysts' sound estimates of most probable Soviet reactions to likely US measures, including the successful blockade (or "quarantine") ultimately selected by the president. They predicted—also accurately—that Soviet reactions would concentrate on "political exploitation" and that any Soviet military responses would not occur beyond Cuba itself.[37] Analysts did not advocate one policy option or another, but they successfully illuminated the likely outcomes of the major policy options available to the president and his crisis decision makers.

Of course, this characterization of analysis as policy-neutral oversimplifies a more complicated and subtle problem often referred to as the politicization of intelligence. Not all policymakers see analysts quite the same way. Seen from the policymakers' trench, intelligence analysis should support policy, so independent analysis may not always be welcome when it is perceived to undermine a preferred policy choice. In this way, providing intelligence is risky in high-stakes policymaking. Intelligence is most helpful when the policy-level customer is genuinely searching for understanding and is not committed to a particular policy course of action. Once committed, the policymaker tends to evaluate the usefulness of intelligence in direct proportion to the extent that it advances the favored policy objective.[38] It is sufficient at this point to establish that the aim of intelligence analysis is to advance the policy process through the provision of unique information packaged to enhance understanding and to reduce the uncertainty of policy decisions, not necessarily to influence the selection or support (or rejection or undermining) of any particular policy choice. For the most part, policymakers seem to appreciate the studied objectivity they can generally expect from intelligence analysts.[39]

Timeliness

A fourth value-added aspect of intelligence in policymaking is getting the information to policymakers in time so that they can act on it if immediate action is needed. For example, if the Soviet missiles had been discovered in Cuba *after* they had already become operational—or worse, publicly announced by an emboldened Nikita Khrushchev as a strategic fait accompli with an accompanying ultimatum—American policymakers would have faced a very different and far less favorable set of options. The timeliness attribute is at the heart of *warning* intelligence, where analysis plays every bit as critical a role as collection because *both* must work for warning to succeed. In spite of a flawed estimate in September that failed to anticipate the Soviet gambit, the timely and success-ful U-2 overflights in October, and the trenchant and accurate analysis that followed, show the Cuban Missile Crisis to have been an outstanding intelligence-warning and crisis-support success.

WMDs in Iraq: Confronting Intelligence Failure

As the successful Cuban Missile Crisis case shows, intelligence can provide unique value added to policymaking through special collection, insightful analysis, strictly objective policy relevance, and timeliness. But failure is also part of the record. If intelligence always worked as effectively as it did during the Cuban Missile Crisis, there would be no controversy over whether it was worth the billions it costs every year, over the episodic clamor for intelligence reform, or especially over its putative value added for policymak-ers. Intelligence failures are disquieting. They shake the confidence of those who argue that the intelligence community is worth the investment and the risk that it takes to pro-vide the most useful information to policymakers.

An especially disturbing failure was the erroneous estimates of WMDs in Saddam Hussein's Iraq. The now well-known October 2002 NIE on Iraq made major errors in assessing Iraq's WMD programs. This NIE erroneously judged that Iraq had stockpiled as much as five hundred tons of chemical weapons (CW) and had an ongoing CW pro-gram; that Iraq had an active biological weapons (BW) program with BW agent stored there, along with mobile BW labs; that Iraq was reconstituting its nuclear weapons pro-gram; that Iraq had a program of unmanned aerial vehicles that was probably capable of delivering BW agent to foreign shores, including to the United States; and that Iraq had missiles whose range exceeded permissible limits under United Nations (UN) sanc-tions.[40] Only the last of the five major judgments (on missiles) proved to be correct. Four were completely wrong. Estimates—correct or not—so closely tied to a US deci-sion to take military action are necessarily in the spotlight and rightly so. But even if this estimate had not been central to the debate over the Iraq invasion, it would still merit attention because of what it uncovered about the state of US intelligence analysis as the twenty-first century began.

Why were the key findings so wrong?[41] Briefly, it was a significant *collection* fail-ure because both human and technical intelligence collectors had failed to penetrate Iraq's WMD programs and because collection had also provided some wrong and mis-leading information. It was also a significant *analysis* failure. Reviewing the record, we find that analysts were more dependent on faulty collection than they comprehended, failed to question their past assumptions, and drew erroneous conclusions from dated,

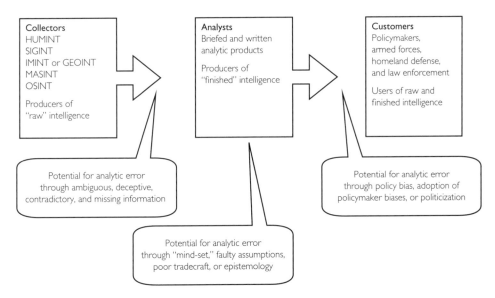

Figure 1.2 From Collection to Customer: The Analyst's Pivotal Role

wrong, and poor information.[42] In short, on two key measures of unique value added—special collection and expert analysis—intelligence failed almost completely. Whether it also failed a third key test, strict objectivity, remains a matter of dispute. Major inquiries by the Senate Select Committee on Intelligence and another by the Silberman-Robb WMD Commission have given analysts a clean bill of health. Both concluded that they had found no evidence whatever of politicization—that is, that policymakers had not apparently influenced intelligence judgments favorable to the war decision.[43] But other observers think this is a more complex and nuanced problem, and even if there was no obvious arm-twisting by policymakers, anticipation caused by the omnipresent war preparations surely distorted analysis.[44] As figure 1.2 illustrates, then, the possibility for analytic errors can occur in three critical areas: where there is poor or missing information, where unchallenged mind-sets or assumptions exist, or where bias may interfere with analytic objectivity. These three areas are explored throughout this book.

Analyzing Intelligence Analysis

Whether we focus on missiles in Cuba in 1962, on WMDs in Iraq forty years later, or on other major successes and failures of analysis, the central questions are whether the vast amount of intelligence analysis is succeeding or failing to give policymakers what they most need and how professionalizing analysis can help in this regard.

This book draws on the individual and collective experience of many intelligence experts—most of whom have enjoyed long careers as successful analysts themselves, some as senior managers of analysts and others who are scholars of the issues we pose here. The book explains how analysis has been conducted and how it can improve.

We examine how intelligence analysis has evolved since its origins in the middle of the last century, including attention to its traditions, culture, and track record. We examine how analysis supports the most senior national security and military policymakers, how analysts must deal with the perennial challenges of analytic bias and foreign denial and deception, and how they must become masters rather than victims of an ever-changing collection environment. We propose new ways to address perennial issues in warning analysis and emerging analytic issues such as domestic intelligence and homeland defense, and we suggest new approaches to supporting national strategy and new forms of analytic outreach in a global intelligence environment. We introduce specific new ideas for using structured analytic tradecraft for both strategic- and tactical-level analysis and for developing self-corrective techniques to improve analytic reliability. We examine the evolution and enhancements in analysis since the creation of the Office of the Director of National Intelligence in 2005 and the importance of building a common analytic culture in sixteen agencies. We also underline much-needed improvements in analyst training and education, as well as further professional development for a new generation of intelligence analysts, which can get the IC closer to the standards of a maturing discipline.

If this book can illuminate the less well-known or poorly understood attributes and issues of the intelligence analysis process and then point to promising ways to improve it, we believe it can help to raise the quality and reliability of analysis. Simply put, our principal objective in the following chapters is to provide a better understanding of analysis for both the producers and users of intelligence.

Notes

1. National Research Council, *Intelligence Analysis for Tomorrow: Advances from the Behavioral and Social Sciences* (Washington, DC: National Academies Press, 2011), 24.
2. There were many judgments made in both the Cuban Missile Crisis and the Iraq WMD case. Some were incorrect, notably the September 1962 national intelligence estimate on Soviet offensive weapons in Cuba that underestimated the possibility of intermediate-range nuclear ballistic missiles on the island and the flawed 2002 estimate of nonexistent chemical and biological weapon stockpiles in Iraq. Other judgments were correct, such as those about the state of readiness of Soviet weapons on the island (once discovered) and whether Saddam Hussein's missiles exceeded allowable range limits, as well as the intelligence community's forecasts regarding the post-Saddam regional and domestic conditions. As in most intelligence controversies, analysts are never entirely correct or entirely wrong.
3. See, for example, chaps. 5–7 and chap. 13 on warning.
4. Sherman Kent, "The Need for an Intelligence Literature," reprinted in *Sherman Kent and the Board of National Estimates*, ed. Donald Steury (Washington, DC: Center for the Study of Intelligence, CIA, 1994), 14–15.
5. Michael Warner, "Wanted: A Definition of Intelligence," *Studies in Intelligence* 46, no. 1 (2002): 15–22.
6. Douglas MacEachin, "Strategic Analysis," in *Transforming U.S. Intelligence*, ed. Jennifer E. Sims and Burton Gerber (Washington, DC: Georgetown University Press, 2006), 117.

7. Jack Davis, "Intelligence Analysts and Policymakers: Benefits and Dangers of Tensions in the Relationship," *Intelligence and National Security* 21, no. 6 (December 2006): 991–1021 at 1007.

8. Jennifer E. Sims, "Understanding Friends and Enemies: The Context for Intelligence Reform," in *Transforming U.S. Intelligence*, ed. Jennifer E. Sims and Burton Gerber (Washington, DC: Georgetown University Press, 2005), 16.

9. This way of depicting the intelligence process as a cyclical phenomenon greatly oversimplifies how it works in practice. For a critique of this approach, see Rob Johnston, *Analytical Culture in the U.S. Intelligence Community* (Washington, DC: Center for the Study of Intelligence, CIA, 2005), and Mark M. Lowenthal, *Intelligence: From Secrets to Policy* (Washington, DC: CQ Press, 2000), 50–51. The depiction of the intelligence cycle in figure 1.1 omits one of the customary five stages: processing (between collection and analysis).

10. Davis, "Intelligence Analysts and Policymakers," 999.

11. Richards J. Heuer Jr., *Psychology of Intelligence Analysis* (Washington, DC: Center for the Study of Intelligence, CIA, 1999).

12. Johnston, *Analytical Culture in the U.S. Intelligence Community*.

13. See especially Stephen Marrin, *Improving Intelligence Analysis: Bridging the Gap between Scholarship and Practice* (Oxford: Routledge, 2011).

14. Richards J. Heuer Jr. and Randolph H. Pherson, *Structured Analytic Techniques for Intelligence Analysis* (Washington, DC: CQ Press, 2011). More specialized works on methods are provided by David A. Schum, *Evidence and Inference for the Intelligence Analyst* (Lanham, MD: University Press of America, 1987), 2 vols., and Morgan Jones, *The Thinker's Toolkit: 14 Powerful Techniques for Problem Solving*, rev. ed. (New York: Three Rivers, 1998).

15. Robert M. Clark, *Intelligence Analysis: A Target-Centric Approach* (Washington, DC: CQ Press, 2010).

16. Classics both, see Hal Ford, *Estimative Intelligence: The Purposes and Problems of National Intelligence Estimating* (Lanham, MD: University Press of America, 1993), and Cynthia Grabo, *Anticipating Surprise: Analysis for Strategic Warning* (Washington, DC: Joint Military Intelligence College, 2002). A still valuable if somewhat dated treatment of analysis is Roy Godson, ed., *Intelligence Requirements for the 1980s: Analysis and Estimates* (Washington, DC: National Strategy Information Center, 1980).

17. Richard K. Betts, *Enemies of Intelligence: Knowledge and Power in American National Security* (New York: Columbia University Press, 2007), and Robert Jervis, *Why Intelligence Fails: Lessons from the Iranian Revolution and the Iraq War* (New York: Columbia University Press, 2010).

18. Joshua Rovner, *Fixing the Facts: National Security and the Politics of Intelligence* (Ithaca NY: Cornell University Press, 2011).

19. Paul R. Pillar, *Intelligence and U.S. Foreign Policy: Iraq, 9/11, and Misguided Reform* (New York: Columbia University Press, 2011).

20. Thomas Fingar, *Reducing Uncertainty: Intelligence Analysis and National Security* (Stanford CA: Stanford University Press, 2011).

21. Robert M. Gates, *From the Shadows* (New York: Simon & Schuster, 1996), and Russell Jack Smith, *The Unknown CIA* (New York: Berkley Books, 1992).

22. The 9/11 Commission's somewhat cryptic recommendation that the intelligence community "bureaucratize imagination" leaves a lot to be desired in the way of practical measures.

See *The 9/11 Commission Report* (New York: Norton, 2003), 344–48. One interpretation is that the commissioners meant to encourage the development of more analytic units whose sole mission would be to challenge conventional interpretations (analytic lines) held by agency analysts. These units would in a sense regularize the use of "contrarian" thinking techniques (e.g., Devil's Advocacy or Team A / Team B analysis) and "thinking like the adversary" (so-called Red Team Analysis). However, the commission was never very clear about what it meant by the phrases, nor has any commissioner subsequently explained it.

23. Commission on the Intelligence Capabilities of the United States Regarding Weapons of Mass Destruction, *Report to the President of the United States, March 31, 2005* (Washington, DC: Government Printing Office, 2005) (hereafter, *WMD Commission Report*), 12 (emphasis in the original). Full disclosure: James Bruce served as a professional staff member on this commission and participated on the analysis working group and on others as well.

24. Ibid., 389, emphasis in the original.

25. Ibid., chap. 8. The findings on Iran and North Korea are not reported in the unclassified volume.

26. National Research Council, *Intelligence Analysis for Tomorrow*, 8.

27. Often "raw," or unanalyzed, intelligence from a sensitive human or technical source is provided directly to senior policymakers. This kind of intelligence can be ignored, or it may have an impact on policy debates. Sometimes this raw intelligence—provided without sufficient vetting, context, or other analytical evaluation—can be both influential and wrong.

28. Mark Lowenthal, "Tribal Tongues: Intelligence Consumers, Intelligence Producers." *Washington Quarterly* 15, no. 1 (Winter 1992): 157–68.

29. National Research Council, *Intelligence Analysis for Tomorrow*, 4 and chap. 6.

30. Intelligence collection and its relationship to analysis are given expanded treatment in chap. 10.

31. See Mary S. McAuliffe, ed., *CIA Documents on the Cuban Missile Crisis, 1962* (Washington, DC: History Staff, CIA, 1992); James G. Blight and David A. Welch, eds., *Intelligence and the Cuban Missile Crisis* (London: Frank Cass, 1998); Dino A. Brugioni, *Eyeball to Eyeball: Inside the Cuban Missile Crisis* (New York: Random House, 1991); Jerrold L. Schecter and Peter S. Deriabin, *The Spy Who Saved the World* (Washington, DC: Brassey's, 1995); and Michael Dobbs, *One Minute to Midnight: Kennedy, Khrushchev, and Castro on the Brink of Nuclear War* (New York: Viking, 2009). In *One Minute to Midnight*, Michael Dobbs offers the most up-to-date and well-researched treatment of the crisis.

32. The erroneous 1962 estimate on Cuba, both a collection and an analysis failure, is examined as a case study in chap. 10.

33. Raymond L. Garthoff, "US Intelligence in the Cuban Missile Crisis," in *Intelligence and the Cuban Missile Crisis*, Blight and Welch, eds., 27; and *Spy Who Saved the World*, Schecter and Deriabin, 334–35.

34. The three added days are the conclusion of CIA's Richard Helms, then deputy director for plans (operations). In addition to bounding the decision-making time frame, analysis of the Penkovskiy documents in conjunction with U-2 imagery enabled extremely valuable intelligence judgments on the key information the policymakers needed, such as missile range (which US cities could be hit), accuracy (1 to 1.5 miles), warhead size (three thousand pounds, or twenty-five kilotons to two megatons), and missile refire rate (five hours). Schecter and Deriabin, *Spy Who Saved the World*, 334–35, 466.

35. The Cuban crisis also illustrates an important analytical failure—namely, the flawed judgment of an estimate produced less than a month before the missiles were discovered that essentially argued that the Soviets probably would not secretly put offensive nuclear missiles in Cuba. Although vacationing, DCI John McCone personally disagreed with that judgment but was unsuccessful in changing it. He was shortly vindicated by the newly discovered facts. This erroneous estimate (SNIE 85-3-62, September 19, 1962), along with other intelligence failings concerning this crisis, is discussed in chap. 10.

36. Sherman Kent observed some fifty years ago that the most important relationship for analysts—that with the policy officials they seek to inform—does not fall naturally in place but requires careful thought to set right and constant efforts to keep effective. See Sherman Kent, *Strategic Intelligence for National World Policy* (Princeton, NJ: Princeton University Press, 1949). Kent articulated the basic challenge to effective ties when he observed that "if analysts get too close to their policymaking and action-taking clients, they would be in danger of losing the independence of mind and the substantive depth and analytic expertise that enabled them to make a distinctive professional contribution to national security. Yet if they stay too far apart from those they are charged to serve, they would be cut off from the feedback and other guidance essential for making that contribution." Jack Davis, "Improving CIA Analytic Performance: Analysts and the Policymaking Process," *CIA Sherman Kent School of Intelligence Analysis*, Occasional Papers 1, no. 2 (September 2002).

37. Garthoff, "US Intelligence," 31–32.

38. Gregory F. Treverton, *Reshaping National Intelligence for an Age of Information* (Cambridge: Cambridge University Press, 2003), 183–85. We explore this issue in some depth in chaps. 5, 6, and 7.

39. See chap. 6 by James Steinberg.

40. National Intelligence Council, *Iraq's Continuing Programs of Weapons of Mass Destruction* (NIE 2002-16HC, October 2002), and Colin L. Powell, "Speech to the U.N. Security Council, New York, Feb. 5, 2003," in *The WMD Mirage: Iraq's Decade of Deception and America's False Premise for War*, ed. Craig R. Whitney (New York: Public Affairs, 2005), 77–106.

41. This failure is discussed more fully in chaps. 9, 10, and 12.

42. *WMD Commission Report*, 157–76; Deputy Director of Intelligence Jamie Misick's "State of Analysis Speech," All-Hands Meeting, CIA Auditorium, February 11, 2004.

43. *WMD Commission Report*, 187–91; Senate Select Committee on Intelligence, *U.S. Intelligence Community's Prewar Intelligence Assessments on Iraq*, 108th Congress, 2nd Session, July 9, 2004, chap. 9. Related inquiries in the United Kingdom and Australia also concluded there was no politicization in the WMD analysis. See, respectively, the Butler report and the Flood report: *Review of Intelligence on Weapons of Mass Destruction*, Report of a Committee of Privy Counsellors, London, July 14, 2004, http://archive2.official-documents.co.uk/documents/dep/hc/hc898/898.pdf, and *Report of the Inquiry into Australian Intelligence Agencies*, July 20, 2004, available at www.pmc.gov.au/publications/intelligence_inquiry/index.htm#downloads.

44. Paul Pillar, "Intelligence, Policy, and the War in Iraq," *Foreign Affairs* 85, no. 2 (March/April 2006): 15–28. Similarly, CIA's Tyler Drumheller argues that Iraq better illustrates a policy failure that sought only supportive intelligence; interview on *Sixty Minutes*, CBS Television, April 23, 2006. He followed with *On the Brink: An Insider's Account of How the White House Compromised American Intelligence* (New York: Carroll & Graf, 2006).

PART I

The Analytic Tradition

CHAPTER 2

The Evolution of Intelligence Analysis in the US Intelligence Community

JOHN H. HEDLEY

The evolution of national-level intelligence analysis in the United States parallels the mid-twentieth-century emergence of the American concept of national security. That concept drove the mushrooming transformation of the United States into a national security state in response to World War II and especially to the Soviet superpower threat to America's survival that emerged in the war's aftermath. Pearl Harbor and the dawning of the Cold War propelled a change in America's understanding of intelligence and of national security as a term encompassing the complex mix of diplomacy, military strength, and intelligence that now would frame and equip America's central role in international affairs. Global threats to US national security would require global information. Intelligence, heretofore thought of essentially in terms of military operations during war, would need to cover not just enemy military forces but also political and economic developments worldwide.

The roots of contemporary all-source intelligence analysis did not take hold until World War II but were being planted even before the Japanese attack on the US Pacific Fleet in Hawaii. Whether or not the United States would be drawn militarily into combat in what clearly could be a war of global dimensions, the US intelligence apparatus was conspicuously inadequate. The United States was new to building national capabilities for global influence. Alone among the great powers, America had no centralized agency responsible for collecting and analyzing foreign intelligence. As a first step toward creating an integrated service, President Franklin D. Roosevelt summoned from private legal practice a personal confidant, William J. Donovan, a former soldier and statesman who undertook overseas missions as the president's personal envoy to appraise the emerging situation and survey America's anticipated intelligence needs. In July 1940, Donovan traveled to England to assess Britain's capacity to resist German subversion and possible invasion, after which he toured the Mediterranean basin. He returned convinced that a regular channel of strategic intelligence information was essential and that political and psychological factors were destined to play a major role in the looming "total" war.[1]

The president agreed, endorsing Donovan's recommendation that there be assembled in Washington a corps of "carefully selected trained minds" with a knowledge both of languages and research techniques. On July 11, 1941, Roosevelt signed an executive order creating the civilian Office of the Coordinator of Information, responsible directly to the president and the Joint Chiefs of Staff. Roosevelt named Donovan to the post and instructed him to "collect and analyze all information and data which may bear upon national security."[2] Within the new office Donovan created a Research and Analysis Branch, naming the president of Williams College, James Baxter, as its head, with an eminent Harvard historian, William Langer, as deputy. Recognizing that a body of expert knowledge could be found in the nation's universities and research institutions, Donovan, Baxter, and Langer set about recruiting scholars.

Staffing the new venture was not a problem. Professors welcomed the chance to serve the war effort with their academic skills. Recruits for R&A, as the branch was called, came from many fields, but especially many were historians, economists, political scientists, geographers, psychologists, anthropologists, and diplomats. Soon after the Office of Strategic Services (OSS) came into existence in 1942, R&A became its analytic arm, and an Enemy Objectives Unit staffed by R&A economists set up shop in London—the first example of forward-deployed analysts—to support the Allied bombing campaign against Germany by analyzing the vulnerabilities of Nazi industry. More than sixty R&A officers served in London, and more than four hundred would eventually serve in a dozen overseas outposts. R&A would grow to more than nine hundred analysts before the war was over, constituting a "chairborne division" of OSS officers whose intellectual inquiry supported combat operations and postwar planning. R&A analysis produced reports on a wide range of issues—for instance, assessing the condition of rail transport on the Russian front, attitudes of the Roman Catholic Church in Hungary, and the political ideas of Charles de Gaulle. Anthropologists studied Japanese films, and psychologists listened to the speeches of Joseph Goebbels. R&A regional specialists studied the Communist Party of India, inflation in Burma, guerrillas in the Philippines, trade routes in the Congo, and rival cliques in the Japanese army.[3]

The authorities and duties of the wartime R&A were limited, however. Its analysts were not all-source analysts; they had virtually no access to the signals intelligence that proved crucial to the Allied victory. The R&A Branch was not a "centralized" intelligence organization; it had no authority to coordinate intelligence for the president. Finally, the OSS was a war-fighting agency, and Donovan never thought of R&A as being "policy neutral." Victory was the goal, and finished intelligence was only another weapon in the US arsenal.

Truman Centralizes

With the war over, President Harry S. Truman promptly dissolved the OSS in September 1945 but retained its analytic capability, transferring the elements of the R&A Branch to the Department of State. Truman wanted a centralized organization to coordinate intelligence, and numerous postmortems on Pearl Harbor had recommended creating a central clearinghouse for all-source intelligence to warn of future threats. R&A's analysts had won many admirers, and even critics of the OSS agreed that R&A had proved that patient research and the collation of mundane information could yield valuable insights for commanders and policymakers.[4] The executive order eliminating the OSS established the Interim Research and Intelligence Service as a holding place for R&A, from whose resources Secretary of State James F. Byrnes was to fashion a new, State Department–based intelligence entity. Truman thus gave State an opportunity to be at the center of what was to become the intelligence community. Instead, a pitched bureaucratic battle broke out. From the outside, the War and Navy Departments insisted that State should not be the center of the new intelligence structure. From the inside, equal hostility came from Byrnes's assistant secretary for administration and many Foreign Service officers concerned that State's traditional diplomatic function would be overwhelmed by the intelligence component.[5]

Truman, impatient with the squabbling and bureaucratic paralysis, took matters into his own hands. In February 1946, he established the Central Intelligence Group (CIG) and authorized it to evaluate intelligence from all parts of the government. The CIG soon got an independent budget and the authority to hire its own workforce rather than merely accept officers offered by other departments. By the end of 1946, the CIG's Office of Reports and Estimates (ORE) had taken on at least three hundred people to correlate and evaluate information and prepare a daily intelligence digest for the president. Although much was in flux, two concepts that have remained key to the US analytic mission were by this time firmly established: Donovan's idea of having smart people work at making sense of all the available intelligence and Truman's insistence on having a central clearinghouse to correlate intelligence for the president and his advisers.[6]

Gaining recognition for the ORE as the central clearinghouse for intelligence was not easy. The White House had authorized the CIG's head—titled the director of central intelligence (DCI)—to "centralize" research and analysis in "fields of national security intelligence that are not being presently performed or are not being adequately performed."[7] This mandate helped to make the CIG the primary foreign intelligence arm of the US government, but it did not give the CIG a controlling role in intelligence analysis. On paper its functions were manifold: to produce national-level intelligence—current, scientific, technical, and economic—and to accomplish interagency coordination of national estimates. The latter proved difficult in the face of institutional resistance from established organizations guarding their information, independence, and prerogatives.

The current intelligence mission, conversely, grew in response to the president's interests with the highest priority: the president himself. On the very day that Truman brought the CIG into existence, he asked it to produce a daily summary of current intelligence. He wanted a single digest to help him make sense of the several departmental summaries crossing his desk. The president received the first *Daily Summary* within a week and was well pleased with it.[8] This modest publication created the precedent for one of the Central Intelligence Agency's core missions—the provision of strategic warning intelligence to the nation's leadership. Truman's interest, combined with the pressure of events in Europe, focused the ORE's efforts on current reporting rather than research or forecasting.[9]

An Independent CIA

In 1947, President Truman signed the National Security Act, creating the CIA, the National Security Council (NSC), and the Department of Defense (DOD). CIA began its existence in September 1947, with Congress (judging from the floor and committee debates over the ratification of the National Security Act) expecting it to provide the NSC—the organization that would coordinate and guide American foreign and defense policies—with the best possible information on developments abroad. Members of Congress said they hoped the new CIA would provide information that was "full, accurate, and skillfully analyzed," as well as "coordinated, adequate" and "sound." Senior military commanders testifying on the bill's behalf used similar adjectives, saying CIA's information should be "authenticated and evaluated," "correct," and based on "complete coverage." When CIA provided such information, it was believed, the NSC would be able to assess accurately the relative strengths and weaknesses of America's overseas posture and adjust policies accordingly.[10]

Congress guaranteed CIA's independence and its access to files in other government departments to give it the best chance to produce authoritative information for the nation's policymakers. CIA was to stand outside the policymaking departments of the government, the better to "correlate and evaluate intelligence relating to the national security." Other departments and agencies would continue to handle intelligence of national importance. But CIA was the only entity specifically charged by the National Security Act with the duty of producing national intelligence for the president. To accomplish this, the DCI was given the right to "inspect" all foreign intelligence held by other agencies, as well as the right to disseminate it as appropriate. If the DCI happened to be a military officer, then he was to be outside the chain of command of his home service. This would help him to resist any temptation to shade his reports to please his superiors.[11]

The creation of CIA made possible a significant expansion of the Office of Reports and Estimates from 300 staff employees in late 1946 to 709 by the end of 1950.[12] In the words of R&A veteran Ray Cline, the future deputy director for intelligence heading analysis at CIA and later a director of the State Department's Bureau of Intelligence and Research (INR), the expansion of the ORE made CIA "a little bigger than before but not much better."[13] Its analytic ranks were thin on experience and credentials. During the critical year of 1948—which saw Soviet-instigated crises in Europe, including the fall of Czechoslovakia and the blockade of land access to Berlin—the ORE's Soviet and East European branch comprised only thirty-eight analysts. Their strength was previous exposure to the Soviet Union: Nine had lived there, and twelve spoke Russian—both high figures for an era when American knowledge of the USSR was limited, even in academia. Only one had a PhD, some had college degrees far removed from intelligence, and a few no degree at all.[14]

Organizing Analysis

Spurring the evolution of intelligence analysis in the United States—and especially enhancing CIA's role as America's independent all-source analytic agency—was the fallout from communist North Korea's surprise invasion of South Korea in June 1950. Suddenly the Cold War had turned hot less than a year after the Soviets exploded an atomic bomb and China went communist. In the fall of 1950, Truman named a new DCI, Walter Bedell Smith, an army general who had served as chief of staff to Gen. Dwight D. Eisenhower in the European theater and subsequently as ambassador to the Soviet Union. Smith was appalled at the slackness of CIA analytic work on Korea, and he soon made sweeping organizational changes. He implemented the recommendations of a 1949 NSC survey report (overseen by OSS veteran and New York attorney Allen Dulles) and divided the ORE into three functional offices: the Office of National Estimates (ONE), whose sole task was the production of coordinated "national estimates"; the Office of Research and Reports (ORR), to support the ONE and conduct basic research; and the Office of Current Intelligence (OCI), to write summaries and other brief products for policymakers.[15]

The ONE had a staff that would draft the estimates, and a board of "wise men" reviewed and coordinated them with the other intelligence agencies. The ONE initially depended on departmental contributions but would rely increasingly on steadily growing CIA analytic resources. CIA drafts were negotiated with other members of the intelligence community, however, and thus gradually became less "CIA" than interdepartmental products.

The ORR amassed reference data and integrated it into such products as the national intelligence surveys as vital "services of common concern" provided for the intelligence community and the US government. The State Department claimed primary jurisdiction in economic as well as political intelligence, but in 1951 it struck a bureaucratic truce with CIA to allow the ORR to analyze the communist economies. The economic arena became the focus of the CIA's research and analysis effort, a development that had a major impact on military and strategic analysis of the Soviet Union.[16]

Current intelligence needed an organizational home but would not fit well in the ONE or the ORR. President Truman was an avid reader of daily intelligence, so DCI Smith directed that CIA must continue doing it well. He made CIA's daily publication an all-source product—for the first time including signals intelligence—and changed its name to the *Current Intelligence Bulletin*. Its success was clear by early 1951, when Truman thanked the DCI for the new publication: "Dear Bedell, I have been reading the intelligence bulletin and am highly impressed with it. I believe you have hit the jackpot with this one."[17]

In January 1952, DCI Smith established the Directorate of Intelligence (DI)—which continues to this day—to formulate strategic intelligence for US policymakers. Within the new directorate, the Office of Current Intelligence produced a daily intelligence publication for the president and senior policymakers, and the Office of National Estimates drafted and coordinated longer-term national estimates. An Office of Scientific Intelligence conducted weapon-related research—despite opposition from the military services, which saw that as their exclusive domain. The Office of Research and Reports did basic research—much of it economic and related to Soviet war potential—and gradually introduced political research, despite the State Department's opposition.[18]

Establishing an Intelligence Profession

Sherman Kent, who became head of the Office of National Estimates in 1952, helped set the tone for that organization for its next decade and a half. A veteran of the OSS's Research and Analysis Branch, a former professor, and an intelligence analyst for more than three decades, Kent left a legacy as America's foremost practitioner of the analytic craft. His 1949 book, *Strategic Intelligence for American World Policy*, explained analysis and the intelligence process in ways that continue to inform intelligence professionals today. His concepts of proper intelligence estimating were rigorous: no policy direction, no shading evidence or slanting analysis to reach a desired conclusion, no slipshod writing or shortcuts.[19]

The Korean War generated pressures for information that spurred a rapid expansion of CIA's DI into the major center of national intelligence analysis. Government-wide demands for reporting and strategic assessments of communist intentions led to dramatic growth that brought the number of DI personnel to 3,338 by the end of 1953.[20] Contemporaries recall the OCI turning out "a flood of the best written, most carefully analyzed intelligence reporting ever to hit Washington desks," which increased with President Eisenhower and his use of the NSC.[21]

Allen Dulles's years as DCI marked a change in the way CIA conceived its analytic functions and duties. In the beginning its leaders and their counterparts in other intelligence agencies wondered if it should be doing analysis at all—perhaps it should only provide current intelligence summaries and various reference services. The long debates in Washington over Soviet strategic forces during the 1950s, however, changed this perspective. No single policy department had the means to penetrate the mysteries shrouding the Soviet defense industries, ballistic missiles, and nuclear weapons, and the DI (aided by advances in collection, particularly the imagery obtained by U-2 aircraft) began to provide this vital service. Having built the essential expertise to do so, it offered policy neutrality—and thus, objectivity—that could transcend the policy pressures that might color departmental analyses. The DI's expansion of assignments and analysts, combined with its independence and direct access to the president, made it increasingly Washington's most visible analytic service, which was to make it more influential but also usually the target for complaints about the quality of intelligence analysis.

At the same time, the Cold War saw other analytic cadres, primarily in the State and Defense Departments, continuing to play key roles as both contributors and competitors. The makers of foreign and defense policy—primarily the secretaries of state and defense—are key intelligence consumers with different intelligence needs reflecting their unique operational responsibilities. These departmental intelligence units ensure that their departmental officials' specific operational intelligence needs are served. They often were working the same strategic issues as the DI but from the perspective of diplomatic and military needs in support of specific requirements. The fact that their work overlapped resulted in a duplication of efforts, but by design that duplication has been tolerated—indeed, encouraged—in the American system as a way of providing checks and balances in the form of competitive or alternative analysis.

The State Department's Bureau of Intelligence and Research (INR) had been the first nonmilitary cadre of intelligence analysts when it took over from the OSS in the 1940s. Indeed, in terms of personnel it was at its zenith during this period of the late 1940s and the 1950s, with a staff of about seven hundred. But INR's analytic focus then was on basic research. Some 40 percent of INR's budget came from CIA and supported analysts whose job was writing for the national intelligence surveys—comprehensive intelligence community studies whose goal was to include everything a warrior or a warrior-diplomat might need to know to fight against or alongside any country in the world. INR's access to the secretary of state was limited until Secretary Dean Acheson instituted daily morning briefings as the Korean War brought INR an analytic transition—as crises invariably do—to an emphasis on current intelligence.[22] Today INR, with fewer than three hundred professionals, retains its all-source analysis but is recognized for the depth of expertise on key diplomatic issues provided by its mix of civil and foreign service specialists. Moreover, as will be mentioned later in this volume, its greater ability to contact foreign policy experts in academia, both in the United States and abroad, has given it a special role in analytic outreach. Senior INR analysts also are in direct contact with policymakers and US ambassadors, and able to support ongoing negotiations in ways not done by CIA and military intelligence agencies.

The DIA Joins the Mix

The creation of the Defense Intelligence Agency (DIA) owed at least as much to a bureaucratic tug of war within DOD as to the idea of centralizing military intelligence to reduce duplication and parochialism. The years following creation of DOD (and CIA) by the National Security Act of 1947 saw a succession of amendments and DOD reorganizations aimed at shifting the balance of power in the Pentagon away from the separate armed services and toward the secretary of defense and the Joint Chiefs of Staff.[23] But the military services were allowed to maintain control of their individual intelligence organizations in recognition of their need for specialized tactical intelligence for combat commanders. Autonomous military intelligence components—the services argued—facilitated flexibility and responsiveness to the disparate intelligence requirements of different service missions.[24] In the waning days of the Eisenhower administration, a joint study group led by Lyman Kirkpatrick recommended combining service intelligence organizations into a single, unified agency, as well as establishing a single CIA-DOD imagery analysis center (later named the National Photographic Interpretation Center).

President John F. Kennedy and his newly appointed secretary of defense, Robert McNamara, were impressed by the study's concept of a strong, single manager. McNamara, coming from a business environment dominated by such an organizational paradigm, ordered the Joint Chiefs to develop a plan. McNamara became convinced of the need to reduce service bias in strategic intelligence and threat assessments, and he hoped to accomplish this by removing the evaluative capabilities from the individual services. They would handle the collection of raw intelligence and some processing, but analytic production and dissemination would occur at higher levels—preferably under the direction of the Office of the Secretary of Defense. He saw the creation of a consolidated military intelligence agency as his primary means of achieving the national intelligence estimates that would be so essential to his strategic reassessment. "I believed," McNamara wrote, "that removing the preparation of intelligence estimates from the *control* of the military services would reduce the *risk* that service biases—*unconscious* though they might be—would color the estimates" (emphasis his own).[25]

As originally conceived by McNamara, DIA would serve the strategic, national intelligence needs of the secretary of defense rather than the narrow, tactical intelligence needs of the Joint Chiefs of Staff. He recognized this plan had to be introduced gradually to avoid disruption and disagreement with the services. In 1961, the first DIA director had only twenty-five analysts assigned to borrowed space in the Pentagon. Even so, by the spring of 1961 there was open conflict between the military services, represented by the Joint Chiefs, and McNamara and his civilian analysts over the future of military intelligence. To end the internecine strife, McNamara agreed—in a significant departure from his previous position—to let DIA report to him *through* the Joint Chiefs rather than directly.[26] In the end, DIA's activation in the early autumn of 1961 as an intelligence support agency carried the day for the Joint Chiefs and the armed services. By the end of 1964, DIA counted approximately 3,600 employees housed in facilities across the Washington area. By 1968, its numbers rose to nearly 7,000, and it was reporting on 127 countries.[27]

In the decades that followed, DIA's analytic mission has grown exponentially. Its director, a three-star general, now serves as the principal adviser on substantive intelligence to both the secretary of defense and the chairman of the Joint Chiefs. DIA's all-source, defense-related analysis encompasses current and estimative intelligence production. Its analytic ranks—a significant segment of the DIA workforce—contribute to IC coverage of the proliferation of weapons of mass destruction, international terrorism, international narcotics trafficking, and defense-related foreign political, economic, industrial, geographic, and medical and health issues.[28]

In an effort to be more responsive to its defense customers, and because of debates over whether it should have a regional or functional structure, DIA has gone through periodic reorganizations.[29] Like the State Department's INR, DIA began providing departmental intelligence uniquely supporting the mission of its department's role in making and implementing policy. At the same time, INR and DIA would critique, coordinate, and contribute their own perspectives to the national intelligence produced at CIA. During the Cold War this was especially the case in the preparation of national intelligence estimates and most especially the case in estimating the military capabilities and the strategic threat posed by the Soviet Union.

Colby's Innovations: NIOs and the National Intelligence Council

William Colby became director of central intelligence in 1973 believing that the Office of National Estimates had become too CIA-centric and had lapsed into an "ivory-tower mentality" detached from the needs and concerns of policymakers. Thus he replaced it with a group of national intelligence officers (NIOs), each to be responsible for coordinating estimates on a particular region or subject. To reduce CIA influence, the NIOs were drawn from "throughout the intelligence community and the academic world to bring to me [Colby] the best ideas and to press the different disciplines to integrate their efforts."[30] Although the NIOs were to assign the drafting of each estimate to the intelligence community's best analysts on the particular subject, CIA officers still filled many of the NIO positions, and CIA analysts did most of the drafting. There followed the creation of the National Intelligence Council, consisting of all the NIOs for regional and functional areas, whose first chairman had previously been the senior official responsible for strategic warning. The logic of this appointment was that warning was the *primes inter pares* mission, and thus the chairman would convene the council to ensure that NIOs would bring warning issues to the attention of the broader intelligence community, as well as senior policymakers.[31] The NIC grew in stature, adding to its NIEs a range of other intelligence products, as well as backstopping senior intelligence officials when they attended NSC and other interagency meetings.

Colby, an innovator, introduced a novel approach to current intelligence with a highly restricted publication in newspaper format aimed at senior policymakers he reasoned were "avid newspaper readers."[32] The DI expanded its twenty-four-hour staffing to make this new *National Intelligence Daily* (which replaced the *Current Intelligence Bulletin*) as timely as possible. Most material was drafted during normal working hours, but each drafting component had someone staying late for updates. Six days a week, teams of two editors each worked shifts of noon to 10 p.m., or 9 p.m. to 7 a.m., to edit drafts and decide on their placement in what was usually a four-page publication slightly smaller than a regular newspaper page. The editors wrote the headlines, gave a final review to the pages pasted onto a light table, and waited while a full-scale offset press in an adjacent room rumbled with the morning's edition as dawn was breaking. The more sensitive articles were included in *President's Daily Brief* (*PDB*) and sent to the White House, while the new *National Intelligence Daily* served others at the top levels of the national security community. Colby also introduced Vice President Gerald Ford to the *PDB*—the most sensitive of daily analytic products—inadvertently paving the way for CIA later to gain daily access to the Oval Office. Having invited Ford to visit CIA in 1974, Colby innocently mentioned the *PDB*—which, it turned out, Ford had never seen! Only then did President Richard Nixon authorize him to receive it, and CIA sent a senior DI officer to take the *PDB* and other pertinent items to Ford early each morning at his residence. When Nixon resigned later in 1974 and Ford became president, Ford continued the practice of having a CIA officer deliver the *PDB*—now to the Oval Office—and discuss items with him.

Ford's second DCI, George H. W. Bush, adopted this practice when he became vice president. He was an advocate and avid reader of the *PDB* throughout the administration of Ronald Reagan, when a CIA officer with the *PDB* would sit down at the beginning of each day separately with the vice president, the president's national security adviser, the secretaries of state and defense, and an added recipient, the chairman of the Joint Chiefs of Staff. When he became president, Bush made the *PDB* his first order of daily business in the Oval Office—a practice that has continued under his successors to varying degrees of regularity.

Reorganizing CIA Analysis

Under President Reagan's choice as DCI, William Casey, CIA's analytic directorate was revamped along geographic rather than functional lines, both to more closely align it with the State Department's regional bureaus and to integrate political, economic, and military experts into offices analyzing the Soviet Union, Europe, Africa, Latin America, the Near East, South Asia, and East Asia. A new Office of Global Issues would tackle "transnational" topics. Analysts suffered a rough period of sorting out responsibilities and space while maintaining the quality and quantity of their work. Hundreds of analysts had to relocate and learn to work with different colleagues. They adjusted, and the restructuring succeeded in enhancing interdisciplinary research and analysis.

The geographic structure meant that CIA's country analysts now worked together, but the attention required to cover transnational problems such as terrorism soon exceeded the capabilities of a single Office of Global Issues. Collectors needed regional and country analysis in order to target operations more effectively. Further innovation was needed to integrate analysis with fast-moving law enforcement issues. The answer came in the creation of "centers," each focused on a single transnational issue and including representatives from other intelligence community organizations. The centers brought analysts of various academic disciplines and area expertise to work side by side with collectors, operations officers, and representatives of law enforcement. The new Counterterrorism Center's success at using this integrated team approach in the mid-1980s became a model for additional centers. It was followed in 1989 with the Counternarcotics Center (it was later expanded to the Crime and Narcotics Center) and other DCI centers addressing counterintelligence, proliferation, arms control, and environmental concerns.[33]

Post-Soviet Search for Relevance

The reordering of priorities to which CIA analysts—still the largest collection of all-source analysts in the intelligence community—responded put actionable intelligence at the top. This applied not only to support for the military but also to law enforcement and CIA's own clandestine operations. Expectations intensified for analysts throughout the community—not just at CIA—to warn of looming threats, to target collection and operations, and to give US officials greater leverage in international negotiations. "Opportunity analysis" was to identify actions or events that could be turned to the advantage of the United States. Analytic products reflected the new emphasis, and increasing numbers of analysts went on rotational assignments to the various centers, policy agencies, and overseas.

New intelligence priorities placed further emphasis on education and further steps toward professionalization of analysis. The long-standing recognition of the importance of training and education was reflected in DIA's Defense Intelligence School, which was renamed the Joint Military Intelligence College (JMIC) in 1993 and the National Defense Intelligence College (NDIC) in 2003.[34] In 2010, the NDIC became the executive agent for the DNI-created National Intelligence University.[35]

At CIA, John McLaughlin, as deputy director of intelligence from 1997 to 2000, established the Sherman Kent School of Intelligence Analysis, CIA's most intensive effort to teach the tradecraft of analysis and learn from the lessons of the past.[36] McLaughlin also established the Senior Analytic Service to provide a professional career track by which analysts could advance to senior grades on the basis of expertise and performance alone, rather than by opting for staff and managerial assignments.

Underlying all these efforts were debates over issues that probably never will be resolved, such as how best to organize analytic components, the proper balance between current intelligence and in-depth research, and whether analysts should tell policymakers which issues are important—or the other way around. During much of the Cold War, long-term research on the relatively stable Soviet target was a necessary focus of analytic assessments. Since then the organizational pendulum has swung toward closer involvement of analysts in support of collection, operations, and policy objectives. On September 11, 2001, counterterrorism took top priority for the indefinite future. The attacks that day on the World Trade Center in New York and on the Pentagon in Washington underscored the growing challenges to intelligence in an era of international terrorism in which small groups of individuals can inflict destruction once wielded only by nation-states.

Post-9/11 Analytic Reforms and Trends

America's terrorist tragedy in 2001, combined with the Iraq/WMD analytic mistakes, led to a scramble to enact the Intelligence Reform and Terrorism Prevention Act of 2004. Most notably, this legislation created the position of the director of national intelligence as a promised institutional corrective for the facts that the vast US national intelligence apparatus did not somehow prevent the terrible events of September 11 and that it failed a year later to grasp that Saddam's presumed WMD capability was actually a bluff. The inquiries explored what went wrong and what might be done about it.[37] Their overriding conclusions with respect to intelligence analysis were that there had been a failure of imagination—that is, analysts had become too risk-averse and disinclined to consider possible surprises. Recommendations included better use of open-source information, improved information sharing, and closer integration of analytic efforts across the now sixteen-member US intelligence community.

Among other initiatives, President George W. Bush approved a 50 percent increase in analytic positions for CIA, along with rapid growth in counterterrorism operations there and across the community. More analysts were assigned to CIA's Counterterrorism Center (CTC), as well as the newly created National Counterterrorism Center (NCTC). More analysts were also forward-deployed to support ongoing counterterrorism operations as well. Indeed, there developed a new analytic discipline called "targeting analysis," to reflect the strong push to place analysts closer to collectors and counterterrorism operators.

The creation of the Office of the Director of National Intelligence (ODNI) has focused on improved integration and collaboration in intelligence analysis, rigorous analytic standards, and more information sharing among analysts across agency lines. A later chapter in this volume details some of those innovations, but suffice it to say that the DNI has brought more central direction aimed at rising above the bureaucratic fiefdoms that had prevented the sharing of HUMINT sources and analytic perspectives.

Today under the DNI there are competitive all-source analytic centers—predominantly CIA's DI, DIA's Intelligence Directorate, and INR, but including the National Security Agency (NSA), the National Geospatial-Intelligence Agency (NGA), and increasingly the NCTC and other intelligence community agencies. This not only helps to override purely parochial views but also to experiment with a continuum of analytic methods and structured techniques. The National Intelligence Council—already a recognized center of strategic analysis producing national intelligence estimates and other intelligence community assessments—has increased emphasis on peer review and the use of outside experts. A major change has been the ODNI's management of the *PDB*—once the exclusive preserve of the CIA analysts—which is now a community product that allows DIA and INR analysts to both contribute to and produce items of presidential interest.

Along with CIA, DIA has gone through a major transformation since the 2011 attacks and the prosecution of wars in Afghanistan and Iraq. Following 9/11 DIA mobilized major support efforts to Operation Enduring Freedom, deploying hundreds of analysts to Afghanistan for in-theater support and document exploitation. In 2009, DIA created the Afghanistan-Pakistan Task Force to coordinate military intelligence activities throughout the region and to be more responsive to military intelligence requirements. Likewise, DIA mobilized hundreds of analysts to support Operation Iraqi Freedom's combat operations, as well as staff the Iraq Survey Group's investigations into Iraq's WMD programs.

Overall, DIA saw a dramatic increase in the number of its employees deployed overseas to improve its deployment-related capabilities for the war efforts. This is merely the latest iteration of its "combat support" responsibilities that began as far back as the 1970s.[38]

One additional but often overlooked change in the US analytic community was the significant increase in the role of the Federal Bureau of Investigation (FBI) in domestic intelligence analysis. Following the 9/11 attacks, the FBI's role in detecting and combating domestic terrorism led to a massive increase in the number of analysts assigned to work with FBI headquarters and field offices. Initially the FBI required significant support from CIA and other analytic agencies to train a new cadre of FBI analysts. As described in a later chapter, the FBI quickly developed its own counterterrorism division and built up a cadre of almost three thousand analysts in Washington and around the country in joint counterterrorism task forces. Reflecting this new community focus, the NIC also conducted more national estimative projects focused on domestic terrorism threats, to which the FBI made major contributions.

The Challenge of Rebalancing Analysis

Today's analytic community is filled with more new faces, its ranks having expanded rapidly to fill additional positions approved by Congress to help fight the global war on terrorism while still providing coverage of events, issues, and trends worldwide. New developments and capabilities in information technology enable analysts to work in new ways within a classified environment that struggles to keep up with the ever-accelerating pace of available technology. The war on terrorism, and especially a decade of US combat operations in Iraq and Afghanistan, had put terrorism-targeting current intelligence in the forefront, again raising questions of emphasis in comparison with longer-term, in-depth research. With those wars in Iraq and Afghanistan winding down in 2013, there appears to be a call to rebalance intelligence analysis, as well as collection, toward more coverage of noncombat areas, from which the next set of crises could potentially arise.[39] More attention is likely to be focused on other regional challenges, especially in light of Washington's "pivot" or "rebalancing" toward the Asia-Pacific region. Thus this decade, like all previous ones, is sure to provide opportunities for more analytic adjustments and advances to deal with the new international realities.

Notes

The author wishes to thank Roger Z. George for assisting with updating this chapter to reflect additional changes that have occurred in the analytic mission since 2007.

1. Barry M. Katz, *Foreign Intelligence: Research and Analysis in the Office of Strategic Services, 1942–1945* (Cambridge, MA: Harvard University Press, 1989), 2.
2. William J. Donovan to Franklin D. Roosevelt, "Memorandum of Establishment of Service of Strategic Information," June 10, 1941, in *Donovan and the CIA: A History of the*

Establishment of the Central Intelligence Agency, Thomas F. Troy (Frederick, MD: University Publications of America, 1984), 420.

3. Katz, *Foreign Intelligence*, 18.

4. Dean Acheson, *Present at the Creation: My Years in the State Department* (New York: Norton, 1969), 157–63.

5. Mark Stout and Dorothy Avery, "The Bureau of Intelligence and Research at Fifty," *Studies in Intelligence* 42, no. 2 (1998): 18–19.

6. John H. Hedley, "The DI: A History of Service," in *The Directorate of Intelligence: Fifty Years of Informing Policy: 1952–2002* (Washington, DC: CIA, 2002), 3. This chapter draws heavily on the content of the author's essay in that commemorative volume.

7. National Intelligence Authority Directive Number 5, July 8, 1946, reprinted in *Central Intelligence: Origin and Evolution*, ed. Michael Warner (Washington, DC: CIA, 2001), 24.

8. Harry S. Truman, *Memoirs*, vol. 2, *Years of Trial and Hope* (Garden City, NY: Doubleday, 1956), 58. See also Arthur B. Darling, *The Central Intelligence Agency: An Instrument of Government to 1950* (University Park: Pennsylvania State University Press, 1990), 81–82. The *Daily Summary* did not include signals intelligence, but by the end of 1946 the editors were able to check draft articles against signals intelligence reports. See Russell Jack Smith, *The Unknown CIA: My Three Decades with the Agency* (McLean, VA: Pergamon-Brassey's, 1989), 34–35.

9. Much of the publicly available information on the organizational history of CIA analysis appears in a 1975 history produced by staffer Anne Karalekas for the Senate Select Committee to Study Governmental Operations. Her draft was based in part on histories written by CIA's history staff, and it was reprinted under the title "History of the Central Intelligence Agency" in *The Central Intelligence Agency: History and Documents*, ed. William M. Leary (Tuscaloosa: University of Alabama Press, 1984), 10, 26.

10. Lyle Miller, "Legislative History of the Central Intelligence Agency: National Security Act of 1947," declassified draft, Office of Legislative Counsel, CIA, July 25, 1967, 40, 45, 47, 48, 50.

11. See section 102 of the National Security Act of 1947, which is reproduced in Warner, *Central Intelligence*, 30.

12. A table of organization with these figures, dated December 20, 1950, is cited in *Assessing the Soviet Threat: The Early Cold War Years*, ed. Woodrow J. Kuhns (Washington, DC: CIA, 1997), 12.

13. Ray S. Cline, *Secrets, Spies and Scholars: Blueprint of the Essential CIA* (Washington, DC: Acropolis Books, 1976), 92.

14. Kuhns, *Assessing the Soviet Threat*, 1.

15. Karalekas, "History of the Central Intelligence Agency," 28–34.

16. Ibid., 90.

17. Harry Truman's letter to DCI Smith, March 8, 1951, quoted by John L. Helgerson, *CIA Briefings of Presidential Candidates, 1952–1992* (Washington, DC: CIA, 1996), 27.

18. Ludwell Lee Montague, *General Walter Bedell Smith as Director of Central Intelligence* (University Park: Pennsylvania State University Press, 1992), 92–95.

19. Smith, *Unknown CIA*, 75–76.

20. Karalekas, "History of the Central Intelligence Agency," 35.

21. Cline, *Secrets, Spies and Scholars*, 146, 151–53.

22. Stout and Avery, "Bureau of Intelligence," 17, 19.
23. Keith C. Clark and Lawrence J. Legere, eds., *The President and Management of National Security* (New York: Praeger, 1969), 175.
24. Walter Laqueur, *A World of Secrets: The Uses and Limits of Intelligence* (New York: Basic Books, 1985), 33, quoted by Patrick Neil Mescall, "A Creature of Compromise: The Establishment of the DIA," *International Journal of Intelligence and Counterintelligence* 7, no. 3 (Fall 1994): 253.
25. Quoted from personal correspondence with Mescall, ibid., 263.
26. Ibid., 265–66.
27. Blue Ribbon Defense Panel," Report to the President and the Secretary of Defense on the Department of Defense," July 1, 1970.
28. Defense Intelligence Agency, www.dia.mil.
29. See James R. Clapper, "Reorganization of DIA and Defense Intelligence Activities," *American Intelligence Journal* (Autumn–Winter 1993–1994): 13–14.
30. William Colby and Peter Forbath, *Honorable Men: My Life in the CIA* (New York: Simon & Schuster, 1978), 351–53.
31. Author's conversation with former Deputy Director of Intelligence
32. Colby and Forbath, *Honorable Men*, 354.
33. Office of Public Affairs, CIA, *Consumer's Guide to Intelligence* (Collingdale, PA: Diane Publishing, 2000), 13–14.
34. This was renamed the National Defense Intelligence College in 2003 and is now a fully accredited program.
35. Defense Intelligence Agency, www.dia.mil/college.
36. In 2000, the then–deputy director of intelligence, Douglas MacEachin, initiated the first major analytic training program throughout CIA's analytic corps. The two-week long Tradecraft 2000 workshops became the basis for later development of structured analytic techniques. See Roger Z. George, "Fixing the Problem of Analytical Mindsets," in *Intelligence and the National Security Strategist: Enduring Issues and Challenges*, ed. Roger Z. George and Robert D. Kline (Washington, DC: National Defense University Press, 2005), 315–16.
37. E.g., see *9/11 Commission Report: Final Report of the National Commission on Terrorist Attacks upon the United States* (New York: Barnes & Noble, 2004), and *Report of the Commission on the Intelligence Capabilities of the United States regarding Weapons of Mass Destruction* (Washington, DC: Government Printing Office, 2005). See also Richard A. Posner, *Preventing Surprise Attacks: Intelligence Reform in the Wake of 9/11* (Lanham, MD: Rowman & Littlefield, 2005), and Richard A. Posner, *Uncertain Shield: The U.S. Intelligence System in the Throes of Reform* (Lanham, MD: Rowman & Littlefield, 2006).
38. DIA began deploying personnel to combat zones in 1973 when nearly a hundred analysts staffed the Intelligence Branch in the Defense Attaché Office in Saigon. The next major deployment was in 1990 and 1991, when a like number was sent to the Persian Gulf to support Operation Desert Shield and Operation Desert Storm. This trend accelerated from 2003 to 2005, when DIA deployed no fewer than 1,500 people as part of the Iraq Survey Group, rising to 5,500 in 2010 with the intensification of the Iraq War. See www.dia.mil/pdf?DIA-2001-calendar.pdf.
39. See David Ignatius, "David Petraeus: CIA Needs Post-Petraeus Intel Fix," *Washington Post*, November 15, 2012.

CHAPTER 3

The Track Record of CIA Analysis

RICHARD J. KERR AND MICHAEL WARNER

Academic efforts to evaluate the performance of the intelligence community (IC) are inevitably complicated by the secretive nature of its activities and by an understandable unfamiliarity with the cultures, art forms, and work practices used by intelligence analysts. Moreover, as Richards Heuer explains, we all suffer—critics and defenders alike—from hindsight biases. Indeed, any career professional with decades of producing and managing analysis can suffer ironically from too much familiarity with the topic.[1] John Hedley explains as well in chapter 2 that the Central Intelligence Agency (CIA) and the IC underwent huge organizational and personnel changes in response to shifting demands from the policy community. The period under review witnessed numerous coups, major revolutions, minor rebellions, and countless terrorist incidents. Add in as well the rise of other global issues, some of which had no end, while others persisted for weeks, months, or years. We can only hope to provide here a sense of CIA's analytic performance based on direct experience, as well as on our official duties as an independent consultant on controversial intelligence problems and an historian of intelligence.

To assess that performance, one must begin with a reasonable set of standards. The reader should note three things that strategic analysis does:

- Assess the significance of new developments as they relate to US policy. Identifying opportunities for US policy is also part of this job.
- Provide warning of dangerous situations to policymakers, perhaps the most difficult task of the intelligence analyst.
- Develop longer-term assessments of major political, military, economic, and technical trends. Research is like an intellectual savings account that not only trains and builds a knowledge base for analysts but also forces them and their customers to challenge existing mind-sets and to imagine alternative outcomes.

One must also realize there is rarely any such thing as "CIA analysis" per se. CIA's analytic role has always been part of a much larger story of government-wide efforts to collect, analyze, and respond to foreign challenges. CIA employs all-source analysts who earn their pay by making sense of the data collected and the evaluations prepared by their own agency, by other components of the IC and the US government, or shared by other governments. This is not an excuse so much as an explanation for how hard it can be for analysts of foreign affairs to see the complete picture when many of the activities they observe themselves are influenced by the actions of other US domestic, diplomatic, or military organizations (as well as those of allies).

Why then concentrate on CIA analysis at all, much less appraise it for whether it guided wise policies or warned of impending threats? Because CIA's Directorate of Intelligence (DI) has long been the proverbial "top of the intelligence food chain," as a senior agency analyst once explained to one of the authors. CIA is the only formally independent intelligence element in the IC (all the others belong to a governmental department), and it has a long tradition of providing direct analytic support to the president and the nation's most senior national security policymakers. On almost every important topic, the DI usually had more access, more objectivity, more resources, or more expertise than other IC agencies. Its product is typically received as the gold standard for American intelligence analysis, and whether the DI was right or it stumbled, the consequences often had national implications. In short, on-target or off, CIA analysis mattered.

Characterizing decades of analysis can only be done with the benefit of hindsight. What that shows is that US intelligence, especially when compared with foreign intelligence services, has provided American presidents and their lieutenants with the broadest and most comprehensive information offered to any government. This record has witnessed failures, naturally, but more successes, some of them unrecognized because they seemed (after the fact) so commonplace. No president can afford to neglect CIA and other agencies' analysis without risking grave missteps. It helped to reduce the uncertainty surrounding many world events, to raise the level of understanding of participants in key policy debates, and to alert decision makers to critical issues they might have overlooked.

The Soviet Union: Its Rise and Fall

The strategic threat posed by the Soviet Union marked the most pressing intelligence challenge during the Cold War. Though the superpowers avoided a direct military clash, many international crises and proxy wars had their roots in this rivalry, and for decades Washington perceived nearly all events in the context of the struggle with the Soviets. This was the original mission of CIA analysis, conferred upon analysts in CIA's predecessor, the short-lived Central Intelligence Group (CIG) in 1946, just months after President Truman asked the CIG's director for a daily digest of intelligence reports. The challenge of monitoring and forecasting the behavior of heavily armed dictators thereafter remained a constant of CIA analysis. Little was known about the secretive Soviet Union in the 1950s, however, and early CIA officials characterized the challenge as making an "inventory of ignorance."[2] For them to do their job, the IC had to build a panoply of systems to collect data from human sources, as well as imagery, communications, and other technical sources. Analysts who knew what data were needed and who understood the collection systems' capacities gradually constructed a knowledge base on the USSR that was without equal in the free world.[3] Using it, CIA analysts tried to help US policymakers understand internal Soviet policy and leadership developments, the defense-dominated economy, and Moscow's attempts to expand its worldwide reach and alter the balance of power with the United States.

Assessing the strength and readiness of Soviet strategic and conventional military forces (including doctrine, tactics, capabilities, and intentions) constituted the main intelligence effort during the Cold War. Seen in retrospect, CIA's work was impressive in scope and often prescient. There were few major weapon systems—out of the hundreds of strategic missile, tactical missile, submarine, aircraft, land warfare, and air defense systems—that were not identified and had their capabilities assessed in considerable detail. CIA analysts dispelled the notion of a "missile gap" and later discovered the Soviet nuclear missiles covertly placed in Cuba in 1962. New satellite collection programs boosted analytic understanding of Soviet nuclear programs and even made it possible for the United States to negotiate verifiable arms control deals that eventually reduced the size of the Soviet arsenal.

Soviet strategic power rested in turn on that nation's economic vitality, which meant that estimating the former inevitably dictated an analytic campaign to understand the latter. Since the early 1950s, CIA largely created the discipline of studying centrally planned economies; one observer told Congress decades later that the intelligence community's quest to understand the Soviet economy "may well have been the largest single social science research project in the history of humanity!"[4] CIA had its critics before and after the Cold War; some felt it underestimated the size of the Soviet economy and the burden of related military spending, while others contended that CIA exaggerated those measures, many of which were made public in presentations to Congress's Joint Economic Committee.[5] A panel of outside economic experts found flaws in CIA economic models and methods but reported to Congress in 1991: "We find it hard to believe that anyone who has read CIA's annual public reports on the state of the Soviet economy since 1975 could possibly interpret them as saying that the Soviet economy was booming. On the contrary, these reports regularly reported the steady decline in the Soviet growth rate and called attention to the deep and structural problems that pointed to continued decline and possibly to stagnation."[6]

In theory, Soviet political and strategic intentions should have mirrored Moscow's own assessment of its military capabilities and economic strength. Thus CIA analysis of the thinking of the men in the Kremlin should have been enhanced by all the hard work of the agency's military and economic analysts. Often it was; CIA analysts concluded in the 1960s and 1970s that the Soviets were bent on achieving strategic parity with the United States rather than seeking a preponderance of power. CIA's analysis of the Soviet military and economy was more methodologically sophisticated than anything available to analysts of Soviet political and leadership issues, however, and sometimes Soviet leaders acted in ways that seemed utterly contrary to their own interests. Perhaps the most challenging and least satisfactory analytic efforts were assessments of how Soviet policymakers calculated the risks and opportunities they faced. Debates raged throughout the Cold War over Moscow's putative contemplation of nuclear "war fighting" versus its alleged acceptance of American concepts of deterrence. Premier Nikita Khrushchev's deployment of nuclear missiles to Cuba in 1962, the most dangerous moment in Soviet brinksmanship, came as a major strategic surprise. In a September 1962 national intelligence estimate, analysts incorrectly assumed that Khrushchev understood the risks he faced in directly confronting the Kennedy administration in the Western Hemisphere.[7] Similarly, a later generation of analysts found themselves underestimating a different Soviet leadership's willingness to intervene in Afghanistan's growing turmoil in 1979, having judged that the Kremlin would neither jeopardize détente nor undertake a risky occupation of the country.[8] Soon both CIA and the key Kremlin players themselves did not realize the degree to which the Communist Party, the economy, and the political system in general had become dysfunctional in the late 1980s. The continuing Soviet investment in strategic military forces and Soviet troublemaking throughout the world preoccupied intelligence analysts. Moreover, early signs of civil unrest and its implications for stability were identified by some analysts but initially dismissed by CIA analysts who believed the Soviet regime could easily quell any unrest by suppressing dissidents or otherwise appeasing the Soviet public.[9]

Even when surprised, however, agency analysts provided good situational awareness. Analysts monitored the Soviet invasion of Czechoslovakia (1968) and the Polish crisis (1980–81) as they unfolded, after having provided strategic warning to policymakers about Moscow's desire to curtail liberalization in both countries. In the Polish case, analysts were aided by sensitive human intelligence regarding Soviet plans.[10] Despite reporting on a day-to-day basis, however, they did not predict when martial law might be imposed. US policymakers also failed to act on information they had at their disposal or to publicize what they knew of Moscow's intentions, which might have altered Polish or Soviet calculations. CIA analysis was good in following crucial leadership changes in the 1980s, as well as the democratic revolutions that swept Eastern Europe in 1989. In fact, the failings of the Soviet system were repeatedly and clearly documented in a running stream of assessments.[11] Thus the breakup of the Warsaw Pact and disintegration of the Soviet Union probably were better assessed by CIA than even the Soviet leaders in the Kremlin. From 1987 until 1989, CIA reports documented the steep rise in labor unrest from a few dozen strikes to more than five hundred, involving hundreds of thousands of workers. President George H. W. Bush's advisers were not eager to hear senior CIA officers' views on President Mikhail Gorbachev's declining influence in the face of Russia's increasingly popular Boris Yeltsin. Yet throughout this period, the analysts' aim was objectivity—namely, to understand the strengths and weaknesses of an adversary, not to paint the picture policymakers expected to see. Gorbachev himself did not know how the story would end, nor did he intend to bring down the Soviet system.

The record does not seem to support the famous charge by the late senator Daniel P. Moynihan (and others) that CIA had exaggerated not only the Soviet economy but also the Soviet threat.[12] On the whole, CIA and IC estimates of Soviet strategic nuclear programs were good. Estimates in the late 1960s and early 1970s were somewhat low, while in the early 1980s they erred on the high side before being adjusted downward.[13] CIA analysts also heard charges that they were minimizing the Soviet threat. For example, President Richard Nixon and Secretary of State Henry Kissinger criticized CIA analysis that did not support their defense objectives, which would have been aided by more alarming assessments of Soviet modernization programs.[14] A few years later the "Team B" study group (a team of cleared outside experts convened in 1976 by the President's Foreign Intelligence Advisory Board—later the President's Intelligence Advisory Board) implicitly accused the analysts monitoring Moscow's strategic modernization of systematic bias and a misunderstanding of Soviet objectives.[15] Even DCI William Casey disbelieved his own analysts' insistence that Soviet oil pipeline deals with Europe were unstoppable and that there was no evidence of a Soviet hand in the 1981 papal assassination attempt.

In the final assessment, the fact that the Warsaw Pact and the Soviet Union broke apart without a major war attests to the basic soundness of US policy and the quality of the intelligence supporting it. Former national security adviser Brent Scowcroft, long a principal customer, felt well served by the intelligence community during this tumultuous period, noting that "its purpose is to inform and narrow the range of uncertainty within which a decision must be made . . . and keep policy within reasonable bounds."[16] Here was an instance where intelligence got little publicity because it was so well integrated into successful policy.

Asia: Wars and Nuclear Weapons

The vast intelligence effort to follow the Soviet Union had direct application to other emerging challenges. Agency analysts acutely felt the difficulty of assessing the intentions and capabilities of communist regimes and of convincing policymakers of the objectivity and accuracy of their evaluations.

China's rise to world power was closely monitored by CIA but with the disadvantage of having even less hard information than was available to analysts watching the Soviets. One longtime CIA China watcher explained that in the early Cold War, "intelligence analysts enjoyed few advantages over their academic and journalistic counterparts on the question of the inner workings of the Communist Chinese Party."[17] After a disastrous failure to spot China's intervention in the Korean War (1950), the agency's growing analytic effort was able to provide policymakers with assessments of Mao Zedong's hold on power, the internal Communist Party struggles, and the emerging Sino-Soviet split. A Soviet military analyst in CIA was one of the first to detect the growing tensions between China and the Soviet Union, and the agency monitored China's disastrous Great Leap Forward and later the chaos of the Cultural Revolution. Analysts spotted the internal pressures and disagreements inside the Chinese military leadership and were quick to develop the story about the attempted defection of Vice Premier Lin Biao (Mao's designated successor) to the Soviet Union in 1971.

Analysts also watched China's growing military strength. They judged that China would pursue its goal of assimilating Taiwan and would continually test Taiwanese and

American resolve—but they saw little evidence that Beijing would attack Taiwan so long as doing so risked drawing in the United States. This was a deadly serious issue; Washington publicly mentioned the possibility of a nuclear retaliation if China attacked the island of Quemoy in 1955. Analysts correctly predicted a Chinese nuclear program would emerge in the early 1960s, but it advanced more rapidly than analysts expected. Equally challenging to analysts was understanding where it might lead. As a 1967 NIE explained, "There is little evidence on Chinese thinking with respect to the role of nuclear weapons in [its] overall strategy."[18] CIA correctly judged that Beijing was not seeking "strategic parity" with the United States but rather desired a modest nuclear arsenal for the prestige and deterrence it conferred.

Given the difficulty of assessing intentions in Moscow and Beijing, CIA's mixed record with regard to the smaller communist regimes in Asia looks understandable. Analysis of North Korea didn't really begin until its 1950 surprise attack on South Korea, and analysts have been wary of forecasting Pyongyang's actions ever since. Despite evidence of war preparations in that year, analysts judged it unlikely that Kim Il Sung would act independently of Moscow, which to their minds had no interest in a war on the peninsula.[19]

Vietnam analysis during the height of the American military involvement there in the 1960s was essentially a subset of USSR and China analysis, with even less hard evidence from which to work. DCI Richard Helms recalled that from "the onset, the intelligence directorate and the Office of National Estimates held a pessimistic view of the military developments."[20] CIA assessments of the weak South Vietnamese governments and the comparatively resolute North Vietnamese intentions and capabilities were equally pessimistic, as well as generally accurate.

Making believers out of policymakers during the Vietnam War proved perhaps as tough as analyzing Hanoi's intentions. CIA assessments of the war challenged Johnson and Nixon administration assertions that American and South Vietnamese policies could succeed, judging that time and resolution were on the side of North Vietnam.[21] The agency won grudging respect for its objectivity, especially in comparison with the judgments of military analysts in the Pentagon and Saigon. In 1965, Secretary of Defense Robert McNamara and the chairman of the Joint Chiefs of Staff quietly asked CIA to produce independent assessments of North Vietnam's strength and to confer with military colleagues in hopes of improving the accuracy of the US government's order-of-battle figures.[22] Subsequent debates over the numbers of combatants on the communist side have become famous for their intensity—although what is less well-known is that all American analysts were grasping at straws, even if CIA's effort looks more intellectually honest in retrospect.[23] Collection shortfalls hobbled analysis. As elsewhere in the communist world, reliable data on the magnitude of North Vietnamese infiltration and resupply were not yet available to anyone. After signals intelligence improved in 1969, the debates subsided somewhat, although two years later CIA and military analysts were still underestimating the communist infiltration of men and materiel into South Vietnam.[24] Although CIA assessed the deteriorating political and military situation accurately, it did not forecast the surprise Tet (New Year) Offensive in January 1968. In addition CIA was wrong in its assessment that Cambodia was not a principal route for arms entering Vietnam, and it clung to that error in the face of some persuasive evidence.[25] President Richard Nixon himself took notice of this failure, and after a coup in Cambodia surprised Washington in 1970, he roared at his aides, "What the hell do those clowns do out there in Langley?"[26]

After Mao's death, analytic attention turned toward the growing capabilities of the Chinese military and China's emergence as an economic power. As economic modernization advanced and political reforms did not, analysts pondered the question of whether internal disorder might result. The tough response of the Chinese leadership to the Tiananmen Square protests in 1989 was anticipated, if not the student unrest itself. Intelligence carefully monitored the replacement of unreliable troops in Beijing and the crackdown on protesters. CIA analysis of China's leadership reported its conviction not to make the mistakes that Gorbachev had in combining economic reforms with political reforms. This remains a key intelligence question—namely, how China will manage economic modernization and its sociopolitical ramifications. Although one has to be careful not to carry the comparison too far, Beijing has now replaced Moscow as the single most important geopolitical rival—with far different military, economic, and regional characteristics—and one that requires rigorous intelligence analysis.

CIA analysts in that same period alerted policymakers to the advancing nuclear plans and likelihood of a military clash between Pakistan and India. In May 1990, President George H. W. Bush dispatched to South Asia a senior envoy who used alarming US intelligence reports of Pakistani-Indian conventional buildups to bring both sides to their senses. Another key intelligence question in the late 1980s was whether or not Pakistan had nuclear weapons. Intelligence was clear that Pakistan had an aggressive program by 1987 to develop such a capability. Reagan and Bush administration officials, however, worked to avoid acknowledging this, as it would trigger a break in American aid to Pakistan while that nation was critical to US efforts to drive the Russians out of Afghanistan. India's nuclear program proved tougher to assess. Clinton administration officials were shocked by New Delhi's May 1998 nuclear tests. Pakistan quickly followed suit, and CIA analysts caught the blame for not alerting the administration to India's test. An inquiry chaired by retired admiral David Jeremiah found that analysts had misjudged the newly elected Indian government's eagerness to test, even though its election campaigning promised precisely that. What was left unsaid, however, was that analysts had all along acknowledged India's technical ability to test at any moment and had warned the Clinton administration; moreover, earlier diplomatic efforts had seen US diplomats sharing imagery with New Delhi to convince the previous government not to test. Information provided through these demarches ultimately enabled Indian scientists to conceal their testing practices, which US analysts had used to successfully warn of their nuclear preparations just three years earlier.[27]

North Korea's nuclear ambitions and missile programs have prompted analytic speculation since the 1980s. CIA assessments were heavily "caveated" but left open the possibility that North Korea might have enough plutonium to make a small number of weapons. The Clinton administration pressed the North Koreans to halt their program in exchange for pledges to supply reactors incapable of producing weapon-grade plutonium (and some say also to contemplate strikes on the North's nuclear facilities). Pyongyang averted a confrontation by accepting the 1994 Agreed Framework, but suspicions remained about how much the North Koreans were adhering to those agreements. North Korea then surprised defense and intelligence officials by launching its Taepodong-1 missile in 1998, demonstrating that its ballistic missile program had progressed far faster than most analysts believed possible. This seemed to verify the concerns of the Rumsfeld Commission, which had lambasted a 1995 NIE for allegedly downplaying the likelihood that prospective nuclear states (for example, Iran, Iraq, Libya, and North Korea) would deploy long-range ballistic missiles by 2010.[28] Since then, senior intelligence officials have acknowledged mistakes and claimed that CIA analysts have responded to criticisms and characterized uncertainties, alternative scenarios, and warnings in a more forthcoming manner.[29] Advocacy of Red Teaming Analysis and Alternative Analysis by the previously mentioned Jeremiah study was another useful impetus for CIA to reestablish more analytic tradecraft training—an area that is richly described elsewhere in this volume.

Not surprisingly, as China's political, economic, and military rise has continued, so too has the attention given to CIA's analysis and the question of whether it too is "politically biased."[30] Congressional criticism has been leveled against CIA for soft-pedaling the Chinese military threat, and in 2000 a congressionally mandated commission (known as the China Futures Group), headed by retired US Army general John Tilelli, spent a year examining CIA's record. Agency analysis has followed Chinese military modernization, and analytic resources have grown as a reflection of the importance this subject holds for US policymakers. To make the point, the DCI's congressional testimony in 2004 typified the "tough-minded" analysis that CIA has been conducting: "Our greatest concern continues to be China's military build-up, which continues to accelerate. . . . China's announced annual defense budget has grown from some $7 billion ten years ago to over $25 billion today. Moreover, we assess the announced figure accounts for less than half of China's actual defense spending. . . . China is downsizing and restructuring its military forces with an eye toward enhancing its capabilities for the modern battlefield. All of these steps will over time make China a formidable challenger if Beijing perceived that its interests were being thwarted in the region."[31]

With regard to North Korea, analysts provided evidence that Pyongyang had a covert program to circumvent its earlier pledges; indeed in 2003, CIA judged that "North Korea has produced one or two simple fission-type nuclear weapons."[32] CIA analysts warned of the low-yield atomic test in October 2006.[33] Analysts still monitor indicators of a possible surprise attack against the South and assess North Korea's military capabilities; they must almost plan to be surprised by North Korea's seemingly different strategic logic and way of approaching the international community. North Korea's unprovoked and unpredictable aggression against the South in the past several years highlights how important it remains to monitor military developments on the Korean Peninsula.

The Middle East: Wars, Terror, and WMDs

CIA analysis of the Middle East and terrorism grew steadily in focus and sophistication with the region's increasing importance to American interests. From a sideshow in the early Cold War to the theater of major and ongoing US military operations, the region has seen events and social changes that have tested agency analysts to their limits.

Israel and its Arab neighbors fought four major wars from 1948 to 1973. In the latter two, Israel received significant US support, and US intelligence worked to warn policymakers downtown about what was coming and to provide daily situational reporting. The 1967 Six-Day War remains a case study in "getting it right." Analysts correctly assessed the building pressure on Arab leaders to fight the Israelis again. Egypt's Gamal Abdel Nasser and his generals laid plans with Syria, Jordan, and other Arab states for joint attacks. Analysts in Washington read the signs correctly and alerted the Johnson administration in time; they even predicted the decisive Israeli victory and the war's quick ending almost to a day.[34] Getting it right in 1967, however, might have lulled analysts into complacency. Evidence soon began hinting that the Egyptians and Syrians wanted desperately to recoup their lands and reputations. Ironically, analysts convinced themselves (and policymakers) that the Arabs would not launch a war in the face of certain military defeat. Israel and other Arab states thought likewise.

The fall of the shah of Iran and the rise of fundamentalist Shi'ite Islam in 1979 rank among the most dramatic events of the last half century. The CIA office following Iran in the 1970s employed experienced analysts who foretold some of the coming developments. The shah had alienated the clergy, confiscated lands, and secularized many aspects of the country's life, and Iran's military and intelligence services only looked strong. Unfortunately for American intelligence, much of its reporting came from people close to the shah's regime, both American officials and other insiders. Scant attention was directed toward what was happening in the street or being said in the morning prayers. "We could not give away intelligence on Iran before the crisis," quipped one CIA analyst.[35] In fact, analysts in those days had little understanding of the potential force of religion in politics—or of the charisma and impact that an old and seemingly unimpressive ayatollah named Ruhollah Khomeini would have on Iran and the world. Since then CIA has developed more analytic capability to monitor political Islam.

Once burned, CIA heeded the rise of Islamic extremism. Accordingly, CIA warned the Reagan administration of the precariousness of Anwar Sadat's regime in Egypt and even suggested in oral briefings that an assassination attempt could not be ruled out.[36] Sadat's murder by the Egyptian Islamic Jihad in 1981 also drove journalists to predict the early demise of his successor, Hosni Mubarak, but CIA judged that Mubarak and his regime in Cairo would weather the challenges. He did for three decades.

Terrorism from the Middle East thus came in two main varieties after 1979: secular-Leninist and fundamentalist. The former resembled (and shared ties with) would-be leftist revolutionaries in Europe such as West Germany's Baader-Meinhof Gang and the Red Brigades in Italy, and to a lesser degree the Provisional Irish Republican Army and the Basque separatists ETA. Terrorists of both ilks typically had some degree of state-sponsorship: Iran, Iraq, Syria, and Libya provided training and support. CIA analysis was clear in its judgment that the objectives of most Middle Eastern terrorism were ending the Israeli control of Arab populations in Palestine, reducing the US presence in the region, and radicalizing local regimes. In 1986, DCI Casey moved analysts together with operators into a Counterterrorist Center (CTC). Together they had impressive success in working with foreign intelligence organizations to preempt attacks against a variety of international organizations, US embassies, airports, and other government facilities. Analysts also helped bring terrorists to justice, even years after their attacks. The bombing of Pan Am flight 103 over Scotland in 1988 was traced back to Libya in an impressive intelligence investigation benefiting from a critical clandestine source.

CIA missed the Iranian Revolution but did not miss hints that Iraq would assault its neighbors in Iran (1980) and Kuwait (1990). Analysts provided adequate, if not early, warning of the Iraqi invasion of Iran. This bloody, eight-year conflict probably inclined analysts to believe that Iraq was too war-weary to consider more than a border incursion. Therefore, when Saddam Hussein deployed forces opposite Kuwait, analysts—not to mention Iraq's neighbors—expected a classic bluff aimed at economic blackmail. While most analysts were not expecting a large-scale invasion, the IC duly reported the Iraqi buildup two weeks before Saddam's invasion of Kuwait, reporting almost daily until the troops invaded. But allies in the area, the US ambassador, and others were not convinced that Saddam would take such a dramatic step, and time was at a premium in any event—possibly contributing to policymakers' inability to fashion a policy solution. Once the international coalition committed forces to ousting Iraqi forces from Kuwait, some American commanders and planners complained that CIA's appraisal of Saddam's capacity to resist a counteroffensive seemingly differed from that of the theater commander, Gen. H. Norman Schwarzkopf. The debate reached the White House almost on the eve of the coalition's ground assault.[37] President Bush rightly deferred to Schwarzkopf's judgment of battlefield conditions, and days later the war ended in a rout of the Iraqi forces. Schwarzkopf showed little magnanimity, however, complaining in his bestselling memoir a year later, "If we had waited to convince the CIA, we'd still be in Saudi Arabia."[38]

Few at the time realized that CIA actually had little experience at crafting tactical and operational (as opposed to strategic) military intelligence. In fact, the collectors, secure communications, and collegial ties required to produce such analysis in Washington and share it with the combatant commands were only just developing. Accepting some of these criticisms, CIA since 1992 has substantially improved support to the war fighter, not only in collection but also by beefing up analytic support to the commands and creating a CIA office whose sole mission is supporting Defense Department customers.[39] As mentioned elsewhere in this volume, military analysis in the commands has improved over its rudimentary state in 1991. Today combatant commanders typically control substantial in-house analytic shops that are well connected with colleagues across the IC.

Barrels of ink have hardly sufficed to explain the IC's failure to warn of the terrorist attacks in the United States on September 11, 2001. Less attention has focused on the agency's hunt for Osama bin Laden before 9/11; CIA took the early lead in developing a campaign against him and his al-Qaeda colleagues. The agency used all sources of intelligence and close cooperation with other intelligence agencies to monitor bin Laden's activities and target him.[40] If anything, this tactical focus on a deadly threat might have distracted attention from the larger strategic danger that al-Qaeda posed to the American homeland. As noted by the 9/11 Commission's report, "though analysts assigned to [the CTC] produced a large number of papers, the focus was support to operations."[41] After 9/11 CIA organized the Afghan opposition to bring down the Taliban and has helped to capture more than a thousand al-Qaeda operatives worldwide. None of this would have been possible without competent analysts who could identify, monitor, and target suspects for arrest and rendition.

Problems with the intelligence on Saddam's weapons of mass destruction (WMDs) before the coalition's 2003 invasion of Iraq still dominate discussions of analytic pathologies a decade after the events in question. The Silberman-Robb Commission's 2005 inquiry highlighted the collection shortfalls, flawed analytic tradecraft, and management problems that contributed to the IC's erroneous conclusion that Saddam retained stockpiles of banned munitions and was trying to reestablish a banned nuclear weapons program. Indeed, much of the flawed analysis relied on dated information. With poor information and long-held assumptions remaining unchallenged, analysts produced faulty judgments. Often overlooked, however, is the proficiency of intelligence produced about the consequences of a war with Iraq, as well as the generally seamless tactical and operational analytic support to US military commanders from Washington and the field.[42] In fact, given good and timely collection, the analysts were capable of excellent work, as they showed in guiding the intelligence operation that convinced Libyan strongman Moammar Qaddafi in 2003 that his troubled WMD program was transparent to the West and had to be dismantled.[43]

What Can We Learn?

Reviewing the history of CIA analysis can help us recognize some of the inherent limitations of analysis and develop realistic expectations for how intelligence can help decision makers. Appreciating these limitations should help in developing better analytic techniques. The record shows challenges involving warning, politicization, information gaps, mind-sets, and expertise building. Let us look briefly at each, bearing in mind the scale of the historic challenge to agency efforts in evaluating some of the most unpredictable and heavily armed regimes on earth—and in providing clarity to urgent and contentious debates in American public life.

Warning remains the most difficult challenge that analysts face. In some cases CIA got it right and effectively warned policymakers; in others it monitored developments but did not recognize them for what they were or did not sufficiently emphasize the implications of an adversary's moves or convince policymakers that action was needed. Flawed mind-sets, inadequate warning mechanisms, and poor intelligence–policymaker relationships were at the heart of such failures. These challenges deserve constant attention and are addressed elsewhere in this volume.

Politicization turns out to be a rare occurrence—but one that grabs headlines if it crops up during a major policy debate. Logically, intelligence analysis should serve as the basis for major judgments on the most important matters of state. Nonetheless, the issues that confront intelligence analysts are complex, contentious, and fraught with political and military risks for the United States, the easy questions having been answered long before they required the IC's attention. All parties in such controversies passionately want "the facts" to support their viewpoint, and they try to construe the intelligence in the most helpful, if self-serving, ways. Analysts and their managers must understand this reality, just as policymakers at both ends of Pennsylvania Avenue must respect the analysts' diligence and patriotism.[44]

Information gaps, partly the result of poor analytic understanding of what they mean, lie at the heart of nearly every major intelligence failure. Whether it is the Cuban Missile Crisis, the 1990 Gulf War, or the 9/11 attacks, analysts must constantly be asking whether there is missing information, whether denial and deception are occurring, and whether their judgments must be qualified based on the paucity or poor quality of the information available. Analysts do not have the luxury of *not* reaching judgments when incomplete or ambiguous information is all they have to go with. The better analysts understand the collection environment; those who do not merely report what they see.

Mind-sets that prevent analysts from asking the right questions often result when poor information forces analysts to rely on an adversary's past behavior or what analysts previously judged to be an intelligence target's most likely course of action. Sometimes analysts were expected to know the plans of enemies who had not yet fully developed them. Analysts tried to put themselves in the position of Soviet—as well as other autocratic—leaders to imagine how they might assess the risks and gains of taking political or military steps that challenged US interests. Not surprisingly, although American analysts have struggled to "think like the enemy," they sometimes failed to understand how those decision makers could miscalculate or reason differently than Western analysts. Asking the right questions about the motivations of the Soviets in Cuba, the Egyptians in the Sinai, or the Iraqis in the Gulf would have required abandoning views about how "risk-averse" America's opponents might be or how they make calculations "just like us." Challenging conventional wisdom through the regular use of better and more transparent analytic tradecraft can reduce—if not eliminate—the hazards of unconscious mind-sets.

Expertise building cannot be achieved quickly or easily. Analysis is a "people business" that requires hiring, training, and leading the best thinkers. CIA has sought people with area expertise, technical training, and linguistic skills to assemble the most complete knowledge of important security issues. But these hires were necessarily American citizens, who were raised in a distinctly American culture and with corresponding habits of mind. Realistically, security requirements still prevent the IC from hiring non-Americans with local knowledge of the Middle East and Asia or "street smarts" about drugs and thugs. To compensate for this, CIA must conduct research and build networks with nongovernmental and foreign experts through outreach efforts, independent study, and overseas assignments. A more adept mining of open sources and use of new technologies must also be part of the research agenda. Incentives to develop such expertise-building skills and experiences must be made available to all analysts.

Policymakers will ultimately judge whether intelligence analysis has served them well or poorly. That said, analysts and their leaders must strive to educate the policy world about the limitations they work under and help those in the executive and legislative branches become more sophisticated consumers of analysis. Demonstrating that analysis can inform policy, but not guarantee its success, is a realistic goal for CIA and the intelligence community. Policymakers should expect no less, but they should also demand no more.

Notes

The authors thank Roger George, Martha Kessler, Brian Latell, and Tom Wolfe, among others, for providing early insights and suggestions to enrich this chapter.

1. Hindsight bias works in at least two ways. Outsiders reviewing the IC's performance can forget that less was known or appreciated at the time of an assessment as later became apparent. Conversely, analysts can recall their past reporting as more accurate than it was or as containing more prescient statements than were, in fact, appreciated at the time by policymakers or themselves. See Richards Heuer, *Psychology of Intelligence Analysis* (Washington, DC: Center for the Study of Intelligence, CIA, 1999).
2. Quote attributed to Max Millikan, founding director of CIA's Office of Research and Reports in 1951 and 1952; Noel E. Firth and James H. Noren, eds., *Soviet Defense Spending: A History of CIA Estimates, 1950–1990* (College Station: Texas A&M University Press, 1998), 13.
3. Chapter 10 examines the importance of the analyst–collector relationship, demonstrating how analysts and collectors are dependent on each other.
4. Testimony of Nicholas Eberstadt of the American Enterprise Institute for Public Policy Research on US policy toward North Korea before the US House of Representatives (Committee on International Relations), hearing on "U.S. Policy toward North Korea," September 24, 1998.
5. Critics included Franklyn D. Holzman and William T. Lee. Holzman accused CIA of overestimates, while Lee claimed CIA was underestimating Soviet military spending. Franklyn D. Holzman, "Politics and Guesswork: CIA and DIA Estimates of Soviet Military Spending," *International Security* 14 (Fall 1989): 101–31, and William T. Lee, *The Estimation of Soviet Defense Expenditures 1955–75: An Unconventional Approach* (New York: Praeger, 1977).

6. Dan M. Berkowitz, "An Evaluation of CIA's Analysis of Soviet Economic Performance 1970–1990," *Comparative Economic Studies* 35, no. 2 (Summer 1993): 35.

7. This major analysis failure is elaborated as a case study in chapter 10, along with similar failures that illustrate the dependency of analysis on collection. Other cases examined there that are discussed in this chapter include the 1973 Yom Kippur War, the 1979 Iranian Revolution, the 1998 Indian nuclear tests, the 9/11 attacks, and the erroneous Iraq WMD estimate in 2002.

8. CIA analysts reported a buildup of troops on the Afghan border and warned that Moscow might introduce small forces, but they did not expect a major military campaign and long-term occupation of the country. See Douglas MacEachin and Janne E. Nolan, "The Soviet Invasion of Afghanistan in 1979: Failure of Intelligence or Policy Process?" Institute for the Study of Diplomacy Working Group Report 111, September 26, 2005, 4. See also Douglas MacEachin, *Predicting the Soviet Invasion of Afghanistan: The Intelligence Community's Record* (Washington, DC: Center for the Study of Intelligence, CIA, 2002).

9. An early and controversial paper (now declassified) on this theme was the National Intelligence Council's memorandum "Dimensions of Civil Unrest in the Soviet Union" (NIC M-83-10006, April 1983), which documented rising levels of strikes, food riots, and other forms of public dissidence that signaled the growing systemic failures that were to become obvious under Mikhail Gorbachev's leadership; see www.cia.gov/library/center-for-the-study-of-intelligence/csi-publications/books-and-monographs/listing-of-declassified-national-intelligence-estimates-on-the-soviet-union-and-international-communism-1946-1984/1983.htm. See also Gerald K. Haines and Robert E. Leggett, eds., *CIA's Analysis of the Soviet Union, 1947–1991* (Washington, DC: CIA, 2001). This volume contains key estimates and CIA assessments that illustrate the scope and depth of CIA's work during the Cold War.

10. For the remarkable story of this sensitive human source, Ryszard Kuklinski, see Benjamin Weiser, *A Secret Life: The Polish Officer, His Covert Mission, and the Price He Paid to Save His Country* (Cambridge, MA: PublicAffairs, 2004).

11. See especially Benjamin B. Fischer, ed., *At Cold War's End: US Intelligence on the Soviet Union and Eastern Europe, 1989–1991* (Washington, DC: CIA, 1999), for representative examples.

12. Daniel P. Moynihan, *Secrecy: The American Experience* (New Haven, CT: Yale University Press, 1998), 197–99.

13. "Intelligence Forecasts of Soviet Intercontinental Attack Forces: An Evaluation of the Record," April 1989, in *CIA's Analysis of the Soviet Union*, Haines and Leggett, eds., 290–91.

14. Memorandum from [name not declassified] of the Central Intelligence Agency to Director of Central Intelligence Helms, June 18, 1969, reprinted as Document 191 in Department of State, *Foreign Relations of the United States, 1969–1976, Volume II: Organization and Management of U.S. Foreign Policy, 1969–1972* (Washington, DC: Government Printing Office, 2006).

15. Illustrative of the critiques was an article by Albert Wohlstetter, "Is There a Strategic Arms Race?" *Foreign Policy* 15 (Summer 1974): 3–20. See also US Senate Select Committee on Intelligence, Subcommittee on Collection, Production, and Quality, *The National Intelligence Estimates A-B Team Episode Concerning Soviet Strategic Capability and Objectives* (Washington, DC: Government Printing Office, 1978), 1–12. Team B was composed of

critics of CIA estimates and, as the Senate committee concluded, "reflected the views of only one segment of the spectrum of opinion."

16. Brent Scowcroft, letter to the editor, *Washington Post*, January 12, 2000.

17. See John K. Allen, John Carver, and Tom Elmore, eds., *Tracking the Dragon: National Intelligence Estimates on China during the Era of Mao, 1948–1976* (Washington, DC: CIA, 2004), xii. This volume contains declassified NIEs on Chinese leadership, politics, economics, and military programs.

18. Ibid., xii.

19. See P. K. Rose, "Two Strategic Intelligence Mistakes in Korea 1950," *Studies in Intelligence* 11 (Fall/Winter 2001): 57–65. See also Richard A. Mobley, "North Korea's Surprise Attack: Weak US Analysis," *International Journal of Intelligence and Counterintelligence* 13, no. 4 (2000): 490–514. Mobley quotes Ray Cline, then deputy director for intelligence, as saying that the "CIA had written some warnings about the possibility of North Korean attack . . . but they were insufficiently emphatic to capture the NSC audience they should have reached."

20. Richard Helms, *A Look over My Shoulder: A Life in the Central Intelligence Agency* (New York: Random House, 2003), 311.

21. Harold Ford, a longtime CIA Asian expert, recounts the CIA's long history of challenging presidential optimism in his article "Why CIA Analysts Were So Doubtful about Vietnam," *Studies in Intelligence* 40 (1997): 85–95.

22. Harold Ford, *CIA and the Vietnam Policymakers: Three Episodes* (Washington, DC: CIA, 1997), 87–89.

23. Sam Adams, the leading Vietnam military analyst at the time, became notorious for challenging the US military's assessments of enemy manpower. His book *War of Numbers: An Intelligence Memoir* (South Royalton, VT: Steerforth Press, 1998) became part of the legend of CIA confrontation with the military. See also Helms, *A Look over My Shoulder*, 328. For another view on the order-of-battle problem, see James J. Wirtz, "Intelligence to Please: The Order of Battle Controversy during the Vietnam War," in *Strategic Intelligence: Windows into a Secret World: An Anthology*, Loch Johnson and James J. Wirtz eds. (Los Angeles: Roxbury, 2003), 183–97.

24. Bruce Palmer Jr., "US Intelligence and Vietnam," *Studies in Intelligence* 28 (1984): 91; Thomas R. Johnson, *American Cryptology during the Cold War, 1945–1989: Book II: Centralization Wins, 1960–1972* (Ft. Meade, MD: NSA, 1995), 539–40.

25. Thomas L. Ahern Jr., *Good Questions, Wrong Answers: CIA's Estimates of Arms Traffic through Sihanoukville, Cambodia, during the Vietnam War* (Washington, DC: CIA, 2004), 39–48.

26. Richard Nixon, *RN: The Memoirs of Richard Nixon*, vol. 1 (1978; repr., New York: Simon & Schuster, 1990), 447.

27. George Tenet with Bill Harlow, *At the Center of the Storm: The CIA during America's Time of Crisis* (2007; repr. New York: Harper, 2008), 44–45. See also the transcript of Adm. David Jeremiah's press conference on the results of his inquiry, June 2, 1998, www.fas.org/irp/cia/product/jeremiah.html, accessed November 28, 2012.

28. "Emerging Missile Threats to North America during the Next 15 Years," Director of Central Intelligence, NIE 95-19, November 1995, forecast that "no country, other than the major declared nuclear powers, will develop or otherwise acquire a ballistic missile in the next 15

years that could threaten the contiguous 48 states and Canada." An independent panel of senior military, diplomatic, and scientific experts led by former DCI Robert Gates concluded that the NIE—although not "politicized"—had inadequately addressed the motives and objectives of governments developing missile programs. In 1998, the Rumsfeld Commission also concluded that "the threat to the US posed by these emerging capabilities is broader, more mature and evolving more rapidly than has been reported in estimates and reports by the Intelligence Community." See *Report of the US Commission to Assess the Ballistic Missile Threat to the United States*, Executive Summary, July 15, 1998, www.fas.org/irp/threat/bm-threat.htm.

29. Robert Walpole, national intelligence officer for strategic and nuclear programs, "North Korea's Taepo Dong Launch and Some Implications on the Ballistic Missile Threat to the United States," speech delivered to the Center for Strategic and International Studies, Washington, DC, December 8, 1998.

30. Bill Gertz and Rowan Scarborough, for instance, claimed that a senior CIA analyst had been advocating "conciliatory" positions toward China and had discouraged analyses critical of China's human rights record and warning of China's rising military power. "Inside the Ring: NSC Predicament," *Washington Times*, November 3, 2005.

31. Testimony of DCI George J. Tenet before the Senate Armed Services Committee, "The Worldwide Threat 2004: Challenges in a Changing Global Context" (as prepared for delivery), March 9, 2004, www.cia.gov/news-information/speeches-testimony/2004/tenet_testimony_03092004.html, accessed November 25, 2012.

32. CIA statement to Congress, August 18, 2003. See also Larry A. Niksch, "Korea: US-Korean Relations—Issues for Congress," Congressional Research Service Issue Brief, April 14, 2006, 2–3.

33. Statement by DCI John Negroponte, October 18, 2006. See also "US Intelligence: Air Samples Confirm N. Korea Nuke Test," *USA Today*, October 16, 2006.

34. Richard Helms recounts that President Lyndon B. Johnson invited the DCI to attend future policy discussions after this episode; Helms, *A Look over My Shoulder*, 298–305. See also David S. Robarge, "CIA Analysis of the 1967 Arab-Israeli War," *Studies in Intelligence* 49 (2005).

35. Quoted in Robert Jervis, "Why Intelligence and Policymakers Clash," *Political Science Quarterly* 125, no. 2 (Summer 2010).

36. John Helgerson, *Getting to Know the President: Intelligence Briefings of Presidential Candidates, 1952–2004* (Washington, DC: CIA, 2012), 115.

37. Richard L. Russell, "CIA's Strategic Intelligence in Iraq," *Political Science Quarterly* 117, no. 2 (2002): 199, 202–3.

38. H. Norman Schwarzkopf with Peter Petre, *It Doesn't Take a Hero* (1992; repr., New York: Bantam, 1993), 501.

39. Analysts are now routinely deployed with US forces throughout the world. According to CIA's website (accessed November 23, 2012), after the 9/11 attacks CIA merged two military offices and "formally established the joined elements under the Associate Director for Military Affairs (ADMA) in 2007. Today, ADMA is jointly manned by Agency and uniformed military professionals, operating as one team to coordinate, plan, execute, and sustain joint CIA and DOD worldwide activities based upon priorities established by the Director of the CIA, to achieve National Security objectives."

40. Richard Kerr adds: As one of two people asked by the CIA's deputy director for operations to assess that program, we said at the time that the activity was impressive and a good example of interagency cooperation and innovative use of operational assets and intelligence analysis. A firsthand account from a former operations officer is in Henry A. Crumpton, *The Art of Intelligence: Lessons from a Life in CIA's Clandestine Service* (New York: Penguin, 2012), chaps. 8 and 9.

41. National Commission on Terrorist Attacks upon the United States, *The 9/11 Commission Report* (New York: Norton, 2004), 92.

42. Richard Kerr, Thomas Wolfe, Rebecca Donegan, and Aris Pappas, "Issues for the US Intelligence Community: Collection and Analysis on Iraq," *Studies in Intelligence* 49, no. 3 (Fall 2005): 1–9.

43. *Final Report of Commission on the Intelligence Capabilities of the United States Regarding Weapons of Mass Destruction* (the WMD Commission), March 2005, 251–52.

44. Richard Kerr adds: "In my own career I have seen little to be terribly alarmed about this. A professional analyst should have no problem turning down any blatant policy request that he or she tailor the analysis to suit a policy preference. And clearly I never had any such problem and believe that analytic integrity is the single most important attribute of solid analysis. Although I personally could not agree with every judgment reached by CIA analysts in my thirty-two years of service, there was never a time when I felt we had compromised our integrity."

CHAPTER 4

Is Intelligence Analysis a Discipline?

REBECCA FISHER, ROB JOHNSTON, AND PETER CLEMENT

A mong the many efforts to improve analysis, there has been a long-standing desire to transform intelligence analysis into a full-fledged discipline. Indeed, the intent of this book is to advance the state of knowledge about analysis and promote further "professionalization" of analysis along the lines that Sherman Kent had suggested as much as half a century ago.[1] Though many practitioners have espoused the goal of creating a more rigorous discipline, few have considered what a discipline actually requires.[2] The steps toward creating a discipline, however, should be informed by what such a goal actually entails, and upon closer inspection practitioners will be heartened to see that such a goal is not as distant as some might assume.

What Is a Discipline?

Disciplines emerge as systems for maintaining order, routinizing methods, and codifying actions. They are found in communities that recognize and seek to minimize the extent to which the welfare of persons or groups of people is put at risk because of the actions of individuals. The development of professional standards, best practices, consensus statements, and practice guidelines are the logical result of this risk mitigation. We need not look far to find examples of how disciplines such as law, medicine, and library science have evolved to the level of their present-day sophistication and development from what were once largely unregulated practices performed ad hoc.

Though closely associated, the words "profession" and "discipline" convey a nuanced but significant difference in meaning. A profession is widely regarded as a life's work that requires specialized knowledge and often long and intensive vocational or academic preparation. For our purposes, we define the word "discipline" as a type of profession but one in which specialized knowledge and rigorous preparation are operationalized by the introduction of formal or informal governing bodies that are responsible for developing rules of a mandatory or voluntary nature that serve to guide, inform, and ensure the highest possible quality professional conduct and activity. Disciplines are professions that retain the collective wisdom of practitioners and establish standards for archiving and accessing that knowledge. Disciplines distinguish themselves by externally and internally derived licensing and credentialing practices, ethical standards, and continuing education requirements. Insofar as "intelligence analysis" lacks these attributes, the answer to the question "Is intelligence analysis a discipline?" would have to be "No." But perhaps the better question is "Should it be?" This chapter looks to other professions-turned-disciplines and makes the case for an affirmative answer to that question.

The Legal Profession

The American legal profession as we know it began to take shape in the nineteenth century. Prior to the 1870s, practicing law was the domain of the upper class, set apart and venerable; the philosopher Alexis de Tocqueville wrote in 1835, "In America . . . lawyers . . . form the highest political class and the most cultivated circle of society."[3] But around midcentury a backlash against the elitism associated with the profession, together with the country's burgeoning growth and increasing demand for legal services, democratized the profession, making it much more accessible. What had been a profession of the privileged few was suddenly open to many. Requirements for becoming a lawyer grew arbitrary and, in some jurisdictions, practically nonexistent.[4]

The American legal profession was in considerable disarray by the latter half of the nineteenth century. Widespread corruption underscored such unseemly conduct as unruly behavior and indecorous speech and dress in the courtroom. In its report to the Bar of the City of New York, the Committee on the Admission to the Bar wrote, "The general standard of professional learning and obligation was high during the first forty years of the nineteenth century. About 1840, it began to decline, and its tendency was steadily downward until about 1870, when it reached its lowest ebb, when even the Bench was invaded by corruption and found support in a portion of the bar."[5]

The first milestone in the restoration of law to its present status as a profession of the educated and regulated was the creation of bar associations. The first of these, the Bar of the City of New York, instituted "rigorous scrutiny of qualifications for membership . . . to maintain the honor and dignity of the professions,"[6] with the overarching goal of assuring the expeditious administration of justice. This turning point was the first of many more bar alliances, most notably the formation of the American Bar Association (ABA) in 1878. The ABA appeared on the American scene at a time when "no uniform code of ethics governed [lawyers'] conduct [and] few institutions for common effort were available,"[7] but by the turn of the twentieth century, the organization had successfully drafted legislation, set standards for law reform, and—most notably for our purposes—established the requirements for legal education in America. By the late nineteenth century, 176 more bar associations had formed. Changes in the way law was taught and the publication of textbooks on specialized topics such as negligence law, taxation, and personal property followed. Each innovation represented a layer of oversight and governance that would transform the profession of law into a discipline.

In keeping with the implementation of educational standards was the systematization of the profession's shared knowledge, establishing the body of case law that came to characterize Western jurisprudence as possibly the world's first "knowledge management" system. Each case generates a unique record of participants, proceedings, and decisions upon which every subsequent case will be based, argued, or rendered null, forming a body of scholarship accessible to any and all. But at its lowest ebb, the legal profession had no uniform and organized system for researching this scholarship; the American Digest System and the National Reporter System, now available in various electronic and print permutations, did not exist. These resources emerged on the American scene in 1872 with the foresighted and entrepreneurial work of John B. West. West's Key Number system, an indexing method still in use, utilizes seven general categories (persons, property, contracts, torts, crimes, remedies, and government)—further divided into four hundred major topics (for example, civil rights, securities, criminal law) and divided further still into nearly a hundred thousand subtopics—to enable researchers to surface relevant, accurate information out of a confusing tangle of data.

The systematization of legal knowledge and the development of methods for retrieving it marked another passage in the transformation of the legal profession from dilettantism to discipline. One of the major advantages of West's system was its ability to accommodate the ever-evolving status of case law. The system's foundation—a dynamic, adaptable taxonomy—allowed the inclusion of new terms and technologies as they emerged. Another benefit was the product's ability to be updated; printed updates that easily slipped into and out of three-ring binders assured that practitioners' legal references would always reflect the current disposition of the law under study. Over the years West's product, eventually called the *National Reporter*, became known as "the authoritative source of case law, legislation, and most things jurisprudential."[8]

Parallels to intelligence are abundant in law. Substitute the words "intelligence" for "law" and "analysts" for "students" in the excerpt below, and you have a more than adequate impression of the current state of US intelligence:

> The law is, after all, a complicated web of interrelated doctrines and often contradictory interpretative texts. First year law students frequently lack the contextual understanding necessary to discover and evaluate all the extant decisions necessary to develop a full analysis of the issues presented to them. In addition to trying to acquire this broad overview of the law and the way it works, they must simultaneously grapple with a multiplicity of challenges: unfamiliar surroundings, a curriculum seemingly designed to keep them off-balance, new ways of thinking, and teachers speaking a new language or, at the very least, a dialect of English with which they are unfamiliar. And, of course, each student is located at a different point along a skills continuum. Legal research is a demanding discipline requiring excellent legal researchers to be curious, persistent, flexible people and these attributes are not universal even, or especially, among lawyers or law students.[9]

Perhaps the most relevant aspect of such a comparison is the notion that although intelligence community members may indeed be overwhelmed in confronting a "multiplicity of challenges" in a world seemingly designed to "keep them off balance," the urgent call for systematizing both resources and methods persists if intelligence analysis is to achieve "discipline" status with all the rigor, tenacity, and high standards such a designation connotes.

In law, organized resources and systematic research methods, governing bodies that established professional standards and ethical guidelines, and boards impaneled to assure that appropriate levels of education and competence preceded admission to the bar earned the profession its modern-day stature. A discipline—Law, writ large—ultimately emerged, with the benefit being homogeneity and predictability in the manner in which state, federal, and international law is administered and practiced in the United States.

The Medical Profession

The medical community's parallel to intelligence analysis may be more apt owing to the temporal nature—often an urgency—with which members of each group must confront difficult challenges of decision making in life-or-death and high-risk situations. Reliance upon years of training, individual experience, and consultation with colleagues has prevailed for centuries in medical decision making—an "apprenticeship" learning model of the highest order—forming a pattern of acquiring expertise and finding support for one's decisions that is remarkably similar to what goes on in the intelligence community.

Training, individual experience, and the advice of one's peers—no matter how well intentioned or informed—do not equal evidence. Ferreting out the hard data that should drive the decisions that ultimately bear on whether a patient lives or dies was not always the norm in medicine, any more than it is in intelligence analysis. Here, as in the case of the legal profession, we see that one of the planks of professionalism—as it becomes a discipline—is access to and proper use of a rich body of scholarship.

As with case law, it was not as though medical scholarship did not exist. Pamphlets, reports, and books shaped the practice of medicine from the time of Hippocrates. But a modern-day data repository only began to emerge in 1818 when Joseph Lovell, the first surgeon general of the US Army, began collecting books and journals to serve as a reference library for the surgeons under his command. His collection seeded what was to become the National Library of Medicine (NLM), a collection of millions of journal article references, monographs, audiovisual materials, and specialized collections on topics such as toxicology, environmental health, and molecular biology. Today the NLM, which uses an indexing system called Medical Subject Heading (MeSH)—not unlike West's Key Number system—serves health professionals, scientists, librarians, and the public. Its servers host over 1.5 billion literature searches every year on an annual budget of approximately $338 million.[10]

Still, a profession's literature—merely because it exists—does not automatically mean its aggregate membership comprises a discipline. Pressure arising from within its own ranks to improve methods and outcomes is also an integral part of any profession's progression toward becoming a discipline. This type of internal agitation appeared in medicine, as it had in law, in the form of widespread demand for improvements and standardization in education and credentialing. Paul Starr, the Pulitzer Prize–winning author of *The Social Transformation of American Medicine*, noted that deficiencies in medical education had existed for decades—that in 1875 anyone with a high school diploma could attend medical school and that the two years' coursework could be completed in any order the student preferred. New knowledge was not, by design, mandatorily built on previous knowledge, which would have ensured a more vertical understanding of medical phenomena and techniques.

The lack of governing boards and credentialing systems common to both late-nineteenth-century medicine and present-day intelligence is not where their similarities end. Starr's observation that the most significant failure of the apprenticeship model—the fact that the "medical faculty had no control over preceptors"—resonates in an intelligence environment where subject-matter experts face serious constraints in their efforts to train novices in the secrets of "tradecraft" while performing their regular work, the demands of which are in constant flux and various states of urgency. In intelligence, emerging governing bodies and oversight systems—for example, peer review and "tradecraft" specialists whose principal duties focus on analytic skills and training issues—help to compensate for some of the gaps and weaknesses in the apprenticeship model by producing tradecraft standards and practice guidelines. But their general absence only exacerbates an already vexing problem.

But medicine did begin to close these gaps and fortify the apprenticeship model as early as 1901, with the formation of the American Medical Association's (AMA's) Council on Medical Education. At its first meeting, the council produced standardized education requirements and set about developing the "ideal medical curriculum."[11] Several years later the "Flexner Report" was issued, the product of Abraham Flexner's rigorous tour of 155 medical schools over the course of eighteen months. Here Flexner remarked that while American medical practitioners were not inferior to their European counterparts, there was "probably no other country in the world in which there is so great a distance and so fatal a difference between the best, the average, and the worst."[12] Flexner's recommendations were implemented in the form of codified processes of training, credentialing, and board-certifying physicians, and the body of shared medical knowledge grew in the form of books, papers, and monographs. Thus the medical profession's metamorphosis to "discipline" stature had begun in earnest.

Yet training, credentialing, or board certification alone and access to the profession's collective knowledge (while absent at various times in their histories from both medicine and law) fail to address the danger of resting on one's proverbial laurels in an ever-evolving world of discovery and innovation.[13] In the case of medicine, the manner in which important clinical information (for example, that contained in Medline, an online medical resources guide and on the shelves of countless medical libraries across the country) was acquired, used, and shared became the hallmark of a discipline, beginning with the realization that evidence rather than opinion needs to gird medical decision making. Before the dawn of evidence-based practice, the idea was that when a physician faced a patient, by some fundamentally human process called the "art of medicine" or "clinical judgment," the physician would synthesize all of the important information about the patient, relevant research, and experiences with previous patients to determine the best course of action. "Medical decision-making" as a field worthy of study did not exist. Analytical methods and mathematical models were limited to research projects. Guidelines were merely a way for experts to pass occasional pieces of advice to non-experts. Coverage and medical necessity were defined tautologically; if the majority of physicians were doing it, it was medically necessary and should be covered. Diseases did not require any management beyond what physicians were already providing, and performance was taken for granted.[14]

The terms "art of medicine" and "clinical judgment" are every bit as nebulous here as the term "expertise" is among analysts in the intelligence community. What is expertise exactly? How is it measured? Can it be taught? Or is it so arbitrary that you only "know it when you see it"? These are questions the medical community was forced to ask itself when the British obstetrician and epidemiologist Archie Cochrane published his landmark 1973 book *Effectiveness and Efficiency: Random Reflections on Health Services*.[15] In the bold, outspoken style for which he was known, Cochrane questioned the very manner in which medicine was practiced and called for the rigorous evaluation of *effectiveness* (whether treatments actually work) and *efficiency* (whether treatments represent the optimal use of available resources). This could be accomplished, Cochrane said, by conducting and using results from randomized, controlled clinical trials. Treatment decisions, he held, must always be made consonant with *evidence* rather than on the basis of hearsay, imagined efficacy, or the "standard operating procedure" mentality that so often fails to consider alternative scenarios, derogatory side effects, long-term damage, and blatantly contradictory information. Evidence, here defined as "any empirical observation about the apparent relationship between events"[16] stored in a systematic manner, allows higher-order cognitive processes to build on such "givens" training and access to sage advice. The use of statistical rather than solely anecdotal information supplies a better picture of an entire disease spectrum or process, an increased familiarity with the array of treatment or surgical interventions that might be warranted, and a broadening of the researcher's scope of inquiry—including possibilities that may otherwise have been overlooked. Cochrane's book marked the emergence of the evidence-based medicine (EBM) movement. A discipline-within-the-discipline, EBM uses strict criteria to determine the validity and quality of medical research and encompasses systematic research methodologies such as randomized controlled trials and clinical trials, publications and repositories on EBM practices and studies, and study groups such as a global network of practitioners who share evidence-based resources on particular medical topics.

In medicine as in law, organized resources and systematic research methods coupled with professional standards, ethical guidelines, and accomplished senior practitioners whose job it is to oversee the mentoring of apprentice physicians have earned the profession its much deserved "discipline" designation.

Library Services

Acquiring and organizing resources and employing systematic research methods in order to fully exploit them are at the root of every library's raison d'être. Twenty-first-century practitioners of "library science" are members of a discipline whose professional standards and ethos reflect postgraduate education, training, internships, credentialing, and often membership in a variety of professional associations. The 148,895 librarians at work today in America's 121,169 libraries are generally proponents of ubiquitous access to knowledge and outspoken opponents of censorship.[17] Frequently among the most judicious, discerning, and skeptical consumers of information as well, a good librarian is often a patron's best hope of finding exactly what he or she needs in a sea of information where quality, value, and accessibility are often unknowns.

This role—based on the ability to efficiently deliver high-quality information to information seekers who are less familiar (or completely unfamiliar) with the organization of information—evolved over centuries, achieving its present democratized iteration only late in the nineteenth century. The earliest libraries existed for the use of rulers and the literate elite. The Library of Alexandria, for example, founded in the third century BC and considered the greatest library the world had known prior to the invention of the Gutenberg printing press in 1447, was staffed by highly educated scientists, mathematicians, and astronomers whose access to and familiarity with the library's extensive holdings was—whether intentionally or not—analogous with power and control. As recently as the mid-nineteenth century, to be a librarian—what Ralph Waldo Emerson called a "professor of books"—remained a type of investiture, available to those whose ability to preserve the "library's service to high culture" was assured by their own classical education, training, and superior knowledge.[17] As such, the air of mystery that came to characterize the role of librarians as keepers of wisdom (and others' access to it) endowed them with a certain ideological authority—the validity of which, like "expertise" or the "art of medicine"—was impossible to prove or disprove. Librarianship was the realm of experts, with expertise deriving from extensive reading and schooling rather than demonstrated facility with systematic methods in approaching a body of scholarship.

Though the underlying causes are beyond the scope of this chapter, it is perhaps no small coincidence that the late nineteenth century saw dramatic changes in the professionalization of not only law and medicine but also librarianship. Agitation for change reached critical mass with the appearance of the Dewey Decimal Classification (DDC) system in 1873. Known as the "Father of Modern Librarianship," Melvil Dewey transformed librarianship from a divining to a disciplined activity when he developed a system for organizing knowledge. Today, more than a century later, the DDC is still the most widely used classification taxonomy in the world. But this transformation was neither instantaneously achieved nor initially well received. A class of librarian scholars who espoused a more bibliographic approach to the literatures—that is, continually producing definitive reading lists of the "best books" on any given topic to guide public access and consumption, with themselves as final arbiters—vehemently resisted his approach. The flashpoint at which the two factions' ideologies ignited was the American Library Association Conference of 1886, where William Fletcher of Amherst maligned the Dewey system as "an attempt to substitute machinery for brains."[18] But Dewey persisted in his life-long aspiration to "achieve his goal of educating the masses toward improvement [which entailed] the efficient operation of free public libraries properly stocked with 'good reading,'" starting with taking the mystery out of locating and acquiring information.[19]

With the deployment of the DDC, librarianship went from the exclusive domain of the elite and abundantly well-read to the purview of anyone who could demonstrate expertise in using systematic procedures. Like West's and Cochrane's, Dewey's sentinel work made it possible to find, locate, and evaluate information from an infinite number of resources. Similar to West's Key Number system and evidence-based medicine techniques, the DDC is constantly refined to accommodate new knowledge: every year Library of Congress specialists classify materials using over 110,000 DDC numbers.[20] West's system and the NLM's MeSH taxonomy are maintained under a single authority; similarly, control of the DDC resides under the auspices of the Library of Congress. Expanding and amending these essential taxonomies is performed regularly, based upon the consensus of subject-matter experts.

Modern libraries—filled with books, serials, audio and video files, and an infinite and ever-increasing number of Web pages—provide support for the psychologist George Kelly's 1963 observation that "all our present interpretations of the universe are subject to revision."[21] In fact, modern libraries are the places most likely to contain *both* the original interpretations *and* their revisions. Today's libraries, descended from the Alexandrian Library and its seven hundred thousand scrolls, provide ready access to and portability of an inexhaustible supply of well-organized information. Today's librarians enable the best possible use of all available information resources for all who seek it. Like their fellow professionals in law and medicine, they exemplify a discipline rooted in systems and replicable methods, in graduate-level training, credentialing, and subspecialty pursuit.

"Learning Organizations" as a Discipline

Another way to define a discipline—be it law, medicine, library science, or possibly intelligence analysis—is to think of it as a "learning organization." Whether informal or formal, an effective discipline must be capable of knowledge management, sense making, and what might be called "mindfulness."[22] Along with other established disciplines, intelligence analysis must strive in this direction, and some intelligence organizations are beginning to recognize the significance of these features.

Knowledge management as a system of organizing principles existed in libraries long before it appeared in law, medicine, or intelligence analysis. But it is only relatively recently that "knowledge management" as a pillar of best business practice has arisen, rooted in the work of Karl-Erik Sveiby and Peter Senge in the late 1980s and early 1990s. Sveiby coined the phrase "knowledge management," building on ideas he set forth in his 1986 book *Managing Knowhow*. He had come to realize that his scholarly work no longer depended on "formal structures [in which] managers were in control and output was visible" but rather on "substantial invisible knowledge-based assets"—subject-matter experts whose knowledge was, in reality, the company's most valuable asset. He recognized that a traditional industrial "command-and-control" mentality was difficult if not impossible to sustain in a knowledge-dependent environment, where the product itself arises from access to information that is constantly changing. His early work sought an answer to problems confronted by business leaders who "lack explicit tools [and] manage intuitively, by gut feeling . . . traveling in uncharted territory, and [lacking] even a basic theory of knowledge—an epistemology, as philosophers call it."[23]

Senge's 1990 best seller, *The Fifth Discipline*, expanded the knowledge management concept beyond simply a way to capture, organize, and store information, to talk in terms of "learning organizations." He defined learning organizations as environments in which "people continually expand their capacity to create the results they truly desire, where new and expansive patterns of thinking are nurtured, where collective aspiration is set free, and where people are continually learning to see the whole together."[24]

Now widely known as knowledge management, this organizational phenomenon encompasses a spectrum of practices and technologies that range from converting tacit knowledge into explicit, codified knowledge to establishing systems for knowledge capture in real time and providing after-action review capabilities. But however they are developed, knowledge management systems are now ubiquitous in many major corporations and are every bit as essential to intelligence.

The value of being a learning organization for analytic agencies is undeniable. Unexpected outcomes are just as unacceptable in the realm of national security as they are in business sectors. To avoid surprises, organizations—and their experts—must continually free themselves from the machinery of preconception and rote through continuous organizational learning. To become a learning organization, then, intelligence analysis must not only embrace better management of the tacit knowledge held by analysts but must also create the conditions that encourage continuous learning, exposure to new ideas, and more flexible business practices that can accommodate unconventional thinking styles and forms of collaboration.

Intelligence Analysis as a Nascent Discipline

What we've learned from law, medicine, and library science is that their separate paths to become disciplines demonstrate some commonalities of interest to intelligence analysis. All developed

- governing bodies (for example, the ABA, the AMA), to set quality standards;
- rigorous educational systems to train their practitioners, and continuous training, throughout the duration of their professional practice;

- certification requirements to limit admission to only those who qualify; and
- knowledge management systems to organize information in their domains (like West, NLM and MeSH, and Dewey), and to facilitate information retrieval and expansion.

These are proven standards against which any fledgling profession—for example, intelligence analysis—can be assessed for its approximation to an established discipline.

These examples of law, medicine, and library science are but a handful of professions in which constantly evolving methods and guidelines for utilizing *data* (observations and measurements), *information* (organized data that has been classified, indexed, and/or placed in context), and *knowledge* (analyzed and understood information) have transformed basic aptitudes into formalized, systematized disciplines.[25] The idea that intelligence analysis, closely tied as it is to US national security and public policy, has not yet undergone that transformation is a matter deserving concern and scrutiny. A number of recent calls for change have coalesced, taking the form of greater demand for rigorous methodological standards (analytic tradecraft), increased knowledge sharing, better access to information across components and agencies, and greater accountability.[26] To the extent that intelligence analysis has remained idiosyncratic and lacks oversight mechanisms by which all its practitioners systematically acquire, share, and produce knowledge, it is not yet recognizable as a full-fledged discipline.

Encouragingly, however, intelligence analysis does share many characteristics in common with law, medicine, and library science as these others have evolved into disciplines. A significant step is the effort to create an "intelligence literature," which Sherman Kent described in 1955 as "dedicated to the analysis of our many-sided calling and produced by its most knowledgeable devotees."[27] Kent, a professor of history at Yale prior to joining the Central Intelligence Agency, envisioned the stepwise building of such an evidence-based literature, such that "Major X [would] write an essay on the theory of indicators and print it and have it circulated. . . . A Mr. B [would] brood over this essay and write a review of it, . . . [and] a Commander C reading both the preceding documents and reviewing them both" would provide insights that would enable yet "another man coming forward to produce an original synthesis of all that has gone before."[28] Kent's "systematic literature of intelligence" would be, he acknowledged, "ponderous and a drain on time." However, he also defended the value of precisely such an investment when he wrote, "Taking Mr. X off the current task and giving him the time to sort out his thoughts and commit them to paper will more than repay the sacrifice if what Mr. X puts down turns out to be an original and permanent contribution."[29] In this sense, Mr. X's contribution to the intelligence literature must be viewed as something more than another briefing, paper, or estimate; it is a distillation of his own unique wisdom, filtered through experience, discourse, and debate.

Kent's call for an intelligence literature has been heeded—perhaps more than expected. Many hundreds of books and articles over the last several decades could fill a good-sized library, even if too few address analysis directly. Several scholarly and peer-reviewed journals, including CIA's occasionally unclassified *Studies in Intelligence*, DIA's *Defense Intelligence Journal*, and *The Intelligencer*, published by the Association of Former Intelligence Officers, nicely complement the more academic journals such as *Intelligence and National Security* and the *International Journal of Intelligence and CounterIntelligence*. Additionally, the International Studies Association regularly sponsors panels on intelligence at its yearly meetings. Although analysis is not always featured, these journals and ISA panels help to advance the discipline with in-depth research, histories, case studies, practitioners' perspectives, lessons-learned articles, book reviews, and sharing of information across all segments of the intelligence cycle.

Emerging Attributes of an Emerging Discipline

Sherman Kent's call nearly sixty years ago to create an intelligence literature was a critical and foundational step on the path to a discipline. Much has followed since. Perhaps the most important development between then and now is the growing appreciation that subject-matter expertise, while essential to good analysis, is not sufficient for a true analytic profession. Beyond an in-depth understanding of substance—that is, solid knowledge of specific states, nonstate actors, regions, ideologies, technologies, and social science theories—what analysts also need is an in-depth understanding of how the practice of intelligence itself works: how requirements are made and how to make them; how intelligence is collected and processed through clandestine sources, human and technical; how analysis is best conducted, typically through structured analytic tradecraft, to yield the most valid, reliable, and useful results; and how the customers are best served by the judgments, forecasts, and insights that good analysis should yield.

The best analysts will develop understanding and expertise in the intelligence-collection disciplines (see box 4.1) and the ways that the subjects of their analyses—namely, US adversaries and "intelligence targets"—develop countermeasures to US collection efforts and deny the information sought or manipulate the collected information for deception purposes. They also must comprehend the cognitive processes inherent in conducting analysis and how the cognitive function may affect the analytic process itself, as well as see why openness to contrary opinion is needed and "alternative" analysis is valuable. They must hone their capacity to admit error—and especially to learn from it and from the "best practices" that give good results over the long haul. And far more now than in Kent's day, they should be able to work successfully in collaborative environments.

Each agency follows its own path toward professionalization. In one case, CIA, the reform trend probably started in earnest in the mid-1980s when the then deputy director for intelligence (DDI, later DCI) Robert Gates insisted on providing better analytic support to policymakers, less parochialism in outlook, and began a much more rigorous review process than ever before of all analytic products. This impetus was accelerated under DDI Douglas MacEachin's mandatory two-week Tradecraft 2000 course. Later, DDI John McLaughlin took major steps toward professionalizing the analytic

BOX 4.1   The Analyst and the INTs

A thorough understanding of the unique collection systems and processes that generate much of the information used in analysis is critical to an analyst's work. While there are different ways to categorize intelligence collection techniques, the following "INTs" generally capture their key differences. Each INT's summary is followed by a brief discussion of implications for analysis.

HUMINT: Human intelligence is the gathering of information through human sources. The process however, is both complicated and risky. The clandestine HUMINT cycle is classic espionage. It involves spotting, assessing, developing, recruiting, and running an asset secretly—that is, unknown to the local counterintelligence service. This requires initially identifying a potential source who may have access to specific information, a targeting strategy for developing access to that asset, then (assuming a successful recruitment) vetting that asset to ensure that he or she is who they say they are and that they are not double agents working for the enemy.

Implications for analysis. The information provided by the source can only be trusted if the source is a bona fide agent, having survived a rigorous vetting process. Analysts typically have no access to the operation itself or to the recruited source. They don't know who the source is and rarely get detailed insight into the source's motivation, access, or vetting. Analysts only see the information, but they cannot make a determination about the accuracy or validity of that information independently of knowing something about the source, the manner of recruitment, and pertinent operational dynamics. While most human sources provide good information, and a rare few are truly game-changers, some turn out to be double agents who provide worthless or deceptive information, such as the Cuban sources run by Castro and the Chinese American Katrina Leung run by China. Others can be fabricators like the Iraqi source "Curveball" in Germany, who told believable lies about biological weapons in Iraq that didn't exist. Analysis based on human intelligence requires useful information that analysts cannot always accept at face value or unquestioningly from HUMINT collectors. It might be true, but wishful thinking will not make it so.

SIGINT: Signals intelligence is the gathering of electronic information through the interception of signals traveling between people or machines. SIGINT includes COMINT, or communications intelligence, which is intercepted communications of parties unwitting of the intercept operation. ELINT, electronic intelligence, provides signals from foreign radars such as surface-to-air missile systems—especially useful for military missions to penetrate the airspace protected by these radar systems. FISINT, or foreign instrumentation intelligence, provides intercepted information from telemetry and tracking of reentry vehicles such as missile warheads and helps analysts assess missile accuracy.

Implications for analysis. All intercepts need careful scrutiny, as their intended meaning often requires knowledge of the circumstances of a conversation, including identification of the parties, their relationship, the context of events, and the venue, in order to divine meaning when individuals talk cryptically and to be alert to the possibility of deception. Sometimes sensitive signals and communications are sent in code. In cases of encryption, the above caveats still apply when decryption succeeds. Otherwise there is value in "traffic analysis" of the frequency, pattern, and the location of the signals. English-language translations could also introduce uncertain meanings or other issues of interpretation. Similarly, interpreting collected data from ELINT or telemetry also requires good technical understanding, as well as good communication skills to convey their meanings clearly and accurately to nontechnical customers.

IMINT: Also called geospatial intelligence (GEOINT), IMINT refers to imagery information and data gathered most often through aerial or satellite photography. Overhead imagery has evolved significantly from early black-and-white photography to the use of near-real-time electro-optical imaging and space-borne radar and thermal infrared sensors.

Implications for analysis. The art and science of photo interpretation has evolved considerably since the U-2 pictures over Cuba revealed covert Soviet missile sites and dramatically illustrated the value of imagery. Today analysts using imagery—both GEOINT specialists and all-source analysts—must understand highly complex sensors, including advanced geospatial intelligence (AGI), as well as their platforms, which requires an understanding of orbital dynamics. And they must understand how well or how poorly the intelligence targets also understand imagery collection techniques and deploy denial-and-deception countermeasures to defeat them.

MASINT: Measurement and signatures intelligence represents a wide array of technical collection capabilities designed to detect, identify, and describe the "signatures" of fixed targets, as well as track moving targets. These techniques are not normally included with conventional SIGINT or IMINT collection, although some (such as multispectral or hyperspectral imagery) clearly overlap, and their proper categorization can be debated. Others are more distinctly MASINT techniques, such as the collection of acoustic, infrared, and laser signals, nuclear radiation and debris, reflected light from distant objects, effluents (particulates), magnetic and radiofrequency data, and the radar interrogation of targets.

Implications for analysis. As SIGINT represents the "ears" of intelligence and imagery the "eyes," MASINT is often thought of as providing the other senses—the smelling, tasting, and touching of collection. It is a vital source of information for weapons of mass destruction, for example. It requires not

---

BOX 4.1   The Analyst and the INTs (cont'd)

---

only good technical understanding of what these highly complex capabilities can and cannot do but also the ability to convey their actual meaning and implications to policymakers who typically undervalue specialized technical collection because they do not understand it.

OSINT: While open-source materials do not constitute a collection discipline in quite the same way as the other four, which all have major clandestine attributes, open-source intelligence is increasingly important to analysis owing to the information explosion in the internet age and the powerful search engines that came with it. They constitute all publicly available media, such as newspapers, magazines, books, radio, and television; public data such as government and official reports; and professional and academic studies, conferences, and symposia.

Implications for analysis. Analysts can be overwhelmed with the abundance of open-source materials, and a major challenge is filtering for quality, usefulness, and authenticity. That provides a good place to start, since policymakers and customers may already be well informed by the same open sources that analysts unearth. This will help establish a common information baseline. Of course, there may also be uniquely important information in open sources unavailable in secret collection. Following this, analysts and their customers will be better able to gauge the value added of information derived from the other clandestine INTs.

Sources: Discussion of the technical collection disciplines draws from Robert M. Clark's *The Technical Collection of Intelligence* (Washington, DC: CQ Press, 2010), especially 283–84. OSINT is well covered in Mark M. Lowenthal, *Intelligence: From Secrets to Policy* (Washington, DC: CQ Press, 2009), 103–6.

---

discipline, with the establishment of the Sherman Kent School for Intelligence Analysis and the DI's Senior Analytic Service (SAS) in 2000. But perhaps the most important drivers for greater professionalism in analysis—and this one is IC-wide—were the back-to-back intelligence failures of 9/11, where analysis played a major role in the IC failure to provide tactical warning for the attacks, and of the failed 2002 national intelligence estimate on Iraqi WMDs.[30] One immediate effect of the 9/11 attack was DCI George Tenet's creation of the CIA Red Cell just two days later. The mandate of the Red Cell—which still exists—was to think outside the box and to challenge assumptions and mainline analytic thinking. The Red Cell employed such structured and alternative analysis techniques as Devil's Advocacy. The institutionalizing of this "challenge analysis" unit foreshadowed later reforms that required the regular use of structured analytic techniques (SATs) across the agency's analytic workforce after 2005.

Learning how to conduct quality analysis is a career-long quest. When new analysts show up for their first day on the job, they may already be qualified experts in area studies, academic disciplines, or subject-matter issues, and most arrive at the all-source agencies with advanced degrees. Still they know next to nothing about the nature of intelligence itself. To be fully effective analysts, they must learn about the intricacies of intelligence and the arcane secrets of the craft—and many literally are classified secrets—and this will take years to learn and a career to master. How this is accomplished requires a combination of individual effort, properly meshed with the support systems provided by the emerging discipline. Such systems will nourish their professionalization in a manner similar to the way neophyte lawyers, doctors, and librarians also learned their professions. Support systems encompass knowledge repositories, information standards, guidelines, best practices, communities of interest, and communities of practice. Further, governing bodies of mature disciplines address professional standards, licensing/credentialing, and certification, as well as continuing education requirements and ethics training.

Revisiting the four common themes seen in the more mature disciplines examined above, we can see that intelligence analysis, while notably short of the others, has made discernible headway in recent years.

Governing Bodies to Set Quality Standards

While intelligence practitioners have nothing comparable to the ABA or AMA to set standards, test and certify, and regulate training and education, recent initiatives taken separately by the Office of the Director of National Intelligence (ODNI) and by CIA illustrate a promising start in this direction. For example, the ODNI has established quality standards for intelligence analysis, first mandated in the Intelligence Reform and Terrorism Prevention Act (IRTPA) of 2004, and in a major 2007 directive on analytic tradecraft, Intelligence Community Directive (ICD) 203.[31] These standards are intended to apply to analysis produced in all sixteen agencies in the IC, as well as to the National Intelligence Council operating under the ODNI. Additionally, the ODNI created the Office of Analytic Integrity and Standards (AIS). Each year the AIS conducts a select number of quality reviews of IC analytic products on key issues, and the results are shared across the IC. This review process facilitates a learning organization dynamic, further reinforced by lessons-learned centers in the ODNI and the major analytic agencies. The lessons-learned centers are mostly new and in early phases of identifying best practices and, thus far, have had no or only minimal impact on professionalizing analysis.

While this is more a governing process than a governing body, all agencies exercise strong oversight in analytic production through a review and coordination process. In some it is very rigorous, and the many layers of review by other experts and experienced analytic managers, along with the demanding coordination process with peer experts inside the analyst's agency and across the IC, ensures a solid degree of rigor in both substantive and tradecraft review. This can be even more demanding in some agencies than peer review in academic publications because the result is not an analyst's opinion but rather the official position of an intelligence agency or even the whole IC in cases of an NIE.

For its part CIA established its SAS in 1999, also a major milestone in moving intelligence analysis toward a discipline. By allowing analysts to advance to more senior ranks as substantive experts rather than switching to a management track for surer promotions, this structure accorded professional equality status to the analytic career track. It recognized the centrality of substantive expertise and analytic thinking skills in the broader IC mission. Moreover, entry into the SAS ranks brings with it responsibilities central to ensuring a learning culture, which includes mentoring of other analysts and sharing expertise and lessons learned both on the job and in Kent School analytic training courses.

Educational Systems to Train New Practitioners and Training throughout Careers

Both the Defense Intelligence Agency (DIA) and CIA have established major analysis training programs—and both give a place of prominence to structured analytic tradecraft. Similarly, the NGA College, the NSA Cryptologic School, the FBI, and the Department of Homeland Security (DHS), along with the military services, have focused on improved training for analysts in recent years.[32] The ODNI has developed a two-week foundational course—Analysis 101—to teach structured tradecraft supporting IC-wide analytic standards. A joint course, it enrolls students from all sixteen member agencies and elements of the IC. The ODNI and the creation of the new National Intelligence University, also mandated by IRTPA and housed and administered by DIA, will offer a broad menu of analysis courses.

An important development was DIA's expansion of its intelligence school, earlier called the Joint Military Intelligence College (JMIC), then later the National Defense Intelligence College (NDIC). Unique in the IC, it was accredited in 1997 to offer a bachelor of science degree in intelligence and later a master of science degree in strategic intelligence (MSI), a master of science degree in technology intelligence (MST), and certificates of intelligence studies (CIS). It also offers an advanced program of studies in foreign denial and deception. As the NDIC has been elevated to the National Intelligence University, its substantial intelligence curriculum, extending well beyond analysis, will likely expand, and more important, it will now serve a broader IC-wide need beyond its earlier and narrower DOD-focused curricular aims.

CIA founded the Sherman Kent School of Intelligence Analysis (SKS) in 2000, much expanding the limited analysis curriculum then offered at CIA's Office of Training and Education, predecessor to the CIA University. The SKS created a robust curriculum dedicated to the analytic profession, offering over two hundred courses addressing economic, political, and military intelligence analysis. Core programs include the mandatory seventeen-week Career Analyst Program (CAP) for all incoming analysts. CAP includes modules on analytic writing, tradecraft, collection, denial and deception, politicization, and interacting with policymakers. Additionally, the Essential Skills Program meets follow-on needs of post-CAP analysts with one or more years of experience. The Advanced Analyst Program comprises some dozen courses and is offered to mid- and senior-level analysts with four or more years' experience. The Expert Level Program is for analysts with ten-plus years' experience, while managers can catch up to their younger and possibly better-trained analysts though the SKS Tradecraft Training for Managers Program.

Recent training has emphasized SATs, including the establishment of "tradecraft cells" in all CIA production offices to teach, facilitate, and promote their regular use. A mandatory three-day course on twenty specific SATs is intended to develop a common understanding of them across the workforce—analysts and managers alike. "Analysis of Competing Hypotheses," "Key Assumptions Check," and "Structured Brainstorming" are among the most used SATs. SKS has also stood up tailored training in SATs for all tradecraft cell members—a "teaching and facilitating course"—to ensure a thorough understanding of structured tradecraft and its most effective employment in daily analytic work.

Notwithstanding the many training improvements throughout the IC, continuing education requirements and opportunities remain a major shortcoming in professionalizing intelligence, and nothing comparable to continuing legal education or its counterpart in medical education, for example, is even on the drawing boards.

Certification Requirements to Limit Admission

Here gains in analysis are barely started. Of course, all IC analysts require a *security* certification, including a polygraph for some agencies, even before they can be hired. And advanced degrees for most imply some college- or university-level of substantive certification. But there is little to no certification at all after admission to the IC that addresses professional requirements for conducting analysis. At CIA the SAS system established a rigorous competitive process for entry whereby mid-level and senior applicants must present a strong body of analytic work and answer in writing a series of questions about the analysis profession, methodologies, and how they approach their work. They must also pass an interview by a team of senior peers and managers. This process provides a form of certification, but admission is voluntary and many analysts do not apply, and applicants who do not pass are still permitted to work as analysts, even if their promotion prospects outside of the SAS may not be as promising.

Knowledge Management Systems to Organize Information and Facilitate Retrieval and Expansion

The IC and some of its agencies have taken small but important steps toward developing a knowledge management system. But the complexity of the task—lacking even a primitive word taxonomy and exacerbated by the daunting challenges posed by layers of classified information and a bewildering array of clearances and accesses to the most sensitive information—will impede real progress in the foreseeable future.[33] Against these odds, the DNI's most important contribution in moving intelligence analysis from information pandemonium toward discipline status is the creation of the Library of National Intelligence (LNI). This ambitious repository of all published IC intelligence analysis may eventually get closer to the comprehensive knowledge bases of the legal and medical professions, but the system is still in its infancy.

When completed, the LNI will be intended to provide IC analysts access to all published products. Studies with especially sensitive or compartmented intelligence data are limited to analysts whose work directly requires such access. Related innovations are I-Space (formerly A-Space) and the Analytic Resources Catalog (ARC). I-Space, a digital workspace open to all fully cleared analysts, enables access to topical reports and databases throughout the IC; it uses social networking tools to facilitate collaboration and allows analysts to locate other analysts working on similar topics. ARC provides a "yellow pages" of the entire analytic community, allowing analysts to quickly identify and contact IC experts on virtually any subject covered by the IC.

In sum, a starting point for assessing intelligence analysis as a discipline is to acknowledge that the medical, legal, and library disciplines took decades to reach the point of serious governance, training, certification, and knowledge capture. It will not work as fast in government. Intelligence analysis is presently a nascent discipline at best. As civil servants, analysts enjoy job protection that private-sector professionals do not, but they also face more resistant bureaucracies, which can add obstacles to professionalization when scarce resources and bureaucratic change are at stake. Still, the gains made in recent years toward professionalizing analysis and building toward a real discipline are both notable and preliminary. With the stand-up of the ODNI, CIA's pioneering SAS, and structured analytic tradecraft gaining traction throughout the IC, governance and quality standards are more explicit and much improved. Analyst training and education have also expanded and deepened, if unevenly. Knowledge management, started only recently and from near zero, has shown important gains but represents only a modest beginning. Of all the key attributes of mature disciplines, certification is perhaps least in evidence. So, with limited but discernible progress offset by serious and persistent shortfalls, the overall record is mixed. Moreover, in a time of shrinking resources, the gains could also be fragile, short-lived, and by no means have an assured future. Dependent on public funding, conducting daily work in a classified and necessarily nontransparent environment, and in need of consistently visionary and forceful leadership to lead the charge for bona fide disciplinary goals—all highlight nontrivial obstacles on the path to discipline status.

Disciplines are responses to a shared sense of need and the collective agitation for systemic improvement. Generally speaking, disciplines do not develop by mandate but rather emerge where professionals combine their lived experiences and learning with those of their colleagues, establishing performance standards and searchable repositories of aggregate knowledge. They adopt "best practice" methodologies used to build and access their hard-won knowledge, whether tacit or explicit, which remain "best" only until better information, experience, or methods become available and supersede what was best before. Therefore, transforming intelligence analysis from a series of ad hoc activities with inconsistent results into a more mature discipline must be seen as an ongoing process rather than a once-and-for-all solution. Still, intelligence analysis is an emerging discipline, however early in the process.

Notes

1. See Sherman Kent, *Strategic Intelligence for American World Policy* (Princeton, NJ: Princeton University Press, 1949), and Jack Davis, "Sherman Kent and the Profession of Intelligence Analysis" (CIA/CSI, Sherman Kent Center for Intelligence Analysis), Occasional Papers, vol. 1, no. 5, November 2002.
2. A notable exception is Stephen Marrin, an early advocate of building an intelligence analysis profession in part by paying attention to the experience of others, beginning with medicine. See Stephen Marrin and Jonathan D. Clemente, "Modeling an Intelligence Analysis Profession on Medicine," *International Journal of Intelligence and Counterintelligence* 19 (2006): 642–65, and Marrin's *Improving Intelligence Analysis: Bridging the Gap between Scholarship and Practice* (London: Routledge, 2012), especially chap. 8.
3. Alexis de Tocqueville, *Democracy in America* (1889; repr., Washington, DC: Regnery, 2002), 221.
4. Harry J. Lambeth, "Practicing Law in 1878," *American Bar Association Journal* 64 (July 1978): 1016.
5. Quoted in ibid., 1016. In 1850, all that was necessary to practice law in Indiana, for instance, was "good moral character" and registration to vote.
6. Ibid., 1018.
7. Whitney North Seymour, "The First Century of the American Bar Association," *American Bar Association Journal* 64 (July 1978): 1040.
8. Jason Krause, "Towering Titans: LexisNexis and West Are Still Battling for Dominance," *American Bar Association Journal* 90 (May 2004): 50.
9. Ibid.
10. NIH National Library of Medicine Programs and Services Fiscal Year 2010 Annual Report, www.nlm.nih.gov/ocpl/anreports/fy2010.pdf, and H.R. 2055—the Consolidated Appropriations Act, 2012, Public Law 112-74, http://officeofbudget.od.nih.gov/pdfs/FY13/Appropriations%20Language-2012.pdf.
11. Andrew H. Beck, "The Flexner Report and the Standardization of American Medical Education," *Journal of the American Medical Association* 291 (May 5, 2004): 2139.
12. Ibid., 2140.
13. For example, see Stephen P. Marrin and Jonathan D. Clemente, "Improving Intelligence Analysis by Looking to the Medical Profession," *International Journal of Intelligence and Counterintelligence* 18 (Winter 2005): 707, and Marrin and Clemente, "Modeling an Intelligence Analysis Profession": 642.
14. David M. Eddy, "Evidence-Based Medicine: A Unified Approach," *Health Affairs* 24 (January–February 2005): 9.

15. See A. L. Cochrane, *Effectiveness and Efficiency: Random Reflections on Health Services* (London: Nuffield Provincial Hospitals Trust, 1973).

16. G. H. Guyatt, R. B. Haynes, R. Z. Jaeschke, D. J. Cook, L. Green, C. D. Naylor, M. C. Wilson, and W. S. Richardson, "Users' Guides to the Medical Literature: XXV—Evidence-Based Medicine: Principles for Applying the Users' Guides to Patient Care; Evidence-Based Medicine Working Group," *Journal of the American Medical Association* 284 (September 13, 2000): 1290.

17. Bernd Frohmann, "'Best Books' and Excited Readers: Discursive Tensions in the Writings of Melvil Dewey," *Libraries & Culture* 32 (Summer 1997): 349.

18. Ibid., 352.

19. Wayne A. Wiegand, *Irrepressible Reformer: A Biography of Melvil Dewey* (Chicago: American Library Association, 1996), 33.

20. "Introduction to Dewey Decimal Classification," OCLC (Online Computer Library Center), www.oclc.org/dewey/versions/ddc22print/intro.pdf.

21. George A. Kelly, *A Theory of Personality: The Psychology of Personal Constructs* (New York: Norton, 1963), 15.

22. "Sense making" was introduced by Brenda Dervin and further developed by Karl Weick, who also developed the related concept of "mindfulness." See Brenda Dervin, "Sense-Making Methodology Site," http://communication.sbs.ohio-state.edu/sense-making, and Karl Weick, *Managing the Unexpected: Assuring High Performance in an Age of Complexity* (New York: Jossey-Bass, 2001).

23. Karl Erik Sveiby, *The New Organizational Wealth: Managing and Measuring Knowledge-Based Assets* (San Francisco: Berrett Koehler, 1997), x.

24. Peter M. Senge, *The Fifth Discipline: Mastering the Five Practices of the Learning Organization* (New York: Doubleday, 1990), 3; revised in 2006 and published with a new subtitle: *The Art and Practice of the Learning Organization*.

25. For this rendition of the three components of intelligence, see Edward Waltz's important work on knowledge management in the intelligence and military communities, specifically his *Knowledge Management in the Intelligence Enterprise* (Boston: Artech House, 2003) and *Information Warfare: Principles and Operations* (Boston: Artech House, 1998).

26. Various works seeking the improvement of intelligence analysis include Rob Johnston, *Analytic Culture in the U.S. Intelligence Community: An Ethnographic Study* (Washington, DC: Center for the Study of Intelligence, CIA, 2005); National Research Council, National Academy of Sciences, *Intelligence Analysis for Tomorrow: Advances from the Behavioral and Social Sciences* (Washington, DC: National Academies Press, 2011); Commission on the Intelligence Capabilities of the United States Regarding Weapons of Mass Destruction, *Report to the President of the United States, March 31, 2005 (WMD Commission Report)* (Washington, DC: Government Printing Office, 2005), chap. 8; Steven Rieber and Neil Thomason, "Toward Improving Intelligence Analysis: Creation of a National Institute for Analytic Methods," *Studies in Intelligence* 49 (2005): 71; and Marrin and Clemente, "Improving Intelligence Analysis," 707.

27. Sherman Kent, "The Need for an Intelligence Literature," *Studies in Intelligence* 1 (Fall 1955): 3.

28. Ibid., 7.

29. Ibid., 10.

30. The two authoritative studies are commission reports: National Commission on Terrorist Attacks upon the United States, *The 9/11 Commission Report*, authorized ed. (New York: Norton, 2003), and the *WMD Commission Report*.

31. ICD 203 is discussed by Tom Fingar in chap. 17 and is provided in box 17.1. Related ICDs on improving analysis include 205 on analytic outreach, 206 on sourcing requirements, 208 on writing, and 209 on production and dissemination.

32. See chap. 15 for the US Marine Corps experience with tradecraft development and training and chap. 18 for an elaboration of training.

33. Early efforts to systematize knowledge in the IC include Rob Johnston's, "Developing a Taxonomy of Intelligence Analysis Variables: Foundations for Meta-Analysis," *Studies in Intelligence* 47, no. 3 (2003): 61–71, revised in chap. 3 of Johnston's *Analytic Culture*. In the related field of private sector (or "competitive") intelligence, the Society of Competitive Intelligence Professionals (www.scip.org) recently developed a *Book of Knowledge* and a certification process for its membership.

PART II

The Policymaker–
Analyst Relationship

CHAPTER 5

Serving the National Policymaker

JOHN MCLAUGHLIN

There is no phase of the intelligence business that is more important than the proper relationship between intelligence itself and the people who use its product. Oddly enough, this relationship, which one would expect to establish itself automatically, does not do this. It is established as a result of a great deal of persistent conscious effort, and it is likely to disappear when the effort is relaxed.

—Sherman Kent, *Strategic Intelligence for American World Policy*

If it is true, as I believe it is, that analysis is where all aspects of the intelligence profession come together, then it is equally true that dealing with the policymaker is where all the components of analysis come together. It is at the nexus between intelligence and policy that we test everything from the substantive merit of the product to the quality of our tradecraft to our effectiveness in training and managing analysts. And it is also where an analytic profession that strives for objectivity, civility, thoroughness, and balance is likely to meet up with the some more jarring qualities: urgency, impatience with nuance or equivocation, and, yes, sometimes even politics. But if this relationship turns sour—if the policymaker does not feel the need for the analytic product—then there is no reason for doing analysis at all. It goes without saying, then, that it is worth thinking about what makes the relationship work and what renders it dysfunctional.[1]

The first thing that must be said is that the relationship between intelligence analysis and the national policymaker is a complex one. Many elements are at play: the very different "cultures" of intelligence and policy, the expectations policymakers bring to the table regarding intelligence capabilities, the analyst's degree of insight into the policy process, the receptivity of both sides to different points of view, and the intangible factors of personality and presence that influence all that happens in Washington.[2]

The Policy Culture versus the Intelligence Culture

The different cultures of policy and intelligence hold the potential to inject a great deal of misunderstanding and tension into the relationship. The culture of the policy world is marked by elements of realism but is essentially—and necessarily—a culture of optimism. Policymaking is a contentious business marked by lots of competing ideas and frequently by heavy intellectual combat. A lot of bureaucratic blood is often on the ground once a particular course of action wins out.

Alternatively, a given policy is often in place mainly because an election has affirmed—or can be portrayed as affirming—the central idea. Indeed, policymakers live in a world heavily influenced by political considerations, and intelligence is only one factor weighing in their decision calculus, as Sherman Kent years ago reminded analysts who thought their views were being discarded.[3] In any event, once a given policy course is set, its advocates earnestly want to achieve its objectives, and they work hard to ensure that they do. They are not blind to obstacles, but their first instinct is to work hard to overcome them, and they are almost always optimistic that they can. It is not that policymakers never question the course they are on—it is that a higher value is assigned to keeping on course and getting to the finish line.

In my thirty years in the intelligence business, I encountered many types of intelligence consumers in the policy world. They fell into two broad categories: those who knew how to interpret and use intelligence, and those who did not or would not, despite considerable understanding of the craft.

Policymakers who know how to use intelligence generally have a realistic view of what it can and cannot do. They understand, for example, that intelligence is almost always more helpful in detecting trends than in predicting specific events. They know how to ask questions that force intelligence specialists to separate what they actually know from what they think they know. They are not intimidated by intelligence that runs counter to the prevailing policy but see it as a useful jog to thinking about their courses of action.

Policymakers who use intelligence less effectively are a more diverse and complicated lot. I dealt with one very senior State Department official some years ago who thought, often justifiably, that he had a more comprehensive and sophisticated understanding of the issues than intelligence specialists. The result was that he almost never requested intelligence support and was content with just an occasional briefing from a trusted senior intelligence officer. To give such policymakers their due, it is likely that their disinterest resulted from some disappointing past experience with intelligence that regrettably closed them off to further use of it.

Other policymakers I dealt with simply could not abide analysis or reporting that ran counter to their own view. In the mid-1990s, I told an eminent Russian specialist who had simply dismissed assessments of growing corruption in Russia that he ought to consider the analysis "his friend" rather than the "enemy" that he obviously perceived it to be. My point was that his violent disagreement with it at least sharpened his understanding of his own point of view and his ability to argue it effectively—in effect the analysis laid out the opposing argument. Finally, when the news was bad, policymaker concerns deepened, particularly in the White House or the National Security Council, when we wrote it down in formal intelligence assessments. The concern, common to administrations over the years headed by both parties, was that bad news would leak, causing embarrassment and lending ammunition to those who preferred a different course.

In one case, for example, senior administration officials in the Clinton administration argued strenuously over the words we chose to use in describing the status of a particular missile system by a developing country. If we termed it "deployed" and if that leaked, the administration fear was that it would have been used by critics to argue that the United States should impose sanctions on an important country whose cooperation was important on other matters and with whom the United States was close to achieving potentially beneficial economic agreements. Intelligence officers, of course, can never yield to such entreaties—and we did not in that instance—but this is one of many factors that can heighten tensions in the policy–intelligence relationship. Given the great controversy over leaks during the Obama administration, it does not seem that this problem has abated.

Such potential frictions are compounded by the culture of the intelligence world. In contrast to the fundamentally optimistic thrust of the policy culture, the culture of the intelligence world is marked by skepticism. The requirement to warn of dangers—and the heavy criticism when warning fails—encourages a darker view than is ever instinctively the case in the policy world. I once heard Robert Gates, during his tenure as director of central intelligence, define an intelligence analyst as someone who "smells flowers . . . and then looks for the coffin." In short, analysts are trained, and indeed are required, to look for trouble—regrettably often at the expense of opportunity—and are thought to have failed when they do not detect it.

To be sure, there is often contentiousness in the analytic world equal to that in the policy arena, with similar quantities of bureaucratic or intellectual "blood on the floor." But unlike the variegated inputs to policy—everything from domestic politics to personal relationships with foreign leaders—the contention over analytic conclusions is entirely about substantive matters: over what is confidently known, what is not, and what it all portends. In short, the battles in the analytic world always center on what things mean and not—as in the policy world—on what to do.

I saw the results of this frequently as I conveyed intelligence to policymakers. During the Reagan administration, a senior State Department official complained to me about our assessment of the prospects for progress in negotiations to settle the long-running dispute between Greece and Turkey over their respective rights in Cyprus—a dispute that had involved military operations and had shown few signs of easing through ten years of talks. He said, "All you do is interpret the data, lay out the problems, and tell me that the situation is bleak. I know that. What I need from you is some assessment of what my leverage is with these guys—of what I should do!" I came to see this as a justifiable complaint. Below I will discuss ways for intelligence officers to be helpful in such circumstances while still observing the prohibition against prescribing policy.

Given such dynamics, the chances are high that analysts and policymakers will bring many misconceptions to the table—or at least high potential for misunderstanding.

Policymakers, for example, can interpret the analysts' hesitation to weigh in on policy as evidence that they live in an ivory tower world. And when policymakers make their choices on some basis other than the intelligence assessment, analysts can conclude that policy counterparts either are not interested or are simply ignoring the intelligence.

Bridging the Divide

The potential for these kinds of problems suggests that it is worth having deliberate strategies to avoid them—ways through which analysts can gain a greater understanding of what makes analysis helpful to policymakers and what does not. And for the policymaker, ways must be developed to give them a better appreciation of what analysis is and is not, what it can reasonably be expected to deliver and what it cannot. In this effort, the larger burden must fall on the analyst community. Just as any producer of product in the private sector must take the initiative to understand the consumer, so the analyst as the provider of service has the responsibility to understand what is needed and the most effective way to present it. This can be done in any number of ways, ranging from surveys of recipients to formal processes for sleeping requirements to exit interviews with departing policymakers.

In my personal experience, however, the most effective way for analysts to understand what policymakers need is to live and work among them for a period of time. It pays enormous dividends in mutual understanding to deploy some portion of the analyst workforce on temporary rotational assignments into the policy community. These can range from assignments of several months' duration supporting an overseas embassy to a year-long stint in one of the executive branch agencies.

My conviction about this comes from direct experience. During Gates's tenure as deputy director for intelligence (the analytic wing of the Central Intelligence Agency, or CIA) in the early 1980s, he insisted that anyone who wanted to compete for a senior-level promotion ought to have a tour in the policy community. As part of this program, I was deployed to the State Department for an extended tour. While serving there as a special assistant to a senior officer in the Bureau of European Affairs, I had an inside look at how CIA's work was received on a wide range of issues. I heard our work both praised and scorned and sought to understand why it sometimes elicited the latter reaction. It seldom had to do with the narrow substance of the message.

Such negative reactions more often had to do with other problems. For instance, the State Department officer had already read the raw reporting on which the analysis was based and found little new in what we wrote. Or a particular assessment was simply too long and complicated for a harried policy officer to absorb. Or the analysis was written without a clue as to what policymakers were thinking or doing about the problem and therefore appeared naive, abstract, or uninformed. Or the analyst had pointed out all the problems surrounding an issue but paid no attention to what points of leverage or opportunities the United States might have.

There were obvious learning points in all this. To succeed, the analysis had to be timely, digestible, and informed about the policy context while stopping short of pandering to or prescribing the policy, and it needed to help policymakers in their search for leverage. Ideally, analysts serving in positions like the one I held should not be in policymaking positions but instead serve as onsite analytic resources for policymakers, with the capacity and authority to reach back into the intelligence agencies for analytic support. Analysts who have this experience gain a keen appreciation for the qualities that their work must possess in order to be taken seriously and have an impact. The experience led me in subsequent leadership positions to keep 5 percent to 10 percent of my analysts deployed to the policy community in order to gain understanding of the qualities needed to make assessments more helpful to policymakers struggling with difficult dilemmas. As will be discussed below, these qualities range from accuracy to timeliness to clarity about what is confidently known and what is not.

Efforts also should be made to educate policymakers—particularly new people in an incoming administration—about intelligence capabilities. This has frequently been discussed, but incoming senior officials are usually so overwhelmed with requirements and material—drinking from the proverbial "fire hose," so to speak—that it is very hard to ensure that "education on intelligence" is a priority.

That said, the intelligence community should offer, to incoming officials at the assistant-secretary level and above, a course on what to expect of intelligence and how to use it—along the lines of the orientation Congress offers its newly elected members on congressional rules and procedures. This could be devised and administered by the director of national intelligence or by one of the agencies' institutions, such as CIA's Center for the Study of Intelligence or the Sherman Kent School of Intelligence Analysis. In the meantime, analysts and their leaders must seize whatever opportunities their work presents to help policymakers understand how the intelligence system works and what they can reasonably expect from it. My understanding is that the intelligence community was able to do this more successfully in the past than at the beginning of the Obama administration.

Hitting the Target

What must the analyst produce to effectively serve the national policymaker? The key is that such support is always about informing policy, not prescribing policy. And it takes many forms. Obviously, the product will be delivered in a variety of publications, but it might also come as a briefing, a response to a specific question, or a telephone call. Essentially, we are talking about the interaction between analysts and policymakers, and in the real world this takes place in all these channels. First and at the most general level, what analysts produce should help policy officials think through the issues and the choices facing them. This is especially true at this moment and will, in all likelihood, continue to be true well into the twenty-first century.

Over the years, I have attended probably hundreds of meetings in the White House Situation Room at the deputies and principals levels, and I can attest that the challenges facing policymakers—and the intelligence officers supporting them—have become steadily more complex.[4] To be sure, the period of competition and confrontation with the Soviet Union had its share of life-and-death situations, controversies, and, of course, existential threat to the United States and its allies. But it also allowed most things to be viewed through the prism of our concerns about the Soviet Union. Some connection to the Soviet threat was what got intelligence questions to the front burner, both as requirements and as subjects for assessment.

In the post-Soviet, post-9/11 world, countries and issues have to be dealt with for what they are in and of themselves, and so the range of issues to which both policymakers and analysts must be attentive has grown in scope and complexity. Policymakers' questions and concerns today and for the foreseeable future are likely to involve not just countries in the aggregate but also issues associated with cultures, regions, tribes, ethnic groups, and other particularistic aspects of foreign affairs.

This trend began to emerge in the early 1990s with the growing importance of non-state actors (terrorists, organized crime, and the like) and accelerated throughout the decade as the post–Cold War thaw yielded problems such as Bosnia and Kosovo. This period also saw shifting alliance patterns, the growing prominence of rising powers such as China and India, and the blurring effect that 9/11 had on the traditional foreign/domestic distinctions for intelligence—all against a backdrop of technological revolution and globalization. It takes little study to appreciate that in dealing with current issues such as homeland security, the proliferation of dangerous weapons, terrorism, and specific troubled regions and countries—the Middle East, South Asia, North Korea, Iran, Syria, Iraq, China, and Russia—policymakers today do not have many clear-cut choices or obvious options, nor is there a national consensus about priorities and policy choices.

Analysts can take a number of steps, well short of prescribing policy, to help policymakers think through choices. First, analysts can use a series of conceptual approaches to help policymakers think through complex problems, for example:

- *Test the case.* This involves marshaling data to test whether the policymaker's theory of the case corresponds to reality as it appears to the analyst. If policymakers are considering an effort to alter the behavior through economic sanctions of countries such as Iran, Syria, or North Korea, what do intelligence analysts know about the practical impact of the sanctions on the economy of these countries? What do they know about the past effectiveness of sanctions in altering the behavior of these countries or comparable ones? What do they know about the preparedness and capability of other countries to enforce the sanctions?
- *Provide pointers.* In the example above, if analysts conclude that sanctions would not alter a country's course, they can delineate areas of greater salience for a country's behavior—such as the diplomatic influence of neighboring states, the country's strong desire for security guarantees, and how internal dissent may alter the country's path.

- *Assess underlying forces.* When the future direction of a country or an evolving issue is particularly cloudy—say, just before a major leadership transition—analysts can lay out the forces at work beneath the surface that will constrain or buoy future leaders and have a strong bearing on how a fluid situation is likely to break. What is known, for example, about public opinion, strengths, or weaknesses in the economy that may foreclose some options, or about friction with a neighboring country that may tie down the new leadership and render alarming rhetoric less so in practice?[5]

These and other analytic approaches allow policymakers to map issues, grasp context, and see the problems they are wrestling with from multiple angles.

The second step that analysts can take to help policymakers think through choices is to effectively warn of impending dangers. There is of course a formal intelligence community warning process, complete with a national intelligence officer to oversee the effort. I am concerned here less with that effort and more with every analyst's duty day in and day out to be thinking about dangers that need to be brought front and center for consumers in the policy world. This obviously places a heavy burden on intelligence analysts—but one that has been part of the job since the day President Harry Truman decided that guarding against another Pearl Harbor required a centralized national intelligence system. Because it is impossible to warn of every significant shift on every problem, the analytic community has to establish some formula for "cannot miss" priorities.

It would be safe to assume that anything that threatens the lives of our citizens, threatens to engage or harm our military forces, or threatens the physical security of the United States would be at the top of any policymaker's list. That obviously involves an intense focus on issues such as terrorism, foreign weapon systems and their proliferation, unconventional weapons, and the possible conjunction of these realms. One way to think about priorities, as I have discussed elsewhere, is to divide global issues into four categories: urgent, important, emerging, and maintenance (the latter meaning sufficient effort to enable a quick "ramp up" if needed).[6]

But beyond these obvious focal points for warning and the heavy emphasis it places on detecting danger, every analyst on every issue needs to bear in mind that what policymakers hate most is surprise. If they are surprised about key foreign developments, even when they do not involve life-and-death issues, it forces them into a more improvisational posture and increases the potential for policy error.

Serving policymakers on this dimension means, therefore, that analysts must constantly ask themselves what is changing in their area of responsibility. It is easy, especially when dealing with something like the fluid politics now prevalent in a country such as Egypt, to fall into the trap of thinking that a clear and digestible description of the current situation is analysis. It is—up to a point—and even that is not always easy. But to serve national decision makers, the analyst must focus equally on incremental changes that could gradually become trends and eventually achieve a critical mass likely to generate surprise. In intelligence, surprise—another term for intelligence failure—is almost never the result of an easy-to-detect precipitate shift. It almost always creeps up on you. When analysts are not attuned to this, the result is something like the surprise that resulted from the fall of the shah of Iran in late 1978.[7] An example of success in detecting pivotal trends is the prescient CIA analysis in 1989–91 that pointed to the likelihood of a coup against Mikhail Gorbachev and the probability that it would fail.[8]

In bringing such trends to the attention of the policy consumer, the intelligence officer must build in an explicit statement of his or her underlying assumptions. Assume that the analyst has been arguing that country X is highly stable. The analyst should understand explicitly what combination of evidence and logic leads him or her to this view and make that clear in the assessments that reach the policymaker. A judgment projecting stability, for example, might rest mainly on the iron control exercised by a country's leader, a high rate of economic growth, the absence of a charismatic and effective opposition, or some combination of these. As the analyst detects changes on these dimensions, they should be brought to the attention of the policy customer with explicit judgments about the likely implications for stability in country X. Policymakers want always to be several steps ahead of potentially surprising changes in the area for which he or she is responsible. It is the intelligence officer's highest duty to ensure that they are.

The third step that analysts can take to help policymakers think through choices is to point out opportunities. As important as it is for the analyst to detect key changes and warn of dangers, chances are that policymakers will stop paying attention if the analyst never does anything but warn. This is the point my State Department contact was making in his complaint about our bleak assessment of negotiation prospects in the mid-1980s. He was basically asking that we alert him to opportunities that might not have been apparent to officials caught up in the hectic game of implementing policy. For instance, a policymaker is grappling with ways to end a costly military conflict, achieve an arms control breakthrough, or end a humanitarian emergency and is frustrated by the obstinacy of the parties. If the analyst's expertise leads him or her to discern what it would take to move one side or the other to compromise—a particular concession, intervention by a third party, or rephrasing of some document—it is perfectly legitimate to advance this view. For example, a senior CIA analyst played a key role in advising the George W. Bush administration in 2001 on the wording of communications with China as the administration sought to end the standoff that resulted from China's holding a US spy plane that had gone down on Hainan Island following an accident with a Chinese fighter plane. Analysts can also legitimately suggest how a country would react to a range of actions by the United States. Such approaches fall well short of prescribing policy and is one of the analytic achievements that policymakers appreciate most. In other words, policymakers appreciate and need more than warning. Otherwise, they begin to experience what might be called "warning fatigue."

In serving the policymaker in these three ways, the analyst's work should have certain characteristics to be most helpful and achieve the maximum impact. Most senior policymakers live in an extraordinarily hectic world. They do not have a lot of time to absorb information or to reflect on it at length. They often do not have the luxury of avoiding or postponing decisions. Analysts must be mindful of all of this as they prepare assessments. This imposes certain analytic standards on the analytic community for accuracy, clarity, timeliness, revising judgments, and alternative views. Let us look briefly at each.

Accuracy

The first requirement, of course, is for accuracy. I mean this largely in an epistemological sense. That is, beyond simply knowing and conveying the facts, the analyst must think about the limits and validity of what is actually "known." Are the "facts" reported iron-clad, observable, and not open to challenge (for example, a foreign leader said something, and it was recorded on television or in a published speech)? Or are they derived from an intercept where there is no question about what was said but where the context may be obscure? Does the information come from a human source whose motivation might be questionable? Does something seen in imagery from space represent reality, or is it being staged for purposes of deception?

I recall once cautioning a senior policymaker not to refer in a public speech to certain things as "facts," even though they were derived from a series of seemingly credible intelligence reports. Though I did not at the time have strong doubts about the basic thrust of the intelligence, I did have in mind the very high standard that must always be used when characterizing intelligence reporting from a range of diverse sources as "factual."

Clarity

A corollary requirement for the analyst is clarity about the uncertainties and what is unknown. Being explicit about this is critical to the policymaker's understanding of how much weight to place on the analysis among the various factors bearing on a decision. A lack of clarity on the uncertainties carries risks for both the policymaker and the analyst; the former may make faulty decisions based on an unwarranted degree of confidence in the analysis, and the latter runs the risk of ultimately being charged with being misleading or, worse, with "intelligence failure" if he or she has left the impression of greater confidence than the available information warrants.

Timeliness

It is equally critical that the analysis be prepared and arrive in a timely manner. The windows of opportunity for senior policymakers to absorb information and make decisions are often very small. Because analysts are almost always dealing with incomplete information, there is a natural tendency and desire to wait for the latest data. But often this is a classic case of the "perfect being the enemy of the good." An assessment that is correct and complete in every way but arrives too late to affect the policymakers' decision is one of the most regrettable outcomes in the analytic profession.

The tension between the need for timeliness and the requirement to spell out uncertainties does not excuse the analyst from telling the policymaker what he or she thinks—providing a bottom line, even if it must be qualified. Otherwise the work will simply be ignored, except in those rare instances where all concerned recognize that a situation is too fluid for anything other than sheer reportage—in other words, the classic "situation report." On the way to a bottom-line judgment, however, it is critical for the analyst to distinguish between what he or she knows and does not know, and then to spell out what he or she thinks in light of that.

Revising Judgments

The policymakers' desire for bottom lines does not excuse the analyst from another ingredient crucial to the success of policy support efforts: letting the policymaker know when the analysts view has changed and, equally important, why. Especially when new data become available and alter an assessment, the analyst needs to be quite explicit about it. Policymakers for their part need to understand that intelligence assessments are highly susceptible to change because they are almost always based on incomplete data from an information stream that the intelligence community is constantly seeking to enlarge. This is a crucial part of the "intelligence education" that has to be delivered to the policy community. That intelligence assessments will change seems obvious, but to people outside the daily ebb and flow of the intelligence business, it may not be. On one occasion when an important assessment changed, a senior policymaker in the George W. Bush administration told me with dismay that I was "moving the goalposts." In fact, I was only factoring in new data.

Alternative Views

While responding to the policymakers' desire for a bottom line, the analyst also needs to give some evidence that he or she has examined all the alternative interpretations of the situation. It is seldom the case that intelligence evidence is so complete and clear as to point convincingly to only one outcome. Policymakers deal with such fluid situations that they instinctively understand this, and analysts should at least evince awareness that there are alternative interpretations of the data, especially when there are significant differences among intelligence professionals about how to interpret them.

It is always best to alert policymakers to these differences and why they exist. Generally policymakers appreciate knowing this and often find the analysis more interesting if they understand the differences on the intelligence side. Ideally, though, a description of such differences should not be presented in an "on the one hand, on the other hand" manner or in a way that suggests "anything can happen." This will not be seen as helpful, and as when afflicted with "warning fatigue," policymakers will simply turn off.

Conclusion

When analysts are generally confident of conclusions and are in a warning posture, it is important that what they present be persuasive. An analytic colleague told me years ago that, confronted with charges of intelligence failure, she said to a former secretary of state that she had indeed told him in advance of an impending war, to which he replied: "You told me, but you didn't persuade me." This at first might seem like a dodge on the policymaker's part, but the remark contains an important point: Analysts must do more than merely state their opinions. Their conclusions have to be laid out in a way that gives the policymaker transparency on many of the factors discussed above: how the evidence and logic are connected, what are the alternative explanations and why have the analysts discarded them, how much of the conclusion is derived from firm evidence and how much from reasoning, and what is the role of precedent and why does it apply or not apply in this case. All these things contribute to the persuasive quality of the argument that the analyst hands the policymaker. Without them the analyst risks having the policymaker dismiss his or her conclusions as mere hunch or intuition that may not have any more value or authority than what he or she reads in the morning paper.[9]

This brief checklist underlines the enormous challenges faced by today's intelligence analysts. A summary way to say all this is that successful support to the national policymaker requires the analyst to

- understand the policymakers' world better than the policymaker will typically understand the intelligence world and
- deal with enormously complex subjects in a highly sophisticated manner, even when given only limited time, space, and data.

Few intellectual tasks in the intelligence business are more demanding than effectively serving national policymakers. But few pursuits are more important, because what ultimately hangs in the balance is the worth of the intelligence support to policymakers, as well as the relevance of the intelligence community to the security policies of the United States.

Notes

1. For a broader discussion of intelligence support to policy, see Roger Z. George and Robert D. Kline, eds., *Intelligence and the National Security Strategist: Enduring Issues and Challenges* (Washington, DC: National Defense University Press, 2004), 417–47.
2. For our purposes, national policymakers will include the president, the vice president, cabinet officers, and those who support them in senior positions: undersecretaries, assistant secretaries, deputy assistant secretaries, senior directors, and directors at the National Security Council. At any one time this amounts to some three to four hundred people. These are the primary executive branch recipients of major intelligence analytic products and the primary requestors of analysis, although clearly hundreds of other officials—office directors and desk

officers in various departments, for example—also have access to large amounts of analytic product and levy tasks on the intelligence community. In addition, Congress in recent years has become a heavy consumer of intelligence, particularly members of the Senate and House intelligence oversight committees and the armed services and foreign relations committees. In a typical year, congressional requestors receive well over a thousand briefings from members of the intelligence community.

3. Sherman Kent, "Estimates and Influence," in *Sherman Kent and the Board of National Estimates: Collected Essays*, ed. Donald P. Steury (Washington, DC: Center for the Study of Intelligence, CIA, 1994), 33–42.

4. National Security Council meetings involving the deputy secretaries of state and defense, the deputy national security adviser, and the vice chairman of the Joint Chiefs of Staff, along with others, came to be called "deputies meetings." The "principals meetings" comprised the secretaries of state and defense, the national security adviser, the chairman of the Joint Chiefs of Staff, and often the vice president.

5. This discussion of techniques that analysts can employ to help policymakers think through issues and choices benefited from a presentation on this subject by James Steinberg, deputy national security adviser in the Clinton administration, at a conference on "The Role of Intelligence in the Policymaking Process" convened by the Ditchley Foundation in the United Kingdom, January 28–30, 2005.

6. John E. McLaughlin, "Spying 2.0 and All That," in *Global Brief: World Affairs in the 21st Century*, February 6, 2012.

7. For a discussion of this, see Gregory F. Treverton and Richard Haass, "The Fall of the Shah of Iran," Kennedy School of Government Case Study Program, C16-88-794.0, 1998.

8. Bruce D. Berkowitz and Jeffery T. Richelson, "The CIA Vindicated," *The National Interest* 41 (Fall 1995): 42–43. Berkowitz and Richelson cited declassified analyses to argue against the oft-repeated view that CIA simply missed the fall of the Soviet Union. This point is also made in chap. 3, this volume.

9. For discussions of the qualities that contribute to effective analysis, see Mark M. Lowenthal, *Intelligence: From Secrets to Policy*, 2nd ed. (Washington, DC: CQ Press, 2003), 108–9, and *Tradecraft Review* 1, no. 1 (August 2004), published by the Directorate of Intelligence, CIA.

CHAPTER 6

The Policymaker's Perspective: Transparency and Partnership

JAMES B. STEINBERG

Policymakers crave good intelligence. Why? Because they believe it can and should make the crucial difference between success and failure, at both the policy and personal levels. This should be the recipe for a match made in heaven between the intelligence analyst and the policymaker. Yet the reality, as many of the contributors to this volume show, is often quite different. Analysts typically feel underappreciated, ignored, or misused by policymakers, while policymakers in turn often feel misled or underserved by intelligence.

Why Is There a Problem?

This chronic tension has flared into the public spotlight in the past six years as a result of the terrorist attacks of September 11, 2001, and the Iraq War. Why, ask the policymakers—and the public—did the intelligence community fail to warn us about the possibility that terrorists would use airliners as flying bombs? Why did they overestimate Saddam Hussein's capability for weapons of mass destruction (WMDs)? Why, ask the analysts, did the policymakers ignore our warning about the risks and dangers of an occupation of Iraq? Why did they set up alternative analytic units to hunt for links between Saddam and al-Qaeda when the established intelligence community repeatedly concluded that none existed?[1]

The result of these two deeply unsettling experiences has led to a rash of proposals for reform of the intelligence community, some welcome and overdue, some merely solving yesterday's problems but of questionable value in meeting the yet unknown problems of the future. Yet few of these efforts have focused on the complex interaction between the policymaker and the analyst. For example, the Silberman-Robb WMD Commission's mandate explicitly excluded the question of how the policymakers used—or misused—the intelligence with which they were provided.[2] And the 9/11 Commission treaded lightly on the question of why the national security adviser could claim—with all sincerity—that no one had warned her about the possibility of terrorist attacks by airplanes, when the Central Intelligence Agency itself had been threatened with just such an attack only six years earlier.[3]

To some extent the reluctance to delve into these uncomfortable questions comes from a healthy desire to avoid the "blame game." Given the enormous consequences of the evident breakdowns apparent in both the September 11 and Iraq events, however, it is vital that practitioners on both sides try to understand the challenges inherent in the policy–intelligence interaction and how to overcome the gulf and suspicion that haunts this critical relationship. In chapter 5, John McLaughlin, one of the consummate intelligence professionals during the Bill Clinton and George W. Bush presidencies, gives us vital insights from one side of the divide.[4] In this chapter I try to complement his analysis and recommendations from the perspective of someone who has served in both the intelligence and the policy communities.

Sources of the Problem

There are a number of reasons for the disaffection between policymakers and intelligence analysts. To an important degree, the problem arises because policymakers want something that intelligence analysis cannot provide: certainty. But the disaffection is also a product of each community's failure to understand what the other has to offer and to work as an organic whole, rather than as two opposing teams volleying a ball back and forth over a high and opaque wall. Helping each side understand the other's needs, capabilities, and limitations is critical to assuring that intelligence analysis can play its rightful, important place in policymaking.

As mentioned above, policymakers crave certainty and abhor surprise. They come to office with more or less defined policy objectives that they hope to attain. They want to work on their priority agenda, not be sidetracked or deflected by unanticipated events. They look to the permanent civil service bureaucracy of government, including the intelligence community, to help them achieve those goals and feel let down that they do not get more help. Why? There are three main reasons.

First, and most important, policymakers harbor unrealistic expectations. There is a tendency among some policymakers to hold the intelligence community to a standard of omniscience and to be let down if the answer is "I don't know." They believe that the enormous sums of money the nation invests in technical and human intelligence collection and in an army of analysts should produce strong, reliable results, and they fault managers and analysts when they do not do so, rather than looking to the inherent limitations of what can be known. At the same time, policymakers are equally vexed if the analyst expresses confidence but his or her judgment is subsequently proven to be wrong.

Second, there is a perception by policymakers that the analytic community views its role as one of cautioner (or worse, naysayer) rather than a support to policy. McLaughlin refers to this as the policymakers' culture of optimism versus the analysts' culture of skepticism. Another way of thinking about this is that policymakers rarely have the luxury of throwing up their hands and saying "too hard" or deferring decisions until the intelligence becomes clearer. Often they must act even if the choices are muddy and the consequences are unpredictable.

Policymakers look to the intelligence community to uncover the facts that will help them achieve their goals. Contrary to the views of some critics, most policymakers do not resist bad news if it is reliable and timely, because they know they cannot succeed by sticking their heads in the sand and pretending that adverse developments will go away if they simply ignore or dismiss them. But often policymakers feel that the intelligence community views its mission as solely being the bearer of bad news or "warning"—that is, telling the policy community about all the obstacles to achieving their objectives, rather than identifying opportunities and how to make the best of the situation to achieve them. Yet for many analysts such a role is tantamount to "supporting" the policy and thus violating the most sacred canon of analytic objectivity and policy neutrality.

Third, policymakers often sense that the analytic community is too insulated from the "on the ground" reality that provides the context for policy. These officials live in the world that they are trying to shape: they meet with leaders of foreign countries and other important actors, travel to trouble spots to observe challenges with their own eyes, and confer with experts in and out of government. Many have also built a considerable body of experience and expertise from their work before assuming office. They believe they have important insights that can inform the analytic process and assess the reliability of other intelligence inputs. By contrast, many intelligence community analysts have had little or no firsthand experience with the problems and people at issue, a product of the recruitment and retention policies in the intelligence community and fears of compromising security.[5] Yet policymakers believe that analysts and intelligence managers resist incorporating their views into the estimative process for fear of "tainting" the product.

No Panaceas

There are no surefire cures for these difficulties. Many are inherent in the nature of policymaking, yet there are a number of things that both the policy community and the intelligence community can do to reduce the frictions and build a more constructive, collaborative relationship that preserves the integrity of the analytic process while enhancing its utility. Let us look briefly at four main things that can be done in this vein.

First, the policymaker needs, and is entitled to, the intelligence community's best judgment. Most policymakers understand that many things are hard to know, and some things are inherently unknowable. Even policymakers know (or can be educated to know) the difference between a puzzle and a mystery.[6] But what is important for policymakers to understand is the degree and nature of uncertainty and, where possible, what steps might be taken to reduce that uncertainty. To take the Cuban Missile Crisis example discussed in chapter 1, the number and state of readiness of the Soviet missiles was a fact that was knowable but difficult to know with absolute certainty. Steps were taken (such as overflights and human intelligence activities) that helped reduce that uncertainty. What Nikita Khrushchev would do in response to various US policy alternatives was inherently unknowable—because it was contingent on actions by others, as well as his own assessment of the Soviet Union's interests. Yet even with respect to future intentions, the intelligence community may be in a position to help policymakers. For example, in the case of the Cuban Missile Crisis, there could have been intercepts of Soviet officials discussing various policy options or prior analogous examples of how Khrushchev had faced other tests of wills.

Analysts are often reluctant to venture onto this treacherous ice. To some extent it is a product of their training, which repeatedly emphasizes the uncertainty around the intelligence exercise, a worthy caution. Unfortunately, sometimes it is a product of a desire to escape accountability—making assessments so hedged that they are incapable of being proven wrong. The collective nature of many intelligence "community" judgments tends to further blur assessments, in the effort to achieve consensus at the expense of crispness. Rather than blurring conclusions to achieve broader acceptance or relegating nonmajority views to footnotes, finished analysis should *highlight* the alternative views within the intelligence community (including in executive summaries, which are the products most frequently read by policymakers) and prominently feature the proponents' underlying arguments for their conclusions.

Some try to bound the problem of uncertainty by assigning probabilities to facts or outcomes. I am somewhat skeptical of what I believe is a false sense of concreteness implied in assigning numerical probabilities to individual events, particularly contingent outcomes that depend on choices others have yet to make. But some sense of the degree of confidence (likely, unlikely, hard to judge, and so forth) can give a feel for the degree of uncertainty. More helpful is providing some insight into alternative pathways that might be consistent with the data, along with an explication of why the analyst believes one path is more likely than the alternatives.

Second, as other chapters suggest, the policymaker needs and is entitled to analytic transparency from the analyst. Why was the judgment reached? What assumptions lie behind it? What are the sources of uncertainty? This transparency is the necessary complement to the judgment. By providing transparency, the analysts should feel more comfortable with providing a bottom line or best guess, and the policymaker should feel more comfortable in either accepting or challenging it. Although there is constant pressure from policymakers to "keep it short" given the demands on their time, the intelligence community has an obligation not to let this legitimate consideration lead to products that are misleading by omission. Because this approach will lead to better policymaking, I believe that the policy community will be open to somewhat lengthier analytic products.

One important but controversial element of transparency concerns sources. The intelligence community is rightly concerned about protecting intelligence sources and methods. Compromises can destroy the value of enormously expensive technical collection tools and, in the case of human assets, not only wipe out years of patient cultivation but also endanger lives. The policy community is the ultimate loser from leaks because the loss of the sources will over time lead to less intelligence and so to less well-informed policy. The track record of protecting such vital sources and methods secrets is unacceptably poor. Although policymakers are responsible for the lion's share of such disclosures, the intelligence community is not without blame. Nonetheless, as the Iraq WMD experience suggests, opaqueness about sources can lead to overreliance on highly questionable sources with their own motivation to "influence," as well as inform. Although the intelligence community should continue to have the primary responsibility for evaluating the reliability of intelligence and the sources that provide it, the policymaker's stake—as well as the insight that the policymakers themselves can bring to assessing the value of sources—requires more transparency than the intelligence community has traditionally been comfortable providing.

Third, the policymaker needs *indicators* from the analysts that will help assess the validity of any judgment going forward. If the judgment is correct, what should we expect to see in the future? More important, what future developments might undermine the validity of the judgment and/or support one of the alternative hypotheses? Disconfirming facts are a far more important, but an often overlooked, part of the analysis process. They are important not only because they have stronger probative value but also because they are the best antidote to the structural problem of wishful thinking or "cherry picking" that infects even the most conscientious policymaker's approach to intelligence. This kind of support is crucial for policymakers to be able to make midcourse corrections or even reverse course if a key assumption turn out to be false.

Fourth, a closely related need is for the analytic community to provide peripheral vision and temporal perspective. How might a US action, which looks well suited to deal with a pending specific problem, affect other US policy actions or foreign actors elsewhere? What will be the likely longer-term effects—the second and third moves by others—if the policy is implemented? The stove-piped and time-constrained nature of the policy process too often precludes such examinations. The intelligence community is uniquely well placed to think about linkages and knock-on effects that might change policymakers' calculations about the costs and benefits of different courses of action. This is true of both horizontal and vertical/temporal linkages. In producing finished analysis, the intelligence community can include analysts who specialize in geographical regions other than the area or country that is the obvious focus of the problem at hand, as well as those with a broad range of functional expertise. Ideally, similar efforts to expand the circle would take place in the policy community as well, but for reasons of time and turf this often proves impracticable. Long-range planning would also benefit from regular meetings between key intelligence community analysts and the leading policy planners in the executive branch.[7]

How Policymakers Can Help

If the relationship is to work successfully, policymakers must take on at least four main types of obligations and responsibilities toward the intelligence community if they expect that community to do a better job of supporting policy. First, the policy community needs to understand what intelligence can and cannot do. As analysts often say, intelligence is not fortune-telling. McLaughlin and other practitioners rightly stress the importance of educating policymakers about the intelligence process. His chapter notes that this is hard to do the moment new officials come into office. However, the intelligence community could do a better job of identifying those who are likely to hold such roles in the future and begin exposing them to these issues even before they come to office. Stronger partnerships with professional schools and graduate programs, as well as outreach to emerging leaders (such as the American Assembly's Next Generation Program) are fertile grounds for such an effort. For current holders of policy jobs, regular briefings on intelligence capabilities and shortfalls are essential.

Second, the policymaking community needs to clearly communicate its goals, priorities, and needs. Analysts are not mind readers; they have limited resources and must make judgments about how to use them most productively. They need to know what is important to the policymaker. A formal requirements process—such as the procedures for identifying and ranking collection priorities that were established by Presidential Decision Directive 35 (PDD-35) issued by the Clinton administration—is a useful and important way to align policy and intelligence collection/analysis priorities, but it is not sufficient. These exercises tend to be static and overinclusive, and they sometimes fail to convey what is really on the policymaking community's mind.[8] Of course, the analytic community's work cannot be confined solely to the policymakers' current agenda—there is a need to think about problems and opportunities that have not yet crossed the policymakers' radar screen.

Third, policymakers need to recognize their value to the intelligence community as sources in their own right and thus keep analysts informed of information and impressions drawn from their own experience. Information sharing is a two-way street. Just as analysts tend to carefully shield their sources from exposure to the policy community, policymakers also tend to fear disclosure to the intelligence community of sensitive diplomatic negotiations and other policy maneuvers. The result is not only inferior analytic product but also one that appears largely irrelevant to a policymaking community, which is working on the basis of a different set of facts and assumptions.

Fourth, and closely related to the third measure, is the need for policymakers to keep intelligence representatives "in the room" when policy is debated. Although analysts rightly take a vow of silence with respect to policy prescriptions, they need to hear the underlying assumptions and beliefs that inform policy, both to correct errors of fact that may creep into policy and to provide policymakers with insights into the factors that might lead them to question or change those assumptions as events unfold. The real danger in the ongoing debate about the danger of "politicizing" intelligence is that both sides will overreact and create a "Chinese wall" that cuts off the analysts from firsthand access to policy debates. McLaughlin suggests one way to achieve this goal—namely, to embed more analysts in policymaking units, not as policymakers themselves but as part of the day-to-day activities of key agencies. For policymakers to gain the benefit of such embedded analysts, they need to appreciate and respect the fact that these analysts are different from other members of the policymaking team and thus should not be subject to the same tests of loyalty or ideological affinity that may be appropriate for "political" appointees—and even more, should not be punished or ignored for putting forth skeptical perspectives or inconvenient truths.

These four suggested measures are even more important in today's national security policy environment, where the challenges are more fluid, the actors (especially nonstate actors) are more diverse and unpredictable, and the sources and quantity of information are growing exponentially. Two key post-9/11 insights—the importance of information sharing and the need to form flexible, horizontal communities for collaboration that can adapt to fit changing problems—are as relevant to the policymaking–intelligence interaction as they are to the intelligence community itself. In its 2002 report, the Markle Foundation Task Force on National Security in the Information Age (on which I served) stressed the importance of taking into account the needs and unique problems of integrating the policymaker into the newly emerging information-sharing environment mandated by the Intelligence Reform and Terrorism Prevention Act of 2004.[9]

Structural Fixes: Two Modest Proposals

Many of the prescriptions I have offered here are primarily a matter of educating both policymakers and analysts to each other's needs, limitations, and capabilities, and of breaking down the barriers between the two cultures. But two structural reforms that would facilitate a better working relationship are worth adopting.

Perhaps most important is the crucial role that the Intelligence Directorate at the National Security Council can and should play to facilitate building the "cross-cultural" community advocated here. Because of the Intelligence Directorate's proximity to key policymakers (including the president) and its ability to participate in all interagency deliberations irrespective of subject matter, it can provide a vital bridging role, thus facilitating the transmission of policymakers' needs to the intelligence community and of intelligence capabilities, limitations, and insights to the policymakers. The directorate can also serve as a translator, particularly in helping policymakers with limited experience in the intelligence world understand the value (and limits) of what the intelligence community has to offer. In recent years this crucial function has largely been abandoned. The Intelligence Directorate should be given an ongoing seat in the interagency process, not simply be confined to intelligence community matters (for example, resources, requirements, and covert action).

A second important structural development is one that has begun to be implemented through the National Counterterrorism Center, which is a novel blending of intelligence and policy planning roles that brings both functions into one organization while retaining two distinct reporting lines—to the director of national intelligence for intelligence and to the president through the Homeland Security Council and the National Security Council for policymaking.[10] This reporting arrangement is uncomfortable to some who fear that it will blur roles and accountability, but it is an appropriate reflection of the need to integrate the policy and analysis function in an area where policy is crucially dependent on both tactical and strategic intelligence.[11]

Minimizing the Risks of Politicization

The approach I have suggested here will seem perilous to some. The traditional arm's-length relationship between policy and intelligence protects against politicization and enhances the protection of sources and methods but at a high cost of irrelevance. Policymakers need to rigorously engage analysts if they are going to have confidence in their judgments. Analysts, in turn, must be prepared to respond to the probing and challenges raised by policymakers; otherwise their work can be too easily dismissed as irrelevant or flawed. Strong internal protections within the intelligence community are the best way to minimize the politicization risk, starting with a director of national intelligence who is seen as a nonpartisan professional with real experience in intelligence and not as someone who is selected by virtue of policy loyalty. Both rigorous oversight by Congress and internal inspector-general procedures need to be maintained to protect analysts from the danger of abuse. However, a failure to establish the deep engagement between the two communities would run the even greater danger that we will fail to marshal all the hard-won intelligence and analytic resources available to us as a nation to address the daunting challenges of the future. The cost of this outcome would be less well-informed policymaking when exactly the opposite should be our highest priority.

Notes

1. See Seymour Hersh's discussion of the Pentagon's Office of Special Plans. Seymour M. Hersh, "Selective Intelligence," *New Yorker*, May 12, 2003, 44.
2. "Second, we were not authorized to investigate how policymakers used the intelligence assessments they received from the intelligence community. Accordingly, while we interviewed a host of current and former policymakers during the course of our investigation, the purpose of those interviews was to learn about how the intelligence community reached and communicated its judgments about Iraq's weapons program—not to review how policymakers subsequently used that information." Commission on the Intelligence Capabilities of the United States Regarding Weapons of Mass Destruction, *Report to the President of the United States*, March 31, 2005, 8. The report does discuss the need to communicate analysis better to policymakers, but this is largely in terms of the format and process of preparation of finished analysis, rather than about the interaction between analysts and policymakers. It also concludes that in the case of Iraq at least, "in no case did political pressure cause [analysts] to skew or alter any of their analytic judgments. That said, it is hard to deny the conclusion that intelligence analysts worked in an environment that did not encourage skepticism about the conventional wisdom." Ibid., 11.
3. See, e.g., the following exchange between National Security Advisor Condoleezza Rice and a reporter: "Q: 'Why shouldn't this be seen as an intelligence failure, that you were unable to predict something happening here?' Dr. Rice: 'Steve, I don't think anybody could have predicted

that these people would take an airplane and slam it into the World Trade Center, take another one and slam it into the Pentagon; that they would try to use an airplane as a missile, a hijacked airplane as a missile." White House Press Office, "National Security Advisor Holds Press Briefing," May 16, 2002, www.whitehouse.gov/news/releases/2002/05/20020516-13 .html. The 9/11 Commission briefly reviewed the prior intelligence and analysis on the possibility of using an aircraft as a weapon and concluded that the problem was the failure to implement tried-and-true strategies for "detecting then warning of surprise attack." But it fails to answer the question of why the considerable body of information on past plots was never communicated (or at least not effectively communicated) to policymakers. National Commission on Terrorist Attacks upon the United States, *The 9/11 Commission Report*, July 22, 2004, 344–48.

4. For another thoughtful analysis of the policymaker–intelligence community relationship, see Jack Davis, "Intelligence Analysts and Policymakers: Benefits and Dangers of Tensions in the Relationship," *Intelligence and National Security* 21, no. 6 (December 2006): 999–1021.

5. In my own experience as a negotiator for the United States, I met frequently with senior foreign officials, as well as leaders of all the concerned political parties in the region, and traveled regularly there to meet with community leaders. The available intelligence reporting relied heavily on "secret" information provided by indirect sources, rather than by direct engagement with the key actors themselves.

6. Joseph Nye identifies a mystery as "an abstract puzzle to which no one can be sure of the answer." See Joseph S. Nye Jr., "Peering into the Future," *Foreign Affairs* 73, no. 4 (July/August 1994): 82–93.

7. During the Clinton administration, Joseph Nye, then chairman of the National Intelligence Council, and National Security Adviser Tony Lake established a process involving policy planners at the State Department, NSC senior directors, and the intelligence community to select and analyze key long-term policy issues on regular basis. Although the effort was pointed in the right direction, it depended too heavily on the national security adviser's own involvement, which was difficult to sustain over time. One adaptation that might overcome this difficulty would be to establish a distinctive policy planning office at the NSC that would participate in this kind of intelligence community–policy community exercise. If the NSC senior director for policy planning then had an automatic seat at the interagency table—just as I suggest for the senior director for intelligence—this perspective could be interjected in the policymaking process in a timely and effective manner.

8. For a critique of the PDD-35 process, see Eleanor Hill (staff director, Joint Inquiry Staff), "Joint Inquiry Staff Statement: Hearing on the Intelligence Community's Response to Past Terrorist Attacks against the United States from February 1993 to September 2001," October 8, 2002, www.fas.org/irp/congress/2002_hr/100802hill.html.

9. See Markle Task Force on National Security in the Information Age, *Mobilizing Information to Prevent Terrorism: Accelerating Development of a Trusted Information Sharing Environment*, third report of the Markle Foundation Task Force (New York: Markle Foundation, 2002), 48–49, www.markletaskforce.org.

10. See National Counterterrorism Center, "What We Do," www.nctc.gov/about_us/what_we_do.html.

11. In the Clinton administration this team approach was used with considerable success on policy issues such as Russia and the Middle East.

CHAPTER 7

Serving the Senior Military Consumer: A National Agency Perspective

JOHN KRINGEN

Over the past decade or so, the relationship between the major national intelligence agencies—the Central Intelligence Agency (CIA), the Defense Intelligence Agency (DIA), the National Geospatial-Intelligence Agency (NGA), and the National Security Agency (NSA)—in supporting the US military has become both closer and more complex. This trend reflects a variety of factors, including constant US involvement in two land-based wars, the unique capabilities and authorities that national intelligence agencies bring to bear in the fight against violent extremists, and the broadening role of US military organizations in missions that extend well beyond combat operations. This enhanced engagement provides greater opportunities for improved national agency support to senior US military customers, but success is not automatic. Understanding military customer needs and identifying areas where national agencies and components of the US military provide unique "value added" are critical. Given the budgetary challenges that both the US military and the intelligence community are likely to face in the years ahead, the requirement to leverage the respective capabilities of all parts of the intelligence enterprise will only grow.[1]

For those intelligence organizations designated as combat support agencies (CSAs)—DIA, NGA, and NSA—their role in providing support to the US military is codified in policy. And to ensure appropriate attention to support of military commanders and their staffs, the defense intelligence enterprise has developed a set of institutional relationships, formal resource-allocation processes, and mechanisms for facilitating a flow of uniformed intelligence staff between the CSAs, the services, and the combatant commands. The result is that each of the CSAs has specifically designed roles and missions in supporting various components of the US military and the senior civilian leadership in the Department of Defense.

CIA, which is not designated as a CSA, has had since its inception a mission to provide intelligence support to the US military, but its relationship with the military has been more complicated. The complexities of CIA's relationship with the military reflect elements of history as well as the reality that CIA's mission of providing intelligence support extends well beyond the military customer. Military opposition to the creation of

CIA and its predecessor organization, the Office of Strategic Services (OSS), reflected in part a reluctance to rely upon a civilian agency to support military requirements—an issue that has occasionally resurfaced over the years since.[2]

In the 1990s, criticism of the performance of the national intelligence agencies in providing support to military commanders in Operation Desert Shield and Operation Desert Storm provided an opportunity to examine the potential for improvement in national agency support. While there is general agreement that US military commanders of these campaigns benefited from levels of national intelligence support far beyond what was provided during the Vietnam War, a number of shortfalls involving the national agencies and Central Command (CENTCOM) were identified.[3] A subcommittee of the House of Representatives criticized the CIA for being less than fully engaged in "joining in the organized support given combat commanders."[4] As a consequence of such criticism, CIA in 1992 created a new organization—then called the Office of Military Affairs—that was composed of both CIA and US military officers to "enhance cooperation and increase information flow between CIA and the military."[5] Currently, the associate director for military affairs, who is a general officer detailed to CIA, oversees these functions and serves as the principal focal point for CIA engagement with the Department of Defense.

Drivers of Closer Collaboration

Of the factors driving closer collaboration between national agencies and military customers in recent years, the most important has been the nearly continuous engagement of US military forces for more than a decade in military campaigns in Afghanistan and Iraq. These campaigns not only highlighted the value of collaboration between the US military and CIA in light of their respective authorities and capabilities, but also brought to the fore the intelligence requirements to provide precise knowledge of adversary networks and to develop a broad understanding of societal factors that go well beyond the military order of battle. Some of the increased military requirements for national support reflect daily operational requirements (such as collection or analytic support to identify where the adversary is located). Many others reflect the need for a broad multidisciplinary perspective that takes into account political, economic, social, psychological, and cultural dimensions.

A January 2010 assessment by Lt. Gen. Mike Flynn, and two US intelligence officers then serving with him in Afghanistan with the International Security Assistance Force (ISAF), highlighted the critical need for better understanding of the Afghan political, economic, and cultural environment.[6] While the authors criticize the performance of the intelligence community in supporting the counterinsurgency (COIN) requirements of military commanders in Afghanistan, the national agencies can and do provide military leaders with a wider range of collection capabilities and analytic resources than commanders directly control. Indeed, some have argued that Iraq and Afghanistan experiences to some degree flipped the traditional roles of the national intelligence agencies and the military, with strategic assets being used to help answer an array of tactical military questions and the military tasked to provide social and cultural insight into foreign operating environments.[7]

The priority given to civilian oversight of these military operations has also been a factor for more engagement between the national intelligence agencies and military commanders. Because the national agencies are involved in providing intelligence support to the senior policymakers at the Pentagon and the White House who constitute the National Command Authority for military operations, those decision makers have appropriately sought to ensure that all those involved—including the senior military leaders—have as mutual an intelligence understanding of the situation as is possible. In both Iraq and Afghanistan, senior US military leaders—and US ambassadors—were often given drafts of intelligence assessments prepared by CIA and other national agencies for their review and comment before publication.[8] The policy intent was to guarantee that senior policymakers had, in a single product, the combined benefit of the formal intelligence community assessments and the military commander's perspectives.

Another important driver has been the significant role of the national intelligence agencies in worldwide efforts to counter violent extremism since September 11, 2001. In the early days in Afghanistan, for example, a key component of the success that was achieved in 2001 in expelling the Taliban and al-Qaeda was the establishment of combined teams of CIA officers and US special operations troops to engage and assist Afghan forces opposed to the Taliban and to facilitate greater precision in US air strikes on Taliban and al-Qaeda fighters.[9] More recently, public accounts of the Osama bin Laden operation in 2011 provide the most visible expression of the partnership among CIA, NSA, NGA, and US special operations forces in bringing him to justice, but a similar dynamic applies in other parts of the world. Given CIA's unique responsibilities and authorities with regard to execution of the counterterrorism mission, maximizing transparency and coordination is a necessity. The requirements for success involve not only daily coordination of counterterrorism operations but also having a shared understanding of the threat at global, regional, national, and even local levels.

Beyond combat operations, increased national-level support to military customers reflects the reality that the US military is frequently engaged in a wide range of activities that extend well beyond combat or preparation for future combat operations. An often-heard term of art in military circles is "whole of government." The frequent use of this phrase reflects the reality that the activities of the US military are inevitably nested within broader US policy objectives and often require capabilities that reside outside the Department of Defense. The geographic combatant commands—Africa Command, Central Command, Northern Command, Pacific Command, and Southern Command—have significant responsibilities for what might be characterized as "military diplomacy":

- In this role, military leaders are responsible for engaging military counterparts on behalf of US policy objectives. These objectives often involve assisting partner militaries in building their capabilities so that they can be effective partners—activities known as "security cooperation" or "building partner capacity." But US military leaders and their staffs also serve such objectives as encouraging foreign military counterparts to support specific US policies and providing publicly visible indications of US policy support. Nowhere is the role more evident than in that of the supreme allied commander for Europe (SACEUR), who also serves as the commander of European Command (EUCOM). A significant portion of the SACEUR's time is focused on engaging our NATO allies to ensure requisite policy and operational alignment.

- When circumstances require, the US military also plays a significant role in providing humanitarian assistance and disaster relief. In the past few years at the request of the State Department, the US military has provided significant assistance in the wake of major disasters in Pakistan (2010), Haiti (2010), and Japan (2011), but it has also delivered US humanitarian aid in numerous other, less visible operations. Intelligence support to these sorts of operations typically involves the provision of insight into local political, economic, and social circumstances that can affect their planning and execution.

While the termination of US military engagement in Iraq and the drawdown of US forces in Afghanistan will inevitably reduce the opportunities for US military–national agency engagement, we can expect that the relationships that have developed will provide the basis for continued productive engagement. Iraq and Afghanistan brought together significant numbers of military leaders and intelligence professionals early in their careers, resulting in an improved understanding of respective capabilities, organizations, and cultures that will last for many years and hopefully mitigate the usual jockeying associated with government bureaucratic politics. Moreover, the enduring quality and intelligence-driven nature of addressing such transnational threats as counterterrorism and counterproliferation means that important drivers of closer collaboration will continue.

Facilitators of Closer Analytic Engagement

While the drivers noted above constitute the array of external factors pushing greater collaboration between the national agencies and the US military, a number of developments have occurred within the US intelligence community that have facilitated improvements in analytic support by the national intelligence agencies to senior military leaders.

Improvements in Intelligence-Dissemination Technology

Since the Gulf War, the national agencies have made tremendous strides in using Web-based capabilities on the Department of Defense's Joint Worldwide Intelligence

Communications System (JWICS) to make their products available to military consumers at all levels. While not all intelligence products are posted on this system, which is cleared for top-secret/sensitive compartmented information (TS/SCI), the overwhelming majority are. This means that military consumers at combatant commands around the globe can get access to intelligence assessments and intelligence reporting about as quickly as senior policymakers in Washington can.

In this regard, I observed during my time at European Command (EUCOM) that the intelligence staffs of the EUCOM seniors—including that of SACEUR—would on a daily basis search through CIA's World Intelligence Review and other national agency websites for analytic products and individual intelligence reports that they judged of value to their leaders. Senior EUCOM leaders needed analytic assessments on topics that extended well beyond such immediate threats as terrorism or the activities of other military forces and defense organizations in EUCOM's area of responsibility (AOR). For example, in the wake of the Arab Spring, the political upheavals in North Africa and the Middle East that began in 2011, EUCOM leaders needed to have a broad understanding of the potential for political instability that might require planning to support potential noncombatant evacuation operations (NEO) in countries bordering the Mediterranean. With only limited staff expertise at EUCOM on the Middle East and North Africa, EUCOM was able to leverage the broader pool of expertise that resided at the national level and other combatant commands. And by pulling assessments from multiple analytic components, there were greater opportunities for military commanders to get insight into broad lines of analytic consensus, as well as any potential analytic differences in the IC.

Enhanced Analytic Collaboration

Beyond such electronic connectivity, support to the US military consumer has also benefited from the improved analytic collaboration that has occurred in Washington in the wake of the 2004 Intelligence Reform and Terrorism Prevention Act (IRTPA). A particular driver of this greater collaboration has been the decision to make the *President's Daily Brief* (PDB) a community, vice CIA, product. While this evolution has made what has always been a demanding *PDB* process into an even more demanding one by significantly expanding the number and range of analytic participants, the benefits of expanded coordination and collaboration have been evident, particularly in assessments of wartime developments in Afghanistan and Iraq. The requirement that assessments being provided to the president have to be fully coordinated with the IC has inevitably yielded greater transparency and collaboration, as well as an enhanced effort to define collaborative boundaries between DIA and CIA, the principal all-source analytic organizations with expertise in military analysis. And this collaboration has built organizational engagement that extends beyond the *PDB* itself. Because DIA is the national-level representative of military intelligence, opportunities for the intelligence staffs at the combatant commands and the four military services to engage have also expanded.

Expansion of Target Analysis Capabilities outside the Military

As greater analytic collaboration has occurred among the various analytic components, there has also been an expansion of the analytic skill sets that have applicability to combat operations. While DIA, NGA, and NSA have long had in place structured analytic processes to support kinetic targeting, CIA has historically tended to be less engaged at the tactical level. To a significant degree, the 9/11 attacks changed that. As CIA's counterterrorism mission expanded significantly, so did the analytic subspecialty at CIA called "target analysis."

Rather than focusing on the preparation of analytic assessments to support the policy decision process, target analysts within the intelligence community seek to develop detailed understanding of individuals, networks, and organizations for operational purposes. Those operational objectives can range from developing plans to collect further intelligence on the persons or organizations involved to designing operations to disrupt their activities. Good target analysis goes well beyond summarizing detailed information about a target to provide a nuanced assessment of potential vulnerabilities, operational opportunities, and desired effects. Prior to September 11, 2001, the biggest cadre of target analysts in CIA's Directorate of Intelligence resided in the Crime and Narcotics Center, where they prepared assessments of drug trafficking organizations around the world. After 9/11 many of these officers were shifted to help jump-start CIA's expanded targeting efforts against al-Qaeda. Today, target analysis at CIA is an established analytic subspecialty whose missions include counterinsurgency, counterterrorism, counterproliferation, counternarcotics, and cybersecurity. As a consequence, these analysts provide an additional pool of expertise that has been involved in supporting not only CIA operations but also military operations in such theaters as Iraq and Afghanistan.

Greater Military Leadership of the IC

Finally, I would offer the probably controversial observation that the placement of senior military leaders and former senior military leaders as heads of the ODNI and CIA has been a positive development in terms of fostering national agency analytic support to senior military leaders. In recent years some apprehension has been expressed publicly and privately about the appointments of Michael Hayden and David Petraeus to head CIA and the appointments of Mike McConnell, Dennis Blair, and James Clapper as directors of national intelligence (DNIs). Of particular concern has been the possibility that these officers might resist or squelch the views of the analytic communities they oversee.[10] I have not observed that to be the case. In fact, I judge that having these officers serve as heads of the civilian intelligence agencies has on the whole improved the quality of analytic dialogue with military leaders.

Nonetheless, in my view the health of the whole intelligence enterprise inevitably rests on a base of diversity in experience and perspectives. Absent that diversity, there are two risks. One is that intelligence support may get tilted in favor of one set of customers over others. The second is that having spent most of their careers in organizations that emphasize the importance of a commander's intent and direction, they may be insufficiently attentive to the criticality in the intelligence business of fostering a workforce that is not afraid to challenge the conventional wisdom and senior leaders' views.

Best Practices in Supporting the Military Customer

The Prime Directive: Understand the Commander's Needs

As with any intelligence customer, the foundation in providing quality analytic support to a military commander begins with an understanding of the commander's needs, preferred methods of receiving information, the environment in which he or she operates, and his or her decision cycle. This is sometimes easier said than done, particularly if one is physically distant from that consumer, but it is still vital. For those analysts who have not served in the military, simply developing a basic understanding of military processes and terminology (including acronyms) can be a challenge. While desk references of military terminology and acronyms exist, new terminology is constantly being developed, it may differ by service, and mastery of its usage can take years.

More important than mastering such basic organizational knowledge is to identify opportunities in the military planning and operational cycles where intelligence analysis and reporting can make a difference. Such opportunities fall primarily into two realms:

- *IPB: intelligence preparation of the battlespace.* Developing plans for complex military operations at the combatant command level is a lengthy process involving a variety of technical specialties (such as targeting, communications, and logistics) that are typically drawn from staff with a variety of military service backgrounds. Intelligence is just one of the inputs into the planning process, and it can be a challenge to identify the best opportunities for engagement by national intelligence agencies in the planning process.
- *Assisting operations.* On the other hand, when operations have commenced, the command staff early on establishes a set battle rhythm whereby the opportunities for national intelligence input are readily identifiable and typically welcomed. A major challenge is to adjust the production and delivery of intelligence products to meet these often demanding timelines, particularly if the intelligence producers are located in another time zone, as they typically are. Another challenge revolves around the commander's desire to have visibility into the sources of information for the reports that he receives and the desire, particularly among human intelligence (HUMINT) professionals, to protect the identity of their sources to the maximum degree.

Having intelligence impact may also require adjustment in how analysis is provided. There is a tendency among some analysts at national intelligence agencies to scorn the use of the PowerPoint briefings of which the US military is so fond. Nonetheless, if one wants to have one's analytic voice heard when decisions are made, it is important to be able to adapt to the communications media that the military commonly uses. Military counterparts are typically appreciative and more receptive when analysts are able to display concepts and information in graphic presentations that readily highlight the key issues and analytic conclusions. Likewise, within the all-source analytic community, there is sometimes a tendency to want to draw firm lines between intelligence analysis and intelligence reporting. As is the case with regard to support for our most senior policymakers through the *PDB*, the timely provision of an intelligence report, accompanied by a brief analytic comment, may have more impact than a fully coordinated intelligence assessment that comes after the time for decision has passed.

Successfully Straddle the Challenge of Being a Team Member

The US military is all about ensuring that there is a cohesive team effort and that there is a common understanding—from the most junior to the most senior staff—of the commander's intent. Senior military officers are known to ask one another whether the national intelligence agency representatives located at their commands are "full members of the team." At the same time, the senior military leadership at a command values the role of civilian agencies precisely because they provide external perspectives that they may not be able to get from their own staff.

The challenge then is to be a member of the commander's team but one whose role is somewhat different. Being seen as a member of the team inevitably rests upon having the trust of the senior leaders. At one point in my career, the head of the local internal security service advised me that "transparency breeds confidence." Although this is a valid statement for all successful professional relationships, it is perhaps particularly true for relationships among intelligence organizations and between national intelligence agencies and most elements of the US military. Within a command, a relationship of transparency and trust with the J2—the command's senior intelligence officer—is particularly critical.

Many of the staff officers at a combatant command are in their first "joint duty" assignment, and unless they are intelligence specialists, they typically have limited experience in working with the national intelligence agencies. In this sort of environment, it is particularly important to be as transparent as circumstances permit. When, for example, some intelligence analysis or reporting can only be shared with a subset of the staff, it is important to apprise the key players of these ground rules. At EUCOM, for example, the senior leadership wanted their key subordinates to receive the same information that they did; on the few occasions where that was not possible, we made sure that the commander and his subordinates were aware.

Being a member of the team, however, means more than being transparent; it requires being both a visible and an active participant. An excellent way to develop credibility in both of these areas is to participate in the key military exercises of a command. For the US military, exercises are intended to provide staff the training vital to the successful execution of their plans. In that regard, the participation of analysts from the national intelligence agencies in military exercises provides the foundation for successful national agency engagement when the proverbial balloon goes up. For example, at EUCOM an experienced Middle East expert participated in a 2010 exercise involving a potential NEO for a country located on the Mediterranean. Her contribution to the success of that exercise led US Naval Forces Europe (NAVEUR) to describe such direct national agency support as one of the key "lessons learned" of the exercise. Later, when the crisis in Libya occurred, there was ready command acknowledgment of the critical need to bring in similar expertise to support the navy commander in charge of US military operations.

Balance "Responsibility to Provide" and "Responsible Information Sharing"

Compared with CIA and other national intelligence organizations, most elements of the US military are exceedingly transparent. This reflects both culture—ensuring that the whole team understands the commander's intent—as well as basic mission requirements. Because much of the business of military logistics requires calling upon the services of commercial firms, significant activity supporting military operations necessarily has to be done at the unclassified level. Beyond logistics, most planning and oversight of operations occurs in communications channels protected at the secret level.[11] An additional complication is that many US military campaigns involve the participation of non-US forces. In contrast to the US military and its foreign partners, the US national intelligence agencies typically conduct the vast majority of their business in communications channels protected at the top-secret level. And all of them both produce and use information in special top-secret compartments.

This information-sharing challenge has been a constant topic of discussion for over a decade. And in the wake of the public compromise by Wikileaks of massive volumes of classified and sensitive information, many elements of the US government have become even more concerned about placing sensitive information on Department of Defense computer systems that have tens of thousands of users.[12] While there is no simple or comprehensive fix, some steps are being taken to ameliorate the problem. Combatant commands where coalition involvement has been an essential element of their operational profile (for example, EUCOM and PACOM) have invested technical and personnel resources to be able to effectively transfer volumes of intelligence information across classification domains and audiences. National intelligence producers have expanded the use of reporting formats that facilitate dissemination to broader audiences at lower levels of classification. At the same time, it remains the case that the best intelligence on the highest-priority topics often comes from sensitive sources of information—both human and technical—that can be readily compromised with increased exposure.

In this environment the best that analysts at national agencies can do is to engage in continuous dialogue with their military counterparts to identify the topics on which greater sharing is both needed and feasible. During the war in Iraq, CIA analysts forged direct connections with a wide variety of military counterparts deployed in the combat zone. And given the numerous and serious terrorism threats to Europe, there has developed a growing understanding in recent years between the national agencies and the EUCOM staff about how to appropriately share very sensitive information on the terrorism threat with an appropriately restricted audience, while at the same time providing more generalized insight to the broader communities that needed to have visibility. Unfortunately, there is no easy way to do this except on a case-by-case basis that builds upon established relationships of trust.

Leverage Insights from the US Military

The typical way to picture the relationships between the national agencies and components of the US military is as a one-way transmission. The world is, however, more complicated. One of the observations of the critique of Afghan intelligence support cited earlier was that significant information relevant to the development and execution of an Afghan COIN campaign was unavailable to higher US military commanders, not to mention the national intelligence agencies. Accordingly, this report recommended that teams of analysts be established to collect information from US government elements operating at the local level, such as provincial reconstruction teams (PRTs), military training teams, and infantry battalions.

Sending teams of national agency analysts to collect information from the field was a concept that was successfully employed in wartime Iraq. CIA's Office of Iraq Analysis (OIA) sent several small teams of analysts over several years to Iraq to collect information from US military officers, other US government personnel, and others in Iraq to fill information gaps on key intelligence requirements. These small teams of typically senior Iraq specialists—which were called strategic field assessment teams—disseminated their findings in numerous individual reports, as well as broader assessments in which the unique information that they collected was prominently featured. These efforts covered a wide array of topics. While limited in size and scope, this effort demonstrated the value of engaging the nonintelligence components of the US military to elicit their insights on high intelligence priorities and is worth pursuing in the future.

Similar approaches have also been applied outside of the war zones to good effect. As noted earlier, senior US military leaders are typically key interlocutors with partner militaries. As such, they can develop insights into the dynamics of militaries around the world. While much of this conversation is scripted by partners to deliver particular messages to the US government, it can be valuable to capture even such scripted messages. Military leaders are typically willing to pass along such insights, but the national agencies may need to take the lead in setting up the processes to capture and disseminate this sort of information.

Provide Real Value Added to the Commander

Because they have broad geographic or functional responsibilities, senior military leaders want the best insight from whatever source and could not care less about where that insight comes from. The practical requirement often then is to identify those areas where the national agencies have particular value added to contribute beyond what a commander can get from his or her own intelligence staff. A particular value-added contribution that national agencies may be able to provide, beyond the products that their own agencies produce, is insight into national-level policy or intelligence deliberations that may frame the choices that the commander has to make. While decisions about dissemination of the *PDB* are the prerogative of the White House and the DNI, military leaders always want to know what intelligence the president and secretary of defense are receiving.

Other things being equal, senior military commanders appreciate the value of having intelligence products that incorporate both the shared views and divergent perspectives held by the intelligence community as a whole. For example, national intelligence estimates and other assessments that the National Intelligence Council produces tend to be well received by military customers. The number of these products is, however, necessarily limited and may not reflect the unique requirements of a specific command. In these circumstances even less formal assessments that pull together a range of national analytic resources can meet a requirement. When Adm. James G. Stavridis arrived as the new EUCOM commander in 2009, the command expressed interest in developing a broad understanding of the future environment it would face as it contemplated possible changes to its organizational structure. To address this requirement, the national agency representatives at EUCOM pulled together a team from DIA, NSA, NGA, and CIA to prepare an assessment of what the security environment for EUCOM's area of responsibility might look like in 2020. By tailoring the focus to the command's mission and bringing together a broad range of expertise, this effort allowed the command staff to have a well-received strategic picture of the possible threats and opportunities the command might face in the future.

Beyond providing community-coordinated assessments, a real strength that the national agencies can bring to bear is their depth of analytic expertise on a wide variety of topics. Most military intelligence staffs do not have the resources and staffing structure to develop and retain the highest level of technical expertise in such specialized areas as proliferation, cyber warfare, energy security, illicit finance, and underground facilities. The challenge for the national agencies is to develop the opportunities to showcase that kind of expertise to the senior military leaders. In some cases this may simply involve a focused briefing by a senior expert. In other cases it may involve the application of unique methodologies or modeling capabilities to problem sets of priority military concern. For example:

- One of the operational challenges in the Gulf War was developing the means to limit the environmental damage that Saddam Hussein could inflict by destroying Iraq's oil fields and refining facilities. In this circumstance, CIA assessment of Iraqi facilities permitted a more precise application of US airpower, which helped reduce subsequent environmental damage.

BOX 7.1   A Model of National Intelligence Agency Analytic Engagement with a Combatant Command

Supporting a combatant command from a national agency located in Washington can be a particular challenge. Physical distance and requirements to support other Washington-based customers make customer focus and engagement particularly problematic, although secure video teleconferencing can facilitate some level of direct engagement. As EUCOM became more involved in missile defense, CIA developed a strategy of engagement that had several lines of activity resulting in a level of support and engagement that optimized collaboration:

- Provision of a constant flow of analytic assessments relevant to EUCOM's missile defense mission.
- Periodic briefings—both in Washington and in Europe—of the senior EUCOM leaders. These sessions ensured that there was full transparency of national and combatant command assessments and provided EUCOM leaders with opportunities to engage on areas of concern.
- Customized briefings by Washington-based technical experts.
- Robust engagement with EUCOM's intelligence staff.
- Direct analytic engagement with air force, army and navy planners.
- Debriefing sessions with EUCOM staff.

- A current and growing challenge for the US military is coping with the ballistic missile threat. Because ballistic missile defense has such limited time windows for execution, much of the associated decision making has to be exquisitely planned in advance and be based upon an understanding, however imperfect, of the effectiveness of the adversary's ballistic missile forces (see box 7.1). In this regard, national assessments of Iranian ballistic missile forces have helped inform US military planning with regard to ballistic missile defense.

The Virtue of Alternative Analysis

In addition to providing a broader community perspective and bringing depth of expertise and understanding in certain topic areas, the national intelligence agencies, along with their military intelligence counterparts, assist military leaders by providing analysis that challenges existing approaches and conventional wisdom. In my view, a reasonable "first principle" of intelligence analysis is that the best predictor of future behavior is past behavior. However, as illustrated by the apocryphal story of the twentieth-century Belgian military intelligence officer who was only wrong twice about the threat of invasion, the more difficult analytic challenges are to identify the circumstances under which historical patterns may not hold and to outline possible alternative scenarios. There are, as has been identified elsewhere in this book, a variety of analytic techniques that can be used in such circumstances. Often the best approaches to challenging conventional wisdom are the simplest.

Understanding the Enemy

One of the principal challenges in a military campaign is getting as firm a picture as possible of the opposing forces, particularly their motivations. After the defeat of Iraqi government forces during the Iraq War, determining the motivations that were fueling the insurgency that subsequently emerged became a major intelligence issue. Given the imperfect knowledge that the IC had of these groups at the time, one technique that CIA Iraq analysts used to address this issue was to develop a series of profiles of the various types of individuals who supported the insurgency. Because it ended up being discussed publicly, the most noteworthy of these profiles was that of "Kamal the tailor," who became a supporter of the insurgency partly as a response to the military occupation of Iraq after Saddam was deposed.[13] This profile illustrates the value that even simple analytic techniques can have in helping policymakers and senior military leaders understand key determinants of campaign success or failure.

Assessing Progress in the Campaign

A key intelligence question in wartime is developing frameworks and metrics that allow policymakers and military leaders to understand how the campaign is going. As the Afghanistan intelligence study cited earlier noted, there is a need to go beyond tracking levels of violence. To help address this challenge in the Afghan campaign, CIA's Afghan analysts developed a framework for assessing the degree of control exercised by the Afghan government and the Taliban. This assessment was, of course, critically dependent upon having adequate reporting, and the quality of such information varied.

But developing and applying this framework had significant value on its own. Having accompanied these analysts on briefings of several military officers, I could see that one important payoff was that such meetings tended to focus discussion at levels where assessments of reporting could be readily compared and important conversations could occur regarding the potential factors that were driving trends one way or the other in particular parts of the country.

Pushing the Envelope

Given the significant investment of resources that military staffs invest in planning, another issue is "confidence testing" of the assumptions that underlie their plans. The requirement to undertake such examinations is manifest in the "red teams" that are a common feature among command staffs and a part of major military exercises. The national intelligence agencies (such as DIA and CIA) have had similar efforts that employ a wide variety of analytic techniques—for example, Devil's Advocacy and "What If?" Analysis—in order to push the analytic envelope and identify potential surprises that might emerge. When focused on issues of military concern, the products of these efforts typically have a receptive audience among senior military leaders. Such efforts need not be limited to government expertise. National intelligence agencies such as the Bureau of Intelligence and Research at the State Department typically have well-developed relationships with experts in academia or other parts of the private sector that can be leveraged to provide alternative views.

Looking to the Future

With the prospect of reductions in intelligence budgets in the coming years, it will be important to look holistically at how the national intelligence enterprise can be made both more efficient and more effective. The obstacles to developing greater synergies between the national intelligence agencies and military intelligence organizations in supporting the senior military leadership are significant—ranging from organizational structure and culture to budget authorities and competing demands to support policymakers with nonmilitary responsibilities. Moreover, there is a risk that, in tough budgetary times, both the national agencies and the US military will disinvest in efforts that have facilitated successful collaborative engagement.

Nonetheless, the increased involvement of national intelligence agencies with the US military in recent years suggests the merit of some rethinking of the roles of national agencies in supporting military leaders. As reductions in staffs and contractors occur at the combatant commands, for example, there may be a need to examine whether more value can be leveraged from the national agencies for the military commander. Moreover, collectively we are facing a number of challenges, such as the need to devise efficient and effective approaches to making sense of the exploding world of social media, where a collaborative effort is required. We have the analytic capabilities and the basic information infrastructure to permit us to be more agile in how we provide intelligence support to military customers. This chapter has suggested some ways to do so.

Notes

The perspectives presented in this chapter reflect the personal experience of the author in his thirty-plus years of government service in various assignments. Of particular importance are his tour as a senior intelligence adviser to the US European Command from 2008 to 2011, his service as director of intelligence at CIA from 2005 to 2008, and his assignment as director of imagery analysis at the NGA, then known as the National Imagery and Mapping Agency (NIMA), in the late 1990s. The views presented here should not be seen as capturing the full range of national intelligence agency support to senior military customers and may inevitably indicate a CIA-oriented prism.

1. Ben Wachendorf, Ajay Patel, and Tiffany Chiang, "Looming Defense Budget Cuts: Separating Fact from Speculation," *Monitor National Security Perspectives*, November 10, 2011, www.monitorns.com/perspectives/.

2. Thomas F. Troy, *Donovan and the CIA: A History of the Establishment of the Central Intelligence Agency* (Frederick, MD: Aletheia Books, University Publications of America, 1981).

3. House of Representatives, Oversight and Investigations Subcommittee of the Committee on Armed Services, "Intelligence Successes and Failures in Operations Desert Shield/Storm," 103rd Cong., 1st sess., 1993 (Washington, DC: Government Printing Office, 1993).

4. Ibid., 6.

5. "CIA Support to the US Military during the Persian Gulf War," Persian Gulf War Task Force, June 16, 1997, www.cia.gov/library/reports/general-reports-1/gulfwar/061997/support.htm.

6. Michael T. Flynn, Matt Pottinger, and Paul D. Batchelor, *Fixing Intel: A Blueprint for Making Intelligence Relevant in Afghanistan* (Washington, DC: Center for a New American Security, 2010), www.cnas.org/files/documents/publications/AfghanIntel_Flynn_Jan2010_code507_voices.pdf. General Flynn is now the director of the Defense Intelligence Agency.

7. Adam Cobb, "Intelligence Adaptation," *RUSI Journal* 156, no. 4 (August 2011): 54–62.

8. To make sure that this evolution did not result in any tilting of the analytic process, the analysts involved were advised that comments from military commanders did not constitute "coordination" that required them to adjust the substance of their analysis. When commanders disagreed with intelligences assessments (which sometimes occurred), their comments were incorporated in the written product as their personal views, not as the intelligence assessment.

9. Henry A. Crumpton, "Intelligence and War: Afghanistan, 2001–2002" in *Transforming U.S. Intelligence*, ed. Jennifer E. Sims and Burton Gerber (Washington, DC: Georgetown University Press, 2005).

10. See, for example, David Ignatius, "Can Petraeus Handle the CIA's Skepticism on Afghanistan?," *Washington Post*, September 1, 2011.

11. The clear exceptions to this pattern are the special operations community and US military intelligence elements that operate at the TS/SCI level. Moreover, the US military relies heavily on JWICS—a TS/SCI network—for its video teleconferencing connectivity.

12. For a view from a State Department officer on the impact of Wikileaks, see Bowman H. Miller, "The Death of Secrecy: Need to Know . . . with Whom to Share," *Studies in Intelligence* 55, no. 3 (2011), posted on the CIA website on November 11, 2011.

13. Jim Hoagland, "Tailor-Made for the CIA," *Washington Post*, February 13, 2005.

PART III

Diagnosis and Prescription

CHAPTER 8

Why Bad Things Happen to Good Analysts

JACK DAVIS

Intelligence analysis—the assessment of complex national security issues shrouded by gaps in authentic and diagnostic information—is essentially a mental and social process. As a result, strong psychological influences intrude on how analysts faced with substantive uncertainty reach estimative judgments, coordinate them with colleagues, satisfy organizational norms, and convey the judgments to policy officials. Effective management of the impact of cognitive biases and other psychological challenges to the analytic process is at least as important in ensuring the soundness of assessments on complex issues as the degree of substantive expertise invested in the effort.

An understanding of the psychological barriers to sound intelligence analysis helps answer the question of critics inside and outside the intelligence world: How could experienced analysts have screwed up so badly? Ironically, after the unfolding of events eliminates substantive uncertainty, critics also are psychologically programmed by the so-called hindsight bias to inflate how well they would have handled the analytic challenge under review and to understate the difficulties faced by analysts who had to work their way through ambiguous and otherwise inconclusive information.

An Introduction to Methodology and Definitions

This chapter benefits from numerous discussions the author has had with Richards Heuer about his groundbreaking book *Psychology of Intelligence Analysis*, which consolidates his studies during the 1960s and 1970s on the impact of the findings of cognitive psychology on the analytic process.[1] The chapter also takes into account recent reports on what Central Intelligence Agency analysts did wrong and how they should transform themselves.[2]

The chapter's insights are essentially consistent with the authorities cited above. However, they were independently shaped by my half century of experience at CIA as practitioner, manager, and teacher of intelligence analysis—and from hallway and classroom discussions with CIA colleagues with their own experiences. Informal case studies presented by analysts in the seminar on intelligence successes and failures—a course the author ran for CIA from 1983 to 1992—were particularly valuable.[3] Discussions of intelligence challenges on an early 1980s electronic discussion database called Friends of Analysis also were informative.

"Bad things" are defined for this chapter's purpose as well-publicized intelligence failures, as well as major errors in analytic judgments generally. As a rule, little is made publicly of the failure of analysts to anticipate favorable developments for US interests, such as the collapse of the East German regime and reunification of Germany, or Slobodan Milošević's caving in to NATO after more than two months of bombings. But the pathology of misjudgment is much the same as with harmful "surprise" developments, and because the hindsight bias is again at play, sharp criticism from intelligence and policy leaders often ensues.

"Good analysts" are defined as those well-credentialed practitioners of intelligence analysis who have earned seats at the drafting table for assessments on war and peace and the other issues vital to national security—a prerequisite for turning instances of estimative misjudgment into an intelligence failure.

Take, for example, the senior political analyst on Iran who said in August 1978, five months before revolutionary ferment drove the pro-US shah from power, that Iran was "not in a revolutionary or even a 'pre-revolutionary' situation." The analyst had worked on the Iran account for more than twenty years, visited the country several times, read and spoke Farsi, and kept in general contact with the handful of recognized US academic specialists on Iran in the 1970s. More than once in the years before 1979, I had heard CIA leaders wish they had more analysts matching the profile of the senior Iran analyst.[4]

Key Perils of Analysis

This chapter examines the psychological obstacles to sound estimative judgments that good analysts face in four key stages of the analytic process:

- When analysts *make judgments* amid substantive uncertainty and by definition must rely on fallible assumptions and inconclusive evidence
- When analysts *coordinate judgments* with other analysts and with managers who are ready to defend their own subjective judgments and bureaucratic agendas
- When analysts, in their efforts to manage substantive uncertainty, *confront organizational norms* that at times are unclear regarding the relative importance of lucid writing and sound analysis
- When analysts whose ethic calls for substantive judgments uncolored by an administration's foreign and domestic political agendas seek to *assist clients* professionally mandated to advance those agendas

To be sure, the countless postmortem examinations of intelligence failures conclude that better collection, broader substantive expertise, and more rigorous evaluation of evidence would have made a difference. However, if good analysts are most often held responsible for intelligence failures, then such improvements would be necessary but not sufficient conditions for sounder analytic performance. When one is dealing with national security issues clouded by complexity, secrecy, and substantive uncertainty, the psychological challenges to sound analysis must also be better understood and better managed.

The emphasis should be placed on substantive uncertainty, inconclusive information, and estimative judgment. To paraphrase a point made recently by former CIA director Michael Hayden: When the facts speak for themselves, intelligence has done its job and there is no need for analysis.[5] It is when the available facts leave major gaps in understanding that analysts are most useful but also face psychological as well as substantive challenges. And especially on such vital issues as countering terrorism and proliferation of weapons of mass destruction (WMDs), US adversaries make every effort to deny analysts the facts they most want to know, especially by exercising tight operational security and by disseminating deceptive information. In short, it is in the crafting of analytic judgments amid substantive uncertainty where most perils to intelligence analysts exist.

Assigning Blame

One does not become an apologist for intelligence analysts if one proposes that an experience-based "scorecard" for analytic failure should generally place the blame on those most responsible for not managing psychological and other obstacles to sound analysis:

- If regularly practiced analytic tradecraft (that is, "methodology") would have produced a sound estimative judgment but was not employed—blame the analysts.
- If analytic tradecraft was available that would have produced a sound judgment but was not regularly practiced because of competing bureaucratic priorities—blame the managers.
- If analytic tradecraft was available that would have produced a sound judgment but was not employed for political reasons—blame the leaders.
- If no available tradecraft would have produced a sound judgment—blame history.

Psychological Perils at the Work Station

To paraphrase Mark Twain's observation about the weather, everyone talks about the peril of cognitive biases, but no one ever does anything about it. No amount of forewarning about the confirmation bias (belief preservation), the rationality bias (mirror imaging), and other powerful but perilous shortcuts for processing inconclusive evidence that flow from the hardwiring of the brain can prevent even veteran analysts from succumbing to analytic errors. One observer likened cognitive biases to optical illusions; even when an image is so labeled, the observer still sees the illusion.[6]

In an explanation of why bad things happen to good analysts, cognitive biases—which are essentially unmotivated (that is, psychologically based) distortions in information processing—have to be distinguished from motivated biases (distortions in information processing driven by worldview, ideology, or political preference). These cognitive biases cluster into the most commonly identified villain in postmortem assessments of intelligence failure: mind-set. More rigorous analysis of alternatives as an effective counter to cognitive biases is discussed later in the chapter. Though there is no way of slaying this dragon, analysts can learn ways to live with it at reduced peril.

"Mind-set" can be defined as the analyst's mental model or paradigm of how government and group processes usually operate in country "X" or on issue "Y." In the intelligence world, a mind-set usually represents "substantive expertise" and is akin to the academic concept of mastery of "normal theory"—judgments based on accumulated knowledge of past precedents, key players, and decision-making processes. Such expertise is sought after and prized.[7] The strategic plans of CIA's Directorate of Intelligence invariably call for greater commitment of resources to in-depth research and more frequent tours of duty abroad for analysts—which amounts to building an expert's mind-set.[8]

True, a mind-set by definition biases the way the veteran analyst processes increments of inconclusive information. But analytic processing gets done, and thanks to a well-honed mind-set, current and long-term assessments get written despite time and space constraints. In between analytic failures, the overconfidence inherent in relying on mind-set for overriding substantive uncertainty is encouraged, or at least accepted, by analysts' managers. And because most of the time precedents and other elements of normal theory prevail—that is, events are moving generally in one direction and continue to do so—the expert's mental model regularly produces satisfactory judgments. More than one observer of CIA analytic processes and the pressures to make judgments amid incomplete information and substantive uncertainty has concluded that mind-set is "indispensable." That is to say, an open mind is as dysfunctional as an empty mind.[9]

All analysts can fall prey to the perils of cognitive biases. A case can be made that the greater the individual and collective expertise on an issue, the greater the vulnerability to misjudging indicators of developments that depart from the experts' sense of precedent or rational behavior. In brief, substantive experts have more to unlearn before accepting an exceptional condition or event as part of a development that could undermine their considerable investment in the dominant paradigm or mind-set. This phenomenon is often described as the "paradox of expertise." Experts are often biased to expect continuity and are hobbled by their own expert mind-sets to discount the likelihood of discontinuity.

To start, the so-called confirmation bias represents the inherent human mental condition of analysts to see more vividly information that supports their mind-set and to discount the significance (that is, the diagnostic weight) of information that contradicts what they judge the forces at work are likely to produce.[10] "Analysis by anecdote" is no substitute for systematic surveys or controlled experiments regarding analyst behavior. But consider this example from one of CIA's most bureaucratically embarrassing intelligence failures: the assessment informing Secretary of State Henry Kissinger on October 6, 1973, that war between Israel and Egypt and Syria was unlikely—hours after he had learned from other sources that the Yom Kippur War was under way.

CIA analysts were aware of force mobilizations by both Egypt and Syria, but they saw the military activity across from Israeli-held lines as either training exercises or defensive moves against a feared Israeli attack. To simplify the analysts' mental model: Shrewd authoritarian leaders such as Egypt's Anwar Sadat and Syria's Hafez al-Assad did not start wars they knew they would lose badly and threaten their hold on power. In particular, before launching an attack Egypt was assumed to need several years to rebuild its air force, which Israel had all but destroyed in the 1967 Six-Day War. And besides, the Israelis who were closest to the scene did not think war was likely until Egypt rebuilt its air force.

As it happened, in a masterly deception campaign it was the Sadat government that had reinforced the argument bought by both US and Israeli intelligence that Egypt could not go to war until it had rebuilt its air force. All along, Sadat had planned to use Soviet-supplied surface-to-air missiles to counter Israeli battlefield air superiority.[11]

What follows is an anecdotal depiction of the power of the confirmation bias. A decade after the event, the supervisor of Arab-Israeli military analysts gave his explanation of the intelligence failure: "My analysts in 1973 were alert to the possibility of war but we decided not to panic until we saw 'X.' When 'X' happened, we decided not to sound the alarm until we saw 'Y.' When we saw 'Y,' we said let's not get ahead of the Israelis until we see 'Z.' By the time we saw 'Z,' the war was under way."[12]

The paradox of expertise explains why the more analysts are invested in a well-developed mind-set that helps them assess and anticipate normal developments, the more difficult it is for them to accept still-inconclusive evidence of what they believe to be unlikely and exceptional developments. This is illustrated by two additional anecdotes about the Yom Kippur War.

The chairman of the Warning Committee of the intelligence community was concerned about the prospect of war and was ready, in two successive weeks, to sound an alarm in his report to intelligence community leaders on worldwide dangers. Twice he gathered CIA's Middle East experts to his office to express his alarm, only to bow to their judgment that war was unlikely. After all, he explained, he covered developments all over the world and only recently was reading with any detail into the Middle East situation. They were the experts long focused on this one issue.[13] Similarly, a top-level official later reported that after surveying traffic selected for him by the CIA Watch Office, he smelled gun smoke in the air. But when he read the seemingly confident assessment of the responsible analysts to the effect that war was unlikely, he decided, to his regret, to send the report on to Kissinger.[14]

The paradox of expertise is also demonstrated through the many remembrances of the those who worked on the September 1962 national estimate on the Soviet military buildup in Cuba, the unpublished 1978 estimate on prospects for the shah of Iran, and the high-level briefings given in 1989 on why the fall of the Berlin Wall was not yet likely. In the latter, less well-known case, a senior analyst who "got it wrong" made a frank observation: "There was among analysts a nearly perfect correlation between the depth of their expertise and the time it took to see what was happening on the streets of Eastern Europe (e.g., collapse of government controls) and what was not happening (e.g., Soviet intervention)." These signs could not trump the logic of the strongly held belief that the issue of German unification was "not yet on the table."[15] On November 9, 1989, while CIA experts on Soviet and East German politics were briefing President George H. W. Bush on why the Berlin Wall was not likely to come down any time soon, a National Security Council staff member politely entered the Oval Office and urged the president to turn on his television set—to see both East and West Germans battering away at the wall.[16]

The rationality or coherence bias, also known as "mirror imaging," is another cognitive challenge that helps explain why seasoned analysts can be blindsided by epochal events. Obviously, analysts must understand the modus operandi of the leaders and factions of the countries and nonstate entities that are key to US national security interests, especially regarding adversaries. A great deal of effort is spent on obtaining effective insight into, for example, the intentions, risk calculations, sense of opportunity, and internal constraints of foreign leaders and groups. The effort usually includes tracking speeches and foreign media, reading biographies and histories, parsing human intelligence (HUMINT) reporting, debriefing people with direct experiences meeting such world leaders, and brainstorming with colleagues.

With justification, then, veteran intelligence analysts bridle at charges of "mirror imaging" and of using US values and experience to anticipate actions of foreign leaders and entities. Many of the analysts, for example, who tried to assess the intentions of Soviet leader Nikita Khrushchev in the run-up to the 1962 Cuban Missile Crisis were accomplished Kremlinologists who had spent years trying to capture the operational codes of behavior exhibited by Khrushchev and other Soviet leaders.[17]

These efforts are usually good enough. But the analysts' psychological drive for coherence often causes them to fill in any gaps in understanding with what they, as American-trained rationalists, think would make sense to the foreign leader or group under assessment. The effect that alternative, egocentric, self-deluding, and self-destructive forms of rationality have on what is usually associated with exceptional events or paradigm shifts only becomes clear to analysts after the failure of collective expert mind-set.

CIA analysts, for example, eventually learned that Khrushchev in 1962 thought he faced less risk to his hold on power by ignoring US warnings against placing nuclear weapons in Cuba than he would by rejecting his military's demands that the huge US nuclear advantage be reduced by a crash military production program (that might have destabilized the Soviet economy) or by some other costly means.[18] Similarly, CIA's Middle East analysts eventually learned that Egypt's Sadat in 1973 was convinced he would lose power if he did not risk war with Israel in hopes of restarting negotiations to regain the Egyptian Sinai lost in 1967.[19] And as CIA analysts learned to their regret, Iraq's Saddam Hussein's deliberate ambiguity regarding possession of WMDs in 2002 reflected a seemingly distorted risk calculation in which his fear of Iranian knowledge that he did not have such weapons outweighed US judgments that he did.[20]

To summarize workstation challenges, when normal circumstances prevail, the hardwired cognitive pathways known as cognitive biases provide formidable benefits to good analysts, and their investment in the development, recognition, and defense of established patterns of behavior underwrites timely and useful support to policy clients. These cognitive biases become psychological obstacles for dealing with the relatively infrequent emergence of exceptional or unprecedented, unexpected, or even unimagined developments. And there is no known theory, practice, or methodological tool for infallible determination of whether a normal or exceptional course of events lies ahead.[21]

Perils of Review and Coordination

On intelligence problems and other complex issues, no matter how accomplished the principal researcher, subsequent review by a well-functioning team of diversified experts generally adds substantially to the soundness of an assessment. And as a rule, even CIA's often labyrinthine review processes increase the overall quality of assessments, especially by improving poorly argued drafts. That said, psychological phenomena similar to those already discussed—but this time reflecting the interpersonal dimension of intelligence cadres—can and do cause bad things to happen to good analysts. These phenomena include groupthink, boss think, tribal think, and no think.

Groupthink is a phenomenon on which critics of the analytic performance of the intelligence community have leaned heavily as a psychological explanation of flawed assessments. As originally defined, it depicts the dynamic of a cloistered and like-minded small group that highly values consensus and reinforces collective confidence in what can turn out to be a flawed set of assumptions and conclusions.[22] Such groups exist in the intelligence analysis world. But in my direct and indirect experiences with analytic failures, the process most often involved a large number of analysts from diverse bureaucratic offices—many with a penchant for argument, some under orders from their bosses to "fix" the final text so that it conforms to office or agency interests. For example, Sherman Kent, the renowned chief of estimates at the time, observed that at least a thousand intelligence professionals (probably no more than a score of whom he knew personally) contributed directly or indirectly to the flawed 1962 community judgment that the USSR would not install nuclear weapons in Cuba.[23] Thus the malfunction of analytic groups most often lies in other maladies, such as boss think, tribal think, and no think.

Boss think is not a criticism of the dwindling cadre of CIA gray-haired senior analysts and supervisors who have saved many a junior analyst from flawed assumptions or other analytic errors on an assigned issue. Rather, it occurs when the more senior practitioners who have worked complex substantive issues the longest often act as if they "own" the paradigm through which inconclusive evidence is assessed. Thus boss think can combine with the paradox of expertise at times in causing delayed recognition of a paradigm shift or a mind-set that was built on oversimplified key assumptions. For example, some decades ago, when I was national intelligence officer for Latin America, I delayed the publication of a junior analyst's assessment because it contradicted my view of the country. As it happened, events soon proved me wrong, and luckily the assessment was published in time for CIA to garner praise for being on top of the issue.

Tribal think, as well, is not a criticism of the necessary division of responsibility for substantive issues among many analysts within and beyond an analyst's organizational unit. The process of "coordination" allows analysts with different substantive responsibilities and experiences to critique and, as a rule, improve and enrich draft assessments. However, when an analyst tries to deviate from the prevailing paradigm, colleagues heavily invested psychologically in different parts of the issue can be quick to prevent what they see as misinterpretations of events and reports.

One example of tribal think came several months *before* the battering of the Berlin Wall. A CIA analyst circulated a draft assessment that argued that the well-known obstacles to German reunification were no longer strong enough to keep the issue of reunification "off the table." This was a bold and prescient departure from CIA's prevailing expert opinion. His well-informed and well-intentioned colleagues each asked for "small changes" to avoid an overstatement of the case here and a misinterpretation of the case there. After the coordination process had finished its watering down of the original conclusions by the mending of "small errors," a senior reviewer delivered the coup de grâce by all but eliminating the innovative argument from the paper's key judgments. A reader of the final version of the paper would have to delve deeply into the text to uncover the paradigm-breaking analysis.[24]

In another case, in 1983, eight years before the Soviet Union collapsed, an analyst invested in extensive research and an innovative methodology to conclude that strikes, riots, and other forms of civil unrest were a harbinger of substantial instability. A host of Soviet experts within CIA strongly resisted this departure from the established position that there was no serious threat to regime stability. The original text was watered down considerably during nearly six months of debate. Even after incorporating numerous changes to accommodate the mind-set of the expert critics in CIA, they refused to be associated with even the watered-down assessment, which was then published by the National Intelligence Council without the formal concurrence of the CIA analysts.[25]

No think, as a psychological barrier to sound analysis, is the analysts' conscious or unmotivated resistance to changing an "agreed-on" assumption or estimative judgment that took hours, if not days, of overcoming tribal think to reach. Even if newly obtained information poses a challenge to prevailing opinions, it can be difficult psychologically for the leading analysts to revisit agreed-on language as long as the body of available information remains ambiguous, contradictory, and otherwise inconclusive. The cost of changing the mind-set of one obstinate analyst, much less that of a group of like-minded experts, can be quite high. Rather than calling the consensus view into question, some analysts might prefer not to focus attention on nonconforming information.

Technically specialized experts, considered science and technology analysts, who work on a single aspect of a WMD issue can be especially vulnerable to a combination of boss think, tribal think, and no think. Once the senior regional analysts or the well-respected national intelligence officers set the broad analytic framework regarding an adversary's intentions, then the science and technology specialists set about assessing the available information. They are probably predisposed to put more weight on the evidence that supports the assumptions set out by the generalists rather than any disconfirming evidence that would require rethinking or rewriting.

This tendency was singled out for criticism in the several postmortem examinations of the flawed 2002 national intelligence estimate on Iraqi WMDs. In an interview, one of the CIA's weapon analysts acknowledged accepting as "given" the principal analysts' judgment that the Saddam regime harbored such weapons and sifting through the evidence critically but with the expectation that the case for a particular suspected weapon system was there to be made.[26]

In sum, great deference to the authority of the principal analysts on complex and uncertain issues and their psychological drive to preserve mind-set–driven judgments work well in producing reasonably sound assessments under normal circumstances. But the practice is vulnerable to missing exceptional, at times momentous, developments. Perhaps there is an analogy between analysis driven by mind-set and nuclear power plants. Both are great for ensuring production—in between meltdowns.

Obstacles in the Organizational Culture

As in any large organization, especially one lacking the discipline of a money-based market, CIA's norms on what constitutes distinctive value-added analysis to policymakers have not always been made clear. One key to why bad things happen to good analysts has been conflicting organizational signals regarding promotion of overconfidence ("making the call") versus promotion of more rigorous consideration of alternative hypotheses and the quality of information, and thus more guarded judgments for dealing with substantive uncertainty.

Whatever the formal norms regarding the quality of analysis, the operational norms over past decades usually have prized the volume of production over sound tradecraft. Emphasis on volume (as well as on speed and conciseness) of production in turn has placed a premium on analytic overconfidence. Put in other terms, informal norms have tended to trivialize the complexity and uncertainty of many national security issues by encouraging analysts to depict and defend a single interpretation of complex events or a single forecast of unknowable future developments.

In part this institutional overconfidence reflected the aforementioned organizational acceptance of "assessment via mind-set"—the experienced analysts' view of how things usually work. In part it reflected an unacknowledged conflation of lucid writing and sound analysis. An assessment that read well was given credit, deserved or not, for having analyzed events, trends, and prospects effectively. So the "gold standard" for analysis as found in analyst training, as well as in the evaluation of published product, was often assessments with catchy titles and strong topic sentences that "make the call" and marshal compelling albeit selective reporting that supports that judgment.

This forceful and confident-sounding communication style has worked well enough for reporting current "normal" events affecting US interests. It often sufficed when the continuity of trends allowed the experts' mind-set to provide informed linear interpretations and projections of events. At other times, however, an understating of the complexity and fluidity of political dynamics in countries of concern to US interests led to woefully inelegant judgments. Twice in my years as an analyst I won recognition by timely prediction of military coups against regimes' policymakers considered a threat to US interests. Unfortunately, my subsequent predictions of when the military would turn power over to duly elected civilian governments were off, in one case by twelve years and in another case by more than twenty.

As a result of unprecedented criticism of analytic performance over the past decade, leaders of CIA analysis are working assiduously and with promising initial results to change the operational norms to emphasize quality of analysis over quantity of production. As former CIA director Michael Hayden has indicated, analysts have to distinguish between the issues on which they can use a laser beam (aimed at the right answer) and the issues on which drawing the sidelines within which policymakers will have to operate would be more suitable.[27]

Policy Bias: The Elephant in the Room

As other contributors to this volume—notably John McLaughlin and James Steinberg—have pointed out, tensions between intelligence analysts and policymakers are inevitable. Though they point out that many factors are at play, the greatest tensions arise essentially from conflicting professional ethics and objectives. Analysts, as a rule, are charged with assessing events abroad without conscious biasing of conclusions to either support or oppose an administration's foreign policy and domestic political agendas. As a rule, policy officials feel obliged to connect and advance these agendas in any way they can. In most cases analyst–policymaker tensions prompt both sides to enhance the utility of their contributions to the national interest. But these tensions can contribute to the perception as well as the commission of flawed analytic judgments.

As noted elsewhere in this volume, analysts have to get close enough to policymaking processes to know where clients are on their learning curves and decision cycles, if their substantive expertise and tradecraft are to have an impact on decision making. That means getting close enough to be exposed to, and at times seduced by, the politics of decision making. Policy officials at times challenge the first cut of analysts' judgment and, among other things, ask them to take another look at the evidence, rethink the judgment, or change the question. As Steinberg makes clear in chapter 6, at times policymakers' criticism is levied because of professional concerns about the quality and utility of the analysis. At times, however, the policymaker's goal is political—that is, to use intelligence as leverage against competing policy colleagues or to ensure congressional and public support of departmental or administration initiatives.

Up to a point analysts should prefer to be challenged rather than ignored by their clients. Historically, however, analysts and managers at times have resorted to politicization in response to criticism by deliberately distorting a judgment to support, or even oppose, presidential policies.[28]

What is of greater concern for this chapter is the influence of unmotivated (psychologically based) biases in the evaluation of evidence and the calibration of judgments. Whether acknowledged or not, there is often "an elephant in the room" when analysts and their managers know what kind of policy support officials would prefer from their intelligence counterparts. In preparing the 1962 intelligence community assessment on Soviet military intentions in Cuba, for example, the drafters knew that President John F. Kennedy would welcome conclusions discounting the threat and allowing him to improve relations with the USSR so that he could run for reelection in 1964 as the "peace candidate." In preparing the Iraqi WMD estimate some forty years later, the drafters knew that President George W. Bush wanted strong emphasis on the threat that lent support to his decision to invade Iraq.

Analysts in these and similar circumstances admit to the presence of policy pressures but tend to deny that the pressures have an effect on their judgments. Yet there is evidence in postmortem reports and academic studies that analysts, in making judgments amid uncertainty at a subconscious level, often are influenced by knowledge of the policy preference of either or both the administration and Congress.[29] My own experiences as a producer and observer of analysis on politically sensitive issues would indicate that. Knowledge of what a president or his congressional opposition wants can subtly influence the analytic process, and this accommodation in evaluating incomplete and ambiguous information in part can explain estimative malfunctions by experienced analysts.[30]

Coping Mechanisms: The Rigor of Alternative Analysis

My earlier reference to the similarity in benefits and risks between nuclear power plants and analysis by mind-set applies as well to the solutions. Redundant safeguards are funded to reduce the threat of power plant meltdowns. Similarly, redundant safeguards are needed to reduce the threat of analytic meltdowns caused by the limitation of the mental faculties of even the brightest of analysts. To ensure against error in established analytic judgments, CIA is vigorously promoting alternative analysis formats, including forms of challenge analysis (for example, Devil's Advocacy) and structured analysis (such as Analysis of Competing Hypotheses). In a complementary effort, CIA is promoting more rigorous analysis of alternatives in first reaching judgments on complex and fluid issues—that is, the systematic generation and critical review of alternative hypotheses, as outlined in chapter 9 by James Bruce on epistemology.[31]

Think of the estimative misjudgments touched upon earlier in this chapter. The requirement for deliberate assessment of a range of plausible explanations of events and projections of developments might have shown gaps and contradictions in the assumptions supporting the prevailing mind-set and a need for rigorous scrutiny of the authenticity and "diagnosticity" of available information. As a rule, the more important the intelligence issue and the greater the uncertainty and information gaps, the greater need for incorporating alternative explanations and projections into the text of an assessment. Even a "high-confidence" judgment implies enough doubt for the properly skeptical analyst to develop a list of tipping points and signposts for one or more "wild card" developments.

Perhaps the most important contribution managers can make when their analysts present a draft assessment based on a paradigm of an issue the managers were proud to have developed in past years is to ask: (1) What new evidence would make you change your key assumptions? (2) Why not review all the evidence through the optic of those altered assumptions? (3) Why not consider the costs and benefits of including that alternative argument in your assessment?

Externally structured analysis—such as the Analysis of Competing Hypotheses, Argument Mapping, and Signpost Analysis—might have overcome the barriers to sound analysis set up by boss think, tribal think, and no think, as well as by the elephant in the room. As a former practitioner of "analysis by mind-set," I bridle at the accusation that my judgments were "intuitive" or not backed by serious thinking. Much deliberative but internalized structuring took place before, during, and after the initial drafting, including via the coordination and review processes. But neither I nor my colleagues could take effective account of hidden and contradictory assumptions and of the overweighting and underweighting of individual reports that supported a hypothesis. If I had committed to external structuring, my sleep these days might be less disturbed by recall of my personal collection of poorly argued or overconfident intelligence judgments.

Challenge analysis—such as Devil's Advocacy, "What If?" Analysis, and High-Impact/Low-Probability Analysis—might have provided analysts and managers with an additional measure of insurance on issues they "couldn't afford to get wrong." Challenge analysis usually is undertaken after the analysts in charge of an issue have reached a strong consensus and are in danger of becoming complacent with their interpretative and forecasting judgments. It is essentially "argument for argument's sake"—that is, a rigorous evaluation of the evidence, including gaps in evidence, from a plausible if seemingly unlikely set of alternative assumptions. As a rule, the primary target audience for challenge analysis is not the policymaker but the analytic community. The primary objective is to test hypotheses and refine judgments or confidence levels and not necessarily abandon judgments.

Challenge analysis serves well even if the exercise only motivates analysts to reassess their previous line of argumentation before deciding to retain their original judgments—as is usually the case. Challenge analysis provides a distinctive service— as is sometimes the case—when it prompts the responsible analysts to alter collection requirements, analytic methodology, or levels of confidence in existing views. In the end, some combination of the often creative insights of analysis by expert opinion (that is, mind-set) and the insurance against cognitive biases provided by more rigorous and structured consideration of alternatives will best serve the reputation of the community of intelligence analysts, the professional needs of policy clients, and the national interest.

Notes

1. Richards J. Heuer Jr., *Psychology of Intelligence Analysis* (Washington, DC: Center for the Study of Intelligence, CIA, 1999).
2. For example, see Commission on the Intelligence Capabilities of the United States Regarding Weapons of Mass Destruction, *Report to the President of the United States, March 31, 2005* (Washington, DC: Government Printing Office, 2005) (hereafter, *WMD Commission Report*); Rob Johnston, *Analytic Culture in the U.S. Intelligence Community: An Ethnographic Study* (Washington, DC: Center for the Study of Intelligence, CIA, 2005); and Jeffrey Cooper, *Curing Analytic Pathologies: Pathways to Improved Intelligence Analysis* (Washington, DC: CIA, 2005).
3. CIA director William J. Casey (1981–87), who had a low opinion of CIA analysts and averred that at least they should learn from their own mistakes, reportedly requested this course. This story was recounted to the author by an agency training official in 1983.
4. The quoted judgment is cited by Gary Sick, at the time the Iran specialist on the National Security Council staff, in his book *All Fall Down: America's Tragic Encounter with Iran* (New York: Random House, 1978), 92. Columbia University professor Robert Jervis, in his unpublished "Analysis of NFAC's Performance on Iran's Domestic Crisis, Mid-1977" (November 7, 1978), comments that "the leading political analyst . . . seems to have had as good a general feel for the country as can be expected" (p. 8); released under the Freedom of Information Act in 1995 as CIA-RDP86B00269R00110011003-425X1.
5. Office of Public Affairs Press Release, CIA, November 30, 2006, www.cia.gov/cia/public_affairs/press_release/2006/pr11302006.html.
6. For a discussion of the impact of these and other cognitive biases on intelligence analysis, see Heuer, *Psychology of Intelligence Analysis*, 111–72.
7. Jack Davis, "Combating Mind-Set," *Studies in Intelligence* 36, no. 5 (1992): 33–38.
8. See John A. Kringen (director of intelligence), "How We Have Improved Intelligence," *Washington Post*, April 3, 2006.
9. Davis, "Combating Mind-Set," 33.
10. Heuer, *Psychology of Intelligence Analysis*, 111.
11. Richard K. Betts, *Surprise Attack: Lessons for Defense Planning* (Washington, DC: Brookings Institution Press, 1982), 71, and Chaim Herzog, *The War of Atonement: October 1973* (Boston: Little, Brown, 1975), 24–25.
12. Interview with CIA supervisor, 1984.
13. Interview with senior warning officer, 1987.
14. Interview with assistant to former CIA official, 2006.
15. Case study presented in a CIA seminar on intelligence successes and failures by a senior CIA briefer, 1990.
16. Ibid.
17. Sherman Kent, "A Crucial Estimate Relived," in *Sherman Kent and the Board of National Estimates: Collected Essays*, ed. Donald P. Steury (Washington, DC: CIA, 1994), 183–84.

18. Fritz Ermarth, reviews of *Essence of Decision: Explaining the Cuban Missile Crisis* by Graham T. Allison and *Victims of Group Think* by Irving L. Janus, in *Studies in Intelligence* 18, no. 1 (Spring 1974): 104 (hereafter, Ermarth, "Book Reviews"), and Max Frankel, *High Noon in the Cold War: Kennedy, Khrushchev, and the Cuban Missile Crisis* (New York: Ballantine, 2004), 8–10.

19. Herzog, *War of Atonement*, 23. The Insight Team of the London *Sunday Times*, *The Yom Kippur War* (Garden City, NY: Doubleday, 1974), chap. 3.

20. See the Iraq Survey Group, *Comprehensive Report of the Special Advisor to the DCI on Iraq's WMD, 30 September 2004* (Washington, DC: CIA, 2004), vol. 1, 4–6.

21. Richard Betts, "Warning Dilemmas: Normal Theory vs. Exceptional Theory," *Orbis* (Winter 1981): 38–46, makes a similar point about academic assessments of foreign policy issues.

22. Ermarth, "Book Reviews," 105–6. I am indebted to Fritz Ermarth for "boss think" and other terms used in this section, although my interpretations may differ from his views.

23. Kent, "Crucial Estimate," 175.

24. Presentation to a CIA seminar on intelligence successes and failures by the CIA office director responsible for analysis of East Germany, 1990; interview with the office senior analyst, 2007.

25. Interview with the principal analyst, 2007. A redacted version of the assessment was declassified and cited as an example of CIA's successful analytic tracking of the pending collapse of the Soviet Union. See Douglas J. MacEachin, *CIA Assessments of the Soviet Union: The Record versus the Charges—An Intelligence Memorandum* (Washington, DC: CIA, 1996), 18.

26. Author's interview with a CIA weapons analyst, 2005. The general point is made in *WMD Commission Report*, 169–71.

27. Kringen, "How We Have Improved Analysis." See also "Opening Statement by Michael V. Hayden before the Senate Select Committee on Intelligence," May 18, 2006, 3, www.globalsecurity.org/intell/library/congress/2006_hr/060518-hayden.htm.

28. Jack Davis, "Intelligence Analysts and Policymakers: Benefits and Dangers of Tensions in the Relationship," *Intelligence and National Security* 21, no. 6 (December 2006): 1008.

29. For example, see Robert Jervis, "Reports, Politics, and Intelligence Failures: The Case of Iraq," *Journal of Strategic Studies* 29, no. 1 (February 2006): 36–38.

30. Davis, "Intelligence Analysts and Policymakers," 1007–9.

31. See also chap. 14 by Randolph H. Pherson and Richards J. Heuer Jr., as well as Roger Z. George, "Fixing the Problem of Analytical Mindsets: Alternative Analysis," *International Journal of Intelligence and Counterintelligence* 17, no. 3 (Fall 2004): 385–404.

CHAPTER 9

Making Analysis More Reliable: Why Epistemology Matters to Intelligence

JAMES B. BRUCE

Another observation I would make concerns what philosophers call epistemological questions: How do we know what we know, and how good is the information that comprises this knowledge? Is it reliable? Is it true? This is the core of the intelligence community's problem.

—John J. Hamre, former deputy secretary of defense, commenting on the failed national intelligence estimate on Iraqi weapons of mass destruction, *Aviation Week and Space Technology*, September 22, 2003

Since intelligence seeks to produce a form of knowledge, analysis must be understood as a knowledge-building activity. Improving analysis thus requires an understanding of epistemology, the branch of philosophy that deals with the theory, origins, and nature of knowledge. This chapter examines how understanding epistemology can help us create more reliable knowledge in intelligence, and why some ways of producing knowledge are better than others. Focusing on an important but failed national intelligence estimate (NIE), it identifies epistemologically induced sources of error in analysis and possible correctives. It also shows how self-corrective mechanisms in analysis can improve reliability and why they should become a more integral part of the analytic process.

Knowledge and Intelligence

Intelligence is *knowledge and foreknowledge of the world around us that allows civilian leaders and military commanders to consider alternative options and outcomes in making decisions.*[1] If *knowledge* and *foreknowledge* are what intelligence agencies are supposed to produce, we should ask, first, what these are and, second, how agencies actually produce—or should produce—them. Epistemology should be a core idea in any discussion of intelligence. It suggests the importance of identifying how different ways of knowing can profoundly impact the judgments that analysis produces.[2]

The centrality of both knowledge and foreknowledge to intelligence was long ago explained by the former Central Intelligence Agency (CIA) director Allen Dulles in his now classic *The Craft of Intelligence*:

> In the fifth century B.C., the Chinese sage Sun Tsu wrote that foreknowledge was "the reason the enlightened prince and the wise general conquer the enemy whenever they move." In 1955 the Task Force on Intelligence Activities of the Second Herbert Hoover Commission in its advisory report to the government stated that "intelligence deals with all the things which should be known in advance of initiating a course of action." Both statements, widely separated as they are in time, have in common the emphasis on the practical use of advance information in its relation to action.[3]

Along with secrecy and espionage, knowledge and foreknowledge are the most durable attributes of the practice of intelligence.

Definitions of knowledge and related terms are provided in box 9.1. The starting point for this discussion is that intelligence analysts work in a world of uncertainty and almost never have all the information they need. In producing finished intelligence, they amass data that typically comprises ambiguous, contradictory, and sometimes deceptive information, and much of what they need is missing. Yet they are called upon to produce judgments, forecasts, and insights that should be reliable enough for policymakers to act on (see chapter 1).

We start with the question: Does finished intelligence, the end product of analysis, actually deliver *knowledge*? The answer depends on the factual content of the judgments and on the methods used to produce them. Certain intelligence questions are binary and can be answered "yes" or "no." For example:

1. Was the crash of TWA flight 800 caused by a missile? (No.)
2. Is Saddam Hussein stockpiling chemical and biological weapons? (NIE: Yes. Factually: No.)

In principle, the intelligence addressing these questions can indeed rise to the level of justified true belief, or knowledge of the highest standard. But there is a difference in the answers to these questions. In question 1, analysts had good access to the facts needed to answer it correctly and with high confidence. In question 2, they did not. Where intelligence judgments are fact-deprived—as most are by necessity, and as illustrated in question 2—the results do not rise to the strict standards required of knowledge. Here, lacking a factual basis for the answer, the reliability of the judgments will depend more on the methods that produce them than on facts they do not contain. As shown below, the methods used in the Iraq NIE were as poor as the "facts" that analysts presented. Knowledge was not the result.

The main thesis of this chapter is that *the reliability of intelligence judgments correlates directly with the level of factual content, the use of reliable epistemology, or both. Said differently, where factual content is low, the reliability of judgments depends heavily on*

BOX 9.1   Definitions

Knowledge (popular definition): Facts, ideas, and understanding, the totality of what is known.

Knowledge (more rigorous definition): Justified true belief.

To know: To perceive directly, to have direct cognition of, to have understanding of, or to recognize the nature of.

Fact: A thing known to be true, to have happened; something to put forth as objectively real.

Foreknowledge: To foresee or to know beforehand; prior knowledge or awaremess of something.

Judgment: Conclusion or inference based on analysis of incomplete and uncertain information; interpretation of facts or evidence that can themselves prove to be accurate or wrong.

Reliability: Dependability, ability to be depended upon; to be able to trust confidently.

Analysis: Judgment under conditions of uncertainty.

Sources: Popular definitions are from the *American Heritage Dictionary and Webster's New Collegiate Dictionary.* Knowledge as "justfied true belief" is in the *Standford Encylopedia of Philosophy.* See also chapter 1 and glossary in this volume.

---

the epistemology. Since epistemology with high reliability is needed most when facts are scarce, it makes sense to ask what makes some epistemologies better than others. The simple answer is the attribute of *self-corrective techniques.* In exploring different ways to build knowledge in intelligence, the key argument made here is that the presence or absence of self-corrective techniques makes some ways of knowing (epistemologies) inherently better than others and that understanding and acting on this core idea is essential to the analytic process. Because each way of knowing has major implications for the accuracy and reliability of analysis, analysts should be acutely aware of precisely which knowledge-building techniques they are using when they research, draft, and coordinate analytic products.

Principal Ways of Knowing

There are only a finite number of ways to produce knowledge. This is as true for intelligence as for any other discipline. For the purposes of this discussion, the principal and distinct ways can be reduced to four: authority, habit of thought, rationalism, and empiricism. A fifth way, science, combines important features of rationalism and empiricism.[4] We examine each in turn.

Authority

When someone "knows" something through authority, the basis of knowledge resides in a reference to something more authoritative than the person who claims to know it. For example, if someone claimed to know that US intelligence was engaged in nefarious or illegal acts at home or abroad because he read it in a newspaper or heard it on a television newscast, then the claim to know relies on the authority of the newspaper or network. Ultimately the validity of that claim will depend on how, for example, the *New York Times* or a network news anchor came to know that particular piece of information. The same is true if the person learned the information from a professor, parent, preacher, or poet—the validity of the information may vary widely, but the method of knowing it is the same: It is authority dependent.

It should be immediately apparent that this way of knowing depends *completely* on the source of the information. If the authority of the information source is valid, so too is the information. If the authority is weak or wrong, so too is the information. For example, in 2002 President George W. Bush and other senior administration officials claimed to know that Iraq possessed a major program of weapons of mass destruction (WMDs). Their claim was based on what the director of central intelligence (DCI) and other US intelligence authorities had told them. The DCI's knowledge, in turn, was based on what the NIE and earlier intelligence products had reported. In this case the authority was the NIE—the most authoritative intelligence product. We will see below that the various ways of knowing used in the estimate on Iraq WMDs also depended heavily on authority. The crippling problem with relying on this way of knowing is that users cannot easily assess any antecedent epistemologies by which the knowledge was created and therefore cannot assess the veracity or sources of possible error. Such antecedent sources of knowledge may or may not be reliable, and if they too are based on authority, they will lack any internal mechanisms for error discovery and correction.

Habit of Thought

The second method of knowing is best characterized by identifying its two most common forms: prejudice in individuals and conventional wisdom in groups. People often claim to know something because they have "always known it" or because they have always thought something to be true without understanding exactly why. As such, prejudice and conventional wisdom may lack specific origins and defy explanation. Stereotypes offer a case in point. For example, before World War II, Western intelligence officers commonly believed that Japanese pilots were unskilled and inept and that Japanese military equipment was of poor quality.[5] Of course the experience of Pearl Harbor and later campaigns proved these stereotypes wrong. Similar ethnic and other prejudices and stereotypes are often based only on habit of thought. If asked to explain how they know this, people may cite "evidence" that is typically anecdotal, and they cannot often identify the origins of such prejudicial information apart from having believed it all along. The source of this knowledge is habitual and based on little else.

Similarly "conventional wisdom" is collective understanding or knowledge that has no more or less of a basis for being valid than whatever formed such habits of knowing in the first place. Once a collective understanding is reached, no matter the original basis for that understanding, it takes on a life all its own. Conventional wisdom can be a factor in producing knowledge of the physical world as well as intelligence. For example, before the full scientific impact of Copernicus and Galileo, the commonly held belief among the learned and illiterate alike since Ptolemy was that the Earth's position in the universe was fixed and that the sun and stars rotated around this stationary planet. This second-century geocentric view hardened into entrenched knowledge and became an extremely difficult position for the later heliocentric advocates to overturn, notwithstanding observational data and logic.[6] Galileo was convicted of heresy for believing differently than the prevailing conventional wisdom. We now know that his views were indeed justified true beliefs—that is, knowledge of the highest standard.

In intelligence, analogous examples of Ptolemaic conventional wisdom having hardened into "knowledge" include the consensus that Soviet behavior into the early 1960s was strategically cautious and that Iranian society into the late 1970s was stable and governed effectively by a strong and capable ruler. Both these examples of knowledge were correct—but only temporarily, because events proved them wrong when the Soviets tried to sneak nuclear missiles into Cuba in October 1962 and the shah's government abruptly fell in 1979. Both these intelligence surprises were rooted in habit of thought as a way of knowing. They also illustrate how errors in knowledge ensure errors in foreknowledge.

As a basis for foreknowledge, habit of thought can be a useful predictor of continuity. For warning intelligence, it has proven a usually reliable—if lazy—way of knowing: The odds generally favor predictions that say tomorrow will look pretty much like today. But this way of knowing inhibits anticipating discontinuity, so major warning failures can be the result. For those cases of abrupt discontinuity such as the Soviet missile emplacements and the Iranian Revolution, habit of thought is an unreliable basis for warning.[7] If habit of thought is wrong, its errors must be discovered by some different way of knowing, because, like authority, it lacks the ability to discover its mistakes by itself.

Rationalism

When knowledge is derived from *reason*, this way of knowing is referred to as rationalism. The great rationalists—Socrates, Plato, Hegel, Descartes, Spinoza, and Kant—differed on methods of reasoning but shared an important attribute: a belief that the human mind can produce knowledge and that knowledge of the physical world is a product of the mind.[8]

Rationalists have devised or identified several *systems of reasoning*, the most important of which are deduction, induction, and abduction.[9] *Deduction* produces inferences or conclusions about particulars that follow from general laws or principles. The best-known example of deductive reasoning is the following syllogism, which illustrates how we can know that Socrates was a mortal:

- All men are mortals; Socrates was a man; therefore Socrates was a mortal.

We have learned nothing from this syllogism because the idea proclaiming Socrates' mortality was already fully contained in the premises. This form of reasoning is empty. Its conclusion cannot state more than what is already known in the premises; it can only make it more explicit.[10] Deductive reasoning can, however, assist in the physical sciences because science, unlike intelligence, does have general laws, such as the law of gravity, from which particular kinds of information may be discovered.[11] But its uses in intelligence are more problematic because intelligence lacks general principles with the explanatory power of Newton's laws. It can assist in generating hypotheses, but analysts will generally find little value in deductive reasoning to help them produce reliable intelligence.[12]

In contrast with deduction, *inductive* reasoning searches *for* general principles or more generalized understandings by reasoning from the particulars to the general:

- Swan 1 is white; swan 2 is white; swan 3 is white. . . . Therefore, all swans are white.

Inductive inference seems to be the dominant choice of reasoning in intelligence analysis. A tool of historians, its intelligence roots are traceable to Sherman Kent.[13] Properly employed, this method can help identify trends, continuity, and change. It helps the analyst make sense of seemingly chaotic data, to discern patterns in behavior and events, and to ascertain possible relationships by searching for connections among things that might otherwise seem disconnected.

Induction, moreover, can help the analyst to move beyond knowledge to foreknowledge.[14] In science, for example, we may predict that after nearly 5 billion years of the sun rising, it is a safe bet that the sun will rise tomorrow morning. We can make this high-confidence prediction based on the sun's unerring track record. Forecasting its arrival tomorrow is foreknowledge we do not have without induction.

But forecasting human events and behavior, such as terrorist attacks, revolutions, and other intelligence issues, invites far less certainty than we find in cosmology. And these uncertain futures highlight David Hume's "problem of induction": that inductive inference is inherently probabilistic and can thus introduce error. Despite having seen many white swans in the past, we cannot know with certainty that all the swans we see in the future will be white. And no matter how many white swans we can count locally, if we visit Australia we will encounter black ones. Unlike deduction, the conclusion is not contained in the premises because it extends to swans yet unobserved. Therefore the reliability of the conclusion cannot be guaranteed.[15] Inductive inference can add knowledge, but it can also lead to error.

Inductive inference presents both strengths and weaknesses. Its most important strengths are its ability to provide tentative explanations for events and outcomes that reveal patterns and to generate hypotheses about future developments.

The most important problem with inductive inference is that different analysts can arrive at different conclusions from the same set of facts or particulars. Another pitfall is linked to probabilism: Without a rigorous effort to bound uncertainty, such as through statistical tools, analysts are always at risk of drawing false conclusions about the probability of an occurrence, such as the probability of finding a nonwhite swan or warning of a terrorist attack. In short, using induction must be more closely linked with more powerful analytic tools. Otherwise we cannot improve. As Collier expressed it, intelligence analysis "seems stuck in the 1950s through the 1960s inductive historical methods advanced by Sherman Kent, instead of adopting the latest social science knowledge."[16] Indeed a major study of the culture of intelligence analysts found resistance to scientific methods and even prejudices against them.[17]

Unlike the venerable deduction and induction, *abduction* is a more recent form of reasoning, developed chiefly by Charles Peirce around the beginning of the twentieth century. Sometimes referred to as "inference to the best explanation" or the "logic of Sherlock Holmes," abductive inference seeks to craft the best hypothesis or inference to "fit" otherwise unexplained facts and occurrences:[18]

- Hypothesis H_1 with fact 1, fact 2, fact 3, fact 4 . . . best explains occurrence A.

Although it can be expressed as a formal system of logic, abduction is chiefly a qualitative technique applying an investigator's approach to understanding disparate phenomena. Intelligence analysts use abductive inference, if often unwittingly, to provide explanations for past, emerging, or ongoing events,[19] and with a view toward understanding the future. Abductive inference outperforms other forms of reasoning in generating hypotheses.

A major weakness of abduction is that, as with induction, different analysts may arrive at different inferences from the same set of facts or give different emphasis to particular facts that lead to different explanations. Abduction also shares another weakness with both induction and deduction: *Reasoning itself does not make something true; it can only identify a possible truth.* For the scientist, establishing what is true—namely, building knowledge—requires an additional step called *verification* (or falsification). *No rationalist technique—neither abduction, induction, nor deduction—offers this crucial step toward gaining knowledge.* Moreover, when logic makes errors, it has only the capacity to detect the *logic* of its errors but not the factual basis of the premises on which its conclusions are based. The knowledge it produces may be correct or incorrect. But because its truth depends on the extralogical content of the facts, knowledge from rationalism alone cannot be trusted as fully reliable. For more reliable knowledge building, we need to turn to the fourth way of knowing: empiricism. It is here that we begin to see the emerging attributes of science, the most reliable knowledge-building technique of all.

Empiricism

The fourth way of knowing represents an important advance in understanding the world. Bacon, Locke, Hume, and Galileo pioneered its early methods. Empiricism is based on what we apprehend from the senses: what we see, hear, touch, taste, and smell. It is about observation, experience, and experimentation. In sharp contrast to the rationalist who believes that knowledge is the product of the human mind, the empiricist insists that "sense observation is the primary source and ultimate judge of knowledge and that it is self-deception to believe the human mind to have direct access to any kind of truth other than logical relations."[20] Rather than dwelling on reason, the empiricist's focus is on observational data. Shifting from an internal mental exercise to externally observable data changes the entire epistemological equation. As Hans Reichenbach explains, the contrast between rationalism and empiricism could not be sharper: "Once empirical observation is abandoned as a source of truth, it is then but a short step to mysticism. If reason can create knowledge, other creations of the human mind may appear as trustworthy as knowledge."[21]

The empirical approach should come easily to the intelligence analyst because the collection disciplines—HUMINT, SIGINT, IMINT, MASINT, and OSINT[22]—are principally sensory. The analyst is awash with empirical data. His or her job is to make sense of it, hypothesize about it, formulate judgments, forecasts, and insights from it, and convey their meanings to customers. In producing knowledge and foreknowledge, analysis relies on collected data—a fundamentally empirical enterprise.

Critics of empiricism sometimes fault "scientific" methods as inappropriate for intelligence analysis and tout the putatively superior virtues of intuition and reason.[23] Other critics point out, rightly, that facts do not speak for themselves and that not all data are valid. Some things are not what they seem.[24] Collected data are only "sampled" data and can be misleading, erroneous, distorted, or unrepresentative—and often are. They can be fabricated. Or elusive. But data-free intelligence is not intelligence. A major challenge of intelligence analysts, therefore, is not only to make judgments *from* the data but first to make judgments *about* the data. We will see below that this important step is not always taken or taken carefully.

To summarize, what authority, habit of thought, rationalism, and empiricism all have in common is a demonstrated capacity for producing error as well as truth. But none of the four has the internal capacity to discover when it is wrong or to prescribe the needed correctives for getting it right. In a historically profound development that combines the third and fourth ways of knowing, rationalism and empiricism, the emergence of science produced a new epistemology that presents a powerful new feature to knowledge building: *self-corrective techniques*. Though all five avenues to knowledge can produce error, *only science has the built-in capacity to identify and correct its mistakes.* The implications for intelligence analysis are obvious and irresistible: These self-corrective techniques can markedly reduce the potential for error in analysis and greatly enhance the production of reliable knowledge.[25]

Science

It is the distinctive ability of scientific inquiry to produce sound understanding and reliable knowledge. As a way of knowing, it combines the best attributes of rationalism and empiricism that yield an array of internal procedures that enable it to check and correct itself. Compared with the other four ways of knowing, its capacity for error identification and correction greatly improves its reliability. This feature should make it of particular interest to intelligence analysts. Significantly a recent study has concluded that developing a science of intelligence analysis would be easier than changing the perceptions of the analysts and managers who oppose it.[26]

This capability of the scientific method for producing reliable knowledge rests on several attributes that other methods lack.[27] Physical and social scientists would generally agree that scientific inquiry must have the following attributes:

- *Use of the hypothesis.* A specific research statement that is falsifiable in principle guides any scientific study. However the hypothesis is initially generated, it must be testable, since the investigator is primarily interested in determining how valid or truthful it is. The investigator will collect observable data to test the hypothesis, using rigorous methods to establish whether it is true or false. He or she may use inferential statistics to establish the probability that its truthfulness is not a chance or random occurrence. Testing may also identify the conditions under which the hypothesis is most likely to be true or false.

- *Objective methods.* A scientist employs rigorous procedures to ensure that data are collected and analyzed in the most objective manner possible to avoid influencing or distorting the test. Scientists are empiricists. The only data used in the research are those relevant to the hypothesis, but neither the data selection nor the analytic methods should influence the outcome of the study to achieve a particular or desired result, nor should they bias the results.

- *Transparency.* Science is a public activity, and its procedures are open to inspection. No study claiming scientific results can shield the methods used to arrive at its findings. Both the findings and the methods used to produce them must be available for public inspection or use. Transparency of methods helps to ensure integrity of the study, as well as its replicability.

- *Replicability.* All scientific investigations must be reproducible by other researchers. If one scientist or group of scientists arrives at any given set of conclusions, another group should be able to repeat the same study, even possibly using different methods, but still reach the same results. If another group cannot achieve the same results, then the initial hypothesis may be doubted and remains open to further investigation.

- *Peer review.* New results do not attain the status of knowledge until other knowledgeable researchers concur that the results are consistent with the methods used and that the methods were empirically sound. Peer review can sometimes be contentious, but studies that survive the review process are more authoritative than those that do not. Rigorous peer review can impede, prevent, or validate the acceptance of findings.

- *Provisional results.* Scientific findings are always subject to modification as procedures are refined, new results come in, and older ones are superseded. This dynamic feature of scientific inquiry is reinforced by the inherently skeptical attitude of the scientist.

This implies an intrinsic readiness to reconsider results when new ideas or information emerge. For the scientist, if ugly facts challenge beautiful theory, facts win.

The upshot of these procedures is vastly improved reliability: When science makes errors—and it sometimes does—it has the inherent capacity to identify and correct them. This self-corrigible capacity was recently demonstrated in the repudiation of two quite public scientific studies: cold fusion in physics and human cloning in biological research.[28] These faulty studies are rare only because they had reached the stage of being announced to the public. Most self-correction in science occurs well before findings become headline news.

Errors in Estimating: Undetected and Uncorrected

The trouble with people is not that they don't know, but that they know so much that ain't so.

—Attributed to Josh Billings (1818–85)

To illustrate epistemological errors that can occur in analysis, we can now examine the ill-fated October 2002 NIE on Iraq's WMDs.[29] It demonstrates how all four ways of knowing each contributed to the NIE's flawed judgments, as well as the consequences of failing to incorporate error-detecting and reducing measures.

This NIE produced faulty knowledge—it knew, in Josh Billings's terms, what "ain't so." Its three most important key judgments were factually wrong.[30] Two of them that described the chemical weapons (CW) and biological weapons (BW) that Iraq purportedly possessed were wrong with "high confidence." And the key judgment on Iraq's efforts to reconstitute its nuclear program was wrong with "moderate confidence." The capacity of each epistemology to yield error appears to be fully realized in the preparation of this deeply flawed NIE.

Authority

The use of authority as a way of knowing played an important and destructive role in all three judgments. Beginning with CW, the principal question at the time of the NIE was, does Iraq possess chemical weapons? The NIE said yes. It judged that Iraq had an active CW program involving the production of mustard, sarin, cyclosarin, and VX, and had stockpiled as much as one hundred to five hundred metric tons of them. The NIE also said that Iraq had produced much of its CW in the year prior to the estimate. Contrary to the estimate's conclusions, we now know that Iraq had no CW at all for about ten years before the NIE was published.

Authority played a significant role in this judgment. According to the Silberman-Robb WMD Commission, the most important CW evidence—and most important source of error—was "over-reliance on a single, ambiguous source (Samarra type tanker trucks) to support multiple judgments."[31] Imagery is a specialized collection discipline, and the imagery analysts who report its findings to all-source analysts are typically regarded as authoritative photo interpreters. The narrow information on the decontamination trucks at suspect CW sites was far from definitive, and precisely for this reason specialized knowledge gave the impression that the information was stronger than it was. The authoritative nature of imagery analysis—a combination of empirical observation and expert judgment—was accepted as a basis for the CW key judgment in the NIE that we now know was wrong.

The high-confidence BW judgment also was heavily supported by authority, in this case a clandestine human source who claimed insider knowledge of Iraq's BW programs. The NIE concluded that Iraq had offensive BW weapons, including mobile BW labs. It also said that all key aspects of the BW program were active and that most program elements were larger and more advanced than they were during the Gulf War. Though other information also supported this judgment, none was more authoritative than the reporting that came from the human source code-named "Curveball," whose intelligence was disseminated in roughly a hundred detailed reports. The WMD Commission found that the intelligence community (IC) had a "near-total reliance on Curveball for its BW judgments" and that serious problems accompanied this source. The fact that Curveball was later exposed as a fabricator meant that the erroneous BW finding was based heavily on fabricated HUMINT.[32] Reliance on any form of authority that cannot be further verified, as is often the case with sensitive collection, is a major vulnerability of intelligence analysis.

The moderate-confidence judgment in the NIE that Iraq had begun to reconstitute its nuclear weapons program and, if left unchecked, would probably have a nuclear weapon during this decade was also based heavily on authority. Understanding nuclear capabilities requires technical expertise provided, in this case by two agencies, both of which provided expert judgment that turned out to be wrong. The Army's National Ground Intelligence Center (NGIC) made the crucial judgment about whether certain aluminum tubes procured by Iraq were intended for use in conventional mortars (NGIC's particular expertise) or for use in a nuclear centrifuge. NGIC's expert authority erroneously concluded that the tubes were suitable for use in a nuclear centrifuge rather than in a conventional weapons application, thereby adding significant credibility to the argument that Iraq was reconstituting its nuclear weapons program. Though the Department of Energy (DOE) disagreed with NGIC on this point, DOE did support the key judgment (on other grounds) that Iraq had begun to reconstitute its nuclear weapons program. As the organization with special expertise in nuclear intelligence, DOE was the most authoritative agency on this issue. The combined weight of DOE's and NGIC's expert status lent significant authority to the erroneous nuclear key judgment in the NIE.[33]

In sum, the role of authority in the CW, BW, and nuclear judgments of the Iraq WMD NIE was crucial, its influence perhaps even expanded given the degree of empirical uncertainty surrounding these issues. A twenty-one-day congressional deadline also imposed a major time pressure for resolution of these complex weapons issues; it almost certainly served to exaggerate this way of knowing even beyond what might have occurred under a more relaxed production schedule. That the coordination session ended on a Friday just before the Monday deadline only added to the intensity for closure.

Habit of Thought

Habit of thought as a way of knowing was probably equally influential in the NIE's key judgments discussed here. Like authority, it too helped in meeting a short deadline. Knowledge of Iraq's WMD program was well established after the post–Desert Storm intelligence in 1991 showed that the IC had actually underestimated the program. The IC consensus on Iraq WMD began to build in the early 1990s, and no compelling evidence had surfaced to challenge it. It seems to have hardened into conventional wisdom by the mid-1990s. Saddam Hussein's own behavior reinforced this IC-wide consensus. He conducted a major denial-and-deception program that both rendered the UN inspection process ineffective and neutralized the effectiveness of US intelligence.[34] This activity only increased Western suspicions that Saddam had weapons he was trying to hide, while a blunted UN inspection system and US intelligence had failed to discover that he had actually eliminated the weapons in the early 1990s.

Habit of thought was effectively admitted by CIA's deputy director of intelligence (the agency's senior manager of analysts) in a speech to analysts, in which she faulted the practice of "inherited assumptions" that went unquestioned in the NIE process.[35] Many of them were wrong. In its scathing review of the NIE, the Senate Select Committee on Intelligence described this phenomenon as "layering"—namely, "the process of building an intelligence assessment primarily using previous judgments without substantial new intelligence reporting" and failing to factor in the cumulative uncertainties through the new assessments.[36]

Overturning a decade of consensus on the weapons would have been a difficult task under the best of circumstances. But analysts lacked good evidence to do so. Worse, to have made the opposite argument—that Iraq had no weapons, which we now know to be the reality—would have stunned policymakers who had been told for years by the IC that Iraq had retained such weapons. The same habit of thought that hobbled intelligence analysts and managers also hobbled the policymakers who had been consuming the erroneous journalistic-style, current intelligence reports on Iraq WMD for years. This particular habit of thought was shared across the intelligence and policy communities.

This habitual way of knowing was not recognized for what it was: a significant barrier to alternative analysis at a time when the impact of authority was also unchecked. Habit of thought, present in all the wrong judgments, was the starting point for an analysis that gave even greater credence to a misguided authority.

Rationalism

The role that reason played in producing erroneous WMD knowledge was probably as strong and error-producing as the first two ways of knowing. By inductive inference, analysts built a cumulative picture of CW, BW, and nuclear reconstitution, all adding up to a significant WMD program. Supported by habit of thought and reinforced by erroneous authority, persuasive reasoning carried the day. Even lacking solid information, analysts concluded that Iraq must have had the weapons even if we were not seeing them. In fact, *not* seeing them seemed to provide evidence that Iraq *had* them. The logic seemed impeccable: We know that Saddam Hussein had them in the past, he is a lying and evil-intentioned dictator, and his pervasive denial-and-deception efforts explain why we are not seeing them. The logic, therefore, added up to evidence *for* a weapons program, not against it.[37] However persuasive, this argument demonstrates that as a way of building knowledge, logic is no better than the content of its premises. If the premises contain error, even the soundest reasoning can only reproduce error.

Empiricism

In contrast to the above three ways of knowing, empirical observations played a startlingly minimal role in the NIEs on Iraq's WMDs: *The IC had no direct evidence of WMDs in Iraq at the time the estimate confidently asserted knowledge of Iraq's weapons programs.* Still, even allowing for the debilitating distortions in the analytic process wrought by the other three ways of knowing, how could the empirical process break down so badly? The answer seems to be that what little observable evidence there was in CW, BW, and nuclear reconstitution was not only overinterpreted but also was not heavily scrutinized or assessed relative to any available evidence to the contrary. A senior defector's reporting in 1995 that Saddam had shut down the WMD programs four years earlier was simply disregarded.[38] Further, aggressive collection efforts in all disciplines kept failing to produce results. This "negative evidence"—that is, the lack of fresh or convincing observable indicators of Iraq's purported weapons despite the concerted search for them—was either explained away as denial and deception or discounted because it did not support the habitual knowledge of a robust and active WMD capability.[39] Called "card stacking" in propaganda, this prosecutor's technique is what passed for empirical analysis in the NIE.[40] But analysts did not actively consider the additional hypothesis that the overwhelming lack of evidence on the key weapons issues might also have meant that Iraq had shut down those programs. Whatever else it was, this analysis was anything but empirical.

In sum, analysis of Iraq's WMD in the 2002 NIE and the analytic efforts leading up to it show that when the empirical component of analysis is low, the impact of other ways of knowing increases—in this case with poor results. It also shows that the NIE was an epistemological "perfect storm": All four ways of knowing—authority (faulty), habit of thought (unquestioned), reasoning (flawed premises), and empiricism (selective or absent)—failed to produce reliable knowledge. The errors that each method produced are expected outcomes of epistemologies whose strengths do not extend to discovering and correcting their own errors. For more reliable analysis, we need to consider what a more scientific approach might offer.

Epistemological Lessons for Analysis

To be successful, intelligence analysis must be able to produce knowledge and fore-knowledge that is reliable. All epistemologies have the potential for producing error as well as truth, as demonstrated in the errors produced in one of the most high-visibility and policy-relevant NIEs in years. Because science, unlike other ways of knowing, possesses unique self-corrective mechanisms intrinsic to its own procedures, how might we adapt these mechanisms to intelligence analysis? The answer can be found in three parts: the role of the hypothesis, the role of coordination, and a prepublication checklist of epistemological vulnerabilities for analysts and managers.

The Hypothesis

Science is careful to distinguish between knowledge, which is justified true belief, and a hypothesis, which might or might not be true. The distinction is crucial. Before the hypothesis can become knowledge, it must survive rigorous testing, including systematic efforts to disprove it (discussed below). A nonscientific approach, like the WMD estimate or a determined prosecutor seeking a conviction in a court, will merely try to "prove" something true. In qualitative research, as most intelligence is, this is often not hard to do. The analyst can select confirmatory facts, disregard or diminish others, and argue like a lawyer to an appropriate standard of proof.[41]

In science the opposite happens. Implementing objectivity rather than trying to prove a point, science actively tries to *prevent* the results from coming out the way the investigator may *want* them to come out. The guiding principle ensuring integrity of results is honest management of the hypothesis under investigation. This process has two parts: hypothesis generation and hypothesis testing.

Hypothesis generation refers to the source of the hypothesis—that is, where it comes from. Hypotheses (statements that can be empirically evaluated) can come from almost anywhere. The most lucrative source of hypotheses is theories and models of behavior (for example, the behavior of states, groups, and people). Apart from explanation, the most important role that theories play is their ability to produce testable hypotheses. This is the test of a good theory. Hypotheses can also be generated by such logical systems as abduction, induction, and deduction as discussed above. They can also be generated by policymakers, pundits, and assorted advocates who are fertile sources of interesting ideas, even if they advocate them. (Note that while policymakers can play an important role in *generating* hypotheses, their biases soundly disqualify them from any role in *testing* them; that role belongs to intelligence, not policy.) Hypotheses can also be produced by intelligence analysts, especially using such SATs as brainstorming, alternative analysis, and scenarios.[42]

Hypothesis testing is one of the most important differences between science and nonscientific activity. The whole idea is to make a sound decision about whether a particular research statement is true or false. Hypothesis testing with statistical tools and quantitative data is, unfortunately, relevant for only a very small number of problems facing the intelligence analyst.[43] The reality is that most intelligence problems are qualitative, not quantitative. This limitation deprives the analyst of powerful statistical tools that can help discriminate between true statements and false ones. Lacking quantitative-like tools for analysis of qualitative issues, can the intelligence analyst still test hypotheses?

The answer is a qualified no: Present tools for qualitative analysis cannot provide the same level of rigor and, therefore, confidence that we find in quantitative techniques. *But the attributes that provide science with self-corrective mechanisms are still largely within reach.* To date, the social sciences have not yet developed qualitative hypothesis-testing techniques that offer the power of quantitative tests. But recent methodological innovations have brought promising new capabilities that can help the intelligence analyst get closer to this standard.

The Analysis of Competing Hypotheses (ACH), as described in Richards Heuer's *Psychology of Intelligence Analysis*, offers real potential for testing qualitative hypotheses. ACH "tests" hypotheses by comparing how well each stacks up against the evidence and by trying to disconfirm them.[44] It evaluates the relative validity of several competing hypotheses—that is, alternative explanations for the same observed phenomenon. Referring to the example of the ill-fated WMD estimate discussed above, had ACH been used during the course of this estimate, the likelihood of achieving the same disastrous results would certainly have been lower.

Because ACH requires the comparison of *multiple* hypotheses, analysts would have been forced to examine more than one. But the flawed estimate tried to find evidence to demonstrate only one: that Iraq possessed WMD. Even to have injected a single *alternative* hypothesis into the estimate drafting and coordination process—such as there were no weapons, which was the correct one—would have much improved the analysis. In addition, ACH would have forced much closer attention to the relationship between the evidence and the NIE's judgments. We now know that the imagery evidence for CW, Curveball's reporting on BW, and the role of the aluminum tubes in nuclear reconstitution did not hold up over time. A much closer examination of these three crucial and, we now know, fragile pieces of information using a "sensitivity check" should have exposed the enormous dependence of these key judgments on such tenuous "evidence."[45]

In sum, whether or not ACH would have brought us markedly different results, we can be fairly sure that it would not have delivered the same wrong results with the same high levels of confidence. Structured tradecraft tools like ACH ward off "card stacking" and proving favored hypotheses. Placing emphasis on generating and testing hypotheses, along with rigorous use of peer review, can help ensure objectivity, transparency, and replicability—all vital self-corrective mechanisms.

Coordination

When analysts meet in a conference room to discuss every sentence in an NIE, the often painful coordination process typically results in a better analytic product. It is the IC's version of science's peer review. *Coordination is the only explicit step in the analytic process that already provides potential self-corrective mechanisms.* But the coordination process is too often corrupted into a linguistic exercise. Analysts and managers often seek agreeable prose crafted to forge agreement among the parties in order to meet a deadline. That emphasis on finding just the right words to facilitate production subverts an otherwise invaluable epistemological process that coordination is intended to achieve. It is the final stage in the analytic process where significant errors can be detected and corrected.

But this important feature of self-correction is lost when the focus shifts from epistemology to language. The coordination process needs to be rediscovered for its intended epistemological function to better ensure the reliability of the knowledge and foreknowledge that policymakers get from intelligence. It should also explicitly identify any judgments that are based on authority or habit of thought for closer scrutiny. And any judgments based on rationalism must confront the factual basis of the premises of the logic and not just the logic itself.

Epistemology Checklist

For major intelligence products that may have significant policy consequences, such as NIEs issued during war planning, analysts and managers should subject themselves to four tests of knowledge—each asking *how do I know that X is true?*—prior to the publication and release of such products:

1. Is X true because analysts believe in the *authority* of the information that says it is true? *Implications:* If so, be sure to understand the basis of the authority. If that is the principal or only basis for this knowledge, then recognize the enormous dependence of the validity of this knowledge on the soundness of the authority. Then try to validate that authority.
2. Is X true because this view is generally believed by most analysts today and it has been *true in the past*? *Implications:* Habit of thought can work to a point, but its origins are often unknown and therefore hard to assess. It is biased toward continuity, resistant to change, and susceptible to blind-side surprise. If this is the principal or only basis for knowing something, then recognize the enormous dependence of the validity of this knowledge on its intellectual inertia. It is often right, but when wrong, it can be very wrong. It should never be accepted uncritically and without challenge.
3. Is X true because analytic logic produced these conclusions? *Implications:* Because no present method of reasoning alone can produce reliable knowledge, it is best to treat any conclusions derived by logic as only hypotheses that deserve further testing. Rationalist approaches are not only vulnerable to error—they cannot themselves determine whether their conclusions are true or false. Hypothesis testing is an empirical, not logical, operation. Good reasoning is essential to knowing, but without good evidence its results cannot be called knowledge.

4. Is X true because the *observable data* gathered suggest it is true? *Implications:* Collection amounts to sampled information whose representativeness is not known. You might have gathered different data that would lead to different, possibly opposite, conclusions. If the data gathering is incomplete and unrepresentative, and key information is missing—in intelligence, it almost always is—you do not have the full story. If it is used selectively to "prove" a point, it probably will. But the point will be no more valid than the distortion techniques that support it. Sound empirical approaches require rigorous testing of multiple hypotheses, not just finding evidence to support a favored one.

As this chapter has shown, a better epistemology—science—is available for intelligence analysis. Its implementation can be advanced through rigorous use of SATs. A more science-based approach to producing intelligence is less error-prone because it consciously seeks to identify and correct its errors. If the experience of the October 2002 NIE on Iraq's WMD offers any guide to the selection of epistemologies for intelligence, then future key judgments should meet stricter epistemological standards before being provided to policymakers. Analysis produced using the self-corrective techniques that science offers will greatly improve the probability of getting reliable results.

Returning to the more rigorous definition of knowledge used in this chapter, justified true belief, we should appreciate what it means for the integrity of intelligence: When judgments are provided to policymakers, they convey the beliefs of the agencies and their analysts that produced them. We owe it to our customers that these beliefs be both true and justified. If they are, then we are providing knowledge that can be relied on. Otherwise our customers should also be fully apprised of the uncertainties—the probabilities and levels of confidence that help them understand what may call the truth or justification of the judgments into question. Customers of intelligence should insist on nothing less.

Notes

The author is indebted to Roy Kirvan, Richards Heuer, and Aaron Frank for very thoughtful critiques of earlier drafts.

1. Briefing, *The Intelligence Community*, on the director of national intelligence (DNI) website, www.dni.gov. A similar knowledge-based definition of intelligence predated the establishment of the DNI: "Reduced to its simplest terms, intelligence is knowledge and foreknowledge of the world around us—the prelude to decision and action by U.S. policymakers." See Office of Public Affairs, CIA, *A Consumers' Guide to Intelligence* (Washington, DC: CIA, n.d.), vii.

2. Epistemology has not been a popular subject in the literature of intelligence, but notable exceptions are Woodrow J. Kuhns, "Intelligence Failures: Forecasting and the Lessons of Epistemology," in *Paradoxes of Strategic Intelligence*, ed. Richard K. Betts and Thomas G. Mahnken (London: Frank Cass, 2003), 80–100; Michael W. Collier, "A Pragmatic Approach

to Developing Intelligence Analysis," *Defense Intelligence Journal* 14, no. 3 (2005): 17–35; and Matthew Herbert, "The Intelligence Analyst as Epistemologist," *International Journal of Intelligence and Counterintelligence* 19, no. 4 (Winter 2006): 666–84.

3. Allen W. Dulles, *The Craft of Intelligence* (1963; repr., Guilford, CT: Lyons, 2006), 1. The author, director of central intelligence from 1953 to 1961, was the longest-serving DCI in history.

4. These can be found variously in the epistemological literature, but I am indebted to David H. Bayley, formerly of the Korbel School of International Studies, University of Denver, who presented the basic argument made here in his research seminar during my graduate studies there years ago. Michael Collier presents a similar list of seven ways of knowing, adding *faith* and *common sense*, which are implicitly covered here in my discussion of habit of thought below, and *intuition*, which I have combined with rationalism. See Collier, "Pragmatic Approach," 19.

5. Roberta Wohlstetter, *Pearl Harbor: Warning and Decision* (Palo Alto, CA: Stanford University Press, 1962), 337–38.

6. For an explanation of the "paradigm shift" from an earth-centered to a sun-centered understanding of the solar system, see Thomas H. Kuhn, *The Structure of Scientific Revolutions*, 3rd ed. (Chicago: University of Chicago Press, 1996), 67–69, 150–55.

7. These cases are further discussed in chap. 10.

8. Hans Reichenbach, *The Rise of Scientific Philosophy* (Berkeley: University of California Press, 1968), 74, chaps. 2–4.

9. A fourth system, dialectical reasoning, was devised by Friedrich Hegel and made famous by Karl Marx but is omitted from discussion here given its limited applicability to intelligence.

10. As Reichenbach explains, "It cannot be overemphasized that logical deduction cannot create independent results. It is merely an instrument of connection; it derives conclusions from given axioms, but cannot inform us about the truth of the axioms." Reichenbach, *Rise of Scientific Philosophy*, 57, 37. Also see Kuhns, "Intelligence Failures," 93.

11. Reichenbach, *Rise of Scientific Philosophy*, 100–103.

12. As Kuhns has pointed out, deductive reasoning that helps identify certain consequences that follow from hypotheses—even if such hypotheses are not general laws—can play a useful, if limited, role in intelligence analysis. Kuhns, "Intelligence Failures," 91–92.

13. Kuhns, "Intelligence Failures," 86. Also see Collier, "Pragmatic Approach," 31.

14. "In addition to deduction, the physicist depends on the use of induction, since he starts with observations and foretells future observations. The prediction of future observations is both his goal and the test of the truth of his hypotheses." Reichenbach, *Rise of Scientific Philosophy*, 114.

15. Ibid., 81–82, 242. Inductive logic rests on theories of probability. See Abraham Kaplan, *The Conduct of Inquiry: Methodology for Behavioral Science* (San Francisco: Chandler, 1964), 232–34.

16. Collier, "Pragmatic Approach," 31. Not all empirically minded analysts agree that the statistical methods used in social sciences are applicable to intelligence analysis. Such skeptics argue that the kinds of variables and relationships studied by intelligence analysts are, more often than not, so specific and complex that they are not easily amenable to statistical treatment. See Richards J. Heuer Jr., ed., *Quantitative Approaches to Political Intelligence: The CIA Experience* (Boulder, CO: Westview, 1978), chap. 1. We return to this issue below.

17. Rob Johnston, *Analytical Culture in the U.S. Intelligence Community* (Washington, DC, Center for the Study of Intelligence, CIA, 2005), 19–20.

18. See John R. Josephson and Susan G. Josephson, eds., *Abductive Inference: Computation, Philosophy, Technology* (New York: Cambridge University Press, 1994), and Peter Lipton, *Inference to the Best Explanation* (London: Routledge, 2001).

19. An outstanding intelligence example of abductive inference is the explanation for the crash of TWA flight 800 in July 1996 over Long Island, disconfirming the hypothesis that it was shot down by a missile. Randolph M. Tauss, "The Crash of TWA Flight 800," *Studies in Intelligence*, Unclassified Special Edition (November 2002), 101–11.

20. Reichenbach, *Rise of Scientific Philosophy*, 75.

21. Ibid., 32.

22. I.e., producing intelligence from human sources, signals, imagery, measurements and signatures, and open sources—the collection disciplines. See chaps. 4, 10, and glossary.

23. An ardent rationalist polemic is argued by David Brooks in "The Art of Intelligence," *New York Times*, April, 2, 2005.

24. Many eyewitness accounts of a missile shooting down the TWA aircraft were simply wrong. There was no missile. Systematic analysis demonstrated this convincingly. See Tauss, "Crash of TWA Flight 800," note 19.

25. James B. Bruce, "Dynamic Adaptation: A Twenty-First Century Intelligence Paradigm," unpublished internal IC paper, 4–5 (winner of a 2004 DCI Galileo Award).

26. Johnston, *Analytical Culture*, 19–21.

27. In the vast literature explaining how science works, an excellent primer is Hugh G. Gauch Jr., *Scientific Method in Practice* (New York: Cambridge University Press, 2002). An especially useful adaptation for social science is Kaplan, *Conduct of Inquiry*. Summaries of the applicability of scientific methods to intelligence analysis are Collier, "Pragmatic Approach," and in Johnston, *Analytical Culture*, 19–20.

28. In the physics case, scientists in Utah had claimed the ability to produce nuclear fusion through an unconventional tabletop process. Subsequent attempts by other physicists to replicate the procedures of "cold fusion" revealed that the original claims could not be upheld by accepted scientific standards. See David Goodstein, "Whatever Happened to Cold Fusion?" *American Scholar* 63, no. 4 (Fall 1994): 527–41. In the human cloning case, a South Korean researcher announced that he had succeeded in cloning human DNA. Hwang Woo-Suk's startling claims were revealed as fraudulent. Nicholas Wade and Choe Sang-Hun, "Researcher Faked Evidence of Human Cloning, Koreans Report," *New York Times*, January 10, 2006.

29. National Intelligence Council, *Iraq's Continuing Programs of Weapons of Mass Destruction*, NIE 2002-16HC, October 2002. Discussion here is based largely on the authoritative Commission on the Intelligence Capabilities of the United States Regarding Weapons of Mass Destruction, *Report to the President of the United States, March 31, 2005* (Washington, DC: Government Printing Office, 2005) (hereafter, *WMD Commission Report*), and on chap. 10 of this volume.

30. The findings that Saddam Hussein had essentially shut down Iraq's WMD programs in 1991–92—its chemical weapons program, its biological weapons program, and efforts to reconstitute the nuclear weapons program—are in the study of the Iraq Survey Group (ISG), *Comprehensive Report of the Special Advisor to the DCI on Iraq WMD*, posted on the CIA

website: www.cia.gov. October 6, 2004, also referred to as the Duelfer Report; hereafter, *ISG Report*.

31. This has been greatly simplified here but is fully elaborated in *WMD Commission Report*, 122–24.

32. *WMD Commission Report*, 87–100; the quotation is on 93. Curveball was an Iraqi emigrant source reporting to the German intelligence service that in turn passed his reporting on to the DIA's Defense HUMINT Service.

33. See full elaboration in the *WMD Commission Report*, 65–79.

34. *WMD Commission Report*, chaps. 1, 7, and 8, and 161–62, 169, 352, 372–75.

35. Jamie Miscik, deputy director of intelligence's "State of Analysis Speech," All-Hands Meeting, CIA Auditorium February 11, 2004, 8–9, released March 2004.

36. Senate Select Committee on Intelligence, *U.S. Intelligence Community's Prewar Intelligence Assessments on Iraq*, 108th Congress, 2nd Session, July 9, 2004, 22.

37. *WMD Commission Report*, 169–70. Robert Jervis, "Reports, Politics, and Intelligence Failures: The Case of Iraq," *Journal of Strategic Studies* 29, no. 1 (February 2006): 42–45. See also Robert Jervis, *Why Intelligence Fails: Lessons from the Iranian Revolution and the Iraq War* (New York: Columbia University Press, 2010).

38. This was reporting of Hussein Kamel, Saddam Hussein's son-in-law, who defected in 1995. He returned to Iraq three years later only to be killed. See *WMD Commission Report*, 52; *ISG Report* 46; and the Butler Report, formally Committee of Privy Counselors, *Review of Intelligence on Weapons of Mass Destruction* (London: Stationery Office, 2004), 47–48, 51.

39. *WMD Commission Report*, 169–70. From June 2000 through January 2003, MASINT sources produced over a thousand reports on Iraqi WMDs, none of which provided a definitive indication of WMD activity, and the reporting before the October 2002 did not significantly inform assessments about Iraq's WMD programs in the NIE. This seems due, in part, "to the tendency among analysts to discount information that contradicted the prevailing view that Iraq had WMD"; 166.

40. For an explanation of how this technique—i.e., using selective evidence to "prove" a favored hypothesis—distorts analysis, see Richards Heuer's reconstruction of how a major Soviet defector was wrongly found to be a KGB penetration instead of a bona fide source. Richards J. Heuer Jr., "Nosenko: Five Paths to Judgment," in *Inside CIA's Private World: Declassified Articles from the Agency's Internal Journal, 1955–1992*, ed. H. Bradford Westerfield (New Haven, CT: Yale University Press, 1995).

41. Lawyers can "prove" guilt or innocence. Mathematicians can offer "proofs" for solving certain problems. But science does not try to prove anything. It only seeks a neutral evaluation to accept a hypothesis as provisionally true or reject it as false through reliable methods—and keeps the issue open to further investigation.

42. See chap. 14 for discussion of SATs.

43. In quantitative analysis where the number of cases (or N) is above a certain number (greater than fifty, according to Collier, "Pragmatic Approach," 26–27), statistical hypothesis testing is a straightforward procedure.

44. Richards J. Heuer Jr., *Psychology of Intelligence Analysis* (Washington, DC: Center for the Study of Intelligence, CIA, 1999), chap. 8. A PDF file is available at www.cia.gov/csi/books/19104/index.html. ACH software is available for computer-aided analysis. ACH tests hypotheses by having several of them compete against each other, then the weaker

hypotheses—i.e., those with most evidence *against* them—are rejected (instead of concluding that those with most evidence for them have been "proven"). Surviving ones have a stronger claim to being true. This follows Popper's more rigorous test of the principle of falsifiability, which requires the disconfirmation of false hypotheses rather than the confirmation of true ones. See Karl Popper, *The Logic of Scientific Discovery* (London: Hutchinson, 1959).

45. This is an explicit exercise—step 6, the sensitivity check—in ACH. See Heuer, *Psychology of Intelligence Analysis*, 105–6. This step should be required in the coordination of NIEs prepared in advance of decision making before armed conflict.

CHAPTER 10

The Missing Link: The Analyst–Collector Relationship

JAMES B. BRUCE

Although considerable attention has long been focused on the relationship between the analyst and the policymaker, a key determinant of analytic effectiveness is found at the nexus of the analyst and the collector (see figure 10.1). This chapter explores this critical relationship through a brief examination of eight cases of intelligence failure. It shows that *when collection fails, the probability of analytic failure increases dramatically*. Better analysis can help reduce this vulnerability. A greater appreciation by analysts for their significant dependency on collected intelligence will help illuminate how attentive collectors and analysts can improve the odds for intelligence success.

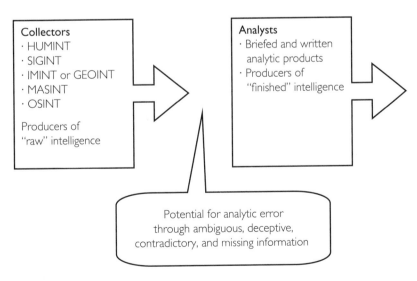

Figure 10.1 The Collection–Analysis Nexus

Intelligence Failure: Eight Instructive Cases

The following case studies of intelligence failure were selected because of their intrinsic importance in intelligence history. They do not constitute a "representative sample" that shows the overall record of intelligence performance over the long period they span, from 1941 to 2002. But they are highly instructive for what they reveal about the important linkage between intelligence collection and analysis. What these cases illustrate, above all, is that collection failures—shown chiefly in the key information that was *not* collected and in some cases erroneous or misleading information that was—are almost certain to result in analysis failures. Other analytic failures can result from information that is collected but is misinterpreted, especially if denial and deception and a faulty analytic mind-set delimit consideration of alternative hypotheses.

From Pearl Harbor to Iraq and a half-dozen major failures between them, we can discern a repetitive pattern of collection shortfalls whose effects can be traced through the analytic process that was itself equally deficient in dealing with them. On the collection side, the single most important factor accounting for failure is the impact of intelligence denial—namely, effective countermeasures taken by an intelligence target that prevented successful collection against it. The impact of denial, as nearly all these cases illustrate, is *missing information* needed for analysis. On the analytic side, the failure to correct for the impact of missing information, when combined with a lack of imagination and the impact of faulty assumptions, are almost surefire predictors of analytic failure. Other factors, too, such as poor collection requirements and poor information sharing also "pile on," helping to ensure intelligence failure.

Pearl Harbor: Failure to Warn of a Surprise Military Attack

The failure to warn US military and political decision makers of the Japanese attack in the early morning hours of December 7, 1941, had many roots.[1] On a just-awakening Hawaiian island where a sizable portion of the US naval fleet lay at rest and vulnerable to attack, several hundred Japanese warplanes appeared without warning and, facing negligible air defenses, systematically and methodically sank or heavily damaged twenty-one vessels, including four battleships. In addition, 164 aircraft were destroyed at four nearby airfields. The capable Japanese bombers and fighters that attacked were launched in darkened skies from six aircraft carriers that had steamed from Japan to Hawaii completely unanticipated and undetected by US intelligence. "Secrecy and deception having effectively screened the movements of the Japanese task force," US intelligence had failed to understand Japanese intentions to attack US territory, as well as the place, time, and strength of the attack.[2] Apart from the enormous loss of naval vessels and army aircraft, more than 2,400 Americans were killed in this historic warning failure, an unprecedented loss of life in a single attack.

How was this large Japanese flotilla, consisting of thirty-three warships and auxiliary craft en route for eleven days, missed when the US military should have been alert to its arrival, and when both the army and navy had in fact collected key information that should have warned decision makers? And, further—even lacking "smoking gun" evidence that an attack was brewing or imminent—when enough information was already in possession of US intelligence to forewarn the military about this devastating destruction of American forces?[3]

For our purposes, the answers explaining this failed warning can be summarized in four key facts:

- *Collection degraded by denial and deception (D&D).* The Japanese prepared and conducted this attack in such a way as to neutralize US intelligence. In concealing their intentions to go to war with the United States along with any tactical information that might have tipped off the attack, their successful denial of important information to US collectors enfeebled analysis. They also conducted related deception operations involving naval and other military forces, as well as deceptive diplomatic activity that further weakened US intelligence capabilities to anticipate attack.[4]
- *Poor sharing.* What information US intelligence did collect that might have made a difference was not fully exploited, in part because it was not shared between the army (reading decrypted Japanese diplomatic cables) and the navy (reading decrypted Japanese naval communications), despite their shared responsibility to warn. Poor sharing of limited collection greatly impeded warning analysis.[5]
- *Signal-to-noise ratio.* Despite the availability of some kinds of information, the signal-to-noise ratio greatly impaired warning: An abundance of marginal or irrelevant information overwhelmed and obscured a few vital pieces that might have enabled successful warning if they had been noticed and properly appreciated for their real worth.[6]
- *Faulty assumptions.* Whatever their capabilities, the Japanese had not conveyed their intentions to attack. Analysts not only did not expect a Japanese attack on Pearl Harbor; some actually assumed that it was a very-low-probability event because an attack on Hawaii would mean, according to a key figure at Pearl Harbor, "national suicide" for Japan.[7]

A retrospective look at the Pearl Harbor warning failure suggests that Japanese D&D success against US intelligence was a vital requirement for a successful surprise attack. The failure to collect any information at all on the massive eleven-day transit of the Japanese task force across the Pacific Ocean deprived analysts of the best possible evidence that would have forewarned of the attack. Distracted by the "noise" of tangential and unrelated information, hobbled by poor sharing of what key information had been collected, and constrained by faulty assumptions, analysts' inability to understand or counter effective Japanese D&D ensured the historic warning failure.

Soviet Missiles in Cuba: Failure to Warn of Covert Emplacements

When the Board of National Estimates considered in September 1962 whether the Soviet Union would attempt to secretly install offensive nuclear missiles in Cuba, just ninety miles off US shores, the resulting special national intelligence estimate essentially concluded that the Soviets would not. Lacking good evidence to show that the Soviet leaders would attempt such a risky military provocation that would dramatically tilt the nuclear balance—and lacking evidence to the contrary—the estimate reasoned that the Soviet leaders would not attempt such a dangerously reckless move that would risk destabilizing the evolving superpower relationship. According to the estimate, a secret missile emplacement in Cuba "would be incompatible with Soviet practice to date and with Soviet policy as we presently estimate it. It would indicate a far greater willingness to increase the level of risk in US–Soviet relations than the USSR has displayed thus far, and consequently would have important policy implications with respect to other areas and other problems in East–West relations."[8]

The analysts who imputed such seemingly rational motives for Soviet restraint were proven wrong when U-2 aerial photography on October 14, 1962, revealed the construction of SS-4 and SS-5 road-mobile missile sites about fifty miles from Havana, less than a month after the estimate was issued. Two factors stand out in explaining why the analysts got it wrong:

- *Collection degraded by D&D.* Key information was missing at the time of the estimate. Effective Soviet D&D prevented US collection from acquiring good evidence earlier that would have better informed analysis.
- *Assumptions misled.* In the absence of good information—that is, empirical evidence—analysts relied on their own assumptions. Thus their reasoning in this case was flawed by faulty assumptions.

Soviet D&D efforts to install the missiles undetected were impressive by any measure. The decision-making process and its implementation were heavily compartmented in the Soviet Union. Only a handful of Politburo members and as few as five military officers were cleared into the planning. The cargo being shipped, and its destination and unloading, were heavily concealed to avert US detection. D&D measures to support this operation included "loading from different docks in Soviet ports, false bills of lading, nighttime unloading of missiles in Cuba, and circuitous routes of delivery. These efforts were complemented by the use of public disinformation campaigns, false media reports and high-level, private Soviet denials and 'reassurances' from [Communist Party of the Soviet Union] General Secretary [Nikita] Khrushchev, Foreign Minister Gromyko, and Soviet Ambassador to the United States Anatoly Dobrynin, who acknowledged in his memoirs that he had not been informed of the delivery of offensive missiles in Cuba."[9]

Supporting deception, successful denial took a major toll on analysis. The lack of information on the emplacement of the missiles over a several-month period (until the October discovery by U-2 overflights) severely impaired the analytic process because failed collection ensured a more prominent role for analysts' assumptions in preparing the estimate.[10] This matters less when the assumptions are identified, explicitly acknowledged, and correct. But when they are hidden, their impact is insidious, and when they are wrong, as they were in this case, they doomed the estimate to a failed warning forecast.

Analysts might have been able to overcome the impact of failed collection with better tradecraft such as the use of structured brainstorming and multiple hypotheses or scenarios to force consideration of more than one outcome.[11] In addition, analysts needed to undertake a vigorous effort to identify their assumptions—in particular those concerning the putative rationality of the Soviets' propensity for risk aversion and the strategic calculus that led the Soviets to underestimate US resolve to preserve the nuclear status quo.[12] Without identifying such critical assumptions—now possible using Key Assumptions Check tradecraft (see chapter 14)—analysts could not easily assess their impact on steering the analytic process to erroneous judgments. These important lessons remain for future analytic puzzles, especially those compounded by major D&D.

The Yom Kippur War: Failure to Warn

When Egypt and Syria joined in a surprise military attack against Israel in October 1973, analysts in the US intelligence community—and worse, in Israel—failed to warn of the well-planned Arab invasion.[13] This failure is especially notable given the high state of tension and political hostilities between the belligerents and the general expectations for an outbreak of war since the Israelis had pounded the Arab states and seized so much of their land in the 1967 Six-Day War. Indeed, the alert levels in Israel were high during the autumn of 1973, and the likelihood of an Arab invasion had been hotly debated in the months preceding the attack. It is also notable because, unlike most of the other cases examined here, collection largely succeeded, and the failure of analysis cannot be easily blamed on poor collection. In light of the political context, the general expectation for war, and good collection, why did warning fail?

Most students of the Yom Kippur War agree that Israeli analysts *did* have sufficient information at hand to justify a clear warning of imminent invasion.[14] But the analysts had failed to make the call, partly out of fear of raising false alarms (the "cry wolf" syndrome) and partly because they clung to false assumptions about Arab intentions, as well as capabilities. In contrast with most of the other cases examined here, Israeli warning analysts had ample information in their possession, but they either disregarded or misinterpreted what information they had.[15]

To be sure, their warning task was greatly complicated by the deception operations that Egypt and Syria had mounted against the Israelis. The ploy of frequent military exercises amassing troops near the borders was reinforced by public complaints of poor military equipment and maintenance, deceptive statements belying the secret Egyptian–Syrian military agreement, and public posturing for Henry Kissinger's peace initiative just one month before the invasion.[16]

For their part, the Israelis were disadvantaged by successful Arab denial of collection that was good enough to impair their full understanding of the Arab deception. They also clung to erroneous assumptions about what they called "the Concept," a view that presumed the necessity of Arab air superiority over Israel prior to attack, which did not exist at that time. The Concept also relied on the credibility of Israel's deterrent posture to an enemy that was undeterred. Analytically impaired with faulty assumptions, Israeli (and US) analysts did not succeed in understanding the Arab mind, to which the "rationality" of the improbable invasion made perfect sense.[17]

Perhaps the key issue in the Yom Kippur War warning failure is the reliance on unquestioned assumptions. This case dramatically illustrates that when assumptions drive analysis—almost always unwittingly—analysts need to identify and aggressively challenge them. It is notable that Israeli intelligence formalized an internal procedure of devil's advocacy following the Yom Kippur warning debacle precisely for this purpose, to ensure that critical but unquestioned assumptions would no longer go unchallenged on important intelligence issues, such as warning of a surprise attack.

Revolution in Iran: Unnoticed

The abrupt fall of the once highly popular Shah Mohammad Reza Pahlavi of Iran to Ayatollah Ruhollah Khomeini, a radical Islamic cleric then living in Paris, marked a genuine revolution that shook the foundation of Iranian society and shattered its body politic. In contrast to the countless coups d'état that populate political instability databases everywhere, a genuine revolution like this one only comes along a few times a century. Yet analysts missed the Iranian Revolution, not fully comprehending its profound meaning until well after it was over.[18]

How did this happen? Again, this case illustrates a core idea of the collection–analysis nexus: Failed analysis is often only one step behind failed collection. But analysis done smartly—even in the face of poor collection—is not irretrievably doomed to failure if it can learn to develop analytic correctives to collection shortfalls.

Of course, the key information that analysts lacked would have revealed the shah's regime as increasingly unpopular—actually hated by growing legions of Islamic radicals—and rapidly losing support among the secular middle classes as well. It would have described a resurgence of Shia Islam in its most fundamentalist strains and a weak and corrupt system of government whose capacity to govern and political legitimacy were increasingly in question. Above all it would have exposed a growing, perhaps unbridgeable chasm between the angry clerics then preaching powerful antigovernment sermons in mosques throughout Iran and a secular and modernizing dictatorship increasingly disconnected from a restive population that it wrongly believed to the end still supported it.

Where was information like this to be found? It was in the "Persian street"—in the mosques and the souks. And it was there for the asking. But US intelligence on Iranian political and societal issues was notably lacking. According to Kenneth Pollack, "the volume of CIA political reporting on Iran in the early 1970s actually dropped below that of the late 1940s, and the US embassy in Tehran had few officers who could speak Farsi or had previously served in Iran."[19] This shortfall was partly by design, as the ten CIA case officers had no real presence outside the diplomatic circles in downtown Tehran, and they focused on Soviet requirements or economic and energy issues. Iran's domestic political issues were effectively off limits to US intelligence, by policy deferential to the

Pahlavi regime. And overdependence on the shah's intelligence service, the SAVAK, to provide the United States with information the shah's regime either did not have or did not want to share was a costly mistake.[20] US human intelligence (HUMINT) collection was blinded to the brewing revolution.

Lacking needed information on the radicalization of Iranian society and the growing subversive power of the clerics, intelligence analysts again were ignorant of reality and comfortable in their assumptions—which were mostly wrong. In retrospect, the analysts involved seemed addicted to the mind-set that the political disturbances in the preceding year were unimportant in the face of a strong and decisive leader who had demonstrated past resiliency and a capacity to take whatever steps were needed to retain control. In fact, this leader was not nearly as strong and decisive as widely believed. Unbeknownst to US analysts (but known to a few French doctors), the leader with a reputation for taking decisive actions against internal unrest was instead terminally ill.[21] Thus a key analytic assumption about the shah's capacity to act was wrong.

In failing to correctly assess a revolution in the making and a declining leader's ability to manage it, this case provides another illustration of the triumph of faulty assumptions over the absence of needed information. This failure, while rooted in poor analyst understanding of limited collection, highlights the dangers of clinging to unquestioned assumptions and the demonstrable lack of analytic imagination.

Indian Nuclear Tests: Surprise on the Subcontinent

The failure to warn US policymakers of impending nuclear tests in the politically volatile South Asia region is also rooted in the debilitating combination of poor collection and poor analysis. But it was aided and abetted by an effective Indian D&D effort that deprived the United States of the kind of information that had successfully tipped analysts to Indian test preparations just three years earlier. Also, deceptive diplomatic statements by India's foreign minister were calculated to reassure Washington that the Indian government had no intentions of testing nuclear weapons.[22]

How did the analysts miss this one? As in the other cases discussed here, the failure begins with successful denial and poor collection. No good intelligence, human or technical, forewarned of imminent testing.[23] But the open press reporting during the elections just months before should have alerted analysts to the campaign intentions of the Bharatiya Janata Party (BJP), which had just come to power, to make India a full nuclear power. Open-source information of decided intelligence interest was either underemphasized or disregarded.[24]

That open press reports did not play a more prominent role in this instance is probably because other collection methods, notably space-borne imagery, had proven so accurate in the past. The attempted 1995 tests had been halted through a forceful US diplomatic demarche that was based on detailed imagery that was also shown—we now know, mistakenly—to the Indians in 1995. This authorized disclosure revealed how US intelligence could detect preparations for testing from space. The lesson was not lost on the Indians, themselves a space power with their own imagery satellites. From this demarche, they learned to prepare their next tests more carefully so as not to repeat their 1995 attempt, which was aborted by outstanding intelligence support to US diplomacy. This time they averted detection by skillfully avoiding satellite observation and by preventing telltale signs beforehand that an imagery satellite might photograph.[25] This adaptation represents sophisticated intelligence denial based on a good understanding of US classified collection capabilities, which the Indians had learned through the backfired demarche process and through damaging press leaks that further disclosed these capabilities.[26]

With previously reliable technical collection now enfeebled and analysts unwitting about these collection limitations, their overdependency on information that never arrived facilitated failure. But it did not guarantee it. Helped along by robust Indian D&D and poor US use of open sources, the failure also relied on an invalid assumption: that the BJP election platform had no greater credibility than any in the United States—an ethnocentric view of how politicians might behave if they acted like Americans, whose fidelity to campaign rhetoric wanes discernibly once the reality of office holding sets in. Not so in this case. Further, the Indians had already demonstrated the technical capability to test just three years earlier. So it is fair to ask why this readiness and capability did not form part of the analysts' understanding of what to expect when a new and hard-line party publicly advocating nuclear weapons had just come to power. This analytic mindset ill served an important warning situation where intelligence collection proved unable to deliver the goods. Better awareness among analysts of their collection dependencies, of the D&D countermeasures that smart intelligence targets can mount against US collection, and of the potential for surprise when discernible political change is afoot would all have mitigated the impact of faulty assumptions.

Soviet Biological Weapons: A (Too) Late-Breaking Story

By the time US intelligence analysts began to understand the enormous scope and scale of the Soviets' biological weapons (BW) program built in the 1970s and 1980s, the Soviet system was about to collapse.[27] Yet during the Cold War, the Soviet government had assembled a daunting capability to research, develop, test, and deploy highly lethal bioweapons. Because BW was such a heavily compartmented program inside the Soviet Union, no one in the West had any understanding at all about the magnitude of the effort and the potential menace it posed to the United States. For US intelligence, the issue was all but missing.[28]

This blissful ignorance changed with startling revelations made by two Soviet defectors, Vladimir Pesechnik and Ken Alibek, who had held senior positions in these programs.[29] Alibek disclosed that the Soviet leaders had begun a huge, secret BW program shortly after signing the Biological Weapons Convention in 1972 that outlawed these weapons. By the time that Alibek defected twenty years later, the Soviets had covertly developed and stockpiled hundreds of tons of anthrax and dozens of tons of plague and smallpox for use as weapons. According to this high-level defector, the Soviets had harnessed BW for single-warhead intercontinental ballistic missiles in the 1970s and had begun in 1988 to develop anthrax, plague, and smallpox for use on the multiple-warhead SS-18 missiles for targeting American cities. The Soviets had also conducted research for deployment of BW warheads on cruise missiles.[30] With the Soviets employing more than sixty thousand people in over sixty installations involved in research, testing, production, and storage of lethal bacterial and viral agents, how did analysts miss this several-decade military effort?[31]

The pattern is familiar: Poor collection foreshadows analytic failure. In this case, before the defectors there was almost no collection at all. But BW was certainly one of the hardest targets in one of the most impenetrable countries because it ranked among the most secret of all Soviet programs. Even as late as 1990, only four members of the ruling Soviet Politburo were even aware of it. The D&D effort itself was massive. The huge program was cloaked in convincing cover stories, such as pharmaceuticals and genetic research; no discernible evidence could have revealed military involvement; and US inspectors were foiled with elaborate ruses. In one instance of an outbreak of anthrax in Sverdlovsk where over a hundred people had died in a BW accident in 1979, a highly thorough cover-up masked all possible indications of a BW connection.[32] Like the rest of the world, US intelligence was clueless.

Until the defectors arrived, analysts had no substantial information to analyze. Still, they did not much hypothesize about the threat possibility either, and there appears to have been scant attention given to it in national intelligence estimates or other analytic efforts that might have addressed this significant threat. It does not seem to have generated meaningful collection requirements or become a worthy analytic issue in the intelligence community.

Apart from the lack of collection that provided no evidence for a BW program, this failure seems equally rooted in an analytic mind-set that combined two key attributes. The first was that there was little or no imagination that a strategically significant and well-funded BW program would have been entirely consistent with a massive strategic military machine that sought superiority over US forces in nearly every way that mattered. The second was that analysts are understandably disinclined to entertain beliefs without evidence, especially because outside experts (notably the prominent Harvard biologist Matthew Meselson) heavily discounted a Soviet BW program, and modest US experience with its own BW effort had been shut down in 1969.[33] So why should intelligence analysts expect the Soviet Union to develop BW on a massive scale?

In light of what we now know about this significant Soviet military program, the failure to understand it when it mattered most to US defense planners reveals a disturbing lack of analytic imagination—an inability to generate high-impact if low-probability hypotheses. This analytic disability can only be addressed through concerted tradecraft and better management practices, as well as fully understanding and addressing collection requirements and gaps. Such approaches could involve Structured Brainstorming, Red Team Analysis, and "worst case" yet unimagined scenarios, then mobilize effective analytic strategies to compensate for poor collection—then demand better collection where analytic concerns may justify it. The Silberman-Robb WMD Commission report warns of insufficient attention to precisely threats of this kind and the need for substantial analytic capabilities worthy of the threat.[34]

September 11, 2001: Echoes of Pearl Harbor

The "Day of Infamy" that President Franklin Roosevelt called the Japanese attack on Pearl Harbor was repeated sixty years later by the successful execution of a terrorist plot in which four seized US commercial airliners were deployed as missiles to topple the World Trade Center towers and smash into the Pentagon.[35] When the dust had settled, three thousand people were dead, overwhelmingly American civilians who did not have a clue that their country was so unprepared for this kind of bolt from the blue. Though many will argue whether the 9/11 terrorist attacks were a strategic warning failure (the character and importance of the terrorist threat was not adequately conveyed to decision makers), others believe that it is at least an open-and-shut case of a tactical warning failure (the event itself was simply not foretold in intelligence). Still others argue that 9/11 was not a warnable event. But there is no disagreement that the warning performance against terrorist attacks before September 11 will not serve the nation after that fateful date.

In diagnosing the intelligence part of the larger government-wide systemic failure, we can see the same four prominent features of Pearl Harbor repeating themselves in 9/11:[36]

- *Collection degraded by D&D.* Al-Qaeda's outstanding operational security was every bit as good as that the Japanese had exercised to mask the surprise attack on Pearl Harbor. In successfully denying intelligence collection against the plot—chiefly foiling needed HUMINT and signals intelligence (SIGINT) penetrations—the terrorist plotters left the analysts largely empty handed when better information would have eased the burden of analysis. The key information—attack planning—was missing.[37]
- *Poor sharing.* A major finding of the 9/11 Commission echoed the Pearl Harbor experience that unshared information degrades warning.[38] Just as the army and the navy were reluctant to provide each other with intelligence in 1941 largely for bureaucratic reasons, the Federal Bureau of Investigation and Central Intelligence Agency appear to have repeated the pattern in 2000 and 2001. Each had information that would have helped the other—and would have helped the nation—had they opted to share it in time.[39]
- *Signal-to-noise ratio.* As Director of Central Intelligence George Tenet told the 9/11 Commission, the system was "blinking red" during the summer of 2001.[40] Among the countless facts, meaningless chaff, and tidbits of terrorist-related intelligence, there were so few pieces of salient information that pointed to the 9/11 planning that they were easily swamped in the surrounding "noise."[41]

- *Faulty assumptions.* The conventional wisdom among most analysts was that terrorist attacks against the United States would most likely occur abroad, not against the US homeland, and that airline hijackings would entail hostage taking. Mass suicide attacks against high-density office buildings in the homeland were not part of the collection or analytic posture.[42]

The convergence of these factors reduced the likelihood of successful warning of 9/11 to near-impossible odds. The 9/11 Commission is certainly correct in emphasizing the importance of imagination in analysis and the lack of it leading up to the surprise attack. But it is misleading at best to characterize the missed warning as a failure "to connect the dots." While they were mired in tens of thousands, perhaps hundreds of thousands, of terrorist threat warnings in 2001, analysts had far too little plot-related intelligence to have specifically warned of the coming catastrophe.[43] The essence of the intelligence problem was less the failure to connect the dots than the overall lack of needed dots—more attack-related dots—in the first place. To connect the dots, we first need to collect them.

However, analysts too have a major responsibility to exercise imagination, to define and direct collection requirements, and to produce more reliable analysis when collection against hard warning problems is likely to come up short. The first crucial step is to notice that collection is coming up short—then act on it.

Iraq's WMDs: The Weapons That Were Not There

Despite the high expectations of finding WMDs in Iraq after the invasion in 2003, US and coalition forces began to face the nettlesome fact that they were coming up dry.[44] A dedicated search team, the Iraq Survey Group, also failed to uncover or locate any WMDs anywhere in Iraq. This would not be so significant were it not for the facts that US intelligence, most notably in a national intelligence estimate (NIE) published in October 2002, had claimed that Saddam Hussein's Iraq possessed fairly significant WMD capabilities across a broad spectrum of prohibited weapons and that the US decision to invade and topple Saddam's regime was predicated on these claims. Intelligence failed.

The 2002 Iraq WMD NIE claimed the following:[45]

- Iraq had an active chemical weapons (CW) program; it was producing mustard, sarin, cyclosarin, and VX; and it had stockpiled as much as one hundred to five hundred metric tons of CW agents, much of it produced in the year prior to the estimate. This judgment, issued with "high confidence," was wrong.
- Iraq had offensive biological weapons, including mobile BW labs; all key aspects of the program were active; and most elements were larger and more advanced than they were during the Gulf War. This judgment, also issued with "high confidence," was wrong.

- Iraq had begun to reconstitute its nuclear weapons program and, if left unchecked, would probably have a nuclear weapon during this decade. This judgment, issued with "moderate confidence," was wrong.
- Iraq was developing an unmanned aerial vehicle capability, probably intended to deliver BW agents, even as far away as the US homeland. This was wrong.
- Iraq had ballistic missiles capable of ranges that exceeded limits allowed under UN sanctions, and it had retained a covert force of up to a few dozen missiles. Wrong on the covert force finding, the NIE's only correct judgment was that the missiles exceeded the UN range limit.

The NIE was wrong on four of the five major WMD issues, so it is fair to ask how analysis had performed so poorly. If we look first at collection, on nearly every measure that counts US intelligence failed. The combined resources of human, signals, and imagery intelligence had performed miserably against an Iraqi regime that wielded a robust D&D capability against them.[46] None of the three major collection disciplines had been able to produce direct evidence of WMDs—or of their absence—at the time of the estimate's preparation in October 2002.[47] Nearly all US collection that characterized Saddam's WMD programs had come much earlier, predating Iraq's covert dismantling of the programs in the early 1990s. *All* evidence afterward was spotty and fragmentary, suggestive, and never conclusive. Analysts seemed unaware of this.

An additional dimension of analytic failure is the unwarranted confidence attached to the major NIE judgments when the evidence for them was so tenuous. The judgments on Iraq's BW and CW programs were characterized as "high confidence" and on nuclear reconstitution as "moderate confidence." We now know that the evidence available at the time simply did not support this exaggerated confidence. In the future, analysts will need to do much better at aligning their confidence levels with evidence and conveying their findings to policymakers with greater specification of analytic uncertainty and the basis for their confidence levels on important issues.

In fairness, where analysts lacked good evidence for such programs, they also lacked good evidence demonstrating that none existed. With the notable exception of a single defector's reporting that the nuclear program had been shut down,[48] analysts were hard pressed to identify persuasive evidence to overturn the prevailing intelligence community consensus, built up over the preceding decade, that the Iraqi regime was hell-bent to assemble a significant arsenal of BW, CW, and soon nuclear weapons—all the more worrisome in the wake of 9/11. Iraq's history and past practices supported this view. Saddam had previously used CW against Iraqi Kurds and neighboring Iran. He conducted a sweeping and effective D&D program that had essentially neutralized US intelligence in Iraq, and he blunted the UN inspection process that had been set up to confirm their destruction—all this conduct reinforcing Western suspicions that he must have had something to hide.

As in the previous cases, lacking solid evidence, analysts relied on weaker assumptions—which again were mostly wrong. But the most egregious failure was to insufficiently challenge the evidence. To do this adequately would have required better tradecraft and a better understanding of the collection process, especially its limitations. Some of the evidence for the nuclear reconstitution hypothesis turned out to be based on forged documents (reporting Iraq's intentions to import yellowcake uranium from Niger). Some of the key evidence for CW was based on poor understanding of imagery collection (misinterpreting Samarra-type trucks with CW transshipments). And the most important evidence for BW was based on fabricated reporting (stories spun by "Curveball" that made their way to the Defense Intelligence Agency from a German liaison).[49]

In hindsight this all looks so clear. But the pressures of a twenty-one-day deadline to produce the NIE encouraged more superficiality than depth, discouraged more "structured" or systematic tradecraft than deadline-driven journalism, and exposed the typically poor understanding that analysts bring to the collection process. Had the crippling collection limitations been highlighted during or, preferably, well before the short-fuse NIE (which structured tradecraft might have done), it is far more likely that analysts would have arrived at more accurate judgments—or at the very least issued the wrong ones with less confidence.

Learning from Failure

Lessons from the cases examined here leave no doubt about the vital role of intelligence collection in the analysis process. The key findings are summarized in the matrix shown in table 10.1.

Collection is incomplete and can only provide a sample. Since all collection is sampling, we don't know how much is missing, and we cannot know whether it is "representative" of what it purports to show or of what we need to fully understand the issue. It is safe to assume it is never complete and almost always unrepresentative. Assuming otherwise can introduce error very early in analysis.

Still, in all the cases examined here, better collection would have helped analysis and in some cases enormously. If only analysts had known of the Japanese carrier task group as it steamed toward Pearl Harbor or that the Soviet Politburo had decided to abruptly overturn the nuclear balance with the United States by sneaking nuclear missiles into Cuba or that Saddam had actually dismantled his WMD program in secret while he used D&D in a policy of calculated ambiguity to hoodwink inspectors, foil intelligence, and deter enemies with weapons he did not have.[50] If only they had known of bin Laden's plot. With more pertinent and better facts to analyze, analysts are more likely to succeed.

But the reality is that while better collection might have been achievable in some cases, in others it was nearly impossible. The practical difficulties of penetrating the top decision-making circles of closed polities such as the former Soviet Union, Saddam's Iraq, or present-day North Korea must be appreciated for what they are. So, too, infiltrating the top ranks of terrorist groups such as al-Qaeda is likely to remain more an aspiration than a reality. Satellites can image a building's roof but cannot look inside or read the minds of human targets we seek to understand or change. Better collection requires

Table 10.1 Explaining Failure: Patterns in Eight Cases

Case	Collection				Analysis				
	Key Information Missing	Information Not Shared	Poor Requirements	Denial and Deception[a]	Poor Imagination	Signal-to-Noise Ratio	Faulty Assumptions	Information Misinterpreted	Uncorrected Impact of Denial
Pearl Harbor		X	X	XX	X	X	X		X
Cuban Missile Crisis	X			XX	X		X		X
Yom Kippur War		X		XX	X		X	X	X
Iranian Revolution	X			X	X		X		X
Soviet biological weapons	X		X	XX	X		X		X
India nuclear weapons	X			X	X		X		X
9/11 attacks	X	X	X	X	X	X	X		X
Iraqi WMDs	X			XX	X		X	X	X

[a]X = Only denial is present; significant deception is not in evidence. XX = Both denial and deception are present.

more effective sources and methods, and far better counter-D&D capabilities than we now have. Better collection also requires greater analyst engagement and expertise, and better guidance and direction in the requirements process where analysts have major, if less well-attended responsibilities.

Where much-improved collection was just not possible in some of the failure cases examined here (for example, Soviet BW and the Cuban crisis) or not needed (for example, in the Yom Kippur War), more caveated judgments and much improved analysis certainly was. How might this have been achieved? The principal correctives for better analysis in the face of major collection deficiencies must begin with a significantly enhanced understanding of the collection process and its limitations. Analysts require a much deeper understanding of the technical collection disciplines, as well as the human recruitment and vetting process.[51] For the most part, however, all-source analysts receive little or no training in collection methods and too few opportunities to learn them on the job. If analysts do not fully comprehend the collection capabilities at their disposal, they cannot fully exploit them. Similarly, if they do not fully understand the collection limitations that impair their analysis, they can neither improve collection nor correct for such impairments in the analyses they produce.

To guard against the pernicious impact of collection limitations, analysts must learn to acknowledge—then correct—an inherent tendency to substitute hidden assumptions for missing information. That this practice is typically unwitting illustrates the importance of identifying hidden assumptions and their effects on analytic results. If the assumptions-to-evidence ratio does not favor evidence, then the tradecraft that analysts use must be good enough to expose and challenge the assumptions that inevitably shape their analysis. The Key Assumptions Check is designed precisely to do this.

Better analytic tradecraft is also a sine qua non for addressing and correcting the inevitable collection shortfalls. Here greater use of "alternative analysis" and other structured tradecraft should be reinforced and even accelerated.[52] If the tradecraft of intelligence analysis is no better than a "classified journalism" that reports and interprets fragmentary information superficially—as it typically does in current intelligence and sometimes estimative products too—then we cannot realistically expect fewer intelligence failures, especially where collection is weak or unproductive against effective denial. Structured and rigorous tradecraft—especially that which exposes hidden assumptions and features alternative hypotheses, interpretations, or scenarios—provides essential hedges against analytic failure.

Along with faulty assumptions, these case studies show that the two most important impairments analysts need to overcome are the failure to correct for the impact of denial and the failure of analytic imagination—each of which can be successfully addressed through the following techniques. Correcting for the impact of denial requires that analysts pose the right questions, consider the deception hypothesis, and brainstorm additional hypotheses:

- When assessing hard problems, the analyst must ask: What key information am I missing? Is it missing because the target is thwarting efforts to collect it? Why is collection not better, and if it were, what might I be seeing? What new information would change my assessment, and why am I not seeing it? How good are the target's denial capabilities against collection, and precisely how, where, and why is the target defeating it?

- The analyst should introduce the deception hypothesis, which, more than any other alternative explanation, will invite a cascade of additional questions that will highlight the target's possible objectives and means, and the collection limitations that may keep them hidden.

- The analyst should enlist the help of his or her colleagues in a group exercise to brainstorm additional hypotheses that may highlight further alternative explanations. Outstanding techniques for this are Structured Brainstorming, Red Teaming, Contingency "What-If" Analysis, and High-Impact / Low-Probability Analysis.

The best insurance against failures of imagination is to generate alternative hypotheses. In the cases examined here, it seems clear that analysts simply did not imagine that the Japanese intended a surprise attack against Pearl Harbor, that the Soviet Union would secretly place nuclear missiles into Cuba, that weakened Arab states would attack Israel, or that a radical Islamic revolution would topple the shah's government and transform Iran. Nor did they imagine that a new ruling party in India would conduct surprise nuclear weapons tests; that the Soviets would secretly build a massive BW program after signing a treaty prohibiting them from doing so; that suicidal terrorists would seize US commercial airliners, slam them into office buildings, and kill three thousand people; or that Saddam Hussein would shut down his WMD programs in secret while thwarting efforts by the UN and Western nations to find that out. We've seen that poor collection greatly elevates the importance of analytic imagination. To achieve it, analysts must significantly increase their use of SATs to generate hypotheses about unlikely but consequential events, even—perhaps especially—if they are otherwise hard to imagine.

The integral relationship between collection and analysis is the overarching lesson of the cases examined here. To summarize, when collection fails, it greatly increases the probability that analysis too will fail. The responsibility to produce analytic judgments on the basis of ambiguous, contradictory, and missing information is a tall one. Of the three, handling missing information is the most difficult. We currently have no analytic model or tradecraft that addresses this issue. And most analysts are poorly equipped to deal with effective denial. Like the patients whose terminal disease takes root long before the symptoms are noticed, many analysts do not even know denial when they experience it.

This chapter has focused exclusively on intelligence failures.[53] We can surmise a counterpoint lesson: When collection improves, so too will analysis. When analysts can better appreciate the limited collection on which they are basing their arguments, they will do a better job of assessing the possible outcomes and placing more credible probabilities against a variety of outcomes. The intelligence community would be wise to invest in a more robust lessons-learned program that unpacks successes as well as failures.

Such studies should identify an optimal relationship between analyst and collector when things go right.

The most important first priority for any analyst when assigned a new portfolio is to prepare a thorough assessment of how good or poor collection is against that target. Where and how is collection weak? What are its major limitations and shortfalls? He or she should ask: How can I learn more about these capabilities? What can I do to better exploit them? Can I do anything to help direct or improve them? What D&D counter-measures does my target use to defeat them? How should my analysis adjust for this?

Lacking another collection revolution in the twenty-first century to match the technical breakthroughs that began fifty years ago, smart and seasoned analysts and collectors alike will appreciate why much improved collection is not likely to magically appear on our doorstep in the foreseeable future. Because analysts will have to live with underperforming collection as far out as we can see, they will be well served to comprehend its implications and prepare themselves for much more challenging analysis that can surmount the collection roots of intelligence failures.

Notes

1. Key sources for this case study are Roberta Wohlstetter's classic, *Pearl Harbor: Warning and Decision* (Palo Alto, CA: Stanford University Press, 1962), and John Hughes-Wilson, *Military Intelligence Blunders* (New York: Carroll & Graf, 1999), chap. 4.
2. Cynthia M. Grabo, *Anticipating Surprise: Analysis for Warning Intelligence* (Washington, DC: Joint Military Intelligence College, 2002), 123.
3. This example of Pearl Harbor along with the Yom Kippur War case below together represent only two of eight cases examined here where there was arguably enough information to have made the call. Of course we only know this in hindsight after a reconstruction of events reveals what the analysts *should* have known. But the cases also illustrate other factors at work (discussed below) that greatly reduced their probability of getting it right.
4. Wohlstetter, *Pearl Harbor*, 121–22; also see box 12.1 in chap. 12 for a summary of Japanese D&D.
5. Ibid., 394.
6. As Wohlstetter explained it in her famous study, "in short, we failed to anticipate Pearl Harbor not for want of the relevant materials, but because of the plethora of irrelevant ones." Wohlstetter, *Pearl Harbor*, 387. Another historian explained it similarly: "The salient fact about the intelligence disaster at Pearl Harbor is that most of the evidence was hidden by a blizzard of other information at the time. . . . Quite simply, the clamor of other voices drowned out the Pearl Harbor material." Hughes-Wilson, *Military Intelligence Blunders*, 73.
7. Adm. Husband E. Kimmel, the senior naval officer at Pearl and commander in chief of the Pacific Fleet, quoted in Wohlstetter, *Pearl Harbor*, 55.
8. *The Military Buildup in Cuba*, Special National Intelligence Estimate No. 85-3-62, September 19, 1962, 2, from declassified excerpts in *CIA Documents on the Cuban Missile Crisis, 1962*, ed. Mary S. McAuliffe (Washington, DC: CIA History Staff, 1992), 93. Other sources for this case study include articles in *Intelligence and the Cuban Missile Crisis*, ed.

James G. Blight and David A. Welch (London: Frank Cass, 1998), esp. Raymond A. Garthoff, "U.S. Intelligence in the Cuban Missile Crisis," chap. 2, and Sherman Kent, "A Crucial Estimate Relived," *Studies in Intelligence* 8, no. 2 (Spring 1964), www.cia.gov/csi/books/shermankent/9crucial.html.

9. Peter Clement, "The Cuban Missile Crisis," in *The Directorate of Intelligence: Fifty Years of Informing Policy, 1952–2002*, expanded ed. (Washington, DC: Center for the Study of Intelligence, CIA, 2002), 91. See also James H. Hanson, "Soviet Deception in the Cuban Missile Crisis," *Studies in Intelligence* 46, no. 1 (2002), www.cia.gov/csi/studies/vol46no1/article06.html.

10. "There was insufficient evidence to justify a conclusion that Soviet missiles would be (or still less, were being) placed in Cuba. In the absence of clear evidence of deployment, the estimate had to rest on an assessment of Soviet intentions, and the past record tended to support the conclusion that the Soviet leaders would not deploy strategic missiles in Cuba." Garthoff, "U.S. Intelligence," 21.

11. See chap. 14 by Pherson and Heuer for a discussion of relevant SATs. Also see David T. Moore and William N. Reynolds, "So Many Ways to Lie: The Complexity of Denial and Deception," *Defense Intelligence Journal* 15, no. 2 (2006): 106–11.

12. Significantly, aided by HUMINT and sound hypotheses, analysts did help direct collection, notably by focusing attention on the importance of aerial photography over San Cristobal, leading to the discovery of the missile base construction there. Garthoff, "U.S. Intelligence," 53.

13. "The principal conclusions concerning the imminence of hostilities reached and reiterated by those responsible for intelligence analysis were—quite simply, obviously, and starkly—wrong." From the Intelligence Community's Postmortem, December, 1973, quoted in *President Nixon and the Role of Intelligence in the 1973 Arab-Israeli War*, symposium, January 30, 2013 (Washington, DC: Center for the Study of Intelligence, CIA, 2013), 15.

14. For example, Ephraim Kahana, "Early Warning versus Concept: The Case of the Yom Kippur War 1973," in *Strategic Intelligence: Windows into a Secret World*, ed. Loch K. Johnson and James J. Wirtz (Los Angeles: Roxbury, 2004), 153–65. Other sources used in this case study are Hughes-Wilson, *Military Intelligence Blunders*, chap. 8; Michael I. Handel, "The Yom Kippur War and the Inevitability of Surprise," *International Studies Quarterly* 21, no. 3 (September 1977): 461–502; and Avi Shlaim, "Failures in National Intelligence Estimates: The Case of the Yom Kippur War," *World Politics* 28, no. 3 (April 1976): 348–80.

15. Shlaim, "Failures in National Intelligence Estimates," 359.

16. Handel, "Yom Kippur War," 497–98; Shlaim, "Failures in National Intelligence Estimates," 356; and Hughes-Wilson, *Military Intelligence Blunders*, 218–59.

17. Kahana, "Early Warning versus Concept," 154–62.

18. Case materials include James A. Bill, *The Eagle and the Lion: The Tragedy of American–Iranian Relations* (New Haven, CT: Yale University Press, 1989); Kenneth Pollack, *The Persian Puzzle: The Conflict between Iran and America* (New York: Random House, 2004); and Barry M. Rubin, *Paved with Good Intentions: The American Experience and Iran* (New York: Viking Press, 1981). See Robert Jervis, *Why Intelligence Fails: Lessons from the Iranian Revolution and the Iraq War* (New York: Columbia University Press, 2010).

19. Pollack, *Persian Puzzle*, 106.

20. Rubin, *Paved with Good Intentions*, 180; Pollack, *Persian Puzzle*, 95, 136–37; and Bill, *Eagle and the Lion*, 402.

21. Pollack, *Persian Puzzle*, 136; Bill, *Eagle and the Lion*, 403.

22. Sources for this case study are a press conference of Adm. David Jeremiah, who was appointed by the director of central intelligence to examine why the intelligence community failed to warn of the tests, at CIA Headquarters, June 2, 1998, https://www.cia.gov/news-information/press-releases-statements/press-release-archive-1998/jeremiah.html; George N. Sibley, "The Indian Nuclear Test: A Case Study in Political Hindsight Bias," WWS Case Study 3/02, Woodrow Wilson School, August 7, 2002, www.wws.princeton.edu/cases/papers/nuclear test.html; and Evan Thomas, John Barry, and Melinda Liu, "Ground Zero: India's Blasts Dramatize the New Nuclear Age—How Did CIA Miss Them?" *Newsweek*, May 25, 1998, 29–32.

23. Admiral Jeremiah stated at the press conference that India "had an effective denial activity," and later added that "our human intelligence capacity is seriously limited."

24. Note, however, that analysis of campaign promises alone will prove a slender basis for reliable warning and risk more false alarms than accurate forecasts.

25. For an Indian account of how they learned from the 1995 demarche experience to apply D&D countermeasures to beat US intelligence, see Raj Chengappa, *Weapons of Peace: The Secret Story of India's Quest to Be a Nuclear Power* (New Delhi: HarperCollins India, 2000), 403, 413–14, 419–20, 425–28.

26. Jeremiah noted: "With respect to the disclosures, in part from our Ambassador and in part from press reports, I think that whenever there is an opportunity to look at what someone else is looking at in your territory it gives you some insights into what you would want to do to cover that. . . . We may have disclosed certain kinds of indicators. . . . And, of course, you don't have to show every kind of whole card you have." See also James B. Bruce, "How Leaks of Classified Intelligence Help U.S. Adversaries: Implications for Laws and Secrecy," in *Intelligence and the National Security Strategist*, ed. Roger Z. George and Robert D. Kline (Lanham, MD: Rowman & Littlefield, 2006), 403, 413, and Thomas, Barry, and Liu, "Ground Zero," 30–31.

27. Principal case study sources are Ken Alibek and Stephen Handelman, *Biohazard: The Chilling True Story of the Largest Covert Biological Weapons Program in the World—Told from Inside by the Man Who Ran It* (New York: Random House, 1999), and Judith Miller, Stephen Engelberg, and William Broad, *Germs: Biological Weapons and America's Secret War* (New York: Simon & Schuster, 2001).

28. This significant deficit in US understanding is partly reflected in the major estimates and other intelligence assessments, many now declassified, of Soviet military capabilities that omitted mention of the substantial BW program. See, e.g., Benjamin B. Fischer, ed., *At Cold War's End: U.S. Intelligence on the Soviet Union and Eastern Europe, 1989–1991* (Washington, DC: Center for the Study of Intelligence, CIA, 1999), 341–78; Gerald K. Haines and Robert E. Leggett, eds., *CIA's Analysis of the Soviet Union, 1947–1991: A Documentary Collection* (Washington, DC: Center for the Study of Intelligence, CIA, 2001), 229–310; and Donald P. Steury, ed., *Intentions and Capabilities: Estimates on Soviet Strategic Forces, 1950–1983* (Washington, DC: Center for the Study of Intelligence, CIA, 1996).

29. Pesechnik headed an important BW institute in Leningrad; he defected while visiting France in 1989. Alibek served for seventeen years in the Soviet BW program, including as deputy director of Biopreparat, the principal BW organization, from 1988 to 1992, when he defected. Biopreparat was established in 1973, a year after the Soviets signed the BW

convention, to provide civilian cover for advanced military BW research. At its peak, it employed thirty thousand people—half the BW industry. Alibek and Handelman, *Biohazard*, 43, 298.

30. Ibid., x, 5–8, 43, 78, 140–41.

31. Ibid., xii–xiii, 43.

32. Ibid., 70–86.

33. In 1988, nine years after the Sverdlovsk BW accident, a Soviet delegation visiting the United States at the invitation of Meselson persuaded its American audience that the Sverdlovsk deaths were caused by contaminated meats, the official cover story all along. This deception was reported as factual in the April 1988 issue of the authoritative *Science* magazine. Russian president Yeltsin publicly acknowledged the true explanation in a 1993 interview. Ibid., 85–86.

34. Commission on the Intelligence Capabilities of the United States Regarding Weapons of Mass Destruction, *Report to the President of the United States, March 31, 2005* (Washington, DC: Government Printing Office, 2005) (hereafter, *WMD Commission Report*), 503–8.

35. The events of September 11 are best documented in the authoritative National Commission on Terrorist Attacks upon the United States, *The 9/11 Commission Report*, authorized ed. (New York: Norton, 2003) (hereafter, *9/11 Commission Report*). The commission discusses the Pearl Harbor and September 11 warning failures on p. 339 and pp. 346–48.

36. "The most serious weaknesses in agency capabilities were in the domestic arena," notably the FBI, INS, FAA and others. *9/11 Commission Report*, 352.

37. Despite the large number of threats on the radar screen in the summer of 2001, they "contained few specifics regarding time, place, method, or target." *9/11 Commission Report*, 262–63.

38. Ibid., 416–18.

39. In particular, information connecting the domestic and foreign activities of terrorist plotters Khalid al-Midhar, Nawaf al-Hamzi, and Tawfiq bin Attash (aka Khallad). The National Security Agency also had unshared information that could have helped identify Hamzi. *9/11 Commission Report*, 364–66, 417.

40. Ibid., 277.

41. By the spring of 2001, terrorist threat reporting had reached the highest levels since the millennium alert. Threats included attacks against Boston, London, India, US embassies abroad, and the White House. Summer threats focused on Bahrain, Israel, Saudi Arabia, Kuwait, Yemen, Genoa, and Rome. By July, reporting indicated that bin Laden's network was anticipating an attack, something "spectacular." As late as August, most threats suggested attacks that were planned on targets overseas; others indicated threats against unspecified US interests. Ibid., 255–63.

42. Ibid., 344–45.

43. According to Richard Clark, then the top White House official on terrorism, in ibid., 345.

44. This case study is based largely on the authoritative *WMD Commission Report*. The findings that Saddam Hussein had essentially shut down Iraq's WMD programs in 1991–92 are in the study of the Iraq Survey Group, *Comprehensive Report of the Special Advisor to the DCI on Iraq's WMD*, posted on the CIA website October 6, 2004, also referred to as the Duelfer Report after its chairman. See also Charles Duelfer, *Hide and Seek: The Search for Truth in Iraq* (New York: PublicAffairs, 2009).

45. National Intelligence Council, *Iraq's Continuing Programs of Weapons of Mass Destruction*, NIE 2002-16HC, October 2002. Only the key judgments have been declassified. A penetrating critique of the analysis is provided by Jervis in *Why Intelligence Fails*.

46. *WMD Commission Report*, 161–65, 169, 352, 365–84. The effectiveness of Iraq D&D, notably against UN inspectors after Desert Storm in 1990, was well documented earlier in David Kay, "Denial and Deception: The Lessons of Iraq," in *U.S. Intelligence at the Crossroads*, ed. Roy Godson, Ernest R. May, and Gary Schmidt (Washington, DC: Brassey's, 1995), chap. 9; Kay's "Denial and Deception Practices of WMD Proliferators: Iraq and Beyond," *Washington Quarterly* 18, no. 1 (Winter 1995): 85ff; and in Tim Trevan, *Saddam's Secrets: The Hunt for Iraq's Hidden Weapons* (London: HarperCollins, 1999).

47. *WMD Commission Report*, 158–67. A fourth collection discipline, measurement and signatures intelligence (MASINT), possesses unique capabilities against WMD targets, but regrettably its uses in Iraq were negligible, or largely ignored when MASINT reports—unable to find evidence of WMDs—provided only "negative evidence," i.e., the lack of evidence for WMD in Iraq.

48. Hussein Kamel, Saddam's son-in-law, defected in 1995 and explained that Saddam Hussein had ordered the destruction of the nuclear program in 1991 in an effort to have UN economic sanctions lifted. His statements were not believed. Analysts should have revisited their skepticism when Kamel redefected and was killed by the Iraqi regime.

49. *WMD Commission Report*, 75–79 (nuclear), 122–24 (chemical), and 87–108 (biological).

50. Saddam's policy of calculated ambiguity sought to convey contradictory messages to different audiences. He wanted the United Nations and the West to believe that he had destroyed his prohibited weapons, in order to get sanctions lifted. He also sought to purvey doubt to the Iraqi Shias and Kurds and to the Iranians and Israelis that he still possessed a menacing WMD arsenal. His goal to have it both ways failed with the launching of Operation Iraqi Freedom, which cost him his regime, then his life. See box 12.2 in chap. 12.

51. See box 4.1 in chap. 4 for a short summary of the collection disciplines and some of the challenges that analysts face in using them.

52. See Roger Z. George, "Fixing the Problem of Analytical Mindsets: Alternative Analysis," in *Intelligence and the National Security Strategist*, George and Kline, 311–27, and chaps. 8 and 14 in this volume.

53. The study of intelligence successes is beyond the scope of this chapter, but it also represents a significant gap in the intelligence literature more generally. Though attention to failures is necessary to identify pathologies, roots of error, and correctives, attention to successes is necessary to identify "best practices" so they can be repeated with the aim of causing more successes.

PART IV

Enduring Challenges

CHAPTER 11

The Art of Strategy and Intelligence

ROGER Z. GEORGE

If you know the enemy and know yourself, you need not fear the results of a hundred battles.

—Sun Tzu, *The Art of War*

In what is often regarded as the earliest writings on "strategy," the Chinese master Sun Tzu spoke of the need to understand the nature of one's adversary—his strengths and weaknesses—as well as understanding one's own abilities in order to fashion an effective way to subdue or defeat an enemy. Sun Tzu's thirteen chapters on the art of war lay out the commander's skills in knowing all aspects of the battlefield and having his unique collection of "spies" to obtain critical information on the adversary.[1] Later, Western writers on strategy such as Carl von Clausewitz would also write about the need to understand the adversary, the nature of war, and the political context in which wars were to be fought if one is to fashion a successful plan of attack or defense.[2] These writings on strategy underline the integral role that information, insight, and intelligence play in what we would now call a national security strategy. Unfortunately, few writings even today go much beyond this general statement to describe or assess the varied roles that intelligence plays in the formation and execution of current national security strategy. And yet the effective use of intelligence analysis can be a critical "enabler" of national security strategies.[3]

Developing a National Security Strategy

Scholars of military strategy have written extensively on what constitutes "strategy"—a debate that will not be resurrected here.[4] However, the essential features of a national security strategy include the assessment of the international environment in which the United States operates, the identification of principal threats and opportunities to US national interests, and the formulation and prioritization of policy objectives and the selection of courses of action (for example, fashioning the means and employing different forms of power) that will be taken to accomplish the established policy objectives.

This seemingly rational and linear process, even if it can be described in a few sentences or paragraphs, is seldom so simple.

Ideally, a strategist uses a rigorous process to arrive at a well-thought-out plan of action. At its core, strategy matches a state's ends (interests) to its means (power). As Sun Tzu notes, the strategist must know oneself as well as the enemy, so that the state can be sure not to misconstrue its true interests or overextend its power. Accordingly, the strategist must develop a clear picture of the domestic and international environment, the threats and opportunities it poses, and the risks and costs of taking different courses of action to achieve one's strategic ends. Once a strategist has established his objectives, selected his course of action, and begun implementing his strategy, he must be constantly assessing whether the environment has changed, his adversary has behaved as expected, or his expected costs and risks have themselves changed. In sum, as Clausewitz has noted, "even the simple can be difficult."[5]

Analyst as Enabler

The intelligence analyst, however, also has a key role in enabling the national security strategist to accomplish critical objectives. Though the analyst does not presume to define a national security strategy, he or she must be cognizant of what that national security strategy is, how the current set of decision makers are defining American interests and thus threats to it as (well as opportunities), and the key policy objectives of those decision makers. Today the analyst has the benefit—and the challenge—of understanding a long list of explicit US strategies on security, homeland defense, counterterrorism, and intelligence that have been drafted in the wake of the September 11, 2001, terrorist attacks.[5] The 2010 *National Security Strategy* goes further than earlier ones in mentioning the critical role of intelligence in shaping American strategies: "Our country's safety and prosperity depend on the quality of the intelligence we collect and the analysis we produce, our ability to evaluate and share this information in a timely manner and our ability to counter intelligence threats. This is true for the strategic intelligence that informs executive decisions as it is for intelligence support to homeland security, state and tribal governments, our troops and critical national missions."[6] As the 2009 *National Intelligence Strategy* lays out the various missions of the intelligence community, it highlights mission 3 on "strategic intelligence and warning," as critical to the decision maker.[7] An analyst who has studied the strategic thinking of key policymakers is in a better position to enable those strategists to improve their performance at each step of the decision-making and policy execution processes.

Seen in this context, virtually all intelligence analysis is strategic, for it seeks to enable policymakers to achieve their goals with the required means. That is, whether the analyst is describing the general strategic environment, providing warning of some attack, merely describing the details of an adversary's military potential or infrastructure, or providing very tactical targeting information, the endeavor itself is in support of an overall strategy to achieve certain specific ends.

Figure 11.1 displays the distinct and more limited roles that analysts play in the strategy formulation and execution process. The decision maker brings to the strategy-making process a worldview or perceptions about the international environment. The analyst brings expertise and analytic tradecraft to improve the strategist's understanding of that environment. As the strategist seeks to define the national interest and the principal threats and opportunities posed by the international environment, the key function of the analyst is to identify—that is, "warn of"—events or trends that might constitute such threats or opportunities. As strategists formulate policy objectives and courses of action, the analysts support these deliberations by describing the opposing actor's strengths and weaknesses, possible foreign responses to any course of action, and perhaps unforeseen consequences of potential US policy actions—that is, information that relates the real and potential costs and risks of such policy actions.

Finally, after policies are implemented, the strategist must reassess the effectiveness of the policies and refine or restructure the overall strategy. At this juncture the analyst's role is to provide an assessment of how adversaries and allies have reacted to US policies, what intended and unintended consequences those policies might have had, and what future actions foreign state and nonstate actors might contemplate to comply with or oppose US actions.

Deconstructing these four unique ways in which intelligence analysis can enable effective strategy will help to illustrate that intelligence analysis is not a one-size-fits-all proposition. Analysis must be sensitive to the stage at which strategy is being formulated or implemented. Analysis that focuses too much on broad trends when the strategist is

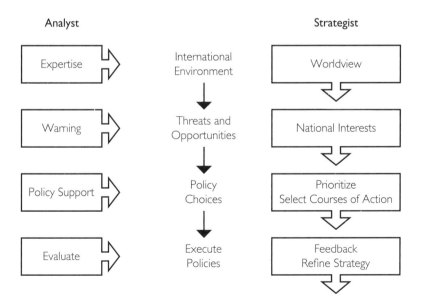

Figure 11.1 Analyst as Enabler: Intelligence and the National Security Strategist

already poised to select courses of action or implement specific policy decisions is likely to be disregarded. If a decision maker does not share the analytic community's general views of a problem early in the strategy-formulation process, then trying to provide policy support can be doubly difficult for the intelligence community.

Shaping the Strategic Context: Analyst Expertise and Tradecraft

The most fundamental goal of both the strategist and analyst must be to comprehend the strategic environment in which the United States and other friendly or adversarial actors are operating. However, the vantage points of strategist and analyst are very different. Whereas the strategist comes to the problem with a well-formed set of values, preconceptions, and policy goals, the analyst must attempt to examine the strategic context from a less explicitly American perspective.

In the Cold War, US strategists were both contemptuous toward and alarmed by the communist system. They could see the faults of the system but may have ascribed more ideology to the factors driving Soviet policy than was actually the case. It was the analysts' responsibility to view the Soviet Union in its totality and understand that its behavior was only partly a function of ideology, as George Kennan pointed out in his groundbreaking "X article," which credited Stalin's actions as much to nationalism and personal paranoia. Also, whereas the strategist might fall prey to a "worse case" view of the Soviet Union's behavior—for example, seeking military superiority, contemplating nuclear first-strikes, or exploiting every potential crisis in the world for the benefit of world communism. The analysts, however, were obliged to assess the limits of the Soviet Union's national economic, political, and military power, to consider how Moscow viewed its own narrow national interest (vis-à-vis other competing communist power centers such as China), and to understand how interest groups inside the Soviet Union (for example, the party, the military, the government ministries) might be competing or working at cross-purposes.

Today, as during the Cold War, the analyst must retain a more dispassionate view of the world than the strategist generally brings to the decision-making process. Analysts must consider the world as it exists, not as one wishes it to be. Moreover, analysts must remain consciously more self-critical than strategists, who can ill afford to show doubt about their policies. That is, an analyst does not have the luxury of asserting some judgment merely because he or she holds a PhD in the subject, speaks the language, or has lived in the region. Those credentials are also held by any number of highly educated policymakers. Moreover, the more expert the analyst, the more prone an analyst becomes to the "mind-set trap"—that is, believing that his or her view of the problem is the best explanation for all behavior. Yet, as many intelligence failures have demonstrated, intelligence experts can become too complacent about their knowledge and too resistant to alternative explanations and thus miss important changes in the international environment or in the attitudes of US adversaries. The analyst must constantly be challenging his or her views on an intelligence subject and using different analytic techniques to check whether key assumptions are flawed, information is incomplete, misleading, or flatly wrong, or the known facts about an issue could legitimately produce multiple thoughts rather than a single conclusion.[8]

Informing the policymaker qua "strategist" about the changing strategic environment is the most all-encompassing role that the analyst performs daily in many forms. Adding knowledge to the policy debate is what Sherman Kent described as the intelligence analyst's goal of elevating the level of the policy debate. Many policymakers do not always acknowledge this quiet yet pervasive function of intelligence, but it is one that intelligence analysts perform almost unconsciously in their everyday interactions with policymakers via finished analysis, oral briefings, or telephone and face-to-face conversations. Sometimes providing a different perspective to a policymaker can be the most important contribution to a strategy debate if it can put the strategist in the adversary's position or demonstrates that the strategist's perspective on an issue is not the only possible interpretation of the current problem.

The strategic environment of the twenty-first century confronts strategists as well as analysts with a very changed world from the one that shaped US postwar security policies and intelligence operations. A world dominated by a single dominant threat—the Soviet Union—gave focus and purpose to US foreign policy; it was the "main enemy" around which much of US intelligence analysis was built. The twenty-first century presents a far more diverse, dynamic, and uncertain set of policy challenges and intelligence requirements. To take just one example, the recently released *Global Trends 2030* report—published by the National Intelligence Council—describes how our world is becoming steadily more multipolar, interconnected, and prone to sudden shocks. It is a world that contains many so-called game changers and black swans—that is, highly uncertain factors and variables—that could produce either very favorable or highly unstable conditions, in which the United States is but one, albeit important, key player.[9] Such a strategic environment suggests that analysts will need to be attuned to a far greater number of trends, issues, and events, even while they must respond even more rapidly to policymakers' requests. Out of necessity analysts will need to collaborate more, as well as rely on outside experts more to understand nontraditional intelligence problems such as climate change, organized crime, global health, or other transnational issues.

Dealing with Threats and Opportunities: The Warning Function

In most cases intelligence analysts are ultimately—if not always fairly—judged on whether they provided adequate strategic and tactical warning of an impending change in the world. For the national security strategist, however, the challenge is far more difficult. The strategist must first decide what are the enduring American interests, which must be protected—a secure homeland, a democratic way of life, a prosperous economy, access to energy supplies, effective alliances and defenses, and the like—and how American hard and soft power will be used to achieve these goals. Defining what are critical national interests at a given moment is not easy, nor is it simple to prioritize, choose among, or balance those interests that might be at times in conflict.[10] If in fact US decision makers have difficulty defining what are the most critical US interests worth defending or advancing, then it stands to reason that intelligence analysts will have an equally difficult time determining which issues need to be watched to provide effective warning or—more positively—notification that an opportunity exists to advance an important US interest.

In the post-9/11 world, it is now axiomatic that a central mission of the intelligence community is warning of any terrorist attack. A huge national effort has been launched to create large analytic centers to identify and prevent such threats from materializing. Not only is there a National Counterterrorism Center to which many national intelligence agencies contribute, but there also are separate, departmental counterterrorism activities throughout the government, most especially at the Central Intelligence Agency (CIA), the Federal Bureau of Investigation, the Department of Homeland Security, the Defense Intelligence Agency, and the State Department's Bureau of Intelligence and Research. So, in this sense, the analysts' mission is clear. However, there is still a long list of other US national interests that must also be protected and advanced, most of which have not been as clearly enunciated as counterterrorism or counterproliferation. How many analysts also should be following and reporting regularly on the international human and drug trafficking, illegal border crossing, and organized crime activity that can harm US citizens? Moreover, are there senior officials paying attention to these issues, to whom analysts might direct their reports?

Analysts—provided they have the necessary resources and information—face two key challenges in providing warning to the strategist. First, does the analyst understand what the strategist believes would be a threat or an opportunity to a key US national interest? At first blush, this might seem a silly question to pose. However, in the past, analytic centers have been established to monitor what senior intelligence community managers considered to be an important challenge to US interests, only to be disbanded when it became clear that senior officials had little or no interest in developing policies against such emergencies. For example, in the late 1990s, CIA briefly established an "environmental center" whose mission would be to track, monitor, and warn about environmental trends or events (such as foreign nuclear reactor accidents like the Chernobyl disaster or other naturally occurring events) that might have geopolitical significance. It became clear that the newly elected administration would have little interest in such activities, so the resources were reallocated to other priority tasks. As global climate change produces extreme weather patterns, there may yet be another call to establish something like a global climate center to assess the impact that rising seas, desertification, tsunamis, and earthquakes might have on affected states' internal stability and their broader geopolitical implications.

Similarly, the spreading "Arab Spring" has posed the question of whether the intelligence community had properly monitored key developments in North Africa and the Middle East and effectively warned of the possible domino effect that a seemingly unimportant event in Tunisia could have throughout the region. The Obama administration had been turning its attention away from Iraq and concentrating on Iran. Presumably, analysts were more focused on the ongoing drawdowns in Iraq and Afghanistan and the rising concern about a nuclear Iran, leaving fewer analysts watching the other states in the region. Postmortems on the Benghazi attacks on September 11, 2012, may well touch off a broader review of how the intelligence community should be allocating its resources to monitor a critical region likely to remain unstable for years.

The second and related challenge is to convince strategists that they have received a serious warning. In the aftermath of many policy failures, there is a temptation for strategists to claim that strategic or tactical warning was not adequately provided by intelligence analysts. In response, analysts often resort to unearthing past assessments that they believe provided adequate "warning" statements had the strategist bothered to pay attention. Who is right? Policymakers' claims that the "warning" was not explicit enough and was buried in an assessment are often juxtaposed by the analysts' lament that their frequent assessments were seldom read or dismissed as "crying wolf." In the *9/11 Commission Report,* controversy swirled around the question of whether "warnings" such as those given in the *President's Daily Brief* during both the Bill Clinton and George W. Bush administrations were in fact explicit enough to be convincing to senior officials (see box 11.1). In part, the problem harks back to the development of the strategic context,

---

BOX 11.1 Two Warnings: Excerpts from the *President's Daily Brief*

---

4 December 1998
SUBJECT: Bin Laden Preparing to Hijack US Aircraft and Other Attacks
Bin Laden and his allies are preparing for attacks in the US, including an aircraft hijacking to obtain the release of Shaykh 'Umar' Abd al-Rahman, Ramzi Yousef, and Muhammad Sadiq 'Awda. One source quoted a senior member of the Gamaa'at al-Islamiyya (IG) saying that as of late October, the IG had completed planning for an operation in the US on behalf of bin Ladin, but that the operation was on hold....The bin Laden organization or its allies are moving closer to implementing anti-US attacks at unspecified locations, but we do not know whether they are related to attacks on aircraft.

6 August 2001
SUBJECT: Bin Laden Determined to Strike in US
Clandestine, foreign government, and media reports indicate bin Laden since 1997 has wanted to conduct terrorist attacks in the US. Bin Laden implied in US television interviews in 1997 and 1998 that his followers would follow the example of World Trade Center bomber Ramzi Yousef and "bring the fighting to America." After US missile strikes on his base in Afghanistan in 1998, bin Laden told followers he wanted to retaliate in Washington.

Note: These excerpts from the only two issues of the *President's Daily Brief* so far declassified can be found in the 9/11 Commission Report, *The Final Report of the National Commission on Terrorist Attacks on the United States,* released on July 22, 2004.

which the analyst must understand and shape to prepare key decision makers to recognize a warning when it is indeed being issued. Too often a strategist can perceive a "warning" as merely a hypothetical, low-probability event and dismiss it as typical intelligence community "worse-case" analysis or "cover yourself" behavior. Only if analysts have put themselves into the mind-set of the strategist and properly couched their assessment in a way that connects their conclusions to the strategist's agenda can they expect their customer to recognize a warning when it is intended.

Strategists often accuse the analytic community of waffling about a specific situation or of not making a "warning" sufficiently grave or frequent enough to be compelling. In the heat of national security policymaking, there also is the problem of "noise," which interferes with a strategist actually comprehending the warning that has been provided. Specific warnings might also be diluted by the variety of other inputs—often contradictory—which come from a variety of sources that the strategist has at his or her disposal. Moreover, in what has become a routinely fast-paced, quickly shifting set of policy discussions, a policymaker will have little time to absorb the latest intelligence analysis and determine whether it merits closer inspection. An interruption, a badly summarized staff note on top of cogently written finished intelligence products, or a very lengthy assessment that is put aside for a time when the decision maker has time to read more thoughtfully can all contribute to inattention to a very critical analytic judgment. In responding to an earlier warning provided but unheeded, former national security adviser Henry Kissinger is reputed to have said, "Well, you warned me, but you didn't convince me." Truly, the challenge for analysts is not only to be prescient and take risks in reaching controversial judgments but also to be convincing.

Providing Policy Support: The Unseen Role of Analysis

Compared to the "warning" mission of analysts, the job of providing support to policy is far more frequent but far less noticed or appreciated by those outside the decision-making process. Yet the reality is that strategists spend far more time on the selection and implementation of courses of action—that is, choosing policy instruments and determining how to apply them—than they do on their initial assessment of the strategic context and identification of principal threats. Once strategists believe they understand the international environment and the principal challenges facing the nation, they are concerned primarily about using the military, diplomatic, economic, and other instruments of power at their disposal.

The role of the analyst, then, becomes one of providing analysis that can enable the best application of courses of action—for example, the imposition of sanctions, the offer or cancellation of foreign military assistance, the threat of military intervention, or the use of public diplomacy. Few writers outside the intelligence community, however, recognize the wide range of analytic contributions to this phase in the policy process, which do not fall into the category of a major intelligence warning or prescient reassessment of an important international development. Jack Davis, for example, has written that literally thousands of so-called transactions between analyst and policymaker fall into the category of policy support. These involve the analyst providing bits and pieces of information and insight on a specific policy issue, whereas the strategist is trying to determine how best to use an instrument such as a foreign aid package or what convincing arguments the policymaker might use in a planned conversation with a foreign counterpart or what possible countermeasures an adversary might take if the United States were to initiate certain actions designed to increase US influence. Few of these activities are transparent to the outside observer.

For the strategist, however, the real contribution of the intelligence community is precisely in this invisible world of policy support, where he or she can rely on the best information and expertise provided by analysts who will not be constantly second-guessing him or challenging his assumptions or arguing with him over whether a policy is well founded or not. Here is where analysts are at their most objective and least likely to be regarded as undermining current policies with critical analysis. Analysts are being mostly instrumental in providing information that "supports" current policy objectives regardless of whether analysts think the policy is correct or likely to succeed. An example of the range of services that can be provided to the strategist is seen in table 11.1, which illustrates possible analytic contributions to the use of a wide range of policy instruments.

As the table illustrates, contributions come from military, economic, and political analysts and provide information about how foreign actors may behave or respond to specific US actions. Monitoring key developments such as sanction regimes and world oil trading patterns, assessing the negotiating positions of important allies or adversaries, or tracking the financial transactions of illicit WMD are part of the daily routine of numerous experts throughout the intelligence community. Moreover, their activities are focused on supporting a specific group of policymakers within the government agencies or in overseas missions. The list of such policy support activities is almost endless and the daily tasking unending. Intelligence community analysts receive such requests or "taskings" at interagency meetings, as a result of one-to-one briefings, and at the end of important telephone conversations with policymakers.

The policy support provided to strategists—if utilized—can be critical to the assessment of the risks and costs of proposed courses of action, which may be selected or are already in train. For example, when considering whether the United States should impose a sanctions regime on a rogue state, analysts will assess the impact such measures might have on weakening that state's ability to acquire or develop weapons of mass destruction, maintain internal control, or threaten its neighbors. At the same time, other analysts are considering the policies and actions of surrounding states, whose compliance with US-sponsored sanctions might impact the effectiveness of the policy. Strategists should also consider a policy's costs to include the economic losses suffered by neighboring states to which the United States is allied.[11] The risks to this course of action are that the sanctions regime might not prove to be effective. Intelligence analysts should be assessing the risk that other US adversaries will try to undermine or circumvent the sanctions regime

Table 11.1 Intelligence as Policy Support "Enabler": Examples from Iraq

Diplomatic power	Economic power	Informational power	Military power
International organizations • Background briefings to P-5 • Demarches on Iraq WMDs • Prepare Iraq white papers	*Foreign assistance policies* • Monitor corruption/misuse • Assess impact on development policies • Identify critical shortfalls	*Public diplomacy* • White papers on WMDs • Review governments speeches • Monitor/report foreign media coverage	*Coercive actions* • Support interdiction operations • Identify key regime vulnerabilities • Support covert actions
International law • Report atrocities, war crimes • Monitor human rights abuses • Support renditions • Support legal actions against Saddam regime leaders	*Economic sanctions* • Monitor border crossings • Assess regional impact • Report on violations	*Political action* • Pinpoint critical weaknesses of adversaries • Assess receptiveness of foreign audiences to media messages	*Paramilitary action* • Assess insurgency • Support counterinsurgency
Alliances/coalitions • Assess strength/weaknesses • Monitor government/public attitudes toward Iraq War • Forecast potential actions and contributions	*International trade policies* • Monitor world market • Forecast impact of oil wealth on regime stability	*Intelligence sharing* • Share assessments with International Atomic Energy Agency • Joint analysis/collection operations against terrorist/WMD targets	*Force start of war* • Support intrusive inspection regimes • Support psychological operations plans/special operations • Identify suspect WMD sites
International negotiations • Assessment of adversaries' negotiation style/posture • Develop US negotiating position	*Humanitarian assistance* • Monitor refugee flows/needs • Forecast economic disruptions caused by war and terrorism	*"Soft power"* • Assess foreign public diplomacy campaigns • Monitor disinformation and propaganda aimed at Western audience	*War plans* • Support OPS plan development • Develop order of battle • Conduct bomb damage assessment

Note: The author has adapted this chart from presentations by Robert Levine of the National War College, who conceptualized the role of intelligence as "enabler" while he was the director of central intelligence's faculty representative and was responsible for instructing war college students in the uses of intelligence.

in order to oppose American policies, bolster their own relations with a rogue state, or merely demonstrate their independence from the American superpower.

Finally, the intelligence analyst also must consider alerting strategists to the unintended consequences of a course of action. In the case of economic sanctions, analysts would inform decision makers of the possibility that a sanctions regime would create new incentives for organized crime groups to profit in illegal shipments of goods, as well as create new opportunities for the rogue state to undermine US stature by claiming that the "unfair" sanctions regime is hurting the average citizens of the country, which would stir up anti-American sentiments in the region. These types of behaviors were observed on the part of Saddam Hussein in the 1990s. In the current context of the comprehensive sanctions imposed against Iran, analysis of Iran's efforts to circumvent them may well highlight new opportunities for US adversaries to benefit from Iran's troubles.

Policy support perhaps is best illustrated as a kind of "scouting" function the analyst can provide to the strategist. In numerous negotiation arenas over the years, strategists have wanted to put themselves into the shoes of the adversary or ally and understand what their negotiating strategy might be. Analysts are often called upon to imagine how the other party will behave in those negotiations, what their bottom lines will be, and what compromises they might be willing to strike. Without suggesting what the US strategist should do, analysts—either as part of a US negotiating team or in written assessments—will often suggest how to play an issue to best American advantage.

Throughout the US-Soviet era of arms control negotiations, CIA analysts were part of the negotiating process, bringing their knowledge of the opposing Soviet delegation and past behavior along with an understanding of Kremlin politics to help shape an effective American strategy. Today one finds many analysts working to support difficult negotiations vis-à-vis North Korea, Iran, and other states, whose intentions and actions require serious all-source analysis and deep expertise.

Refining the Strategy: The Difficult Job of Evaluation

It would be naive to assume that a strategy, once set, runs its course "automatically" until it achieves its stated goals. As military commanders often say, "no plan survives first contact with the enemy." Accordingly, when developing strategic plans, there is the danger that the strategist will fall into the trap sometimes known as the "fallacy of the first move": presuming that the adversary will accept the inevitability of an American action and comply in the ways imagined by its creators.

Sadly, the world is far more complex and less predictable than this. Numerous times confident strategists have proclaimed that a stated policy action would be successful and then were shocked by the persistence of an enemy's resistance or an actor's clever response to some US policy action. The analysts' role in the postimplementation phase of strategy formulation is to report back to policymakers in a timely fashion on the effectiveness of the courses of actions taken. This role is in addition to the earlier role of analytic forecasting; instead, in this case, analysts are required to draw up after-action reporting that strategists can use to reassess or redirect their policies. Not surprisingly, this is a contribution that is needed but seldom welcomed, particularly when it amounts to a failing grade or a less-than-overwhelming success for an American administration. As Richard Kerr has noted elsewhere, "There are no policy failures, only intelligence failures."

Thus the analyst must tread carefully in providing feedback to the strategist if he or she is to maintain the trust of the strategist and survive to provide analysis to policymakers another day. As James Steinberg notes in his chapter in this volume, a smart strategist would be foolish to dismiss analytic evaluations of policy simply because they do not conform to his expectations. However, there are examples of where the strategist's expectations and the analyst's assessment of a policy action were widely disputed. The long record of intelligence community evaluations of US military policies in Vietnam and American policymakers dismissing them has been recorded by numerous intelligence practitioners and policymakers and is mentioned elsewhere in this volume. Intelligence community bomb-damage assessments of the Gulf War, which disputed military claims of destroying nearly all Iraq's Scud missiles, also have been cited as an example where military planners were unwilling to consider the possibility that their air sorties were not nearly as effective as imagined.[12] Likewise, the press heralded a dispute regarding the crisis in the former Yugoslavia in the late 1990s, when the Clinton administration's optimism that Serbian prime minister Slobodan Milošević would cave after three days of bombings met serious questioning by intelligence analysts.[13] In a somewhat ironic twist, the 2007 NIE on Iran's nuclear program—whose declassified key judgments were released—suggested US and international pressure on Teheran might have halted for a time part of Iran's nuclear weapons program, yet policymakers roundly criticized this estimate for undermining Washington's efforts to keep pressure on Iran.

An added complication for the strategist is that his or her role is not simply to calculate the costs of adjusting the strategy in terms of the foreign environment. Unlike the analyst who only thinks about how foreign adversaries and allies are reacting to the policy, the strategist must consider the domestic environment in which the strategy has been fashioned. Among these considerations are a strategy's level of congressional, public, and media support; the morale of the American forces fighting overseas; the budgetary pressures; and the overall credibility of US policies. So when intelligence assessments begin to question the logic or effectiveness of a strategy, there is an immediate tendency to resist such inputs. Highlighting the possibility that a strategy needs to be adjusted because the adversary is not behaving as imagined or because the military or economic tools used were not as effective as predicted causes major strains in the strategist–analyst relationship. Typically these frictions probably surfaced earlier in the strategy-formulation process, as there likely were disagreements among strategists and analysts in their characterization of the strategic environment and differences about the likely effectiveness of different courses of action. Most likely there was some reluctance on the part of strategists to accept the analysts' coaching skills for providing policy support, if they were so skeptical from the beginning of the strategy's underlining logic.

Maintaining the independence of the analytic process is the only real guarantee that strategists will get the unvarnished truth from the intelligence community. Examples of how strategists have not done themselves any favors by hobbling the independence of intelligence services can be seen in the poor advice provided to Stalin or Hitler for fear of retribution. Similarly, it appears that Saddam did not know how weak his military was or how prepared the United States was to bring about a regime change in Baghdad, because his own security services only told him what he wished to hear. One also can imagine that the North Korean intelligence services have a hard time convincing their leaders of the seriousness of American counterproliferation concerns or the likely devastating impact of a war on the Korean Peninsula were Pyongyang to start one.

Improving the Strategist–Analyst Relationship

The model put forward here argues that there should be a close and symbiotic relationship between the strategist and analyst. The reality is that the interactions are anything but smooth and seamless. Too often the strategist and analyst are either working with little appreciation for the other's role or are openly dismissive of the challenges that the other faces in fulfilling his or her respective responsibilities. The strategist can unintentionally, or sometimes willfully, dismiss the analyst's perspective as uninformed about the policy perspective; worse yet, the strategist may not trust the analyst with knowledge about the true strategy and seek instead to keep intelligence professionals at arm's length for fear that they might jeopardize policy initiatives and are likely to see only the negative consequences of some untried course of action. In the same way, analysts are sometimes dismissive of the high stakes that strategists face every day. They do not carry the decision-making burden that their policy customers must assume. Analysts can shrug off the uncertainties implicit in their analyses and posit conclusions that are clearly speculative. However, at the end of the day the strategist must arrive at a decision, select a course of action, and face the consequences.

An improved relationship is only likely to come through mutual understanding of the strategist–analyst model. Though every strategist is by nature his or her own analyst, few have actually worked as intelligence professionals or have experienced the challenges of being an analyst. There are no courses on intelligence offered to incoming US government officials to introduce the policymaker to how intelligence works, the strengths and weaknesses of American collection and analysis, or the various analytic methods used by today's professionals.

For the analyst, in turn, there must be a greater appreciation for the complexities facing policymakers and for the "big picture" world in which they live. Too often the strategist is trying to see how an intelligence briefing or new assessment fits into the broader agenda in which they must operate. Unfortunately, the size and complexity of the intelligence business often results in analysts being responsible for only a "thin slice" of any given intelligence topic. Few analysts are able to give strategists an overriding sense of a specific judgment's impact on the overall strategic landscape they are facing. This narrow account-splitting is contrary to the way the strategist views the world. In his or her domain, everything is connected to everything else. Events happening in one country will have consequences somewhere else in the region and the world. They do not have the luxury of inviting an endless line of experts into the office for their piece of the puzzle to be added to the mix. Therefore, a start for analysts would be to develop broader and integrative perspectives on their issues, so they can put answers into a context that strategist's value. It means real multidisciplinary analysis in each analyst, not just an analytic structure that places narrowly focused military, economic, and political analysts into one unit.

Strategist and analyst must understand each other while maintaining their respective roles. The more we know ourselves, as Sun Tzu noted centuries ago, the more able we are to take full advantage of the knowledge we have developed about our world and America's adversaries.

Notes

1. Quoted from Sun Tzu, *The Art of War*, trans. Lionel Giles, http://classics.mit.edu/Tzu/artwar.html.
2. Carl von Clausewitz, *On War*, ed. and trans. Michael Howard and Peter Paret (Princeton, NJ: Princeton University Press, 1993).
3. "Enabler" is used to distinguish intelligence from the traditional forms of "power," which strategists cite as military, political, economic, and informational. Some writers on strategy consider intelligence a means—that is, a type of "informational" power—whereas others argue it is only an enabler of other means.
4. There are excellent studies on strategy, including Robert J. Art, *A Grand Strategy for America* (Ithaca, NY: Cornell University Press, 2003); Colin S. Gray, *Modern Strategy* (New York: Oxford University Press, 1999); and B. D. Liddell Hart, *Strategy* (Westport, CT: Praeger, 1954). For an excellent survey of strategic thinking, see Peter Paret and Gordon Craig, eds., *Makers of Modern Strategy: From Machiavelli to the Nuclear Age* (Princeton, NJ: Princeton University Press, 1986).
5. For the best articulation of how strategists must systematically examine the strategic environment, set out their objectives, and calculate different courses of action in terms of their costs and risks, readers should consult Terry Deibel, *Foreign Affairs Strategy: Logic for American Statecraft* (New York: Cambridge University Press, 2007). The author wishes to pay tribute to Professor Deibel's education of numerous students and colleagues such as himself in the complexities of strategy development.
6. White House, *National Security Strategy*, May 2010, 15, www.whitehouse.gov/sites/default/files/rss_viewer/national_security_strategy.pdf.
7. Office of the Director of National Intelligence, *National Intelligence Strategy* fact sheet, September 2009, www.hsdl.org/hslog/?q=node/5060. It lays out six key missions: (1) combat violent extremism, (2) counter WMD proliferation, (3) provide strategic intelligence and warning, (4) integrate counterintelligence capabilities, (5) enhance cybersecurity, and (6) support ongoing operations (diplomatic, military and law enforcement).

8. See Roger Z. George, "Fixing the Problem of Analytic Mindsets: Alternative Analysis," in *Intelligence and the National Security Strategist: Enduring Issues and Challenges*, ed. Roger Z. George and Robert D. Kline, 311–26 (Lanham, MD: Rowman & Littlefield, 2005).

9. Office of the Director of National Intelligence, National Intelligence Council, *Global Trends 2030: Alternative Worlds*, December 2012, executive summary, iii-iv, www.dni.gov/files/documents/GlobalTrends_2030.pdf.

10. Today the homeland security debate often focuses on balancing American citizens' right to privacy against their right to feel secure at home. Equally challenging is proper prioritization of domestic well-being in the form of spending on education, health care, or airport security against defense spending or foreign assistance programs designed to avert failing states that can become safe havens for future terrorists.

11. This has occurred on numerous occasions, as when the United States was considering sanctions against Iraq in the early 1990s and Turkey insisted that its losses would be in the billions of dollars. Analysts were also constantly assessing the regional impact of sanctions on Serbia during the Yugoslavian conflict, estimating the amount of humanitarian aid needed to support Bosnian refugees, and even trying to assess how weather patterns would impact UN winter relief activities.

12. Richard Russell, "Tug of War: The CIA's Uneasy Relationship with the Military," in *Intelligence and the National Security Strategist*, ed. George and Kline, 479–93.

13. This is in a March 2000 report titled "Behind the Kosovo Crisis"; see also Allan Little, "Behind the Kosovo Crisis," BBC News, March 12, 2000.

CHAPTER 12

Foreign Denial and Deception: Analytic Imperatives

JAMES B. BRUCE AND MICHAEL BENNETT

We must significantly reduce our vulnerability to intelligence surprises, mistakes, and omissions caused by the effects of denial and deception (D&D) on collection and analysis.

—President's Commission on the Intelligence Capabilities of the United States regarding Weapons of Mass Destruction, March 2005

Foreign denial and deception (D&D) is a fact of life for every intelligence analyst who has ever worked a "hard target."[1] Such targets are objects of high intelligence interest and are considered to be hard because they defy a wide variety of ordinary collection methods and pose the most difficult analytic challenges. The standard collection activities such as human intelligence (HUMINT), signals intelligence (SIGINT), and imagery or geospatial intelligence (GEOINT) are typically less productive against such targets because the countermeasures these targets take against collection reduce, and sometimes confuse, the factual basis for analytic understanding. During the Cold War, the Soviet Union was the exemplary hard target. Today countries such as China, North Korea, and Iran, along with post-Soviet Russia offer the best examples, as well as such nonstate actors as international terrorist groups, including al-Qaeda and other networks that seek weapons of mass destruction (WMDs).

What Is Denial and Deception?

Highly relevant to national-level policymakers and to warfighters, D&D is defined as any undertaking (activity or program) by adversaries—state and nonstate actors alike—to influence or deceive policymaking and intelligence communities by reducing collection effectiveness, manipulating information, or otherwise attempting to manage perceptions of intelligence producers and consumers (for example, policymakers and warfighters). Those who practice D&D seek to shape the decisions and actions of policymakers by manipulating their perceptions. Notably the perceptions of these intelligence consumers can be shaped by influencing the intelligence they receive. More specifically:

- *Denial* refers to activities and programs designed to eliminate, impair, degrade, or neutralize the effectiveness of intelligence collection within and across any or all collection disciplines, human and technical. The goal is to distort intelligence by depriving it of information it requires for a more complete and accurate understanding.
- *Deception* refers to *manipulation* of intelligence collection, analysis, or public opinion by introducing false, misleading, or even true but tailored information into intelligence channels with the intent of manipulating the perceptions of policymakers in order to influence their actions and decisions. The goal is to *influence* judgments made by intelligence producers and thus the consumers of their products.

Since intelligence collection and analysis can play a significant role in shaping policymaker perceptions, intelligence agencies are a key target for the deception planner.

Effective D&D has the potential to significantly degrade US intelligence capabilities by attacking vulnerabilities in collection and analysis. Such vulnerabilities tend to be costly to the targeted intelligence organization as can be seen in previous US intelligence failures. As shown in chapter 10, of the eight cases of failure examined there, deception was a factor in most, and denial was a factor in all. That denial is a factor in all these failures suggests that it is not only pervasive but also consequential. Though deception is far less common than denial—it is held in reserve for only the rare but perfect circumstances—its batting average is extraordinarily high, succeeding more than nine times of every ten it is used.[2]

An important historical example of D&D is illustrated in the surprise military attack that Japan conducted against the United States at Pearl Harbor in 1941. The Japanese denial measures successfully concealed the eleven-day transit of a massive naval task force that conducted the attack, killing 2,400 unsuspecting Americans and bringing the United States into World War II. Deception measures were so successful that even Japanese intentions to go to war with the United States were never comprehended by US intelligence, policy, and military officials (see box 12.1).

It is clear from historical cases as well as more recent ones that analysts who underestimate the power of D&D increase their vulnerabilities to its effects, while those who are equipped to understand and counter the techniques that D&D practitioners use will perform better against not only hard targets but also any targets no matter their complexity. Successfully countering D&D holds the key to avoiding tactical and strategic surprise.

Denial: Foundations for Poor Intelligence

Denial of intelligence collection is a significant impediment to successful analysis. As shown in chapter 10, that denial effectively neutralized collection in major US intelligence failures is one thing. But analysts' failure to understand and correct for successful

BOX 12.1   Japanese Denial and Deception in the Pearl Harbor Attack

Denial: Intelligence was denied through effective operational security:

- Radio communication among ships in the task force were forbidden beginning on November 10.
- Naval call signs were changed twice between November 1 and December 1 prior to the attacks, slowing any US translations of radio intercepts.
- The northern rendezvous point off Etorofu Island was chosen because it was unlikely to be observed, even by Japanese citizens.
- The military concealed the purchase and attainment of clothing, equipment, and supplies for the rendezvous point and for the northern journey toward Pearl Harbor.
- Dumping of garbage or waste into the water from ships in the task force was forbidden to reduce the likelihood of detection.
- Only top Japanese naval planning officers were aware of the Pearl Harbor plan; military Cabinet secretaries were informed only late in the game, and some Cabinet members were never informed prior to the attack.
- Members of the ships' crews were kept unaware of their destination until after their departure.
- Pilots and crews training for the attack knew nothing of the ultimate purpose of their training.

Deception: Expectations of attack were reduced through manipulating information and perceptions:

- Japan sought to create the illusion that the task force was still in training at Kyushu. The main force in the Inland Sea created massive, deceptive communications to manufacture this ploy. This deception was reinforced by allowing a large number of shore leaves in Tokyo and Yokohama for naval men.
- Japanese military commanders in other theaters such as in Indochina were given false plans for military campaigns other than those actually being planned.
- The Japanese navy issued a war plan on November 5 with full and accurate details of planned attacks on the Philippines and Southeast Asia but omitted any reference to the Pearl Harbor mission whose orders had been communicated verbally.
- The Foreign Office announced that one of its largest ocean liners would sail on December 2 to California and Panama to evacuate Japanese citizens, giving the impression that Japan would not commence hostilities while its liner was at sea.
- The Japanese government and press continued to play up the Japanese–American negotiations prior to the attack.

Sources: Roberta Wohlstetter, *Pearl Harbor: Warning and Decision* (Palo Alto, Calif.: Stanford University Press, 1962), 368–85, and Cynthia Grabo, *Anticipating Surprise: Analysis for Strategic Warning* (Washington, DC: Joint Military Intelligence College, Center for Strategic Intelligence Research, 2002), 121–22.

denial is quite another. In general, analysts need a much better understanding of the impact of intelligence denial on their analysis. Often they may not even be aware that needed information has not been collected, even though it may bear directly on the issue that they are analyzing. When denial measures succeed against the collection disciplines, human and technical, the result is that intelligence sought is intelligence denied. We are thus left with "missing information."

But even when we know that certain missing information is the result of effective denial, the *impact* of that denial on analytic processes and findings is often poorly understood. No one doubts that intelligence findings about any difficult issue (for example, in terrorism, WMDs, or warning situations) would be different if more and better information had been collected. But the potential impact on analysis of important information that is *not* collected can also distort results. Analytic judgments based on missing information are inherently uncertain; they may also be wrong. Had analysts better identified the impact of missing information on their analysis of Iraqi WMDs, a more reliable estimate might have been the result.

Targets of intelligence collection that wish to avert discovery or observation generally have two resources at their disposal: knowledge of their adversary's collection capabilities and use of countermeasures against the collection activities they aim to degrade, such as camouflage against imagery or other direct observation. There are good reasons that Iran chose to place its uranium enrichment efforts in underground facilities (UGFs) at Natanz and Qom—UGFs offer excellent means to negate overhead imagery. Good D&D practitioners have countermeasures that work against not only imagery but also human and signals collection efforts. Though much of denial activity is passive, such as practicing good operational security and just "staying below the radar," hard targets are notable for their sophisticated denial capabilities, which are not merely passive but also seek to actively neutralize intelligence collection methods. Their ability to do this entails an understanding of collection programs that cannot normally be attained at unclassified levels. Sophisticated denial capabilities successfully exploit classified information about collection sources and methods that has been compromised in some way or another, often through spies or through press leaks and other disclosures that may or may not have been authorized. The cumulative effects of many and frequently major disclosures enable D&D practitioners to actively deny US collection efforts.

Effective D&D programs thus require good knowledge of the collection that targets them—it is the bedrock of effective denial. Because all collection disciplines save for open sources are intended to work secretly or clandestinely, their effectiveness depends on how well their secrecy works. As intelligence is the collection of secret information by secret means, acquiring the target's secrets (such as plans for surprise attack) presumes that the most effective collection methods remain a secret.

Secrecy is the opposite of transparency. As an intelligence service's methods become more transparent, its loss of secrecy necessarily impairs its effectiveness. A priority objective of smart intelligence targets is acquiring information that compromises the secrecy of intelligence collection sources and methods. All hard targets conduct priority efforts to learn how to defeat collection. This knowledge can be acquired through both authorized disclosures, such as intelligence sharing or diplomatic demarches, and unauthorized disclosures, such as media leaks that disclose classified information.[3] In particular, media leaks, according to the report of the WMD Commission, "have significantly impaired US intelligence capabilities against the hardest targets."[4] When secret collection capabilities are compromised, analysis is also impaired. Analysts are not only denied information later as a result—they also need to understand the impact of compromises at least as well as the D&D practitioners that defeat transparent collection and thereby degrade analysis.

In general, the effectiveness of denial techniques against collection is often better than it seems. As we come to appreciate the impact of key gaps in our information that result from effective denial, both collectors and analysts need a better understanding about unproductive or unsuccessful collection operations in all disciplines and why they are not productive. Overcoming key intelligence gaps produced by adversaries' denial activities will require much more effective counterdenial approaches if analysts are to succeed.

Principles of Deception

If denial is the foundation of D&D, then deception is the silver bullet that almost never misses. Dodging the bullet requires an understanding of how deception works. Based on a comprehensive review of the literature on deception, including a large number of historical cases, Michael Bennett and Edward Waltz have described four fundamental principles of deception:

- Truth. All deception works within the context of what is true.
- Denial. Denying the target access to select aspects of the truth is the prerequisite to all deception.
- Deceit. All deception requires and utilizes deceit.
- Misdirection. Deception depends on manipulating what the target registers.[5]

These principles can be used as a framework for understanding the deception process by examining the relationship between the deceiver and the target of the deception and why deception is almost always successful.

It might seem odd that *truth* should be a principle of deception. But if deception is to work at all, there must be a foundation of accepted perceptions and beliefs about the world that can be exploited. This first principle is based on the study of deception in nature (that is, with plants and animals) and the observation that most organisms expect an honest response when signaling another organism.[6] Such interactions make deception possible when honest signals produce an unexpected or even dishonest response. In D&D the selective use of the truth—supplying the target with authentic data—establishes the credibility of those channels of communication on which the target depends, such as particular collection disciplines and information collected by them.

Denial, on the other hand makes deception possible by creating the opportunities the deceiver needs to manipulate the target's perceptions. Denial conceals selected aspects of what is true, such as the deceiver's real intentions and capabilities, and denial used alone can have serious consequences even when intentional deception is not a factor. Thus, as the Pearl Harbor example illustrates, denial is also the foundation on which deception is carried out.

Together truth and denial set the stage for deception methods associated with *deceit*, the most obvious deception principle. Barton Whaley calls deceit in the form of disinformation the "most important single broad category of ruses."[7] Without deliberate deceit, the target is only the victim of misperceptions due to misinformation and/or self-deception, not deception. But when these first three principles are integrated, they allow the deceiver to present the deception target with what appears to be highly desirable, genuine data while reducing or eliminating the real signals that the target needs to form accurate perceptions of the situation. The end result is that the target must rely on data that has been deliberately fashioned so as to manipulate his perceptions to the deceiver's benefit.

With a few notable exceptions, the strategic deception literature generally does not recognize the fourth principle, *misdirection*, as a distinct concept, although numerous authors consider it to be the very foundation of magic.[8] In magic, misdirection diverts the audience's attention toward the magic effect and away from the method that produces it. The history of deception is filled with examples where the deceiver either deliberately redirects the target's attention or exploits environmental factors that have the same effect. For example, a feint is perceived as a *real* attack (the truth principle), not a false one; it is used to redirect the adversary's attention away from where the real attack will occur.

Used in concert, these four principles are exercised by the deceiver in a way to control what the target of the deception observes and, as a result, what the target registers and thus what the target perceives. When deception succeeds, it causes the target to act to the deceiver's advantage and to his own disadvantage.

Bias Traps and Analytic Vulnerabilities

The deception principles described above illustrate how deceivers exploit very basic human vulnerabilities at several levels. These vulnerabilities can be attributed to biases—systematic errors in perception, judgment, and reasoning—that fall into three major categories: cultural and personal biases, organizational biases, and cognitive biases.[9]

Cultural and personal biases are the result of interpreting and judging phenomena in terms of the preconceptions and beliefs that are formed by the individual's personal experiences. These are further influenced by the knowledge, beliefs, customs, morals, habits, and cognitive styles that the individual acquires as a member of his or her specific social environment—that is, culture. The preconceptions and beliefs that result can be extremely resistant to change, even in the face of large amounts of discrepant information, and they can thus be exploited by deception planners. Such biases also affect the way analysts interpret events. Cultural biases can also influence how people go about solving problems and analyzing situations, and analytic flaws such as mirror imaging may be the result. Such personal traits as overconfidence (hubris) can facilitate being deceived. As Roy Godson and James J. Wirtz point out, the successful deceiver "must recognize the target's perceptual context to know what (false) pictures of the world will appear plausible."[10]

Organizational biases are similar to cultural biases and are generally associated with the limitations and weaknesses of large bureaucratic organizations. These biases are the result of the goals, mores, policies, and traditions that characterize the specific organization in which the individual works and often appear in the form of barriers to the flow of information within and between organizations. An even more insidious bias appears in the manner in which the very nature of the information about a specific topic changes as it winds up flowing through different channels. Such differences in information across linked organizations such as in the intelligence community are even more extreme when classified information is involved. Barriers to information flows and differences in perception due to the uneven distribution of compartmented information, as shown above, contributed heavily to the American failure to anticipate the Japanese attack on Pearl Harbor. Such barriers and differences in perception also played a role in the failure to anticipate the terrorist attacks on September 11, 2001.[11]

Two prominent organizational biases in intelligence agencies are the search for consensus and time pressures. As we have learned in discovering the rationale for alternative analysis, if consensus becomes a goal in and of itself, it may deprive decision makers of important information about potential weaknesses in the analytic judgments presented, as well as the existence and grounds of alternative views. A second bias, time pressure, is inherent in fast-paced analysis, particularly current intelligence. Analysts have always been under pressure to provide timely intelligence. But the post-9/11 threat environment and congressional pressure for a quick answer, as we saw with Iraqi WMDs, may exert added pressure on analysts to make judgments prematurely. Like the pressure for consensus, time pressures may also elevate the impact of cognitive biases that increase susceptibility to deception.

Cognitive heuristics represent a wide variety of adaptation mechanisms that help humans to accurately perceive and understand the world around them on a day-to-day basis. They usually help us by reducing the complexity of difficult problems (for example, assessing probabilities). These same processes, however, also make us vulnerable to optical illusions, magician's tricks, con artists, and, of special interest to us, military and political deception. It is impossible to survey the range of cognitive biases that are relevant to denial and deception here.[12] Fortunately, professor of psychology Thomas Gilovich provides an excellent framework for capturing the role these heuristics and biases play in deception. He summarizes much of the social and cognitive psychology research into what he calls *determinants of questionable and erroneous beliefs* and organizes them into categories, three of which are especially relevant to D&D:[13]

- Too much from too little—the tendency to form judgments from incomplete or unrepresentative information and to be overconfident about those judgments
- Seeing what we expect to see—the tendency for our expectations, preconceptions, and prior beliefs to influence the interpretation of new information in ways to support our present beliefs
- Believing what we are told—the tendency for a good story to seem credible and to bias one's beliefs

The powerful cognitive traps that Gilovich describes here were very much in evidence in the faulty national intelligence estimate that erroneously judged Iraq to have weapons of mass destruction in 2002, more than a decade after the WMD programs had actually been shut down. See box 12.2.

Together the four principles of deception and Gilovich's determinants of questionable beliefs provide a framework for understanding analysts' vulnerabilities as they apply to D&D. They show how a deceiver can exploit each of the deception principles to gain advantage. For example, from the deception planner's perspective, revealing some truth to the target provides several advantages. In the case of *too much from too little*, selective truth can convince a target of deception—for example, that something exists when it does not. The Allies took advantage of this in World War II when feeding information to the Germans in order to create the false order of battle for FUSAG and other elements of the Fortitude deception plan.[14] The *too much from too little* bias sets the analyst up to misinterpret limited information. Providing truthful information also allows the deceiver to exploit the *believing what we are told* determinant. By incorporating real events, people, organizations, equipment, and information into the deception story, the deceiver can increase the story's immediacy and plausibility, thus making it more believable. This also acts to increase the target's confidence in his sources of information, and it is that confidence in those channels that is critical to the success of deception. The deceiver will use those same channels later, such as a controlled source believed by the target to be reliable, to pass false information in order to build up the deception story (the principle of deceit).

BOX 12.2   Iraq WMDs: A Deception Paradox

Deception is characteristically complex. Iraq's D&D overreached, fooled the IC, and backfired.

Saddam Hussein had two target audiences for his deception plan: (1) the United Nations and the West, whom he wanted to assure that he was in full compliance with sanctions and that he had shut down his WMD programs, and (2) his enemies, internally the Kurds (previous targets of his chemical weapons attacks) and the Shiites, and externally Iran and Israel, against whom he wanted to posture as a powerful tyrant and leader in full possession of the robust WMD arsenal he had built before Desert Storm curtailed them in 1990.

The burden of his deception plan was to sustain the contradictory narratives to each audience for as long as possible—to the UN and the West, he had shut down his weapons programs, but to his enemies, he retained them. Both could not be true at once. What was the truth?

The 2002 national intelligence estimate on Iraq WMD acknowledged Iraq's major denial-and-deception efforts and correctly judged them as major impediments to assessing WMDs. But it wrongly concluded that these D&D countermeasures to US intelligence were concealing WMDs. And this erroneous judgment was well supported by Saddam's repeated refusals to provide the UN with documentation supporting his claims that he had destroyed the weapons. In truth these D&D efforts were concealing the *absence* of such weapons, as we later learned Saddam had actually shut down the full range of his CW, BW, and nuclear programs after Desert Storm.

This case illustrates a deception paradox: While analysts correctly understood the scope and impact of the Iraqi D&D program, they misunderstood its purposes. In assuming that D&D was intended to conceal WMDs and not their absence, faulty analysis here illustrates the seduction of the cognitive traps that Gilovich warns against:

- *Too much from too little:* Iraq's successful denial efforts deprived analysts of needed information to understand intentions, so analysts drew unwarranted conclusions about them from too little evidence. His intentions spanned a broader audience than one.
- *Seeing what we expect to see:* Analysts expected to see D&D, which they did, and to see it conceal a major WMD program, which it didn't. They did not expect D&D to conceal the fact that the weapons program had been shut down. In not seeing the weapons, and in concluding that D&D must be hiding them, they judged WMD as present, not absent.
- *Believing what we are told:* Although analysts are inherently skeptical and cannot really be "told" anything, they accepted the past "analytic line" uncritically—namely, that Iraq possessed WMDs before 1990 (which was true) and, lacking convincing evidence to the contrary, believed it must still be true in 2002 (which was false).

These are preventable errors. Good D&D analysis should make use of such structured analytic techniques as Analysis of Competing Hypotheses, Key Assumptions Check, and Structured Brainstorming. This tradecraft almost certainly would have revealed the snare of these cognitive biases and resulted in more accurate analytic judgments.

Sources: For elaboration, see Bruce, "Denial and Deception in the 21st Century," in *Defense Intelligence Journal* 15, no. 2 (2006): note 1, 18–22, and chapter 14, for tradecraft discussion. Michael I. Handel explains how both denial and deception support military intentions and capabilities in *War, Strategy, and Intelligence* (London: Frank Cass, 1989), 314–16 and figure 2.

Denial has its greatest impact through the *seeing what we expect to see* set of biases. Research studies and real-world events have repeatedly demonstrated that individuals consistently fail to appreciate the limits of the data and information available to them.[15] What is unknown, what is out of sight, is out of mind. Effective denial techniques mean that what little information is available, no matter how ambiguous, may be eagerly grasped and fit to existing expectations and preconceptions. Denial, therefore, is the key to making sure that nothing significant occurs to change the target's mind once the deception plan is put into motion.

Deceit is probably the first thing one thinks of with regard to the relationship between deception and *believing what we are told*. After all, it is deceit in the form of double agents, deception operations such as Mincemeat, security "leaks," and exotic camouflage techniques that give deception its historical importance.[16] Analysts and decision makers depend heavily on secondhand information, and this dependence makes them vulnerable to serious biases and errors, especially if those sources are providing false or inaccurate information. More important, deceit exploits the *seeing what we expect to see* bias when analysts readily accept disinformation and fit it to their existing expectations and preconceptions.

Misdirection can be of two general types: one physical, the other psychological.[17] In World War II, for example, the Allies always made sure to pass information to the Germans about the movement of both real and fictional units (that is, truth and deceit) to reinforce their expectations, as well as to distract their attention from the real buildup in southwestern England.

Principles of Counterdeception

To succeed against smart adversaries for whom denial and deception are key weapons in their security arsenals, intelligence analysts must master counter-D&D understanding, principles, and skills, learn to assess the impact of missing information on their analytic judgments, develop significant expertise in the collection disciplines, and adjust for unwarranted dependency on inadequate information. These imperatives find their practical justification in the experience of poor intelligence community performance against foreign D&D and their theoretical justification in sound counterdeception principles.

Bennett and Waltz's review of the deception literature produced not only fundamental deception principles but also yielded four *counter*deception principles, all of which point to the analyst's level of knowledge and understanding:

- Know yourself.
- Know your adversary.
- Know your situation.
- Know your channels.

Understanding and acting on these principles is prerequisite to an analytic posture to reduce vulnerability to D&D and mitigate its effects when it succeeds.

Drawing from the work of Heuer and the cognitive heuristics literature leads to the first fundamental principle of counterdeception: *Know yourself.* Put succinctly, this principle stresses that the analyst's first defense against D&D is a sound understanding of those cognitive vulnerabilities discussed above. Sun Tzu makes it clear that you must know yourself if you wish to have any reasonable hope of success in battle.[18] The same is true for the battle waged between deceiver and target. Whaley has demonstrated how deception can be particularly successful when it exploits the target's expectations and preconceptions (the *seeing what we expect to see* bias).

The *know your adversary* principle should be a constant reminder to analysts and decision makers to consider the means, motives, and culture of their adversary. The means that the adversary has at his or her disposal include doctrine, training, personnel, experience, and technology for concealing or exaggerating intentions, capabilities, and activities. Historically motives have generally included achieving surprise, bluffing, deterrence, seeking prestige or influence, blackmail, and seeking concessions from the target. Today specific D&D motives include concealing WMD capabilities and transactions and planning terrorist attacks. This principle also stresses the need to develop the depth of knowledge of the adversary that makes it possible to begin breaking down ethnocentric biases and come to see things from the adversary's perspective. As Dewar noted, being able to put yourself into the mind of the adversary may be the counterdeception analyst's most effective weapon.[19]

Analysts throughout the intelligence community require a much better understanding of adversarial D&D capabilities than they routinely exhibit. If they do not understand an adversary's D&D capabilities, they cannot be expected to understand how effective—or how hobbled—their nation's intelligence will be when working against that adversary. Analysts who are assigned a specific country or nonstate actor account should make it their first priority to learn all they can about the D&D capabilities that their assigned target can mount against the specific collection disciplines that produce intelligence on that target.

The third principle, *know your situation*, focuses on the necessity for continually evaluating the environment for cues that indicate that deception should be considered as the adversary is formulating strategies, considering options, making decisions, or taking action. An important thing to keep in mind is that analysts are confronted by a continuum of deceptive activity and that most of it, like an adversary's routine operational security measures (denial), is normal and likely to occur no matter what the situation is. Because large-scale, sophisticated deception operations are rare, situational factors may offer important clues to the possibility that the adversary is planning or employing more sophisticated deception operations. These situational factors include

- high-stakes situations;
- asymmetrical power relationships between the participants;

- changes in leadership, motives, political goals, military doctrine, or technological capabilities;
- situations involving potential surprise and risk as high-risk, high-gain strategy; and
- events in the international environment that threaten security or provide opportunity.

The fourth counterdeception principle, *know your channels*, is the conscientious application of this everyday maxim to the channels of information used by intelligence analysts and policymakers. For the analyst, it means above all else having a sound understanding of the collection disciplines—their capabilities and their limitations, and especially their vulnerabilities to denial and deception. *It is critical to understand the extent to which those collection capabilities are known and understood by intelligence targets and are thus vulnerable to being denied and deceived by them.* An in-depth understanding of collection channels and what the intelligence target knows about them is a vital requirement for effective analysis, particularly against hard targets.

Analysts, as illustrated in chapter 10, require a far better understanding of their *dependency on intelligence collection* than they often demonstrate. Briefly, when collection succeeds, it significantly improves the probability that analysis will also succeed. When collection fails—as it did against al-Qaeda before September 11, 2001, and against Iraqi WMDs before Operation Iraqi Freedom—it increases the probability that analysis will also fail. Analysts who do not fully understand the broad range of intelligence collection *capabilities* as well as collection *limitations*, or the enormous importance of their having this special expertise, significantly increase their vulnerabilities to D&D.[20]

Analysts also require a far better understanding of their *dependency on only one or a few key pieces of information.* Sometimes the whole analysis of a complex problem may crumble if a key piece of evidence is removed. If that key datum is unreliable, fabricated, or tenuous—and the analysts are not fully cognizant of its tenuousness or of its potentially exaggerated impact on the analysis—their analysis is likely to be wrong. Their certainty or confidence will also be misplaced. Errors in analysis can sometimes be traced to exaggerated dependence on poor evidence.[21] Because D&D is a major cause of missing evidence, it is also a potential source of poor or deceptive evidence.

Finally, as we know all too painfully from the pernicious effects of the source "Curveball" on the faulty judgments about Iraq's biological weapons capabilities in 2002, sources of intelligence information require better vetting than ever before. Curveball's impact on the erroneous biological weapons analysis in the 2002 WMD national intelligence estimate dramatically illustrates the dependency vulnerability discussed just above. The need to apply more rigorous scrutiny to both human *and* technical sourcing is a key requirement for better intelligence adaptability to D&D. Of course, no intelligence service ever takes information at face value from any source. But sophisticated D&D techniques can be subtle and insidious, and reliable intelligence requires even better *counter*-D&D techniques in the vetting of intelligence collection.[22]

Vulnerable Minds and Vulnerable Organizations

Even the most competent analysts and decision makers have found themselves deceived. To make matters worse, they may find themselves accused of incompetence by those blessed with 20/20 hindsight. To say that we are vulnerable to deception is by no means pejorative, because the concept of vulnerability helps to distinguish the important ways that humans and organizations are open to attack or damage by deception. Therefore, understanding our vulnerabilities to deception can act as a guide to actions we can take to mitigate those vulnerabilities.

Such understanding starts by considering the profiles of the vulnerable mind and the vulnerable organization.[23] The *vulnerable mind*—the one least prepared to counter D&D—sees reality unwittingly shaped by its own biases, preconceptions, and expectations. It understates or ignores the impact of ambiguous, contradictory, and missing information, and exaggerates the importance of the information it expects to see. It is unduly gullible or influenced by a good story. It tends to be overconfident in understanding complexity. And it lacks accurate, in-depth knowledge of its adversary, including especially the D&D capabilities that adversary may wield. These vulnerabilities result in flawed perceptions and judgments that cede advantage to the deceiver. This is a formula for successful D&D.

Similarly, the *vulnerable organization* overemphasizes consensus, consistency, and being decisive. It fails to exploit its full collaborative potential, performing with less than the sum of its parts. It has inadequate learning processes and fails to learn from past performance, including its failures, which it tends to repeat. And it is preoccupied with the present at the expense of the historical or strategic and future perspectives.

Countering Foreign Denial and Deception

With these vulnerabilities understood, we can now develop counterdeception analytic imperatives for transforming vulnerable minds and vulnerable organizations into prepared minds and prepared organizations.

The Prepared Mind

Our desired goal is to deliver better, more accurate judgments that will negate or at least mitigate the effects of denial and deception.

Bennett and Waltz propose two broad strategies for reducing the mind's vulnerability to D&D. The first is to *improve the information available*. Two approaches can accomplish this. One is to improve collection. Multiple intelligence sources and new collection methods increase the likelihood of uncovering flaws in an adversary's D&D attempts. Another is to develop better metadata to support the vetting of our information sources, such as the credibility of a human source.

The second strategy is to *improve analysis* itself. This entails mitigating cognitive biases, adopting the use of a systematic or structured analytic tradecraft, improving intuitive reasoning, and developing "acumen" skills.[24]

The *know yourself* principle emphasizes continuous awareness of the vulnerable mind's most exploitable weakness: its own preconceptions, expectations, and beliefs. One of these weaknesses is the failure of the vulnerable mind to generate adequate hypotheses. And the persisting failure to generate alternative hypotheses is insufficiently recognized in the intelligence community. This failure can be attributed to the use of a suboptimal heuristic of choosing the first explanation that seems to be the closest fit to the evidence at hand ("satisficing" and jumping to conclusions). A major contribution of alternative analysis is that it shows the value of multiple hypotheses.

Just as the failure to generate hypotheses increases vulnerability to deception, so also do confirmation bias and overconfidence. A particularly helpful approach to mitigating confirmation bias and overconfidence is to *restructure the analytic task*. This is aimed at challenging the mind-sets that induce confirmation bias and exaggerate confidence. Several methods of restructuring the analytic task can reduce analytic susceptibility to this kind of error. For example:

- Asking analysts to list reasons why their answers to questions might be wrong.
- Instructing analysts to consider the opposite interpretation of a judgment or forecast, or to engage in *any* second explanation task (for example, explaining a different version of the same outcome).
- Asking analysts to consider what evidence would be required to convince him or her that the interpretation is wrong or what evidence could cause the analyst to change his or her mind.[25]
- Asking analysts to assess any inconsistencies and discrepancies that have been explained away ("bending the map") might indicate that other possibilities are being ignored.[26]
- Having analysts define "tripwires," events that should not be occurring or levels that should not be exceeded if the favored hypothesis is correct. Finding that too many tripwires are tripped could be an indication that the favored hypothesis is wrong.[27]

The *know yourself* principle emphasizes recognizing the assumptions, preconceptions, and expectations that influence analyst beliefs, while the *know your situation* principle focuses on continually evaluating the environment for the cues that deception may be a factor in the situation under consideration. The use of structured analytic techniques (SATs), including Challenge Analysis, also provides another way of restructuring problems so that assumptions, preconceptions, and mental models—that is, factors shaping mind-sets—are not hidden, by making them more explicit so that they can be examined and tested. In particular such SATs include Analysis of Competing Hypotheses, Key Assumptions Check, Structured Brainstorming, Argument Mapping, and Signpost Analysis. Challenge Analysis techniques include Devil's Advocacy, "What If" Analysis, and High-Impact/Low-Probability Analysis.[28] Using such tradecraft can highlight possible biases or situational cues.

A prepared mind will make a conscientious effort to see the problem or situation from the adversary's point of view. It will continually test and retest its judgments, update and evaluate all the evidence at hand, and remain alert to cues and anomalies in the environment that something has changed or is missing. It will not ignore its intuition when something does not quite feel right about a complex analytic situation. And it will diligently update and evaluate the credibility of information sources, stay alert to any channels that may have been compromised, and revisit the issue of source vetting and validation.

The Prepared Organization

To conclude, we want to emphasize four things that an intelligence organization can do to facilitate better counter-D&D analysis and to make itself less vulnerable to denial and deception:

- Prioritize an effective counter-D&D analytic capability and ensure that it is well resourced, incentivized, and protected.
- Enable analysts to better collaborate, access and share sensitive information, and exchange alternative and/or dissenting views.
- Create and encourage a robust analytic learning environment that emphasizes "lessons learned" and structured analytic techniques.
- Emphasize anomaly detection to help ensure that little surprises do not become big surprises.

The prepared organization will be well armed with robust counter-D&D analytic capabilities. Such capabilities can be gauged largely by the strength of the organization's counter-D&D analysis components (or even whether there *is* one), the quality and stature of the analysts who staff them, the skills of fellow D&D analysts in the hard-target components throughout the IC, and the measure of the training resources that directly support the counter-D&D mission. Though the IC has seen wide variation in these capabilities in previous decades, they have been perennially short of critical mass.[29]

A positive step toward creating an intelligence community of prepared organizations is the recent effort of the director of national intelligence to create a "culture of collaboration" that emphasizes greater intelligence sharing among analysts.[30] Greater counter-D&D collaboration must also encourage championing alternative views. A more collaborative and sharing environment must continually challenge and update analysts' expectations, mental models, and situational awareness.

Prepared organizations are also learning organizations. For countering D&D, two types of learning are especially required. First, there should be active learning programs that capture and share lessons learned to help analysts learn from past performance;

these activities should address both previous events and more current issues.[31] The pre-pared organization will also resist pressures of day-to-day distractions and devote time to learning from unexpected events, knowing that if it fails to do so, it will remain vulner-able to later unexpected events. Another important type of learning will provide analysts practice in situations involving D&D before they encounter it. Both types require more robust intelligence community training programs than are now in place.

Finally, reducing vulnerability to D&D surprises requires paying attention to anom-alies, or what Barton Whaley calls "incongruities." Whaley's rule for this is that "when enough evidence is reconsidered in one brief time—in the forefront of the analyst's mem-ory—incongruities, if present, tend to become obvious."[32] Where D&D is concerned, the intelligence community's goal is the same as that in the highly reliable organizations studied by Karl E. Weick and Kathleen M. Sutcliffe—that is, to deal with the small sur-prises before they become big ones.[33] Analysts should always recall what Cynthia Grabo has taught us about warning failures: "While not all anomalies lead to crises, all crises are made up of anomalies."[34]

Implications for the Future

Deception has been a part of life on this planet since its beginnings. It will surely con-tinue to play a significant role in human competition and conflict in the years ahead. His-tory has shown that the use of deception gives the deceiver a significant advantage over both naive and sophisticated targets.

Our adversaries recognize the immense economic, information, and military advan-tages that the United States enjoys. History has shown that deception offers the means of equalizing the kinds of asymmetrical power relationships in favor of the deceiver. The United States now faces a range of adversaries who view deception as a proven force multiplier and a dependable tool of statecraft through diplomacy, military strategy, and other instruments of power.

The explosion of information technology has important implications for both deception and counterdeception. The number of channels available for reaching decep-tion targets is expanding. Increasingly ubiquitous mobile devices, social media, and internet technology, including malware, all multiply ways of reaching out and influenc-ing target audiences or even individuals. Computer-generated imagery is reaching such a degree of sophistication that the phrase "pictures don't lie" may become a quaint anach-ronism. Advances in material science and electromagnetics point to the possibility of "smart skin" camouflage materials and of signature reduction and adaptation techniques that may make "cloaking" devices a reality.

In sum, foreign denial and deception pose major threats to successful intelligence analysis. The best counters to the D&D analytic threat begin with an understanding of the principles of deception (truth, denial, deceit, and misdirection) and require a keen awareness of bias traps and cognitive vulnerabilities to being deceived. By knowing yourself, your adversary, your situation, and your channels, you can greatly reduce your susceptibility to D&D-induced faulty analysis. In particular the prepared mind and the prepared organization together present the best possible assurances of intelligence analysis uncorrupted by foreign denial and deception.

Notes

1. This chapter draws heavily from James B. Bruce, "Denial and Deception in the 21st Century: Adaptation Implications for Western Intelligence," *Defense Intelligence Journal* 15, no. 2 (2006): 13–27, and Michael Bennett and Edward Waltz, *Counterdeception Principles and Applications for National Security* (Boston: Artech House, 2007).

2. This is based on calculations made by Richards Heuer using two databases starting in 1914 compiled by Barton Whaley. One database ($N = 68$) ended in 1968, the other ($N = 93$) in 1972. Both showed a deception success correlation of slightly higher than .9. Donald C. F. Daniel, "Denial and Deception," in *Transforming U.S. Intelligence*, ed. Jennifer E. Sims and Burton Gerber (Washington, DC: Georgetown University Press, 2005), 138.

3. Commission on the Intelligence Capabilities of the United States regarding Weapons of Mass Destruction, *Report to the President of the United States, March 31, 2005* (Washington, DC: Government Printing Office, 2005) (hereafter, *WMD Commission Report*), 381.

4. Ibid. See also James B. Bruce, "How Leaks of Classified Intelligence Help U.S. Adversaries: Implications for Laws and Secrecy," in *Intelligence and the National Security Strategist*, ed. Roger Z. George and Robert D. Kline, 399–414 (Lanham, MD: Rowman & Littlefield, 2006).

5. Bennett and Waltz, *Counterdeception Principles and Applications*, 58–66.

6. R. W. Mitchell, "Epilogue," in *Deception Perspectives on Human and Nonhuman Deceit*, ed. R. W. Mitchell and N. S. Thompson (Albany: State University of New York Press, 1986), 358.

7. Barton Whaley, *Stratagem: Deception and Surprise in War* (Cambridge, MA: Center for International Affairs, Massachusetts Institute of Technology, 1969), 17.

8. See J. Lierpoll, Misdirection Resource Center, www.lierpoll.com/misdirection/misdirection.htm.

9. Bennett and Waltz, *Counterdeception Principles and Applications*, 71–88. Richards Heuer pioneered the early work on how cognitive bias increases vulnerabilities to deception. See Richards Heuer, *Psychology of Intelligence* (Washington, DC, Center for the Study of Intelligence, CIA, 1999), and chap. 8 by Jack Davis.

10. Roy Godson and James J. Wirtz, "Strategic Denial and Deception," in *Strategic Denial and Deception: The Twenty-First Century Challenge*, ed. Roy Godson and James J. Wirtz (New Brunswick, NJ: Transaction, 2002), 3.

11. *The 9/11 Commission Report*, authorized ed. (New York: Norton, 2003), 416–18.

12. For further reading on cognitive biases and deception, see Bennett and Waltz, *Counterdeception Principles and Applications*, chap. 3, and Richards J. Heuer, "Strategic Deception and Counterdeception: A Cognitive Process Approach," *International Studies Quarterly* 25, no. 2 (June 1981). For more on cognitive heuristics and biases, see Daniel Kahneman, Paul Slovic, and Amos Tversky, *Judgment under Uncertainty: Heuristics and Biases* (Cambridge: Cambridge University Press, 1982).

13. T. Gilovich, *How We Know What Isn't So: The Fallibility of Human Reason in Everyday Life* (New York: Free Press, 1991).

14. "FUSAG" refers to Lt. Gen. George Patton's First US Army Group, the notional army unit in southern England preparing for the Allied invasion of Pas de Calais—in reality, the deception setting up the Germans for the invasion of Normandy. R. Hesketh, *Fortitude: The D-Day Deception Campaign* (New York: Overlook, 2000), 193.

15. Gilovich, *How We Know What Isn't So*, provides a good overview of such research.

16. During World War II, Operation Mincemeat successfully deceived the Germans that Greece and Sardinia were the Allies' next invasion target instead of the island of Sicily, the real target. See Ewen Montagu, *The Man Who Never Was* (New York: Oxford University Press, 1996).

17. P. Lamont, and R. Wiseman, *Magic in Theory* (Hatfield, UK: University of Hertfordshire Press, 1999), 36–52.

18. Sun Tzu, *The Art of War*, trans. S. B. Griffith (New York: Oxford University Press, 1963), 84. See also Jennifer E. Sims, "Understanding Ourselves," in *Transforming U.S. Intelligence*, ed. Sims and Gerber, 32–59.

19. M. Dewar, *The Art of Deception in Warfare* (Newton Abbot, UK: David & Charles, 1989), 194–203.

20. *WMD Commission Report*, 409–10.

21. Heuer, *Psychology of Intelligence Analysis*, 105–6. Also see the discussion of the Iraq WMD national intelligence estimate in chaps. 9 and 10.

22. See *WMD Commission Report*, 158–61, 367–72.

23. Bennett and Waltz, *Counterdeception Principles and Applications*, 186–93.

24. Ibid., 200.

25. Gary Klein, *The Power of Intuition* (New York: Currency Doubleday, 2004), 147–48.

26. Ibid.

27. Ibid.

28. See chap. 14 by Pherson and Heuer.

29. James Bruce, foreword to Bennett and Waltz, *Counterdeception Principles and Applications*, ix.

30. See chap. 17 by Fingar.

31. Stever Robbins, "Organizational Learning Is No Accident," *Working Knowledge for Business Leaders Newsletter*, Harvard Business School, 2005, http://hbswk.hbs.edu/item.jhtml?id=3483&t=srobbins.

32. Barton Whaley, "Meinertzhagen's Havesack Exposed: The Consequences for Counterdeception Analysis," unpublished manuscript, 2007.

33. Karl E. Weick and Kathleen M Sutcliffe, *Managing the Unexpected: Assuring High Performance in an Age of Complexity* (San Francisco: Jossey-Bass, 2001).

34. Cynthia Grabo, *Anticipating Surprise: Analysis for Strategic Warning* (Washington, DC: Joint Military Intelligence College, Center for Strategic Intelligence Research, 2002), 31.

CHAPTER 13

Warning in an Age of Uncertainty

ROGER Z. GEORGE AND JAMES J. WIRTZ

What warning really is: The considered judgment of the finest analytic minds available, based on an exhaustive and objective review of all available indications, which is conveyed to the policy official in sufficiently convincing language that he is persuaded of its validity and takes appropriate action to protect the national interest.

—Cynthia Grabo, *Anticipating Surprise*

If the general mission of the analytic profession is to inform decision makers, then the indispensable mission of the professional analyst is to warn effectively. Because it permeates virtually all aspects of analysis, many of this volume's chapters touch on the challenges posed to effective warning, including identifying intelligence gaps, accounting for missing information, considering deception and denial possibilities, and interpreting information properly, as well as considering the role of cognitive biases in preserving outmoded, albeit commonly accepted, analytic judgments. The intelligence–policy relationship also shapes decision makers' receptivity to intelligence community "warnings."

This chapter examines the challenges of warning, including those in the post-9/11 environment.[1] The prevailing view that every analyst has a duty to warn carries with it the presumption that every analyst, and policymaker for that matter, understands the warning function, its enduring difficulties, and its new features in a post-9/11 world. As a senior warning official noted in the 1990s, attention to warning rises after a failure but quickly fades over time until the next failure, when the cycle begins anew.[2] Given the changes that have occurred in the past few years in the US intelligence community's approach to warning, there is a risk that attention is again receding.

Warning is the capacity to alert decision makers to events having significant consequences for US foreign and security policy so that action can be taken to avert such dangers or significantly reduce their consequences. Several assumptions are embedded in this definition. First, it is assumed that the analyst can recognize that an event that threatens US interests or policies is becoming increasingly likely. Second, the analyst must have accurate and timely information and a keen understanding of the target's intentions and capabilities based on a comprehensive review of both past and current

reporting. In other words, a "strategic" warning is rarely the result of only a recently collected, single sensational report; rather it is the considered judgment of seasoned analysts
who can utilize both past and current reporting to detect a significant departure in a
target's standard operating procedures or modus operandi. Warning thus highlights the
growing possibility that the target is about to take actions that had previously not been
evident or credible. These patterns were often characterized as "indications and warning"
factors, which can take the form of lists of specific behaviors and actions that would pre-
cede hostile actions against US interests. These indications and warning processes grew
out of intelligence community monitoring of military forces, although indications and
warning methodology can be applied to new nontraditional challenges as well.

Third, the analyst must be able to communicate quickly to others in the intelligence
community and to important policymakers the judgment that a significant danger exists,
so that countermeasures can be taken. Thus there must be predesignated mechanisms
for sharing warning analysis with other intelligence professionals, particularly collectors who can then direct their efforts to provide further clarity to the warning problem.
Channels for engaging policymakers at an early stage of a potential crisis also must be
available. In examining a number of historical cases, warning practitioners have found
that so-called intelligence failures were less the result of information shortfalls than of an
inability to assess and communicate available information persuasively.[3]

Obstacles to Good Warning

While these steps in the warning process might seem simple, the execution of timely
warning is supremely difficult. Analysts must be confident enough in their judgments
to issue a forceful warning that would lead policymakers to alter their current strategies
and policies or suffer the consequences of not acting. Seldom are the signals so clear that
analysts can provide more than a reasonable guess that such a significant event could
occur. As Thomas Fingar has noted, the analyst can only reduce uncertainty but not
eliminate it.[4] In the aftermath of the 9/11 attacks, critics charged that either the US
intelligence community failed to "connect the dots" or that the George W. Bush administration failed to heed the warnings given by the Central Intelligence Agency (CIA)
prior to the attacks. Defenders of CIA have argued that ample "strategic warning" had
been provided to the Bush administration but that tactical warning on the exact details
of the plot—method, date, time, and place—is beyond the capability of any intelligence
service.[5] And indeed, the argument has been made by senior intelligence officials responsible for warning that when the intelligence community fails, it is most often in providing tactical, not strategic, warning.[6] The debate will continue on whether the attack on
the US embassy in Benghazi was a failure to warn or simply a failure to adopt adequate
security procedures in a dangerous setting. Chances are that the intelligence community
possessed an accurate assessment of the general threat faced by US personnel in Libya,
making this more a tactical than a strategic warning failure.

The Analyst's Responsibility

Not all the causes of warning failure (see box 13.1) reside with the analyst, but many sins of omission and commission can be averted or minimized if analysts understand their targets' history, culture, and the behavior patterns that shape their intentions. This is a greater challenge during a period when many new analysts are being integrated into the intelligence community. While many come with some academic training, they are often not well versed in their targets' past patterns and practices that their predecessors have witnessed. They must become experts on their countries or topics, not just from their first day on the job but going back, in some cases decades, to truly understand the underlying cultural and societal norms that shape their warning challenges. Context is everything when it comes to determining whether a sensational report is of real significance or merely an "outlier" and not to be taken seriously. Analysts must also understand the strengths and weaknesses of the collection environment and whether a target is masking its true motives and capabilities—that is to say, denial and deception is a threat that should always be on the minds of analysts.

BOX 13.1 Surprise's Seven Sins

1. Collection failure: Information on changing behavior or conditions is lacking because of flawed collection requirements or strategies, leaving analysts with major information gaps.

2. Deception: Misinformation provided by an adversary misleads analysts regarding a capability or intention; it takes advantage of known analytic mind-sets to lull analysts into believing there is no need to warn.

3. Denial: Collection gaps are created by an adversary's operational security, making it impossible to develop indicators or monitor changed behavior.

4. Misinterpretation: Analysts interpret intelligence poorly, owing to their inability to consider the role of collection gaps, deception and denial, or personal cognitive bias about the adversary's intentions or capabilities.

5. Poor information sharing: "Need to know" and other compartmentation practices of organizations hamper sharing of critical pieces of data that might have filled important collection gaps for analysts.

6. Muddled messages: Poorly crafted "warning" assessments fail to communicate the dangers or convince policymakers of the significance of a development and its impact on US interests.

7. Policy resistance: Recipients of "warning" assessments dismiss them as worst-case analysis conflicting with their own mind-sets or judge the warnings as designed to undermine their policy preferences.

Perhaps the most important responsibility of analysts is to be able to couch their warnings in terms that policymakers can grasp. One must understand the predilections of decision makers whom one has to persuade to take a warning seriously. Often it amounts to telling senior officials what they do not wish to hear or overcoming policymakers' mind-sets that lead them to minimize the probability and risks of a bad turn of events. "Wishful thinking," the urge for easy consensus, and a predisposition to judge intelligence assessments as "worst-case" analysis make the job of the analyst all the harder.[7]

The Warning Paradox

Often the analyst faces the difficult decision of whether to warn or not. "Damned if you do, damned if you don't" is often the feeling analysts have when they contemplate warning policymakers of the increasing likelihood that some untoward event is about to occur. Should the analyst err on the side of caution and warn repeatedly when some new indicator of change has emerged or wait a bit longer for more information to accumulate? Should he or she take the risk of not alerting a policymaker and be blamed if a spectacular military attack, terrorist event, political coup or financial crisis occurs? Most analysts recognize that there is a need to warn if the chances of an attack or crisis are rising toward better than even. But what about the more typical circumstance, when warning challenges are not black or white? So-called low-probability/high-impact events are the most troublesome. "Crying wolf" will quickly discredit the analyst to policymakers and make it even harder to be taken seriously the next time a warning needs to be issued.

There are many circumstances where the indicators are ambiguous or can be interpreted differently by analysts. Unanimity among analysts is rare on issues as complex as a foreign government's or nonstate actor's decision to launch an attack. For example, Charles Allen, former national intelligence officer (NIO) for warning, has described the difficulty in moving intelligence agencies to issue a "warning of war" message prior to the 1990 Iraq War. Analysts agreed that Saddam's military movements placed him in a position where he could quickly launch an attack, but few were prepared to say he was planning a major invasion. In their minds, this would be another blackmail attempt and there was most likely only a chance of a minor military "incursion" to seize oilfields in order to pressure the Kuwaiti government.[8] In a sense, they couched their warning in terms that made Saddam's behavior more rational and plausible, which minimized the full threat to US interests.

Analysts are often accused, after the fact, of having exaggerated threats when events do not turn out as badly as described in a warning assessment. The paradox here is that we cannot know how much the warning helped to ward off an event because of the actions US policymakers took to prevent a dangerous incident that was anticipated. What appears in hindsight to be an instance of crying wolf might actually be effective warning because it changed US policies, making it unattractive for an adversary to consider moving forward with its planned actions.

There are indeed documented cases of this phenomenon. During the year before the October 1973 Yom Kippur War, Israeli intelligence warned of Egyptian plans—derived from sensitive HUMINT reporting—to initiate military hostilities. Israel subsequently mobilized its forces, and one can surmise that Egyptian president Anwar Sadat determined he could not go through with his war plans. In September 1973, the same HUMINT source again reported Egyptian plans to attack, but this time the Israel Defense Forces did not mobilize and instead celebrated the holy day by permitting many soldiers to take leave. Senior officials seemingly became doubtful of the HUMINT source's veracity; yet, in the end, the intelligence warnings had been on the mark, and only when they were dismissed as inaccurate or exaggerated did Egypt see an opportunity to catch Israel by surprise.[9] Other studies of surprises where policymakers have not acted on intelligence warnings also suggest that had they taken some steps, the events might have been averted, resulting again in analysts being perceived as overly alarmed by the indicators they were watching.[10] Thus the more persuasive the warning, the less likely the event is to occur, if one assumes that the United States has an ability to shape events by changing its defense posture or foreign policy positions. Paradoxically, persuasive warnings, by helping to head off disasters before they happen, can also lead to the perception that analysts are crying wolf, which leads to the emergence of pathologies in the intelligence–policymaker relationship that create the conditions for inaction and strategic surprise.

The Intelligence Community's Track Record

The track record on warning, like that described in chapter 3, is mixed at best. Much of the history of the post-1945 intelligence community is littered with failed or missing warnings, which resulted not only in changes in the US intelligence community but also in damaged credibility of CIA and intelligence community analysis. Most of the cases one typically thinks of have a military dimension, but that is not always the case. Often political, technological, or economic developments have "surprised" US intelligence and led policymakers to charge that there had been major intelligence failures.

The most often cited intelligence failures have involved a failure to warn of the possibility of hostilities. If one thinks about the commonly mentioned military warning failures, there is a long list, including those mentioned below:

- Japan's attack on Pearl Harbor, 1941
- North Korea's invasion of South Korea, 1950
- The Soviet Union's placement of missiles in Cuba, 1962
- The Soviet Union's invasion of Czechoslovakia, 1968
- Egypt's attack on Israel, 1973
- The Soviet Union's invasion of Afghanistan, 1979
- Iraq's invasion of Kuwait, 1990

In these warning cases, there were observable indications of changes in a foreign adversary's behavior and even the movement of military forces or equipment. There were observable military movements or buildups reported to decision makers, constituting strategic warning in the minds of some practitioners. Nevertheless, analysts were not convinced that an adversary's "intentions" had changed, nor was there sufficient information available to them about the purposes or intent of the adversary's changed behavior. In many cases the adversary conducted denial-and-deception operations to mask its intentions; in others the information was too limited or considered unreliable to convince analysts that a real threat was imminent. In a few cases tactical warning was not provided prior to the onset of hostilities; in many others warning came so late in the crisis that policymakers were unable to adjust policies or take action to prevent the adversary's moves. In some of these cases warnings might have even been counterproductive because they alerted policymakers to the minimal threat posed by an opponent's activities, thereby fostering a "wait and see" attitude among officials.

Military surprise is by no means the only type of warning failure. The intelligence community has struggled to understand foreign political developments, which are even less susceptible to technical collection and the development of rigorous indications and warning analysis. The perennial problem of having accurate and timely human reporting on a foreign government's internal stability, the nature and strength of opposition groups, and the possible collapse of order in weak societies continues to frustrate American intelligence analysts. A classic example of this type of warning failure was the 1979 Iranian Revolution. Few intelligence analysts could contemplate the fall of the shah given the dominant mind-set that portrayed him as a pillar of stability in the region. Severely restricted reporting on internal opposition groups and a continuing stream of reporting from Iranian officials designed to reassure US policymakers about the shah's firm control reinforced this frame of mind.[11]

A more recent example of a failure to warn of political change might be the recent turmoil caused by the "Arab Spring." Here was a case where the US government—including intelligence analysts—was caught by surprise when a simple Tunisian fruit merchant's actions kicked off public disturbances that swept North Africa and are even now continuing in Syria and other parts of the Middle East. According to some reports, the administration was already disappointed before the Arab Spring with CIA analysis that straight-lined its judgments and ignored the possibility of radical discontinuities.[12] CIA director Leon Panetta, according to this narrative, had challenged analysts to identify possible triggers for instability. What strategic warning might have been possible, even accepting that predicting the precise "trigger" for unrest might be unknowable? Some senior intelligence officials have already acknowledged that analysts did not judge reporting of evident public dissatisfaction as capable of putting the masses into the streets and squares of Cairo and elsewhere.[13] A more complete postmortem of events leading up to the onset of the Arab uprisings is likely to reveal a number of errors commonly found in other warning cases: a lack of focus and resources on the issue or country, a strong presumption that surface stability—even if a repressive one—would continue, poor understanding of underlying social forces and opposition groups, and little appreciation for how social media magnify the consequences of a small triggering event on other actors and countries.[14] These weaknesses and failings appear eerily similar to the shortcomings that bedeviled analysts in the months leading up to the fall of the shah in 1979.

A final warning challenge relates to technological and economic surprises. Historically the US intelligence community has monitored military developments generally well. As Richard Kerr and Michael Warner note in chapter 3, there are virtually no cases where intelligence analysts missed the development of Soviet weapon systems. Nevertheless, the US intelligence community has been surprised, repeatedly, about the rate at which foreign adversaries develop and deploy sophisticated weapon systems. IC estimates of the Soviet atomic and hydrogen bomb programs consistently underestimated how quickly Moscow would master and build a nuclear arsenal. In like fashion, China surprised analysts by quickly developing its own nuclear arsenal. In the 1970s, the intelligence community did better in terms of monitoring the development of Indian and Pakistani weapon programs. Analysts continued to suffer, however, from surprises regarding the timelines for testing and introduction of new weapons into combat units. Analysts were surprised in 1974, when India tested its first nuclear device. Similarly in 1998, India conducted a series of tests—rapidly followed by Pakistan's own—that caught US policymakers by surprise. This was not a strategic warning failure because the intelligence community had previously warned policymakers that the Indian government had the ability to test a nuclear weapon at any moment without major additional preparations, but it did constitute a tactical warning failure. In postmortems it was clear that India had deceived intelligence analysts in the way it prepared for the tests. However, given the newly installed Indian government's campaign pledge to do so, it would seem that the intelligence community should have been on its guard for efforts to test.[15] One can also consider the intelligence community's flawed Iraq WMD national intelligence estimate in 2002 as a type of warning failure in the sense of it being a false positive. Had intelligence warned policymakers that there was only ambiguous reporting on current Iraqi activities, it might have altered the way the Bush administration proceeded or at least altered the justification for its invasion of Iraq.

Warning on economic crises has been similarly weak. In the mid-1990s, the Mexican peso crisis caught US policymakers by surprise, even though senior American business leaders appeared much better informed about the general state of economic affairs inside Mexico. Intelligence warnings, according to one former intelligence official, "were never very sharply etched and so were dismissed by Treasury and other officials in charge of the issues." The more telling comment was that "information was there. The art lay in interpreting and projecting it."[16] The Asian financial crisis of 1997 proved to be another intelligence surprise. Analysts did not realize that what appeared as merely a currency crisis in Thailand would produce more dangerous social and political unrest in countries throughout Asia and eventually in Russia as well.[17] One consequence of globalization, then, is the reality that economic developments in one part of the world are likely to have repercussions elsewhere. Analysts who focus narrowly on their own country accounts need to collaborate more closely with those responsible for other areas and issues, or else they will fail to detect the possibility of cascade effects as economic, political, or social developments in one country influence events across entire regions or global economic sectors.

Lest one conclude that the intelligence community never successfully warns, one should at least acknowledge that there have been remarkably prescient cases in which warning was provided. The 1967 Arab-Israeli War was forecast by intelligence analysts. The judgment that it would last no longer than seven to ten days (it began on June 5 and ended on June 10) so impressed President Lyndon Johnson that he began inviting CIA director Richard Helms to his restricted policy lunches. Periodically intelligence warning regarding the state of tensions between Pakistan and India on their shared border has resulted in timely intervention by senior US officials to defuse military confrontations that might have resulted in military clashes and potentially the use of nuclear weapons.[18] The 1990 national intelligence estimate on Yugoslavia is a good illustration of very explicit warning but one that was barely heeded. Subsequent estimates on Bosnia were equally bleak, forcing policymakers to get more involved in the deepening crisis there and ultimately bringing the ethnic conflict to an end. More recently, two major intelligence community assessments on post-Saddam Iraq and the regional implications of regime change there were very prescient, yet they too were largely dismissed at the time by policymakers skeptical of analysts' expertise and political bias, as well as convinced that their assumptions regarding the ease of restoring order there were well founded.[19] The intelligence community's early warnings on Russo-Georgian tensions alerted the George W. Bush administration early to the possibility of hostilities between the two countries, which eventually broke out in 2008.

How Has Warning Changed since 9/11?

The 9/11 attacks put a new spotlight on the warning function of the intelligence community. The publication of the 9/11 Commission's report found fault with the way the IC was collecting and analyzing intelligence, as well as how it collaborated and shared information. Much of the Intelligence Reform and Terrorist Protection Act of 2004 was indirectly aimed at improving the community's operation for the purpose of effective warning. It is thus a bit surprising that the specific warning system that had been operating—known as the National Foreign Intelligence Warning System (NFIWS)—remained in place until 2009. This system, which began after the 1973 Yom Kippur War, had been based on a centralized model for warning led by a national intelligence officer for warning who directed a sizable national warning staff that held interagency meetings (known as the National Warning Committee) and issued periodic "alert memoranda" to warn of possible hostilities or damaging events.[20] This system provided a training ground for analysts, which helped them to become more sophisticated in their understanding of warning problems. As late as 2006, the director of national intelligence was still identifying the NIO for warning as his "primary executive agent for foreign intelligence warning and assigned the authority to direct, manage, and certify the capabilities, processes, and performance of the NFIWS."[21] This reaffirmation was occurring even while other intelligence officials were questioning the rationale for a Cold War–style warning system in a post-9/11 world. Discussions within the National Intelligence Council, as well as various outside studies, pointed to the need for an approach that expanded well beyond the military domain, requiring a diffusion of warning responsibilities across the community.[22]

A new system—termed mission management—would eventually lead to the abolishment of the position of NIO for warning and the national warning staff. In its place was the instruction that all analysts were now responsible for warning regarding their accounts. The new philosophy was that the subject-matter experts were in a better position to understand the longer-term trends in their areas than a centralized staff of generalists. Over the years a succession of NIOs for warning had encountered continued resistance from their regional and functional counterparts, who believed that they were the experts on their accounts and should therefore be principally responsible for warning. More often than not, they viewed the NIOs for warning as poaching and pontificating on issues for which they had less expertise than the substantive experts in the National Intelligence Council and the IC's analytic units. Moreover, given that warning was no longer restricted to merely military matters but covered a wide range of political, economic, and social issues, there seemed less reason to place the warning function in the hands of a single officer and warning staff that had largely grown out of a military warning model.

The new system, however, poses new challenges. Without a senior official for warning, who was accountable for actually sounding an alarm? The answer appears to be found in Director of National Intelligence James Clapper's decision to designate the national intelligence managers (NIMs) as being responsible for warning issues in their respective regional and functional areas. NIMs are the senior intelligence officials who monitor both the collection and analysis activities for different regions, as well as country-specific and issue-specific topics. The number of NIMs is not fixed, but in 2012 approximately fifteen individuals were designated as such.

An examination of the NIMs' responsibilities provides a justification for them becoming players in the new warning function. Looking at *Intelligence Community Directive Number 900* (*ICD 900*), which established their positions, it is clear that NIMs' core duties amount to a checklist of challenges to warning—that is to say, their responsibilities to monitor, evaluate, and improve intelligence collection, analysis, and information sharing are precisely the areas that often are cited as having been lacking when an intelligence failure to warn has occurred.[23] Box 13.2 lays out NIMs' key duties. If they fulfill these tasks to the best of their abilities, the prospect of a surprise or a failure to warn would be significantly reduced.

The question becomes, however, whether monitoring both the collection and analysis side of intelligence activities, as well as other duties contained in *ICD 900*, really leave sufficient time for a national intelligence manager to take on the equivalent role of "chief warner" that the NIO for warning formerly held. NIMs may not see warning as their

---

BOX 13.2 National Intelligence Managers: DNI's Chief Warners

Among the duties specified in *ICD 900*, the following include some key aspects of the warning problem:

- Setting collection and analysis priorities for national intelligence related to their assigned missions
- Determining the state of collection against their assigned missions, identifying collection gaps, and developing cross-IC collection strategies to fill those gaps
- Identifying exploitation gaps related to their assigned missions
- Determining the state of analysis on their assigned missions, identifying analytic gaps related to customer requirements, and tasking analysts related to those missions
- Evaluating the quality of analysis and ensuring that competitive and alternative analyses are conducted on topics related to their assigned missions
- Ensuring that intelligence related to their assigned targets is available to and shared with all appropriate IC personnel
- Evaluating the effectiveness of the IC's efforts against their assigned missions, including, but not limited to, collection, analysis, exploitation, dissemination, information sharing, foreign relations, and resources

---

Source: DNI, *Intelligence Community Directive Number 900, Mission Management* (2006).

primary function or use their positions to raise consciousness about the warning mission as the NIO for warning had previously done. A further complication has been the friction between NIOs and NIMs, who now share responsibility to interact with senior policymakers. Where the NIOs were once the senior intelligence officials meeting with senior directors on the National Security Council staff and with assistant secretaries at the State and Defense Departments, now the NIMs would have the responsibility to warn these same officials. A clear division of labor remains to be worked out. At this juncture there is little to suggest that NIMs are replacing NIOs as the principal intelligence advisors to senior policymakers.

The Future of Warning

Warning will remain a core mission of the US intelligence community and of analysts. Already there is some discussion of how to best characterize warning in a post-9/11 world. A traditional military model, based on the NIO for warning and military-style centralized warning staff, appears to be no longer suited to the wide range of issues that are now followed by the IC. But it would be folly if reorganization led to the abandonment of well-established indicators and warning methodologies that can still be used against a range of traditional military targets and perhaps some nontraditional, nonstate actors. It also is clear that China's military potential needs to be monitored closely, as well as the military activities of other known adversaries such as Iran and North Korea. The same can be said of such major military powers as Russia, India, and Pakistan, where there remains the possibility of hostilities on their borders or elsewhere. Thus indications and warning alert lists are useful tools when it comes to monitoring these military forces for signs of war preparations or military interventions.

In the absence of a warning system led by the director of national intelligence, there appears to be growing interest on the part of the Defense Department to develop its own elaborate set of warning mechanisms. Most recently, the Defense Intelligence Agency (DIA) has promulgated new instructions for defense intelligence analysts to reaffirm warning as a core mission and to develop what is being called the Defense Warning Network. This new mechanism will rely upon designated defense warning advisers from combatant commands, as well as combat support agencies (DIA, the National Security Agency, the National Geospatial-Intelligence Agency, and so on), who will constitute a Defense Warning Council, whose responsibilities include providing warning assessments, evaluating the effectiveness of defense warning efforts (both analysis and collection), and conveying warning intelligence requirements from the Joint Staff and combatant commands to the Defense Warning Network. According to these new directives, DIA analysts will be responsible for identifying, assessing, and warning about emerging and potential risks, vulnerabilities, and threats to defense interests.[24]

This Defense Department approach retains the traditional indicators-based warning methodologies, which are readily applied to leading military actors such as China, Russia, Iran, North Korea, India, and Pakistan. But an indicators-based methodology might easily apply to some nonstate actors, which have some of the same characteristics as states. In hindsight we know that al-Qaeda had a well-developed organizational structure, with specific units assigned various military, intelligence, logistics, and operational duties not so dissimilar to organizations found in a country's military and security services; thus these would be significant targets for identification, monitoring, and assessment. Indications and warning methodologies are also under development in the fields of cyberwarfare and cybercrime. It now appears possible to monitor the "prelude" to a major cyberattack or to detect virulent virus and malware outbreaks before they spread across the Web. Responses to indications and warnings of cyberattacks, however, might in some cases have to be virtually instantaneous, creating political, strategic, and technical challenges for analysts and policymakers alike.

It is also conceivable that other nonstate actors such as organized crime groups or terrorist cells would lend themselves to such warning methodologies. For example, deviations could be observed in what constitutes normal activity of various clandestine organizations as efforts begin to focus on launching initiatives, not simply maintaining clandestine cells. Chatter on internet-enabled criminal or terrorist networks might increase as coded messages are relayed to fellow travelers to prepare to face enhanced law enforcement activities and break with "peacetime" command-and-control procedures. Communications within criminal or terrorist circles about the increased likelihood that a major operation is about to unfold might be picked up by informers. Paradoxically, the very absence of signals of normal activity could suggest a sharp increase in operational security that could indicate that military forces, terrorists, or criminal organizations are attempting to hide last-minute preparations to stage a significant operation. The absence of chatter on internet networks or indications that routine activities have inexplicably been curtailed could serve as important signals that the opponent might be changing its readiness posture. The presence of unique signals or the absence of routine signals—the presence or absence of data—could both serve as important indicators that an opponent is moving from a day alert to a generated alert status.

Meanwhile, the rest of the intelligence community is considering how to go beyond the traditional notion of "warning" to capture the new era in which surprises are likely to come from a variety of domains, in addition to direct military threats. At this writing, the director of national intelligence has a small interagency "tiger team" focused on how it can best develop "anticipatory intelligence," which identifies emerging trends that might have significant implications for US interests. In part it is a recognition that some new transnational issues—global health, global climate change, humanitarian issues, and financial crises—do not lend themselves to traditional indicators and warning analysis. Determining how one can monitor these more novel issues remains a work in progress. Some have suggested the use of "horizon-scanning" techniques for monitoring a long list of basic economic, demographic, social, political trends from which one can determine some potentially significant discontinuities, but these techniques remain relatively untried in the United States.

Regardless of the specific techniques or organizational structure used to perform warning, there is no doubt that it will remain a core mission of the US intelligence community. As the analysis profession advances, it must not lose sight of this enduring responsibility. Accordingly, the IC should direct some of its training and education efforts to sensitize every analyst to the importance of communicating warning intelligence to policymakers as early and as clearly as possible. If there is one Achilles' heel to the acceptance of analysis as a true profession, it is the prospect that a future failure to warn will undermine an American president's, or the American public's, confidence in intelligence.

Notes

1. This chapter benefits from interviews held with three former national intelligence officers for warning and numerous other warning experts in the intelligence community.
2. Robert Vickers, "The State of Warning Today," *Defense Intelligence Journal* 7, no. 2 (Fall 1998): 9–15.
3. Douglas E. MacEachin and Janne Nolan, *Discourse, Dissent, and Strategic Surprise: Formulating US Security Policy in an Age of Uncertainty* (Washington, DC: Institute for the Study of Diplomacy, 2006), 109–10.

4. Thomas Fingar, *Reducing Uncertainty: Intelligence Analysis and National Security* (Stanford, CA: Stanford University Press, 2011).

5. See Paul R. Pillar, "Think Again: Intelligence," *Foreign Policy*, January/February 2012.

6. Vickers, "State of Warning," 10.

7. MacEachin and Nolan, *Discourse, Dissent*.

8. Charles E. Allen, "Warning and Iraq's Invasion of Kuwait: A Retrospective Look," *Defense Intelligence Journal* 7, no. 2 (Fall 1998): 36.

9. Uri Bar-Joseph, *The Watchman Fell Asleep: The Surprise of Yom Kippur and Its Sources of Surprise* (Albany: State University of New York Press, 2005), 49.

10. MacEachin and Nolan, *Discourse, Dissent*, 63.

11. See Robert Jervis, *Why Intelligence Fails: Lessons from the Iranian Revolution and the Iraq War* (Ithaca, NY: Cornell University Press, 2010).

12. David Sanger, *Confront and Conceal: Obama's Secret Wars and Surprising Use of Military Power* (New York: Crown, 2012), pp. 280–81.

13. David Shedd, deputy director of DIA, quoted in the *Los Angeles Times*, July 19, 2012.

14. Although in another—nonwarning—context, Lt. Gen. Michael Flynn has criticized the intelligence community for not appreciating the importance of understanding the sociological and cultural basis of the conflict. See Michael Flynn et al., *Fixing Intel: A Blueprint for Making Intelligence Relevant in Afghanistan* (Washington, DC: Center for a New American Security, 2010).

15. Gregory Treverton, "Failing in India," in *Reshaping National Intelligence for an Age of Information* (Cambridge: Cambridge University Press, 2001), 3.

16. Ibid., 96–97.

17. Douglas E. MacEachin and Janne Nolan, "The Asian Financial Crisis 1997–1998: Adapting Intelligence and Policymaking to the Challenge of Global Economics," Georgetown University Institute for the Study of Diplomacy, Working Paper No. 5, February 27, 2006, 9.

18. Allen, "Warning and Iraq's Invasion," 36.

19. Paul R. Pillar, *Intelligence and U.S. Foreign Policy: Iraq, 9/11, and Misguided Reform* (New York: Columbia University Press, 2011), pp. 56–58.

20. According to some former intelligence officials, the NIO for warning was seen to be the primus inter pares of the national intelligence officers, and he shortly became the first chairman of the National Intelligence Council in recognition of his role in convening the council for the purpose of examining warning issues that cut across the diverse regions and issues for which individual NIOs were responsible.

21. Director of National Intelligence, *Intelligence Community Directive Number 201, National Foreign Intelligence Warning System (Effective: 6 June 2006)*, declassified but heavily redacted, www.fas.org/irp/dni/icd/icd-201.pdf.

22. The authors base many of these observations on discussions held with three former NIOs for warning who were involved in discussions leading up to the changes announced in 2009 and 2010.

23. Director of National Intelligence, *Intelligence Community Directive Number 900, Mission Management (Effective: 21 December 2006)*, www.fas.org/irp/dni/icd/icd-900.pdf. This directive states that NIMs are created on counterterrorism, counterproliferation, counterintelligence, Iran, North Korea, Cuba, and Venezuela, leaving open the possibility of others.

Since then others have been established for broader regional areas that more or less overlap with existing regional NIO accounts, which has been a source of some friction between the National Intelligence Council and the DNI. Many NIOs consider themselves also in a position to warn senior policymakers and are not content being somewhat subservient to the NIMs, who appear to have more clout with the current DNI.

24. This guidance is provided in a July 16, 2012, DIA directive, *Instruction on Defense Warning*.

PART V

Analysis for Twenty-First-Century Issues

CHAPTER 14

Structured Analytic Techniques: A New Approach to Analysis

RANDOLPH H. PHERSON AND RICHARDS J. HEUER JR.

Among the characteristics of a true analytic profession, a standardized set of methods must be considered essential. As other chapters in this volume highlight, efforts are under way in many spheres to professionalize analysis through better training and education, as well as to reach out to broader centers of excellence. These important aspects of professionalization, however, need to be matched by the development of more rigorous, transparent, and replicable methods for reaching intelligence judgments. This chapter focuses on the development of structured analytic techniques (SATs), which are being used increasingly among intelligence analysts and agencies.

While self-initiated improvements in analysis have been important, the terrorist attacks of September 11, 2001, and the erroneous 2002 national intelligence estimate on Iraqi weapons of mass destruction prompted a more intense reassessment of how intelligence analysis is done. The commission convoked after the 9/11 attacks criticized the intelligence community for its "failure of imagination," and the WMD commission documented a flawed analytic process that failed to challenge analytic mind-sets, examine key assumptions, consider alternative hypotheses, and detect deceptive reporting. Attention initially focused on the need for "alternative analysis"—techniques for questioning conventional wisdom by identifying and analyzing alternative explanations or outcomes. The US Congress also called for intelligence analysts to adopt competitive, contrarian, or "red cell" techniques to ferret out poor logic, faulty evidence, and other shortcomings in analytic tradecraft.[1]

Origins and Purposes of SATs

Such criticisms were not new to the intelligence community; it had already initiated a process to change the way analysis is done before these failures. As mentioned in an earlier chapter, CIA established the Sherman Kent School for Intelligence Analysis in 2000 to improve the effectiveness of analytic tradecraft.[2] Simultaneously, several contributors to this book were engaged in teaching a workshop on alternative analysis that introduced analysts to a handful of new techniques designed to add more rigor and structure to their analysis. In the wake of the 9/11 attacks and the Iraqi WMD fiasco, the focus on alternative analysis was broadened to encompass a new approach to analytic tradecraft that came to be called structured analysis.[3] Structured analysis employs a variety of techniques by which internal thought processes are externalized in a systematic and transparent manner so that they can be shared, built on, and easily critiqued by others. With transparency each technique leaves an auditable trail that other analysts, managers, and customers can examine to see the basis for an analytic judgment.

Intelligence community methodologists and analysts have used forms of structured analysis for decades, beginning in the 1950s with the RAND Corporation. However, the general use of structured analytic techniques by mainline analysts has accelerated since the late 1990s, when CIA introduced more formal training in such processes, gradually followed by DIA and the FBI.[4] They have now become a staple of most US government and military intelligence training and education programs. SATs have also spread to intelligence and law enforcement organizations in Canada, the United Kingdom, Australia, and elsewhere. A growing number of colleges and universities are introducing these techniques, and a few Fortune 500 companies and nongovernment organizations are incorporating them into their own business practices. The driving forces behind increasing interest in and use of SATs are: (1) an appreciation of cognitive limitations and pitfalls that make intelligence analysis so difficult, (2) prominent analytic failures that have prompted reexamination of how analysis is generated, (3) pressures to adopt more collaborative work processes, and (4) the desire by decision makers who receive analysis that it be more transparent as to how the conclusions are reached.

Overcoming Cognitive Limitations

Intelligence analysts work under time pressure with information that is incomplete, ambiguous, and sometimes deliberately deceptive. This makes them vulnerable to a wide range of well-known sources of analytic error, as described in one of the author's previous books, *Psychology of Intelligence Analysis*.[5] SATs provide a first line of defense against common analytic pitfalls. They help analysts mitigate the proven cognitive limitations, sidestep some of the known analytic pitfalls, and explicitly confront the problems associated with unquestioned mental models or mind-sets. They spur analysts to think more rigorously about an analytic problem and ensure that preconceptions, assumptions, and mental models (or mind-sets) are not taken for granted but are explicitly examined and tested.[6] There is, of course, no formula for always getting it right, but the use of structured techniques can reduce the frequency and severity of error.

Many tools for overcoming recognized cognitive limitations are based on two basic principles: decomposition and externalization. Decomposition means breaking a problem down into its component parts. That is, indeed, the essence of analysis. One dictionary definition of analysis is "the separation of an intellectual or material whole into its constituent parts for individual study; the study of such constituent parts and their interrelationships in making up a whole."[7] Externalization means getting the decomposed problem out of one's head and down on paper or a computer screen in some simplified form that shows the main variables or elements of the problem and how they relate to each other.

The recommendation to compensate for the limitations of working memory by decomposing and externalizing analytic problems is certainly not new. The following quote is from a letter Benjamin Franklin wrote in 1772 to the great British scientist Joseph Priestley, the discoverer of oxygen:

> When those difficult cases occur, they are difficult, chiefly because while we have them under consideration, all the reasons pro and con are not present to the mind at the same time, but sometimes one set present themselves, and at other times another, the first being out of sight. Hence the various purposes or inclinations that alternatively prevail, and the uncertainty that perplexes us.
>
> To get over this, my way is to divide half a sheet of paper by a line into two columns; writing over the one Pro, and over the other Con. Then, during three or four days of consideration, I put down under the different heads short hints of the different motives, that at different times occur to me, for or against the measure.
>
> When I have thus got them all together in one view, I endeavor to estimate their respective weights; and where I find two, one on each side, that seem equal, I strike them both out. If I find a reason pro equal to some two reasons con, I strike out the three . . . and thus proceeding I find at length where the balance lies; and if, after a day or two of further consideration, nothing new that is of importance occurs on either side, I come to a determination accordingly.[8]

It is interesting that Franklin over two hundred years ago identified the problem of limited working memory and how it affects one's ability to make analytic judgments. Franklin also identified the solution—getting all the pros and cons out of his head and onto paper in some visible, shorthand form. The fact that this topic was part of the dialogue between such illustrious intellects reflects the type of people who use such analytic tools. These are not aids to be used only by weak analysts and that are unneeded by the strong. Human cognitive limitations affect everyone. It is the more astute analysts who are most conscious of this and most likely to recognize the value gained by such tools.

Putting ideas into written form ensures that they will last. They will lie around for days goading analysts into having further thoughts. Lists are effective because they exploit people's tendency to be a bit compulsive—most analysts want to keep adding to them. They let us get the obvious and habitual answers out of the way, so that attention is given to thinking of other less obvious ideas. One specialist in creativity has observed that "for the purpose of moving our minds, pencils can serve as crowbars"—just by writing things down in ways that stimulate new associations.[9]

Lists such as Franklin recommended are one of the simplest forms of structured analysis. An intelligence analyst might make lists of early warning indicators, alternative explanations, possible outcomes, factors a foreign leader will need to take into account when making a decision, or arguments for and against a given explanation or outcome. Other tools for externalizing the component parts of a problem include outlines, tables, diagrams, trees, and matrices, with many subspecies of each. For example, trees include decision trees and fault trees. Diagrams include concept maps, mind maps, argument maps, causal maps, influence diagrams, and flowcharts. Other structured techniques usually fall into three broad categories: imagination, diagnostic, and challenge analysis. Imagination techniques spur analysts to think more creatively and synthesize data; diagnostic techniques help analysts distinguish, characterize, or identify a particular activity more precisely often through a process of hypothesis testing; and challenge techniques force analysts to challenge their assumptions, the quality of their evidence, and the soundness of their logic.

Spurring Greater Collaboration

Our current high-tech global environment increasingly requires collaboration among analysts with different areas of expertise and different organizational perspectives. Structured analytic techniques are ideal for this interaction. Each step in a technique prompts relevant discussion, and typically this generates more divergent information and more new ideas than any unstructured group process. SATs' step-by-step process structures the interaction among analysts in a small analytic group or team in a way that helps to avoid the multiple pitfalls and pathologies that often degrade group or team performance.

Analysis in the US intelligence community is currently in a transitional stage from a mental activity done predominantly by a sole analyst to a collaborative team or group activity.[10] The driving forces behind this transition include:

- the growing complexity of international issues and consequent requirement for multidisciplinary input to most analytic products;[11]
- the need to share more information more quickly across organizational boundaries;
- the increased dispersion of expertise, especially as the boundaries between analysts, collectors, and operators become blurred; and
- the need to identify and evaluate the validity of alternative mental models.

This transition is being enabled by advances in technology such as Intellipedia (the intelligence community's classified version of Wikipedia) and other collaborative networks, communities of interest, the mushrooming growth of social networking practices among the upcoming generation of analysts, and the increasing use of structured analytic techniques that guide the interaction between analysts. SATs can guide the dialogue between analysts with common interests as they share evidence and alternative perspectives on the meaning and significance of this evidence. Just as these techniques provide structure to our individual thought processes, they can also structure the interaction of analysts within a small team or group. Because the thought process in these techniques is transparent, each step in the technique prompts relevant discussion within the team, and discussion under these circumstances can generate and evaluate substantially more divergent information and new ideas than a group that does not follow a structured process. In other words, SATs are enablers of collaboration. These techniques and collaboration fit together like hand in glove, and they should be promoted and developed together.

Along with its advantages, team-based analysis also brings with it a new set of challenges comparable to the cognitive limitations and pitfalls faced by the individual analyst.[12] The well-known group-process problems, however, can be minimized by use of structured techniques that guide the interaction between members of a team or group. This helps to keep discussions from getting sidetracked and elicits alternative views from all team members. Analysts have found that the use of a structured process helps to depersonalize arguments when there are differences of opinion. Fortunately, today's technology and social networking programs make structured collaboration much easier than it has ever been in the past.

The Role of SATs in the Analytic Process

The first step of science is to know one thing from another. This knowledge consists in their specific distinctions; but in order that it may be fixed and permanent, distinct names must be given to different things, and those names must be recorded and remembered.

—Carolus Linnaeus, *Systema Naturae*, 1738

Intelligence analysts employ a range of methods to deal with an ever-growing list of topics. Many researchers write about only two general approaches to analysis: qualitative versus quantitative, intuitive versus empirical, or intuitive versus scientific. Others might grant that there are three: intuitive, structured, and scientific. The authors posit four broad categories of analytic techniques based on the nature of the analytic methods used and the type of data that are available (see table 14.1).[13] Although each method is distinct, the borders between them can be blurry. Each, however, usually requires a different type of training:

- *Unaided expert judgment:* Often referred to as traditional analysis, this is the intuitive way most intelligence analysis has been done.[14] Akin to journalism, at its best it includes evidentiary reasoning, most of what is generally considered critical thinking, historical method, case study method, and reasoning by analogy. The key characteristic that distinguishes traditional from structured analysis is that it is usually an individual effort in which the reasoning remains largely in the mind of the analyst until it is written down in a draft report. Training in this type of analysis is generally provided through graduate education, especially in the humanities and liberal arts and often with an area studies focus on some country or language expertise.
- *Structured analysis:* Structured techniques externalize the analyst's thinking in a manner that makes it visible to all, thereby enabling it to be reviewed and critiqued

Table 14.1   Four Types of Analytic Techniques

	Known Data	Unknown Data
Qualitative	*Unaided Expert Judgment*	*Structured Analysis*
	(Critical thinking processes)	*(Imagination, diagnostic, and challenge techniques)*
Quantitative	*Empirical Analysis*	*Quasi-Quantitative Analysis*
	(Data-based computer tools and visualization techniques)	*(Computer-based tools requiring input from experts)*

Source: Katherine Hibbs Pherson and Randolph H. Pherson, *Critical Thinking for Strategic Intelligence* (Washington, DC: CQ Press, 2013), 53. Reprinted by permission of SAGE Publications, Inc.

piece by piece, or step by step, by the author and by other knowledgeable analysts. For this reason it often becomes a collaborative effort in which the transparency of the analytic technique exposes analysts to divergent or conflicting perspectives. Structured analysis is believed to mitigate the adverse impact on analysis of known cognitive limitations and pitfalls. Structured techniques can be used by analysts who have not been trained in statistics, advanced mathematics, or the hard sciences. When used correctly, structured analytic techniques significantly increase an analyst's level of confidence in his or her analytic assessments and key judgments. Most of the training in SATs occurs within the intelligence community where it was largely invented or adapted out of necessity, given the limited applicability of academically inspired techniques designed for more data-rich problems. Most national intelligence estimates, for example, include a core structured technique—the Key Assumptions Check (see box 14.1).[15] A growing number of colleges and universities have incorporated structured analysis into their intelligence, law enforcement, and homeland security studies programs.

- *Quasi-quantitative analysis:* Analysts often lack the empirical data needed to analyze an intelligence problem and must use data generated by experts. In the absence of empirical data, many methods are designed to use quantitative data generated by expert opinion, especially subjective probability judgments. Special procedures are used to elicit these judgments. This category includes methods such as Bayesian inference, dynamic modeling, and simulation. The Coup Vulnerability Methodology, for example, requires analysts to rate fifty-four distinct factors that make up a four-stage process known to contribute to civil-military tensions on a high–medium–low scale to monitor a country's vulnerability to a military coup.[16] Training in the use of such methods is provided through graduate education in fields such as math, information science, operations research, business, and the sciences.

BOX 14.1   Key Assumptions Check

When to Use

At the beginning of a project, alone or with a group of analysts, construct the list of key assumptions, then at the end review the initial list to see if it needs to be modified.

Value Added

Writing the list of key assumptions that underpin the analysis exposes them to critical examination and provides a better understanding of the most important dynamics at play. Analysts discover hidden relationships and links among key factors, as well as identify developments that would undermine the assumptions. It reduces the risk of surprise should new information render assumptions invalid.

The Method

Involve those working the issue, as well as others less familiar with the topic who can openly challenge the key assumptions. List all key assumptions that underlie the analysis and ask how much confidence analysts have that each assumption is valid and why. Identify circumstances that might undermine the assumption and consider if the assumption was more true in the past than it is now. It is important to ask what impact each assumption's invalidation would have on the analysis. Categorize each assumption as basically solid, correct with qualifications, or unsupported—a major "uncertainty." Refine the list by deleting invalid ones and adding newly identified assumptions.

- *Empirical analysis:* Quantifiable empirical data are so different from expert-generated data that the methods and types of problems the data are used to analyze are quite different. Econometric modeling is one common example of this method. Other examples include statistical hypothesis testing using political, economic, demographic, or public opinion data. In intelligence, empirical data are collected by various types of sensors and are used, for example, in analysis of foreign weapon systems. Training is generally obtained through graduate education in statistics, economics, or the sciences.

Techniques from two or more of these categories will often be used in a single analytic project. For example, a structured analysis tool such as Structured Brainstorming (see box 14.2) might identify variables to be included in a dynamic model that uses expert-generated data to quantify these variables.[17] Similarly, analysis of a foreign military threat might combine the use of SATs to assess political motive or intent with a quantitative analysis of technical capabilities.

BOX 14.2   Structured Brainstorming

When to Use

When beginning a project, Structured Brainstorming can help generate a full range of hypotheses and ensure all aspects of a problem are considered. As the project advances, the technique is useful to stimulate new research ideas or avenues of inquiry. When a conventional and static view of an issue needs to be reexamined, this technique can be employed.

Value Added

The brainstorming process can spark new ideas and creative thinking. It can assist an analyst by bringing in outside experts with different backgrounds, perspectives, and skills. Often by broadening the perspectives on a problem, new "unknown unknowns" are identified.

The Method

Brainstorming is most effective when "structured" rather than "freewheeling" or informal. To structure the process, start with a specific purpose and topic. Asking a diverse set of participants to come to the session with a list of ideas in advance can enrich the group process. To benefit from the diversity of ideas, never censor any "odd" or "outlier" notions, as they may be the germ of a new idea that the process can uncover. Including outsiders with different mindsets, data, or culture is essential. The ideas generated should be written down immediately and circulated after the brainstorming session. Those key insights become the basis for new perspectives from which all the participants can benefit.

Building a Taxonomy

Development of a taxonomy is an important step in organizing knowledge and furthering the development of any particular discipline. Rob Johnston developed a taxonomy of variables that influence intelligence analysis. He noted that "a taxonomy differentiates domains by specifying the scope of inquiry, codifying naming conventions, identifying areas of interest, helping to set research priorities, and often leading to new theories. Taxonomies are signposts, indicating what is known and what has yet to be discovered."[18]

Considering that the intelligence community began focusing on structured techniques in the early 2000s to improve analysis, it is fitting to categorize these techniques by the various ways they can help achieve that goal. Structured analytic techniques can mitigate some of the human cognitive limitations, explicitly confront the problems associated with unquestioned assumptions and mental models, and ensure that assumptions and mental models are explicitly examined and tested. They can structure and support the decision-making process, and the documentation of these techniques can facilitate information sharing and collaboration.

A secondary goal when categorizing the structured techniques is to correlate categories with different types of common analytic tasks. In *Structured Analytic Techniques for Intelligence Analysis*, the authors have identified fifty SATs most suited for intelligence analysis. We organized them into eight categories:

- Decomposition and Visualization
- Idea-Generation Techniques
- Scenarios and Indicators
- Hypothesis Generation and Testing
- Assessment of Cause and Effect
- Challenge Analysis Techniques
- Conflict Management Techniques
- Decision-Support Analysis

Core Techniques and Sleepers

Structured analytic techniques constitute a methodology—a set of principles and procedures for analyzing the kinds of uncertainties that intelligence analysts must deal with on a daily basis. Over the past decade, several of these techniques have emerged as core techniques that analysts find the most useful in supporting their daily work. In 2006, CIA's Sherman Kent School initiated a "Train the Trainers" program in which senior analysts spent several days learning how to facilitate the use of a core set of four SATs. The course focused on the following:[19]

- *Structured Brainstorming:* a brainstorming process using sticky notes for generating new ideas and concepts often used to kick off a multiple-scenarios exercise
- *Key Assumptions Check:* a systematic effort to make explicit and question the assumptions that guide an analyst's interpretation of evidence and reasoning about any particular problem
- *Analysis of Competing Hypotheses (ACH):* the identification of a complete set of alternative hypotheses, the systematic evaluation of each, and the selection of the best-fitting hypothesis (or hypotheses) by focusing on information that tends to disconfirm each hypothesis (see box 14.3)
- *Indicators:* a preestablished set of observable phenomena that are periodically reviewed to help track events, spot emerging trends, and warn of unanticipated changes

The Sherman Kent School's selection of these four core techniques was followed by a global business consulting company deciding to integrate three of the four structured techniques directly into its well-honed methodological approach: the Key Assumptions Check, Analysis of Competing Hypotheses, and Indicators. The company also flagged three other techniques as adding major value to the analytic process:[20]

- *"What If?" Analysis:* A technique that posits an event has occurred with the potential for a major positive or negative impact and then explains how it came about, this technique has proven particularly useful for dealing with controversial topics or issues for which much data is missing.

BOX 14.3   Analysis of Competing Hypotheses (ACH)

When to Use

Analysis of Competing Hypotheses can be used on any problem where alternative explanations or outcomes should be examined and weighed. Controversial issues, which require a careful audit trail of how analytic judgments were reached, lend themselves to ACH. Especially when analysts and decision makers disagree over analytic judgments, ACH can help to identify key areas of disagreement.

Value Added

ACH can guard against three common analytic pitfalls: (1) the temptation to accept as an adequate explanation first impressions that are based on incomplete data, (2) failure to identify a range of hypotheses at the beginning of a project, and (3) relying on information that supports an analyst's favored explanation without realizing it might also support alternative explanations. More generally, ACH can overcome "confirmation" bias—that is, a tendency to accept or interpret new information in a fashion that supports the prevailing view. In addition, it can help to identify differences of opinion among analysts on the strength and relevance of evidence.

The Method

Analysts array all the relevant information in a matrix format that displays each item of information on one axis against each of the separate hypotheses on the other axis. Analysts discuss each piece of information and its relationship—or diagnosticity—to each hypothesis. Analysts determine if each data point is consistent or inconsistent with the alternative hypotheses. Once this is completed, analysts can review their work to identify which pieces of information are less diagnostic—that is, cannot rule out hypotheses—and the ones that are highly diagnostic—that is, can only be true for one explanation. Analysts can then decide which hypotheses can be discarded and which best deserve their attention as lead hypotheses.

- *Quadrant Crunching™:* This is a Structured Brainstorming technique for systematically challenging assumptions, exploring the implications of contrary explanations, and discovering unknown unknowns. It also generates large numbers of mutually exclusive alternative scenarios. The technique was developed to help policymakers avoid surprise and anticipate the unanticipated by generating a large number of scenarios and then focusing on those that are most attention-deserving.
- *Premortem Analysis and Structured Self-Critique:* This technique reduces the risk of analytic failure before it occurs by imagining that the paper has been published and that several months or years in the future it has turned out to be a spectacular failure.

The task is to fix the paper before it is published. The value of the technique is that by taking a few hours before a paper is submitted for review and editing, the analyst can avoid devoting days or even months to explaining why the analysis did not turn out to be correct.

Based on the authors' experiences in working with and training analysts, we believe these seven techniques were singled out by analysts in the IC as well as the private sector as core techniques primarily because they (1) added obvious rigor to the analytic process, (2) were transparent and provided an audit trail, (3) made the analysis more compelling, and, most important, (4) saved time for the analysts.

In recent years attention has focused on two other techniques that could emerge as standard in any analyst's toolkit:

- *Indicators Validation* is a simple process for assessing the diagnostic power of indicators. It sorts indicators from most to least diagnostic and helps analysts detect indicators that should not be given to collectors to target. A diagnostic indicator, for example, is highly likely to emerge in its home scenario but highly unlikely to appear in any other scenario. A nondiagnostic indicator could appear in any scenario and would not aid the analysis.
- *Adversarial Collaboration* involves an agreement between opposing parties to work together to try to resolve their differences. They will seek to gain a better understanding of exactly how and why they differ, and this often involves collaboration on a joint paper describing the differences. Each party may then provide this paper to supervisors or other higher authority to seek resolution of the dispute.[21]

When the authors built their taxonomy of techniques, they discovered that several techniques fit comfortably in three or more of the eight categories because they served multiple analytic functions. The Key Assumptions Check, for example, which is grouped with techniques for the Assessment of Cause and Effect, is also used in the domains of Challenge Analysis, Hypothesis Generation and Testing, and Idea Generation. Included in this list of "multidomain" techniques are all four of the core techniques identified by CIA's Kent School, as well as Scenarios Analysis—which was already well established in the IC—and Quadrant Crunching™, a relatively new technique that is quickly gaining popularity with analysts.

Two other techniques that qualify as multidomain techniques but—to the authors' surprise and concern—have not been used widely within the IC are Cross-Impact Matrix and the Delphi Method. Cross-Impact Matrix is most helpful when analysts are trying to sort out a particularly complex situation and need to explore how each factor in a particular context influences the other factors. The authors suspect that the Delphi Method, which requires several rounds of anonymous commentary from a panel of experts, is less widely used because of time and analytic resource costs required to collect and portray several rounds of analysis. Hopefully this obstacle will be overcome with the advent of more powerful Web-based software tools.

Countering Arguments against Using SATs

The most common criticism of SATs is "analysts do not have enough time to use them." The experience of most practitioners and particularly their managers is that this criticism is not justified. In fact, if an analyst stops to consider how much time it takes to research an issue, draft an analysis, coordinate the analysis, and guide the paper through the editing and coordination process, he or she will usually discover that the use of structured techniques almost always speeds the process and also improves the results.

- Many of the techniques such as the Key Assumptions Check and Indicators Validation take little time, while substantially improving the rigor of the analysis.
- Some take some effort to learn, but once that is accomplished their use often saves the analyst considerable time over the long run. ACH provides a good example of this phenomenon. By learning to look for information that can disconfirm a given hypothesis, an analyst can quickly dismiss potential hypotheses when encountering compelling data that is inconsistent with that particular hypothesis, saving considerable time.
- Structured techniques such as the Getting Started Checklist, the Customer Checklist, and Issue Redefinition are especially useful at the start of a project when an analyst may be unsure of how to proceed.[22]
- Structured techniques usually aid group processes and help build consensus in the early stages of framing a paper, thus avoiding major coordination battles later in the process. They also make the reasoning behind the analysis more transparent.

Two of the best examples of structured techniques that save time are Indicators Validation and the pairing of Premortem Analysis with the Structured Self-Critique. The process of validating a set of indicators rarely takes more than an hour or two and invariably identifies a set of chosen indicators (often 10 percent to 20 percent of the indicators typically generated) that are not diagnostic and should not be disseminated to collectors to target. The Premortem Analysis and Structured Self-Critique usually take more time—a couple hours to as much as a day, depending on the complexity of the project—but offer major rewards if they improve the analysis or avoid analytic error. A premortem takes far less time than a postmortem initiated to determine why the conclusions or the recommendations were off track. In the intelligence community and the business world, such postmortems can take days or even months to conclude, while involving more time and much larger numbers of personnel.

Perhaps the best rejoinder to the complaint that analysts do not have enough time to use structured techniques is to ask "Do you mean that you do not have time to do good analysis?" Structured techniques simply add rigor to well-known thought processes. They apply the principles of scientific experimentation—such as hypothesis testing that most of us learned in high school and college—to the analytic process.

When one is working on quick-turnaround items such as a current intelligence brief that must be produced the same day, a credible argument can be made that it is not possible to take time out to conduct a Key Assumptions Check or an ACH exercise. If the analysts had practiced using these techniques in the past when time was less pressing, however, they would have already engrained these new habits of thinking in their minds. By practicing how to apply the concepts embedded in the structured techniques when they had time, they would be more capable of applying them instinctively when under pressure.[23] A good analytic thinker who has mastered the core SATs will instinctively:

1. Know when to challenge his or her key assumptions—which is usually far more often than one would think!
2. Consider alternative explanations or hypotheses for all events—including the null hypothesis and the deception hypothesis when applicable.
3. Look for inconsistent data that provides sufficient justification to quickly discard a candidate hypothesis.
4. Focus on the key drivers that best explain what has occurred or what is about to happen.
5. Anticipate customers' needs and understand the overarching context within which he or she is working.

For example, if an analyst has engaged in several ACH exercises over the past year, he or she might be much more inclined to ask "What would be a comprehensive and mutually exclusive set of hypotheses for explaining this new phenomenon?" or "What key assumptions am I making about the reporting and how well are those assumptions supported?" In the end, most analysts will learn that the use of structured techniques saves them time, makes their analysis more compelling, and increases their confidence in the key judgments they present.

Ensuring Correct Usage of SATs

As the use of structured techniques has spread throughout the US government and around the world, a key concern has been whether they are being used correctly. A few efforts have been made to evaluate the utility of SATs in the intelligence and homeland security communities, but much more work is needed to be done. The Forum Foundation for Analytic Excellence—a not-for-profit organization—launched several pilot programs in 2012 to ensure that SATs are used and taught correctly in the United States and overseas. Students taking courses that involve the application of structured techniques and associated software will be required to take a certifying examination approved by the Forum Foundation. If they pass the examination and meet other specified requirements, they will receive a certificate of proficiency in the use of several core techniques—Brainstorming, Structured Brainstorming, Key Assumptions Check, Multiple Hypothesis Generation, Analysis of Competing Hypotheses, Indicators, and Indicators Validation. A similar process is being developed to certify instructors as competent to teach the same set of core techniques.

Analysts and students seeking instruction in the correct way to use SATs can also find guidance in two books, *Cases in Intelligence Analysis: Structured Analytic Techniques in Action* and *Critical Thinking for Strategic Intelligence.*[24] Both provide detailed examples of how the technique can be applied, as well as valuable tips regarding both the strengths and weakness of using the techniques. Eight more case studies illustrating how to apply structured techniques will be added to the virtual library of case studies offered by CQ Press in 2013.

Building Collaboration

The development of collaborative software for generating multiple hypotheses, conducting ACH exercises, and validating indicators has accelerated the use of these techniques. Work is currently under way to develop additional Web-based, collaborative tools, including Quadrant Crunching™ and a collaborative version of the Key Assumptions Check. In 2013, a suite of freeware tools was available in beta testing on the internet. The suite includes a noncollaborative version of the ACH methodology, a rudimentary version of the Key Assumptions Check, a simple Link Analysis tool, and a tool that helps analysts identify the who, what, how, when, where, and why of a problem, as well as the key assumptions underlying those selections. Analysts are able to move information from one software tool to another without having to reenter the data.[25]

The development of collaborative versions of these structured analytic techniques should not only change how analysts think but also change how IC organizations function. The use of collaborative software can help to overcome serious problems associated with the coordination process by doing the following:

- Prompting analysts to begin by seeking a common definition of the problem.
- Ensuring that analysts from different offices and agencies are all working from the same body of evidence and arguments. This gives every participating analyst an equal opportunity to express his or her views.
- Making assumptions and cognitive biases explicit, and revealing previously unstated differences of opinion as each analyst's input is recorded.
- Exposing differences of opinion by comparing each analyst's matrix or submissions, tracing the origin of the differences, and analyzing how much effect, if any, they have on the final conclusion.
- Providing a framework for the clear presentation of an analytic conclusion or discussion of alternate views at a coordination meeting or in an analytic report.

As collaborative tools are developed for the internet and incorporated into the IC's collaborative information-technology systems, analysts with shared interests working in different agencies or in different parts of the world will be able to establish a common virtual workspace where they can engage each other on issues of common interest long before they become involved in the coordination process. They will be able to organize and access a common set of evidence, identify key assumptions, select the most diagnostic items of information, and engage in interactive virtual "chats" with their colleagues. By opening a new means for interagency collaboration in a virtual workspace where SATs such as ACH can be used collaboratively, the IC can take a big step forward toward changing the current culture of independent analytic fiefdoms.

The development of collaborative software based on SATs will go a long way toward accomplishing a goal set forth by another contributor to this volume—Thomas Fingar, the former deputy director of national intelligence for analysis. In his view, a primary goal of better integration is to "transform the analytic component of our community from a federation of agencies, or a collection of feudal baronies, into a community of analysts, professionals dedicated to providing the best and most timely, most accurate, most useful analytic insights to all of the customers we serve."[26] In other words a more collaborative community.

Conclusions

Structured analytic techniques are called "techniques" because they guide the analyst in thinking about a problem rather than provide the analyst with a definitive answer as one might expect from a method. They make the analytic process more systematic and rigorous, and give analysts confidence that they have not missed something important or failed to present a clear line of argumentation. Many argue that structured techniques are the connective tissue between scientific experimentation and intuitive insight. They are thinking tools that help analysts work their way through a problem. Ultimately, their value is dependent on the expertise, information, tradecraft savvy, and collaboration skills of the participants. They are steadily becoming embedded within the global intelligence and law enforcement communities, and early indications are that they are likely to continue to spread into new domains such as business consulting, medicine, financial analysis, and academia.

As the editors of this book have argued, making intelligence analysis a true profession involves developing a commonly accepted set of practices and procedures, similar to medicine and law. The adoption and use of SATs is part of this professionalization. Developing a common language regarding analysis, its methods, and its standards can only be accomplished through even more widespread acceptance of SATs. Progress made in the past decade suggests that such efforts are taking hold in US intelligence agencies and in university and business communities where work continues in refining their use and applications. One can hope that such advances will help to validate the utility such methods have in reaching reliable analytic judgments and forecasts, as well as improve the profession's track record of providing insights into twenty-first-century intelligence challenges.

Notes

1. See *The 9/11 Commission Report: Final Report of the National Commission on Terrorist Attacks upon the United States* (New York: Norton, 2005), http:govinfo.library.unt.edu/911/report/index.htm, and Commission on the Intelligence Capabilities of the United States regarding Weapons of Mass Destruction, unclassified version of the *Report of the Commission on the Intelligence Capabilities of the United States regarding Weapons of Mass Destruction* (March 31, 2005), www.gpo.gov/fdsys/pkg/GPO-WMD/content-detail.html.

2. Analytic tradecraft is defined as "the principles and tools used by analysts to instill rigor in their thinking and prevent cognitive biases from skewing their analytic judgments." Emphasis was placed on techniques that helped analysts challenge their own assumptions and data, be more creative in order to anticipate the unanticipated, and improve the diagnosticity and rigor of the analysis.

3. A fuller history of structured analytic techniques can be found in Richards J. Heuer Jr. and Randolph H. Pherson, *Structured Analytic Techniques for Intelligence Analysis* (Washington, DC: CQ Press, 2011), 8–10.

4. CIA's Sherman Kent School of Intelligence Analysis was the first to offer a three-day course on advanced analytic tools and techniques, in 2003. In 2004, the FBI started requiring all its analysts, as well as an incoming surge of new analysts, to receive three days of instruction at the FBI Academy on structured analytic techniques. The major schoolhouses in the IC subsequently developed their own, often mandated, courses. DIA's course on critical thinking and structured techniques covers over fifteen different techniques. In 2007, CIA's Directorate of Intelligence established analytic tradecraft cells within the various analytic divisions to support the application of the techniques to current intelligence issues. The ODNI incorporated several SATs, including Argument Mapping and Analysis of Competing Alternatives, into its Analysis 101 course for new analysts and made attendance at a workshop on advanced analytic tools and techniques a requirement of its Advanced Analyst Program.

5. Richards J. Heuer Jr., *Psychology of Intelligence Analysis* (Washington, DC: Center for the Study of Intelligence, CIA, 1999), www.cia.gov/csi/books/19104/index.html. Also see Thomas Gilovich, Dale Griffin, and Daniel Kahneman, *Heuristics and Biases: The Psychology of Intuitive Judgment* (Cambridge and New York: Cambridge University Press, 2002); Robyn M. Dawes, *Everyday Irrationality* (Boulder, CO: Westview, 2001); and Scott Plous, *The Psychology of Judgment and Decision Making* (New York: McGraw-Hill, 1993).

6. The judgments in this paragraph are based on the authors' experience and anecdotal evidence gained in discussion with other experienced analysts. We recognize that there is a clear need for the intelligence community to conduct systematic research on such benefits believed to be gained through the use of structured analytic techniques.

7. *American Heritage Dictionary of the English Language*, 4th ed. (Boston: Houghton Mifflin Harcourt, 2000).

8. Nathan G. Goodman, ed., *The Benjamin Franklin Sampler* (New York: Fawcett, 1956).

9. Alex Osborn, *Applied Imagination*, rev. ed. (New York: Scribner's, 1979), 202.

10. *Vision 2015: A Globally Networked and Integrated Intelligence Enterprise* (Washington, DC: Director of National Intelligence, 2008).

11. National Intelligence Council, *Global Trends 2025: A Transformed World* (Washington, DC: Government Printing Office, November 2008).

12. For examples, see Paul B. Paulus and Bernard A. Nijstad, *Group Creativity: Innovation through Collaboration* (New York: Oxford University Press, 2003).

13. This chart was developed by Katherine Hibbs Pherson and Randolph H. Pherson, and appears in *Critical Thinking for Strategic Analysis* (Washington, DC: CQ Press, 2013), 52–54.

14. The authors had difficulty selecting the name for this category. The term "traditional analysis" does not describe the procedural difference between this and the other categories. "Intuitive analysis" was rejected because the definition of intuition implies "without evident rational thought and inference." That certainly does not apply to the way conscious, deliberative analysis is conducted. Expert practitioners of traditional analysis do a great deal of systematic reasoning. "Expert judgment" is a good term for traditional analysis, but it does not distinguish traditional analysis from structured analysis, because structured analysis also relies on expert judgment. The difference is that the reasoning process in structured analysis is externalized more or less in real time as the reasoning is being conducted. This externalization and systematic procedure is believed to aid the reasoning process and, especially, to help in collaboration with other analysts. That is the basis for calling the more traditional approach to analysis "unaided" expert judgment.

15. How the Key Assumptions Check, Multiple Hypothesis Generation, and Quadrant Crunching™ could have been used in the case of the "DC Sniper" can be found in Sarah Miller Beebe and Randolph H. Pherson, *Cases in Intelligence Analysis: Structured Analytic Techniques in Action* (Washington, DC: CQ Press, 2012), chap. 8.

16. For a more detailed description of the Coup Vulnerability Methodology, see Pherson and Pherson, *Critical Thinking for Strategic Intelligence*, 80–81.

17. For a more detailed description of the Structured Brainstorming technique, see Heuer and Pherson, *Structured Analytic Techniques*, chap. 5. The Mumbai case study that employs this technique can be found in Beebe and Pherson, *Cases in Intelligence Analysis*, chap. 10.

18. Rob Johnston, *Analytic Culture in the U.S. Intelligence Community* (Washington, DC: Center for the Study of Intelligence, CIA, 2005), 34.

19. See Heuer and Pherson, *Structured Analytic Techniques*, for detailed descriptions of all the techniques discussed in this section, when to use them, and their value added.

20. Pherson Associates briefed the company on a wide range of analytic techniques relevant to business consulting in the mid-2000s, and these techniques were selected.

21. For a more detailed discussion of Adversarial Collaboration and a description of six techniques for managing potential conflicts, see Heuer and Pherson, *Structured Analytic Techniques*, chap. 10.

22. A full list of Getting Started techniques can be found in Heuer and Pherson, *Structured Analytic Techniques*, chap. 4, and Pherson and Pherson, *Critical Thinking for Strategic Intelligence*, part I.

23. The Five Habits of the Master Thinker were developed by Randolph H. Pherson in response to a question posed by analysts in the U.K. Cabinet Office who wanted to use the techniques but often had very little time to produce an assessment. The solution to this dilemma, Pherson suggests, is to practice using techniques such as the Key Assumptions Check, Analysis of Competing Hypotheses, and Quadrant Crunching™ when time is available so that practices such as challenging assumptions, looking for disconfirming data, and identifying key drivers become so engrained into one's analytic process that they become instinctive.

24. Twelve case studies showing how to use twenty-three different techniques can be found in Beebe and Pherson, *Cases in Intelligence Analysis*. Case studies for exploring the value of the Key Assumptions Check and Analysis of Competing Hypotheses can be found in Katherine Hibbs Pherson and Randolph H. Pherson, *Critical Thinking for Strategic Intelligence*.
25. Additional information on these tools and their capabilities can be found at www.globalytica.org.
26. Thomas Fingar, speech to the DNI's Information Sharing Conference and Technology Exposition, Denver, August 21, 2006, www.au.af.mil/au/awc/awcgate/dni/20060821_2_speech.pdf.

CHAPTER 15

New Analytic Techniques for Tactical Military Intelligence

VINCENT STEWART, DREW CUKOR, JOSEPH LARSON III, AND
MATTHEW POTTINGER

Tactical intelligence is a key asset of all military commanders.[1] While combat-seasoned leaders supply depth of knowledge, experience, and technical expertise, they must be well informed about the environment in which they operate and the enemy they face. A commander on the battlefield must leverage all assets at his disposal to accomplish the designated mission. This includes effectively employing and integrating intelligence across the information spectrum to generate a reliable, robust, and accurate picture of the battlefield. With comprehensive information and solid analysis on the enemy and the environment, a commander will make better decisions.

National-level agencies such as CIA and DIA have made efforts to improve the quality of analysis through the use of structured analytic techniques (SATs).[2] Many of these developments have been modified, improved, and institutionalized at the tactical level in support of warfighters, altered to reflect the unique environment of combat. This chapter shows how one military service, the US Marine Corps, has designed and incorporated structured analytic tradecraft for tactical intelligence. It explains how the marine corps puts new analytic approaches into practice and how it tests and validates them for wider use. This applied tradecraft is brought to marines worldwide through knowledge vehicles called structured models, approaches, and techniques (SMATs).

Supporting Tactical Military Operations with Intelligence

The contemporary battlefield is a cluttered and congested place where adaptive irregular, hybrid, and conventional adversaries exploit advanced technology and conceal themselves from friendly sensors, creating a complex intelligence puzzle. The modern challenge, and the one addressed throughout this chapter, is discovering and instituting the most advantageous manner of improving intelligence for tactical military operations as the US military moves forward into an increasingly complicated threat environment.[3]

Experience from recent wars confirms what has been known and repeated from wars of the past: The capability for sound, reliable, transparent, and nuanced *analysis* of the enemy and combat environment is critical to operational success. Analysis, as defined in marine corps doctrine, means understanding and contextualizing data and information with respect to a commander's mission and his unit's operations.[4] This is one of the definitive battlefield-intelligence challenges of our era. Among the most critical functions of tactical intelligence is the discovery of answers to complex, subtle, and elusive problems that are not as obvious as they sometimes appear. Unstructured collections of data organized around aspects of situation and time are of little utility unless they are built into a cohesive picture and made actionable. Buried within the data are answers to myriad questions that the analyst must uncover. Using social science principles to help frame problems, the analyst must translate the commander's needs into clear questions that can be answered by exploitation and analysis of this data.

Because the field of tactical military intelligence analysis isn't developed to the same degree as other analytic fields, analysts often rely on an unstructured and intuition-based approach to evaluating complex problems. Such an approach is highly susceptible to cognitive errors, logical fallacies, and biases of the individual analyst or team of analysts.[5] During the wars in Iraq and Afghanistan, military analysts operated forward with infantry battalions, regiments and divisions. They were armed with foundational training in intelligence culture and technology, and they were asked to provide knowledge and recommend courses of action to commanders on complex counterinsurgency topics, including tribal politics, political engagement, targeting of high-value individuals, sophisticated weapons analysis, and pattern identification. Despite their herculean efforts, there was sometimes an undeniable gap between the depth and precision of the analysis that battlefield commanders needed and that which tactical intelligence analysts were equipped to provide. Intelligence analysts, many times operating without methods, approaches, and tools to address commanders' requirements, would instead rely on intuition to solve problems.

Technology has improved, but not solved, the fundamental difficulties associated with tactical military intelligence analysis. From collection assets to battlefield computers to collaborative tools, US intelligence personnel at all echelons have been armed with the most sophisticated technology available. But access to technology does not unilaterally solve all of the problems associated with the tactical military intelligence environment. The reason is simple: Technology enables good analysis but does not replace it. Intelligence analysis requires well-trained, thoughtful human beings to engage technology.[6] Marines, to paraphrase J. C. R. Licklider, still set the goals, formulate the hypotheses, determine the criteria, and perform the evaluations. Technology can only perform the routine work that must be done to prepare the way for intelligence judgments and operational decisions.

With knowledge of what good analysis *isn't* (the product of mere intuition and more computers), the marine corps refocused on how it was educating and training the analysts themselves. It implemented a process for teaching tactical analysts best practices for specific problems. Structuring analysis and providing practical, real-world methods specific to the problem at hand, such as social organization theory for enemy underground analysis, became the new innovation needed to meet the demands of combat intelligence analysts.

The Backdrop: Structured Analysis

The use of more structured analytic approaches for tactical intelligence builds on work from the intelligence community (IC) since the mid-1990s. Then, as a result of internal efforts to improve the quality of analysis, research largely drawn from cognitive psychology was used to help analysts identify weaknesses in their intuition and avoid cognitive and perceptual lapses.[7] The resulting emphasis on "structuring" analysis intended to reduce cognitive error and to improve both accuracy and reliability of analysis. Since then, SATs have become important tools for improving the quality of analysis presented to policymakers. Organized to help analysts think critically, to challenge key assumptions, and ensure that differences of opinion are considered, SATs are now widely used in the IC and by tactical intelligence analysts within the military services.[8]

Structured techniques essentially mimic and enforce aspects of the scientific method of analysis. They assist in separating quality information from bad data, preventing biases, testing hypotheses through competition, improving transparency, adjusting interpretations based on results, and providing feedback. Given the stakes associated with a major, strategic-level assessment, structured techniques are necessary to ensure results are of a scientific quality.[9]

But a problem still remained: Tactical intelligence analysts needed more than good foundational tradecraft in SATs to be useful. They also needed practical examples of good tradecraft that applied to the tactical intelligence questions they were being asked. It wasn't enough to ask analysts in the field to find these answers by using critical thinking techniques or bias checks. Rather, they needed an outline of a *method specific to the problem they faced*, preferably captured in field experience, validated, refined, and taught in an expanding repository of practical, real-world examples that marine corps analysts could use in the field. In short, in addition to foundational tradecraft from SATs, they also needed *applied tradecraft*.

While SATs are excellent tools to produce high-quality analysis and serve the IC well, they are not perfectly suited for tactical military intelligence. Most structured techniques are not designed for the types of problems tactical analysts face. Also, structured methods typically prioritize accountability, complexity, and precision over speed, specificity, and simplicity. At a tactical level, where a commander may require an answer with greater speed at the price of less certainty, and when an intelligence assessment is needed to drive an immediate operational decision, SATs cannot be the only basis for producing analysis on the battlefield. They must be complemented by another form of structured analysis. Furthermore, the analyst that employs tactical techniques is distinct in terms of training, education, and background. Typically, strategic and operational intelligence analysts possess a deeper level of expertise or background in a specific field or geographic area prior to working on an intelligence problem. Even generalists usually bring advanced education and subject-specific knowledge to bear.

But for the tactical analysts working in a different trench, often without appreciable training in social sciences or analytic methods, or lacking a large base of substantive knowledge from which to begin analyzing problems, merely structuring analysis is insufficient. It is akin to a layman conducting medical diagnostic techniques designed for doctors without having received an introductory course in anatomy or biology. Without highly knowledgeable analysts or the luxury of time, SATs in isolation are an insufficient framework for intelligence work at the tactical level.

Threat Finance and SATs

A more concrete, real-world example of this phenomenon in the realm of tactical intelligence is the field of threat finance analysis. Assume a commander approaches a professional civilian analyst at the strategic level and poses an intelligence question: How much money does the Taliban spend annually in Helmand Province, Afghanistan? That analyst, faced with that question, may employ a number of structured techniques to begin assembling a response. Perhaps he or she will use imaginative thinking techniques to develop a hypothesis ("The Taliban spends their annual revenue, derived from poppy, in its entirety on insurgent operations. Therefore, the amount they spend is determined by the amount they raise through taxing and distributing poppy.") He or she may subject that hypothesis to contrarian analysis through techniques, including "What If?" Analysis or Devil's Advocacy. After arriving at a conclusion, he or she must subject that conclusion to a diagnostic test, such as a Key Assumptions Check or quality of information check, to ensure the results match the data.

Initially it is likely that the analyst facing this problem understands some basics in the field of threat finance. He or she will likely know how revenue is generated and intuit some methods for approximating the amount of revenue. He or she will also likely know how the Afghan financial system works, including principles such as *zakat* or how money is transferred via the Hawala network. He or she will likely understand how to read a basic balance sheet, understand how revenue differs from expenditure, and how to identify revenues and expenditures from assorted documents and then calculate how much it costs to operate an insurgent organization and how it finances its operations. At the very least the analyst will have time and resources to assemble a basic body of knowledge on threat finance before delving into the analysis.

Threat Finance and SMATs

Now imagine that a tactical military intelligence analyst deployed in the theater of operations is asked the identical question: How much money does the Taliban spend in Helmand annually? This analyst typically will not have a background in accounting, finance, quantitative methods, or the financial practices of the geographic region. In the theater of operations, the analyst likely will not have access to online libraries, LexisNexis, college economics textbooks, or primers on accounting. The requirement to provide an immediate answer, often within hours, also precludes a consultation with IC peers who may already have the appropriate substantive expertise.

This analyst will require more than structured analytic techniques to look at the problem of insurgent finance. He or she will need a structured method *specific to the problem*. This method may offer techniques for immediately analyzing threat finance with little to no background in the field. These methods may

- define accounting principles such as revenue, expenditure, assets, liabilities, equity, debt, and interest;
- list both licit and illicit categories of obtaining revenue;
- list various cost categories based on a group's activities;
- explain the threat-finance process through existing economic models (such as Leites and Wolf's Economic Model of Insurgency);
- enhance analysis through a graphic portrayal of the steps involved in threat finance analysis;
- discuss developing collection requirements and driving collection of threat finance network–associated information;
- provide more specific information on threat finance organizations and resources within the intelligence community; and
- identify potential weaknesses and vulnerabilities in the adversary's infrastructure of operational significance to the tactical commander.

This method we can call *applied tradecraft*—specific analytic approaches that can be directly applied to produce rapid intelligence across the range of military operations. Such approaches synthesize best practices from the field and are infused with proven techniques and methods derived from the social and physical sciences. Such applied tradecraft is not only structured like SATs—it also provides specific step-by-step guidance for tactical analysts. SMAT tradecraft spans question formation through data gathering from intelligence sources at hand, to the analytic steps needed for tactically relevant answers and the intelligence products needed to convey them to the customer, the battlefield commander. Beyond threat finance, such techniques will focus on specific functional areas such as target identification, enemy and pattern-of-life analysis for human targeting, cultural and political topics, infrastructure, resources, and terrain.

Structuring Combat Intelligence

Like SATs, applied tradecraft represents a form of structured analysis. Applied tradecraft uses a formal methodology that is visible to external observers and helps the analyst frame a situation while providing a way to account for the analytic judgment.[10] Here the methodology is subject-specific and grounded in data, theories, techniques, approaches, and product models, all of which are transparent to other analysts and explicitly linked to the final product. By providing more than general techniques for eliminating cognitive bias, applied tradecraft seeks to infuse analysis with background, theory, models, and examples that an analyst will find relevant to the subject at hand. Most important, applied tradecraft provides specific step-by-step directions in the form of SMATs to guide the analyst through an analytic process to get a rapid answer for the commander.

Composition and Development of SMATs

SMATs are knowledge vehicles that contain specific analytic steps, social science theories, exemplar product models, and other guidance to enable an analyst when using and applying the techniques in a tactical situation. Like SATs, this applied tradecraft for tactical intelligence must meet the hallmarks of quality analysis: It must be structured, reliable, repeatable, robust, timely, capable of being taught and understood by a large audience of diverse practitioners, and vetted through a refined quality-control process. But copying the SAT format was insufficient to incorporate the range of social science, production techniques, and combat-derived insights. In addition, every piece of applied tradecraft should focus on a specific intelligence problem.

After careful deliberation, Marine Intelligence created the SMAT knowledge vehicle, which captures intelligence techniques in a format that allows for growth but is easily taught and applied in a tactical environment. This structured format includes the following:

- *Models:* Representing the broadest form of structured tradecraft, models distill entire subjects into distinct conceptual attributes that mirror a real-world process or activity.
- *Approaches:* Narrower than a model, an approach provides guidance for the creation of intelligence products to inform tactical commanders.
- *Techniques:* The most concrete of the knowledge vehicles, techniques provide well-defined and repeatable step-by-step procedures for analyzing the underlying problem.

Whatever echelon of this taxonomy is employed, SMAT-applied tradecraft includes the following elements:

- *Key intelligence questions.* Analysts in a tactical environment face numerous problems, many of which can be distilled to a distinct subset of specific intelligence questions. The existence of a *specific* question—vice a generic technique or model—differentiates a SMAT from a SAT. The question forms the basis for the steps that follow, and it serves as a guidepost to determine when a technique can be applied.
- *A theoretical basis.* The SMAT defines and explains the theoretical basis (for example, social network theory) for the analytic structure it defines. It guides the analyst in using specific theories to generate hypotheses and enhance understanding (see box 15.1).

BOX 15.1 SMAT Vignette: Social Science Theories and High-Value-Individual Targeting

Assume an analyst with little experience is assigned to a counterinsurgency theater of operations focused on the targeting of specific high-value individuals (HVIs) believed to be supporting the insurgency. With unstructured analysis, HVI targeting entails reading the intelligence reporting, making a rudimentary link chart, and creating a target package based on the perceptions and intuitions of the individual analyst. In an era of enormous quantities of data, much of which is potentially useful, it is doubtful that human labor alone could distill the data, find patterns, and map interactions for that HVI in a comprehensive or reliable fashion.

A social science–based approach would be more complex; it would require the analyst to take the potential HVI through a series of social science–based tools in order to determine if targeting that individual truly meets the command's overall objectives. The analyst would be trained to consider theories relevant to the line of analysis:

Social network theory helps the analyst develop intelligence questions regarding whether certain nodes in a network are more important to the network's survival than others and provide tools to identify HVIs through analysis of these nodes. Tools would include an analysis of that HVI's centrality in a complex system using measures such as degree, closeness, betweenness, and eigenvector centrality.

Spatial models of politics help the analyst develop questions regarding elite power and position, and provide tools to identify key veto players and stakeholders who may become HVIs or can influence them.

Theories of organizational form and behavior help the analyst form questions addressing whether organization form and processes may affect the identities and roles of HVIs, and gather information that will help prioritize the placement of that HVI on a targeting list.

Deterrence theory will help the analyst develop questions as to whether elimination of certain leaders may deter or increase future violence or terrorist group/insurgency membership. It also invites analysis of second- and third-order effects of leadership removal and change.

Spiral-of-violence theories will assist in determining if the HVI targeting is likely to trigger tit-for-tat retaliation and escalating cycles of violence.

- *Guidance for the creation of intelligence products.* In addition to insights from social science theory, the SMAT contains explicit direction as to how to create intelligence products, including the types of raw collection reports used, tools for conducting machine-aided analysis, and guidelines on how to use the specific theories to inform analysis to support operations.

- *Model intelligence products.* SMATs provide structured templates for intelligence products for analysts to convey their findings to commanders in clear, actionable, and precise ways.

Each SMAT is contained and described within a defined structure that includes the following user-friendly documentation, training, and implementation elements:

- A concise paper explains the intent of each SMAT, the theory behind it, and how it is employed. Each paper contains introductory material, background, sources of information, strengths and weakness of the approach, and guidelines for implementation.
- A presentation of the material for formal instruction.
- A practical application exercise.
- An examination that tests the analyst's understanding of each SMAT.[11]

A wide set of SMATs reflects all-source intelligence techniques used in Iraq, Afghanistan, and other expeditionary experiences from 2007 to the present. They include applied tradecraft topics such as organizational analysis, elite analysis, population analysis, and spheres of influence analysis. Applied tradecraft is supplemented by technical intelligence methods and product models, including data aggregation and displays, best practices, and alternative methods of intelligence collection and analysis. Examples of more technically focused applied tradecraft include the COIN (Counterinsurgency) and Conventional Intelligence Summary Product Models, Trends and Tactics Intelligence, Intelligence Support to Prosecution, and Enemy Media Analysis. Examples of highly tactical, applied intelligence tradecraft based on foundational knowledge learned in more basic SMATs include HVI Targeting, Document and Media Exploitation, and Intelligence Support to Humanitarian Assistance and Disaster Relief (HA/DR).

These knowledge vehicles provide specialized subject-matter knowledge and analytic guidance in order to overcome an analyst's knowledge deficit and enable him or her to provide support that matches a real-world battlefield environment. By employing tested methods, SMATs combine much of the advantage of SAT-driven analysis without requiring specialists, while focusing on specific tactical-level problems.

A common but misplaced argument against the SMAT concept is that the resulting analysis is overly structured—that by providing specific theories and factual components, the method subsumes the analyst. In our experience, however, we have found this not to be the case. The analyst will still have to engage in the actions that are distinctly analytic: formulating questions, gathering data, examining sourcing, making intermediate and final assessments, answering intelligence requirements, making judgments and forecasts, and providing recommendations for actions. This is a generational leap from when tactical analysis was unstructured, opinion-driven, and sometimes off target for the commander or operator. It is a natural consequence of conducting intelligence analysis in fields where the analyst has no preexisting expertise that the analysis will be more heavily structured. The investment in quality analysis is not made at the end of the chain (the analyst solving the problem) but rather at the beginning—namely, the development of quality tradecraft skills that will guide less seasoned analysts to reliable and useful answers needed by the battlefield commander. One goes into battle with one's gear already assembled.

Applied tradecraft supplements but doesn't replace existing structured methods such as SATs. At certain times the analyst may decide that a structured analytic technique is the best tool to generate or test a hypothesis. At other times the analyst may determine that applied tradecraft is the best avenue to provide the commander a timely, reliable assessment. One structured model doesn't necessarily negate existing models but instead provides options for the use of varied structured techniques. Generally, applied tradecraft will be utilized in the faster, more diverse, and highly tactical arena of combat intelligence.[12]

Applied analytic tradecraft represents a new class of investment from the already well-developed field of theoretical knowledge. It requires commitment of time and resources to evolve the workforce to the point where tactical intelligence analysts master and hone the techniques they develop, seek to improve them using structured methods, and originate and deliberately grow applied analytic tradecraft to meet analysis requirements in a wide range of fields. With a master menu of applied tradecraft at their fingertips, analysts will more reliably answer difficult questions and provide commanders with actionable intelligence.[13]

Building and Institutionalizing Structured Tradecraft: Aesop's Crow and Combat Innovation

Aesop gives us the oft-repeated maxim that "necessity is the mother of invention." The phrase provides a postscript to a fable in which a thirsty crow finds a water pitcher but is distressed to find that the bottle top is too narrow, preventing it from reaching the water inside. Rather than die of thirst, the crow collects and drops stones into the pitcher in order to raise the water level to the point where drinking is possible. The fable surprises the reader because of the unexpected ingenuity the crow displays in solving a problem that at first glance seems unsolvable. The lesson of the fable is that any thinking organism will innovate to the maximum of its potential when it is forced by circumstance to do so.

Like Aesop's crow, the community of marine tactical intelligence analysts has created novel ways of solving problems in order to survive, even to thrive, in new and uncertain operating environments. As seen in Iraq, Afghanistan, and elsewhere, these analysts have made judgments addressing threats that are adaptive, networked, embedded within unfamiliar cultures, and employ asymmetrical or hybrid combinations of traditional, irregular, and criminal tactics. In order to flourish in this environment, marine analysts have engaged in creative processes of innovation, developing new tools, products, templates, and methods to solve often difficult problems across the spectrum of battle. A small sampling of these innovations includes the following:

- In response to commanders' requirements for host-nation intelligence, analysts have developed systematic and widespread templates for reporting on key leader engagements with tribal and political leaders.

- In response to concerns over threats from improvised explosive devices (IEDs), analysts have developed a standard method of accumulating threat data, analyzing that data, and reporting their assessments to convoy operators and planners in a systematic graphic format.
- In response to commanders' concerns regarding combat momentum, analysts have developed unique methods of analyzing incident reports and attack data to determine the level of insurgent effectiveness in initiating and executing operations.
- In response to concerns over enemy organization and structure, analysts have improved the manner in which they use existing social-science intelligence and collection resources to template an enemy's shadowy underground system of financial support and command responsibility.

These innovations represent a new frontier for tactical intelligence analysis but only if they are properly captured, refined, validated, and institutionalized. While the military services have engaged in detailed postdeployment after-action reports and surveys since the start of combat, their success in capturing the methods of analysis and then improving them for the next generation of analysts has been only sporadically successful. Such innovations too often reside in old boxes of manila folders, dusty shared drives, or outdated and unused Web pages on unmanaged servers.

Capturing and sharing this information is critical. While the story of Aesop's crow is compelling and teaches a valuable lesson about innovation, the solution the crow devises is transient; one knows the next crow facing a similar dilemma will have to reinnovate in order to accomplish the same task. Otherwise, the less innovative crow may die of thirst.

To facilitate the institutionalization of applied tradecraft, the marine corps empowered a new organization with the specific mission of serving as the caretakers, promulgators, and quality managers of SMAT-applied tradecraft developed in the operating forces. This organization—the Center for Marine Expeditionary Intelligence Knowledge (CMEIK)—captures analytic methods developed in the field by marines, including tradecraft groups in the operating forces, and collects others from other IC elements, think tanks, and academia. The CMEIK validates, enhances, and standardizes them, and then creates easy-to-use structured training packages for each SMAT to be used by individuals or units to train with and master.

The marine corps also created analytic tradecraft groups in order to link the newly created CMEIK with forward-operating intelligence elements. They serve as the keepers of tradecraft within marine corps intelligence elements. They are the on-site experts in analytic methodology and applied tradecraft, overseeing the coaching and use of SMATs within their units. As an integral fixture of the units within which they serve, tradecraft groups also engage in the development and improvement of new methods and work closely with the CMEIK.

These organizations work together to develop, publish, and institutionalize SMATs across the marine corps. The SMAT process entails development, validation, and training. In a nutshell it

1. captures analytic techniques and products from the field;
2. evaluates them by submitting them to a panel of military and civilian intelligence professionals and academics at the Marine Corps Intelligence Activity (MCIA) in Quantico, Virginia;
3. further evaluates, refines, enhances, and validates the new tradecraft through an external Social Science Board comprising outside experts with methodological and practical experience analyzing similar problems;
4. creates easy-to-reference training modules with practical exercises and case studies, complete with best practices needed to tackle similar problems; and
5. makes the training packages available to all marine corps analysts, including those in the field who wrote the original product.

Vetting Intelligence Techniques: Evaluation of Tradecraft

Applied tradecraft that emerges in the course of military operations must be objectively evaluated by qualified experts to attempt to discern, to the best extent possible, tradecraft's reliability and transparency. As the CMEIK's *21st Century Marine Expeditionary Intelligence Analysis* states, "Method alone is insufficient to make the enterprise 'scientific'; instead, there must be proof that method is tied to improved accuracy."[14] Therefore a holistic approach to applied tradecraft requires that new methods undergo evaluation, validation, and improvement.

This evaluation process utilizes the Social Science Board's interdisciplinary team of social scientists and subject-matter experts who collaborate with marines on applied tradecraft. The board evaluates and enhances SMAT tradecraft using the following criteria:

- clarifying intelligence questions and analytic objectives
- providing theoretical foundations
- implementing methodological standards for validity and reliability
- clarifying boundaries and links among SMATs and related applied tradecraft
- defining data requirements
- assessing proposed intelligence products

These evaluations follow their own methodology and produce actionable findings. The Social Science Board refines the applied tradecraft to address identified shortfalls using proven social science techniques. Once validated, SMAT tradecraft is added to the arsenal of tools available to tactical-level intelligence analysts.

SMATs in Action: Two Illustrations

Use of structured tradecraft to address tactical-level problems at the height of the COIN campaign in Iraq enhanced the ability of deployed forces to understand and counter insurgents. Two brief examples will illustrate how marine analysts developed and applied SMATs to address specific intelligence issues in insurgency finance and propaganda.

Financing an Insurgency

Returning to the earlier discussion of threat finance, we can see that a concrete example of the SMAT process in action occurred at the height of the war in Iraq when marine corps analysts in Anbar Province were asked to determine how much money insurgents were spending on their attacks. The answer would have implications for how high a priority to place on interdicting terrorist finances and how to do it effectively.

But the marine analysts in Iraq weren't well equipped to tackle the question. Unlike civilian all-source analysts back in Washington, they didn't have a background in finance and accounting, and they lacked direct access to people who did. Thus their rudimentary approach to the question was unsurprising. These analysts exploited existing "raw" intelligence information for finance data, and human intelligence collectors were tasked with asking Iraqi sources of information for estimates and details on insurgent spending. The analysts used critical reasoning and were careful to "show their math" in how they arrived at their assessment. But in the end the assessment they produced was generally thinly sourced, intuitive, and based on guesswork.

What the analysts needed was a structured method *specific to that problem*. To construct that new method, they needed the guidance of an existing assessment that had answered a similar question, with the methodologies spelled out clearly by more experienced analysts. Ultimately, that is what evolved some weeks after their product was submitted through the new SMAT process.

In the first step of that process, tradecraft-qualified analysts back in Quantico received the product from Anbar, reviewed it, and graded it. In consultation with outside experts with practical experience in threat finance analysis, they formulated applicable methodologies for that intelligence issue. They recommended breaking down the constituent parts of a recent attack, from the market cost of ammunition for AK-47s, rocket-propelled grenades, and homemade explosives, to the fuel needed to move fighters by pickup truck. They hunted down recently captured documents—a perennially underutilized resource by the intelligence community—that revealed the levels of stipends insurgents were paid by a local insurgent group. They summarized what existing open-source research showed about terrorist financing models, and they created a graphic portrayal of the steps involved in insurgent financing, making it easier to analyze. All of this "second generation" tradecraft was then captured in a SMAT-applied tradecraft tool and returned to analysts in the field. It led to far more insightful products by analysts in Iraq, and this SMAT on threat finance was used again to generate smart analysis by marines serving in Helmand Province.

This is the essence of *applied tradecraft*—specific analytic approaches contained in clearly expressed, instructional case studies that can be applied to produce intelligence across the range of combat theaters sharing similar circumstances.

Enemy Propaganda

A second successful SMAT module, also from Anbar Province, involved the analysis of insurgent propaganda posted online. For many months marines had been looking at video clips depicting insurgent attacks. Analysts often translated and summarized the claims by insurgents, which was useful but limited in insights. After a number of these products reached Quantico, a group was convened to discern patterns in the propaganda that might yield deeper, actionable analysis. Some interesting trends quickly emerged: By comparing the propaganda to coalition force records of significant events across the field, the group found that the insurgents rarely lied about the attacks they described. Though insurgents often exaggerated the damage they inflicted, they were usually accurate about the time and target, and the name of the group that executed a particular attack. This second-generation analysis led to the revelation that, contrary to analysts' assumptions that al-Qaeda in Iraq (AQI) was responsible for most attacks, some thirty distinct groups were actually attacking—many of them in competition with other insurgent groups. The media analysis yielded important information about the relative strength of these groups and opened up new avenues for coalition forces, helping to stifle insurgent momentum. These lessons were captured in SMAT case studies, or training modules, that are used today in other theaters of war.

Toward Tactical Insight in the Age of Intelligence

Our nation now sits at a unique juncture of international relations and national priorities. Our internal and external environments are changing so rapidly that we cannot rely on old paradigms and outdated practices. The marine corps forecast for the future geopolitical environment envisions that the conclusion of the wars in Iraq and Afghanistan will not usher in an era of international harmony. Threats—conventional, hybrid, and irregular—will not abate, and the continued involvement of the US military on the international scene is inevitable. We will see the emergence of new threats from a variety of arenas, including transnational terrorism, conventional military powers, and nonstate actors. Problems associated with these threats will be exacerbated by emerging global trends in cyberwarfare, poverty, disease, and access to natural resources. How we adjust our practices and organizations to meet this threat will make up the next chapter of US military history. Analysis will play a pivotal role.

In this future the modernization of military intelligence analysis will largely determine the success of US forces on the battlefield. The foundational principle is simple: Successful operations require reliable and actionable tactical intelligence derived from rigorous analysis of raw data, using structured tools and modern technology. Training analysts in the basic skills of analysis and teaching them to read, write, research, and engage in structured thought at the highest levels are necessary but not sufficient conditions for producing reliable intelligence. Instead, a standard for reliability must be found in the repeated and robust use of applied tradecraft: field-derived, experiential learning that has been codified, validated, refined, and taught to tactical intelligence analysts, whose products and professionalism will be a principal determinant of US military success on the battlefield in the twenty-first century.

Notes

1. The *tactical* level of war refers to the "concepts and methods used to accomplish a particular mission in either combat or other military operations. In war, tactics focuses on the application of combat power to defeat an enemy force in combat at a particular time and place. In noncombat situations, tactics may include the schemes and methods by which we perform other missions, such as enforcing order and maintaining security during peacekeeping operations. We normally think of tactics in terms of combat, and in this context tactics can be thought of as the art and science of winning engagements and battles. It includes the use of firepower and maneuver, the integration of different arms, and the immediate exploitation of success to defeat the enemy." Marine Corps Doctrinal Publication 1, *Warfighting*, 27–29. See also Marine Corps Doctrinal Publication 1-3, *Tactics*.
2. See the chapters by Pherson and Heuer, Fingar, and Hedley in this volume.
3. A major advance in tactical-level analysis came when the US Army developed "Intelligence Preparation of the Battlefield" (IPB), published in 1994 in *Field Manual (FM) 34-130*. Initially developed for interstate conflict to defeat nations with rigid and known doctrines such as the Soviet Union and North Korea, IPB presented a leap ahead in connecting conventional warfare with analysis. Still, it was less useful in helping to answer complex questions posed by the counterinsurgency environment and other "nonconventional" battlefields entailing irregular warfare, armed groups, and nonstate actors.
4. For elaboration on the definition of analysis, see US Marine Corps, *Marine Corps Warfighting Publication 2-1: Intelligence Operations* (Washington, DC, 2003), and Center for Marine Expeditionary Intelligence Knowledge, *21st Century Marine Expeditionary Intelligence Analysis* (Quantico, VA: Center for Marine Expeditionary Intelligence Knowledge, 2011), 3–4.
5. These are the same pitfalls experienced in strategic or national-level analysis predating the use of structured analytic techniques, as explained in Richards J. Heuer, Jr., *Psychology of Intelligence Analysis* (Washington, DC: Center for the Study of Intelligence, CIA, 1999), and in the chapter by Pherson and Heuer in this volume.
6. See J. C. R. Licklider, "Man-Computer Symbiosis," *IRE Transactions on Human Factors in Electronics* HFE-1 (1960): 4–11. Licklider argues that computational and technological advantage will supplement but never replace human thought. Specifically, he states that "the question is not, 'What is the answer?' The question is, 'What is the question?' Men will set the goals, formulate the hypotheses, determine the criteria, and perform the evaluations. Computing machines will do the routinizable work that must be done to prepare the way for insights and decisions in technical and scientific thinking."
7. See Heuer, *Psychology of Intelligence Analysis*.
8. For example, CIA's authoritative *Tradecraft Primer*, first published in 2005 by the Sherman Kent School of Intelligence Analysis, identified thirteen tradecraft tools that structure diagnostic, contrarian, and imaginative thinking techniques. It intended to help analysts

overcome cognitive limitations imposed by "mind-set"—mental models inherent in the analytic process necessary to conceptualize reality but that also cause analysts to ignore, overlook, exaggerate, or distort information used in assessing intelligence problems. Military analysts face the same challenges at tactical levels too.

9. The rationale for a science-based approach to intelligence analysis rests on the ability of science to identify and correct its own errors, a powerful feature that is not found in any other way of building knowledge. See chapter 9 of this volume by James Bruce, and National Research Council, National Academy of Sciences, *Intelligence Analysis for Tomorrow: Advances from the Behavioral and Social Sciences* (Washington, DC: National Academies Press, 2011).

10. Stephen Marrin, *Improving Intelligence Analysis: Bridging the Gap between Scholarship and Analysis* (Abingdon, UK: Routledge, 2011), 31.

11. Materials designed for SMAT and tradecraft training are not prepared for public dissemination but are accessible to US government users through the MCIA's Center for Marine Expeditionary Intelligence Knowledge.

12. The choice of analytic tradecraft depends on the intelligence problem, the form of warfare at issue, the amount of time available, the nature of the assessment, the training and education of the analyst, and the analyst's access to resources.

13. Center for Marine Expeditionary Intelligence Knowledge, *21st Century Marine Expeditionary Intelligence Analysis*, 2–3.

14. Ibid., 16.

CHAPTER 16

Domestic Intelligence Analysis

MAUREEN BAGINSKI

There is no official or even agreed definition of *domestic intelligence*. For the purposes of this chapter, the term generally refers to information or activities involving threats that bear on security conditions at or within US borders. Domestic intelligence has a focus inside the United States as to both target and source and is distinguished from, but may sometimes overlap with, foreign intelligence, which focuses on information and activities about the plans, intentions, and activities of foreign powers, persons, networks, and their agents. Domestic intelligence analysis informs the decisions and actions of those charged with defense of US territory at the federal, state, local, and tribal levels.[1] This chapter provides a brief history of US domestic intelligence as seen from an analyst's perspective. It discusses how the absence of a single authority for national intelligence operations as defined in law creates unique conditions for the practitioners of domestic intelligence analysis, and then it examines steps that could be taken to strengthen domestic intelligence analysis.

The principal practitioners of domestic intelligence analysis at the national level are organizations within the Department of Homeland Security (DHS), the Department of Justice, and the Office of the Director of National Intelligence (ODNI). DHS intelligence organizations include two national intelligence community (IC) organizations: the Office of Intelligence and Analysis (I&A) and the US Coast Guard. In addition, individual DHS departments and administrations have intelligence organizations that are not part of the IC, most notably the Secret Service, Customs and Border Protection, and the Transportation Security Administration. The Department of Justice houses two members of the IC: the Directorate of Intelligence of the Federal Bureau of Investigation (FBI) and the Office of Intelligence of the Drug Enforcement Administration (DEA). The Directorate of Intelligence is housed in the larger FBI National Security Branch (NSB), which includes the Counterterrorism and Counterintelligence Divisions and the Weapons of Mass Destruction Directorate. Within the Department of Justice other subordinate elements have intelligence organizations that are not part of the IC, for example in the Bureau of Alcohol, Tobacco, Firearms, and Explosives and the US Marshals Service. Within the ODNI the National Counterterrorism Center (NCTC) performs domestic intelligence analysis activities focused on international terrorism. At the state,

Table 16.1   Domestic Intelligence Practitioners

Federal Entity	IC Elements	Non-IC Elements
Department of Justice	FBI Directorate of Intelligence	Bureau of Alcohol, Tobacco, Firearms, and Explosives
	DEA Office of Intelligence	Marshals Service
		Federal Bureau of Prisons
		Office of Tribal Justice
Department of Homeland Security	Office of Intelligence and Analysis	Customs and Border Protection
	Coast Guard	Immigration and Customs Enforcement
		Citizenship and Immigration Services
		Transportation Security Administration
		Secret Service
Office of the Director of National Intelligence	National Counterterrorism Center	

local, and tribal levels, numerous organizations are charged with domestic intelligence analysis; none of these are members of the IC (see table 16.1).

Legal Framework

In authorizing national intelligence activities, US law distinguishes between the *purpose* for which intelligence is collected and the *information* that comes from those collection operations (see box 16.1). While the term "domestic" intelligence has been used freely since the tragic events of September 11, 2001, there is an argument to be made that there is no provision in US law for the existence of an intelligence discipline called "domestic." When the National Security Act of 1947 was amended and superseded by the Intelligence Reform and Terrorism Prevention Act of 2004 (IRTPA), there was an opportunity to authorize a category of intelligence operations called "domestic." Instead the new legislation left intact the language from the 1947 law that authorizes only two types of intelligence *operations* conducted for the purpose of acquiring two categories of information: foreign intelligence and counterintelligence. That both foreign intelligence and counterintelligence operations are conducted on various geographies, including that of the United States, has always been the case. But intelligence operations for the purposes of producing domestic intelligence information have never been authorized and remain unauthorized under IRTPA. IRTPA confirmed the status quo for domestic intelligence collection operations, leaving those authorities outside of the intelligence community (IC) and primarily within the law enforcement community.

BOX 16.1 Definitions

Foreign Intelligence: The purpose of foreign intelligence operations is to collect information about the plans, intentions, and capabilities of foreign powers or organizations. Foreign intelligence is collected from non-US citizens and residents, except when a US citizen or resident is determined to be an agent of a foreign power under the provisions of the United States Foreign Intelligence Surveillance Act (FISA) Court. In that case, collection operations are authorized under a FISA warrant.

Counterintelligence: The purpose of counterintelligence operations is to prevent hostile elements from collecting sensitive information about the United States. Counterintelligence is collected from US and foreign sources using law enforcement and foreign intelligence authorities, respectively. The lead for counterintelligence operations within the United States is the FBI. The lead organization for counterintelligence operations overseas is CIA.

Domestic Intelligence: Information or activities involving threats that bear on security conditions at or within US borders. Domestic intelligence has a focus inside the United States as to both target and source and is distinguished from, but may sometimes overlap with, foreign intelligence, which focuses on information and activities about the plans, intentions, and activities of foreign powers, persons, networks, or their agents.

Rather than create a category of national intelligence operations for the purposes of collecting domestic intelligence information, IRTPA instead focused on expanding and refining the definition of national intelligence to include information collected for any purpose and in any geography that bears on security within US borders. In the amended definition, the terms "national intelligence" and "intelligence related to national security" refer to all intelligence, regardless of the source from which it derived, and include information gathered within or outside the United States, that "(A) pertains, as determined consistent with any guidance issued by the President, to more than one United States Government agency" and "(B) that involves (i) threats to the United States, its people, property, or interests; (ii) the development, proliferation, or use of weapons of mass destruction; or (iii) any other matter bearing on United States national or homeland security."[2]

With the definition above, IRTPA declared information collected from any source that bears on threats to the nation to be national intelligence information. In addition, IRTPA mandated the sharing of that information with national authorities, specifically with the director of national intelligence (DNI). By mandating this, IRTPA created the conditions for the integrated analysis of information collected from any source that meets the threat standards in the definition above. It is important to note, however, that while the DNI was given authority to receive and analyze all national intelligence *information*, he or she was expressly forbidden from tasking directly other than foreign and counterintelligence operators in the United States to collect that information.

The unauthorized disclosures over the course of two days in June 2013 of two National Security Agency (NSA) surveillance programs illustrates the distinction between the authorities governing the *purpose* of intelligence collection activities and the sharing of *information derived* from that collection. According to media reports, for one program the FBI uses its law enforcement authorities under section 215 of the USA PATRIOT Act to collect bulk phone records—not the content of those communications—from US service providers. The FBI then shares the *information derived* from those collection operations with NSA—a foreign intelligence organization. Authorization to collect this information under the PATRIOT Act requires that the FBI provide a statement of facts showing that there are reasonable grounds to believe that records they seek are "relevant to an authorized investigation"—in other words that the collection is necessary for its law enforcement mission. In the case of the second program, NSA directly collects for *foreign intelligence purposes* the communications of foreigners overseas whose communications flow through the United States, using section 702 of the Foreign Intelligence Surveillance Act.[3]

This legal framework places domestic intelligence analysts operating at the national level in a situation unlike any of their counterparts in the national IC. The collection of the information they are charged with analyzing and the analytic activities they perform are governed by two separate authorities—the DNI and the authority that holds or collects the "national intelligence," most often law enforcement authorities. The analysts' positions are funded by the DNI's budget—the National Intelligence Program (NIP)—and they are rightly held to the DNI's analytic standards. But the information they analyze is collected, disseminated, and shared according to the priorities and policies of law enforcement and public safety officials over which the DNI has no authority. Perhaps most important, the value of their analysis is determined by those same two sets of officials. Thus two different authorities, each with legitimately different views of what information is necessary to provide "decision advantage," both direct and assess the value of domestic intelligence analysts' work. Much has been written about the wisdom of creating a separate national domestic intelligence organization. Although acknowledging its importance, we will not reopen that issue here.[4]

A History in Brief

Prior to 9/11 there was no discernible advocacy for a national domestic intelligence capability. Before then, national security threats were generally not seen as originating from within our own borders. In addition, forays into national domestic intelligence operations historically ended in scandal, such as the improper surveillance of US citizens by NSA, the Central Intelligence Agency (CIA), and the FBI aimed at monitoring or suppressing political dissent in the 1960s and 1970s. These and previous scandals, coupled with the larger sense of security and well-being within our own borders, gave rise to the belief that domestic intelligence operations at the national level not only were unnecessary but also were somehow unsavory. Despite the fact that the FBI's abuses in the 1960s and 1970s arose from mixing intelligence and law enforcement operations, domestic intelligence functions were and remain linked to case-based law enforcement investigations. This appears to be a function of the widely held view that intelligence operators violate the laws of the foreign countries they operate in, while law enforcement and public safety operators must always operate within the law, regardless of the country they operate in. It remains to be seen whether the June 2013 media reports about NSA and FBI cooperation on surveillance programs that appear to target US citizens will change that view.

Our "domestic warfighters"—law enforcement and public safety officials operating at all levels of government—have long recognized the value of intelligence for informing their operational decision making. As a result they dedicated resources and attention to both developing professional intelligence analysts and sharing information long before 9/11. Absent a single national authority for coordinating the operations of national, state, local, and tribal law enforcement and public safety organizations—a product of our federal system—these efforts were and remain largely voluntary.

For example, the Law Enforcement Intelligence Unit (LEIU) was formed in 1956 by twenty-six state and local law enforcement agencies to address the issue of sharing confidential criminal information. These law enforcement professionals understood that organized criminals would take advantage of advancing technologies in transportation and communications, become more mobile, and form geographically dispersed networks that would increase their spheres of influence and criminal activities. These law enforcement officials rightly judged that sharing information about these threats would create a network of law enforcement personnel whose chances of defeating the threats would be higher than those of the individual organizations acting alone. LEIU remains in existence today.[5] The National Crime Information Center (NCIC) database was created in 1967 under the then FBI director J. Edgar Hoover. This system endures today, plays an important role in public safety, and is a key component of the larger homeland security mission. Similarly, the International Association of Law Enforcement Intelligence Analysts (IALEIA) was formed in 1981 "to advance high standards of professionalism in law enforcement intelligence analysis at the Local, State/Provincial, National and International levels." IALEIA remains in operation today.[6]

What the events of 9/11 brought into stark relief was that the era of globalization carried with it the globalization of threats and that indeed threats to our national security beyond espionage and drug trafficking could and would emanate from within our own borders. While the nature of the threat was clear, how to respond to it within the framework of our federal system and constitution was not. Actions were taken and structures created that individually made great sense but in the aggregate created new challenges for the domestic intelligence analyst:

- In 2002, the Department of Homeland Security was created to ensure sufficient barriers are in place to keep threats from entering our borders. Within DHS the Directorate of Intelligence Analysis and Infrastructure Protection (IAIP, now the Office of Intelligence and Analysis, I&A) was created to analyze information from all sources (including national intelligence and law enforcement) to prevent terrorist attacks and understand the nature of the terrorist threat to the homeland, particularly to its critical infrastructure.
- The creation of the Terrorist Threat Integration Center (TTIC) was announced in the State of the Union Address in January 2003. The mission given the TTIC (now the National Counterterrorism Center—NCTC) was identical to the mission given to DHS's IAIP, with the exception of DHS's critical infrastructure focus.
- The FBI created a Directorate of Intelligence (DI) in 2003 and a National Security Branch in 2005 to better integrate foreign intelligence and counterintelligence and law enforcement operations, transforming the FBI into a national security organization that fuses traditional law enforcement and intelligence missions.
- The FBI expanded the number of joint terrorism task forces (JTTFs), which according to the Department of Justice "are small cells of highly trained, locally based, passionately committed investigators, analysts, linguists, SWAT experts, and other specialists from dozens of US law enforcement and intelligence agencies. It is a multi-agency effort led by the Justice Department and FBI designed to combine the resources of federal, state, and local law enforcement."[7]
- A position of director of national intelligence was created in 2005 to oversee, coordinate, and integrate the operations of intelligence community, including those with both law enforcement and intelligence missions.
- State and local governments formed a total of seventy-two intelligence fusion centers[8] to integrate threat information focused not just on terrorism but instead on "all crimes and all hazards."

This proliferation of domestic intelligence authorities and activities has resulted in confusion: DHS's I&A was designated the national authority for coordination with and support to the fusion centers in 2007. The FBI, however, describes its field intelligence groups (FIGs) as "the focal point for sharing information with fusion centers."[9] The FBI in 2008 was designated "the lead agency for domestic intelligence collection, as outlined in Executive Order 12333."[10] And in 2012, the DNI designated FBI special agents in charge (SACs)—law enforcement rather than intelligence professionals—his personal representatives in the United States, despite the fact that the DNI has no authority to directly task those personnel to collect domestic intelligence.

The organizations and structures outlined above all play a critical individual role in defending the nation, and each has made important contributions to that effort. Taken as a whole, however, they reflect the disunity of effort and confusion that results from overlaying a traditional national-level intelligence business model—where intelligence requirements, collection, processing, analysis, and dissemination authorities are resident in a single organization—on a domestic intelligence enterprise where those authorities are held in multiple organizations, each operating under unique authorities and with distinct missions for protecting the homeland. This in turn has had a profound effect on the efforts of domestic intelligence analysts and contributes to the lack of a strong and unified US domestic intelligence analysis capability more than a decade after the tragic events of September 11, 2001.

Impact of Law Enforcement Culture on Domestic Intelligence Analysis

If intelligence analysis can be described as "judgment based on reasoning and evidence"—with evidence defined in its broadest sense to include everything that is used to determine or demonstrate the truth of an assertion—then the state of domestic intelligence analysis, given its placement within law enforcement investigative organizations, should be very strong indeed. That domestic intelligence analysis is linked to law enforcement operations represents simultaneously its greatest potential strength and also its greatest weakness.

Sources

The law enforcement culture of prosecution places a premium on the pedigree of sources, a weakness of foreign intelligence and counterintelligence analysis that is often cited in investigations of intelligence failures, including that of the IC's judgments about Iraq's weapons of mass destruction capability in 2003.[11] The need to present evidence culled from sources in public for evaluation by judge and sometimes jury leads law enforcement professionals to take great care in validating the credibility of especially their human sources. The intelligence analysts who support them follow suit. Intelligence analysts who support case-based law enforcement operations often have greater visibility into the reliability of sources than analysts at other agencies. In fact, they often contribute to source-validation activities. This puts domestic intelligence analysts at a distinct advantage over their foreign intelligence and counterintelligence counterparts who are often denied such source-specific information because of concerns about divulging the identity of a source or method and thereby putting it at risk.

At the same time, the nature of law enforcement operations does not encourage the pursuit of sources beyond their utility for a specific investigation or series of investigations. This presents intelligence analysts with two fundamental challenges: (1) The information on which they base their analysis is inherently limited to the confines of a specific case, and (2) their ability to use intelligence to drive new investigations based on intelligence information is similarly limited. Domestic intelligence analysts thus serve the narrow purposes of a specific case and the apprehension of a suspect or suspects, rather than examining larger strategic issues that may emerge across multiple cases. The implications are far-reaching. As a result, operational and tactical intelligence analysis is optimized at the expense of strategic intelligence analysis that is supposed to produce and share national security information as defined in IRTPA.

The Investigative Process, Intelligence Analysis, and the Scientific Method

Investigative tradecraft has much in common with good intelligence analysis tradecraft and the scientific method. All three of these processes involve using a body of techniques to investigate phenomena, acquire new knowledge, and correct and integrate previous knowledge. Both scientific method and investigative inquiry are distinguished by being as objective as possible in order to reduce biased interpretation of results.[12] In addition, both methods are designed to let the evidence speak for itself, whether it supports a theory or not. Intelligence analysis has been faulted in the past for sometimes lacking the discipline inherent in the investigative and scientific methods, with the Iraq WMD intelligence failure often being cited as an egregious example of this lack of objectivity. Fairly or not, intelligence analysts are often accused of using information to support the preconceived ideas and theories of their customers, rather than letting the information itself substantiate or disprove multiple theories. The colocation of domestic intelligence analysts with law enforcement personnel aligns their analytic approach more closely with the investigative process, thereby creating conditions for greater adherence to scientific methods and objectivity in their analytic product.

The events of 9/11 have often been called a "failure of imagination."[13] We know that imagination is a vital attribute of successful analysis and often a missing ingredient that helps to explain analytic failures.[14] While the law enforcement investigative culture allows for positing hypotheses and allowing hard evidence to prove or disprove them within the confines of a specific case, it specifically discourages that same inquiry absent the framework of a specific case.

The negative effects of this on domestic intelligence analysis tradecraft is perhaps best seen in the inability of the FBI to connect information on suspicious students at flight schools in two US cities prior to 9/11. In early July 2001, the FBI's Radical Fundamentalist Unit and its Osama bin Laden Unit at FBI headquarters received a memo from the Phoenix field office outlining concerns that students with links to a London fundamentalist group were attending flight schools in Arizona. Phoenix suggested a national sweep of such schools for possible terrorists, but no action was taken. Then, in August 2001, a Minneapolis-based flight school reported to the FBI its suspicions about a student— later the suspected twelfth 9/11 hijacker, Zacarias Moussaoui—including that he did not want to learn the takeoff and landing phases, that he had no background in aviation, and that he had paid in cash for the course. The FBI promptly launched an investigation of Moussaoui, but for bureaucratic reasons the Minneapolis office was unable to obtain authority to search his computer and did not receive the Phoenix memorandum that might have allowed intelligence analysts to connect the two cases. While such a situation might not repeat itself today given the FBI's focus on terrorism prevention since 9/11, it is the single case-based nature of the investigative culture that created the obstacles to positing a hypothesis and testing it beyond the confines of a single case.

A History of Voluntary Information Sharing for Law Enforcement Operations

Law enforcement has a strong history of information sharing, dating from the creation of LEIU in 1956. Having spent almost twenty-five years in the IC, I recall being very impressed by law enforcement's approach to information sharing when I joined the FBI in 2003 to lead its then Office of Intelligence. In fact, I often thought that the IC could learn a great deal from the law enforcement approach. This point is perhaps best illustrated by the governance processes that drive the operation of the National Crime Information Center. Law enforcement entities from across the nation have agreed to share elements of personal identifying information held individually within their organizations to strengthen public safety operations nationwide.

Even if unaware of the existence of the NCIC database, one is likely to have encountered this system when purchasing a firearm, for example, or registering a motor vehicle. Have you ever been pulled over for a traffic violation and waited patiently for the officer to emerge from his or her vehicle and approach yours? Have you ever wondered what that officer is doing? He or she is checking your vehicle information against NCIC records to learn as much as possible and inform the decisions that will be made about the manner of approach to you and your vehicle. Such an activity could be legitimately described as "intelligence support to force protection operations." Under NCIC operations, a governing body of law enforcement leaders agrees upon standards for information sharing, including the elements of information, their format, and most importantly sanctions for misuse or improper access to that information. To the best of my knowledge, no similar system has been proposed for sharing personal identifying information derived from foreign intelligence and counterintelligence collection operations across the IC.

Even with its natural tendency to share information in the interests of public safety, law enforcement organizations collect and share information for their own use, often not understanding the utility of that information to others who act in defense of the nation, including intelligence and military organizations. To be sure, there are legitimate reasons for the reluctance to share information outside of law enforcement organizations. State, local, and tribal law enforcement organizations operate under laws and policies that limit the sharing of information, including the Code of Federal Regulations (CFR) 28 Part 23—a federal guideline for law enforcement agencies that operate federally funded, multijurisdictional criminal intelligence systems. 28 CFR Part 23 provides guidance for law enforcement agencies on how to operate criminal intelligence information systems effectively while protecting individuals' privacy and constitutional rights during the collection, storage, and dissemination of criminal intelligence information. That intelligence analysts operate within federally funded fusion centers means that 28 CFR Part 23 sharing restrictions apply to them.

Thus national-level guidance on intelligence sharing for domestic analysts comes to them from two places—and they conflict. So how intelligence analysts are to reconcile the provisions of 28 CFR Part 23 with those of IRTPA is less clear. Little of the difficult policy work to reconcile the conflicting provisions of the two laws has been completed, leaving domestic intelligence analysts to be guided by the more authoritative policies of law enforcement when considering the sharing of their analytic product.

Intelligence Analysis: An Intellectual Virtual Pursuit of Information in a World That Values Physical Access to Information

Despite the similarities between the intelligence analysis and law enforcement investigative processes, they differ in one very important way: Intelligence analysis is at its core an intellectual and sedentary process that leverages vast information stores, while the law enforcement investigative process is marked by the physical pursuit of information, much of which never finds its way into information stores for use by others. This is the result of two phenomena: (1) Despite the success of systems such as the NCIC's, information systems to support law enforcement operations are woefully inadequate, and (2) law enforcement officers value oral information over written information.[15] Unlike their IC counterpart collectors who write prolifically to ensure collected information is shared via appropriate information systems, law enforcement personnel are less inclined to put information in writing, both because they lack access to supporting information systems and because they want to protect the integrity of their case information. For a law enforcement officer, the case is the place where all pertinent information is gathered—a "bucket" of information. There is little difference between an IC professional's views of a collection source or platform and a law enforcement professional's view of the case. Both want to protect their sources and their information. But the IC has spent many years devising policies, procedures, and technologies to both protect sources and to share information with others who need to act upon it. The law enforcement community has far less experience with sharing information while protecting sources and lacks enabling policies, procedures, and technologies to facilitate it.

I recall early in my tenure at the FBI asking a group of agents if they would rather "knock on forty doors, or let intelligence analysis guide it to the right ten doors?" At the time I did not fully understand why my question was greeted with indifference and silence. Sometime later I came to appreciate how strongly the investigative culture is rooted in the physical acquisition of information in support of the case. It then struck me that at NSA I had lived in an incredibly rich information environment that allowed me to do my intelligence analysis without moving from the confines of my office. It also struck me that law enforcement officers and domestic intelligence analysts alike lived in an incredibly impoverished information environment, and budget limitations and the case-based culture strongly limit a change in that situation. One has only to ask a DHS analyst working at the IC's NCTC and a DHS analyst working at DHS headquarters to describe their information environments to grasp the enormity of the difference. The NCTC analyst comments on the large amounts of data she has to peruse each day. The DHS analyst comments similarly on the foreign intelligence stores he uses each day but laments the paucity of homeland intelligence information on which to base his intelligence analysis.

Conducting Analysis: How It's Done in the Domestic Agencies

Intelligence analysis at national agencies is defined by three unique environmental conditions: (1) access to information, (2) the priorities of the operators they support, and (3) the fact that their customers—including the public—operate for the most part in an unclassified information environment.

Information systems within both DHS and the FBI were not designed to allow for the analysis of information across multiple sources. There are very good reasons for this, most of them related to provisions in law and policy that severely inhibit information sharing. Certainly similar obstacles exist at the foreign and counterintelligence agencies, but those agencies have developed systems and policies over many years that allow for sharing consistent with law and policy.

The operators with whom domestic intelligence analysts are colocated judge the value of analytic product in terms of what they themselves can "do" with it. While this is a fair measure of the value of analytic product, it is but one measure. One of the lessons observed but not learned from the tragedy of 9/11 is that information held or produced by one organization is of use to others as well and should be shared with them to enable their operations and prevent harm to the nation. At the FBI in August 2012, for example, Deputy Director Sean Joyce stated publicly that the FBI is the customer for 95 percent of the intelligence analysis it produces. The statement suggests that intelligence analysis at the FBI remains a local support activity instead of a national mission that supports all instruments of national power, including DOD and DHS.

The customers for domestic intelligence analytic product outside of their organizations for the most part work and make decisions in an unclassified information environment. Even when domestic intelligence analysts are encouraged to share their product outside of their organizations with those who act in defense of the homeland, they must do so at the unclassified level, often diluting the impact of the product.

The consequence of these three conditions is that domestic intelligence analysis remains largely an "in-box/out-box," short-term journalism activity. This type of reporting is not without value. In fact, when I arrived at the FBI in May 2003, raw intelligence production of intelligence information reports (IIR) averaged thirty-four per year. Since that time, raw intelligence production has increased by multiple hundreds. The emphasis on reporting and sharing raw intelligence reporting has borne fruit and is to be commended. This focus, however, has left little room for estimative strategic intelligence analysis. Because little value and attention has been placed on strategic intelligence analysis, advanced analytic tradecraft among domestic intelligence analysts remains underdeveloped and unpracticed. Many domestic intelligence analysts have joined domestic agencies after careers as intelligence analysts in the foreign and counterintelligence arenas. These analysts know how to do estimative and strategic analysis, but they also know it is not valued within their organizations. Rational behavior for such analysts is either to leave the domestic agencies or to conduct the type of work that their supervisors value.

The First Decade: An Early Report Card

There is much to celebrate with regard to improvements in the state of domestic intelligence analysis since 9/11. Efforts at all levels of government to improve the state of domestic intelligence analysis clearly have been credited with disrupting numerous terrorist plots targeting the homeland. All citizens of the United States owe a debt of gratitude to those who have worked tirelessly, some making the ultimate sacrifice in our defense. That the efforts to improve domestic intelligence have been sincere and accompanied by hard work and considerable achievement is inarguable.

Two successful homeland terrorist attacks since 9/11 show that despite notable progress, work remains to develop a robust national domestic intelligence analysis capability that not only supports the law enforcement investigative process, but also drives it. On November 5, 2009, Army major Nidal Malik Hasan, a US citizen, entered the deployment center at Fort Hood, Texas, and opened fire, killing thirteen and wounding another thirty-two in the worst terrorist attack on US soil since 9/11. Among other findings pointing to systemic information-sharing issues, a Senate Homeland Security and Governmental Affairs Committee investigation found that "in the Hasan case, the FBI did not effectively utilize intelligence analysts who could have provided a different perspective given evidence that it had."[16] The report concludes that an intelligence analyst–led examination of Hasan's behavior could have uncovered his radicalization and possibly prevented the attack. Investigations continue into the terrorist attack in Boston on April 15, 2013, but early reports suggest shortcomings in both information sharing and the full integration of intelligence analysts in the investigative process.[17]

While a decade seems like a long time, it is unreasonable to assume that a strong domestic intelligence analysis capability should or could be created within that timeframe. The national foreign intelligence and counterintelligence analysis capabilities have existed for over sixty-five years, and no one, including the intelligence analysts themselves, would describe those capabilities as "perfect" and in need of no improvement. Still, foreign intelligence and counterintelligence analysts enjoy certain advantages inherent in their linkage to intelligence organizations. These advantages are the same disadvantages encountered by domestic intelligence analysts because of their linkage to law enforcement organizations, and the disadvantages have not been sufficiently ameliorated in the first decade of intelligence reform. As a result, the state of domestic intelligence analysis, while stronger at the operational and tactical levels, remains weak at the strategic one.

The weakness of strategic domestic intelligence analysis raises questions about the extent to which law enforcement organizations at all levels of government have been successful in transforming their operational focus from the prosecution of crimes that have happened to the prevention of all threats to our nation's security, including crime.

A decade of war at home and abroad has challenged all intelligence organizations to maintain a balance between strategic intelligence analysis and operational/tactical intelligence analysis. This perennial tension has been a hallmark of foreign intelligence and counterintelligence analysis activities, and it is not surprising that the same tension exists in their much younger and less mature domestic intelligence analysis cousins. But the weakness of the strategic domestic intelligence analysis is perhaps of greater concern because the case-based environment in which domestic intelligence analysis takes place tends to discourage and undervalue strategic-level analysis. The principal customers of analysis—namely, law enforcement professionals—judge the value of intelligence in terms of the "leads" that it provides them. What specific actions can they take, what investigations can they open, and what leads can they follow based on the information provided? This is true at all levels of law enforcement organizations, from national to state, local, and tribal.

Strategic intelligence analysis generally does not contain specific "lead" information, both because it is designed to focus on issues that transcend individual cases and because intelligence analysts are trained to avoid policy prescription in their work. Intelligence analysts do not tell decision makers—those charged with taking action on information—which actions to take based on their analysis. As long as domestic intelligence analysis remains tethered to law enforcement operations and its value continues to be judged by its contribution to those operations, strategic-level analysis will remain undervalued and likely will not be produced at all. As a result, those outside of law enforcement charged with defense of the nation will not have the benefit of strategic-level domestic analysis to inform their decisions.

No Unified Threat Picture for the Homeland

Ten years after 9/11, the combination of the distributed nature of US domestic intelligence analysis efforts described above with the weakness of strategic domestic intelligence analysis has prevented the creation of a single, unified picture of threats to the homeland. There are many, but two primary reasons for this: (1) At the national level, domestic intelligence operations have been focused largely on terrorism, while at the state and local level the focus has been on "all crimes and all hazards," and (2) domestic intelligence analysis remains linked to case-based law enforcement operations, which optimizes operational and tactical intelligence analysis at the expense of strategic intelligence analysis. As a result, DHS has its threat picture, the FBI has its threat picture, and the seventy-two fusion centers have their threat pictures. That these entities have even individual threat pictures is a real accomplishment and should be applauded. This progress is the result of visionary leadership, extraordinary dedication on the part of intelligence analysts and law enforcement professionals at all levels of government, and a ruthless focus on the security of our nation.

At the national level domestic intelligence analysts belong to organizations in which intelligence is not the only mission. In these organizations the intelligence analysis function is seen as a support function for the core mission of the agency in question. This holds true at the state, local, and tribal levels. The core mission practitioners understandably view themselves as the main customer for the analytic product. In recent years the partnership between analysts and mission personnel has been strengthened, and tactical operations are better for it. The absence of a unified threat picture for the territory of the United States persists, however, because the individual mission practitioners each have a legitimately different view of what, and how urgent, the threat is. Unless or until those charged with defending US territory have a forum in which to jointly define a common threat picture, this situation is unlikely to change. Under current conditions it is difficult to have confidence that domestic intelligence analysts will graduate from *supporting* tactical operations to *driving* them with their analytic product in an effort to anticipate and prevent new threats.

Intelligence Analysts

Intelligence analysts who operate in the domestic arena may no longer be regarded as "furniture" or "carpet dust,"[18] but much work remains before intelligence analysts in the domestic arena are treated as professionals in their own right—that is, fully on a par with their professional law enforcement partners—rather than as support personnel. This is particularly problematic at the national level, though far less so in state and local law enforcement organizations where "sworn officers" perform the role of intelligence analysts. At the fusion centers, intelligence analysts' positions are often filled by contractors because limited funding for permanent positions makes it easier to staff these positions using federal grant funding. Few fusion centers require their contract intelligence analysts to adhere to the DNI's analytic standards, particularly those for training in analytic methodology. It is worthy of note, however, that professional associations for intelligence analysts, such as IALEIA, not only persist but thrive. FBI intelligence analysts have taken the initiative to form the FBI Intelligence Analysts Association (FBI IAA), giving of their own time and energy to take responsibility for developments that bear on their profession both in the world and within the FBI.[19]

The director of the FBI is required by IRTPA to "afford the analysts of the Bureau training and career opportunities commensurate with the training and career opportunities afforded analysts in other elements of the intelligence community."[20] In 2005, the FBI appropriations bill removed FBI analysts from the jurisdiction of Title V, which limited their promotion potential to GS-12 in the field and GS-13 at headquarters. No longer governed by Title V, FBI intelligence analysts now can advance to the Senior Executive Service as do their foreign intelligence and counterintelligence counterparts in the rest of the IC.

Until recently there was reason for optimism about the FBI's commitment to professionalize its intelligence analyst ranks. In mid-2012, however, the FBI announced that analyst promotions would be frozen at GS-13 pending an evaluation of their work roles and in conjunction with a larger reorganization of the FBI's Directorate of Intelligence. That reorganization is under way and removes all FBI analysts from the direct supervision of the Directorate of Intelligence, placing them instead under dual subordination to FBI investigative organizations at headquarters and in the field. This reorganization not only inhibits an IC cultural connection for FBI analysts and the salience of DNI-driven analytic standards and tradecraft, but it also greatly diminishes the authority of the Directorate of Intelligence, reducing it to a policy organization with no authority to ensure that intelligence drives FBI investigative operations. This appears to be inconsistent with the provisions of IRTPA Title II, which codifies both the FBI's intelligence structure and the responsibilities and authorities of the Directorate of Intelligence.[21] It also raises concerns about the FBI's commitment to a professional intelligence analyst cadre, despite the fact that the FBI has since lifted the freeze on analyst promotions.

From 2006 to 2009, I had the privilege of teaching a module in a DHS intelligence analyst training course. During that time I met many DHS intelligence analysts and had occasion to provide career advice. One DHS intelligence analyst asked me about a career move he was considering. "I am in CBP [Customs and Border Protection] now," he said, "but I am considering a move to DHS." At the time I remember not fully understanding his question; the CBP is after all a DHS component. What his question revealed, however, was something DHS employees, critics, and champions acknowledge freely: DHS is not yet an enterprise but rather a loose confederation of twenty-two former agencies and departments. Because DHS investigative elements and their operations are not an integrated enterprise, there is no imperative for integrated intelligence analysis within DHS. Many DHS elements, such as TSA, CBP, Immigration and Customs Enforcement, and the Secret Service, have intelligence components and intelligence analysts, but neither the components nor the analysts within them are members of the larger intelligence community. Within DHS, only I&A and the Coast Guard are members of the IC. Unlike their FBI counterparts, intelligence analysts in DHS—even those within the IC—have no intelligence career service to guide their professional development, although DHS is attempting to address that gap.

Intelligence Requirements

There is no single authoritative intelligence requirements document to guide domestic intelligence collection and analytic efforts. The National Intelligence Priorities Framework (NIPF) that guides foreign and counterintelligence intelligence analysis operations on behalf of the DNI cannot provide the same guidance for those whom the DNI cannot task directly. In addition, because both the collectors of and customers for domestic intelligence reside in large numbers at the state and local levels and do not possess requisite security clearances, even the NIPF document itself is not readily available to them.

Recent DNI efforts to further IC integration include the creation of national intelligence managers (NIMs) to organize intelligence efforts around issues rather than collection sources. This issue focus holds great potential for unifying domestic intelligence activities and should be applauded. As the Office of the Director of National Intelligence has stated, "regional and functional National Intelligence Managers (NIMs) develop Unifying Intelligence Strategies (UIS) for geographic and topic areas. The UISs serve as a roadmap to help the Intelligence Community work together on the highest-priority intelligence issues."[22] It is worthy of note, however, that the DNI did not create a NIM position for the United States or one for the homeland. Only belatedly has the DNI agreed to "pilot" the concept of a NIM for the homeland, placing that responsibility within the portfolio of the NIM for the Western Hemisphere. The DNI hesitancy is understandable. NIMs are supposed to integrate intelligence analysis and intelligence collection activities. The DNI has no authority over the collection activities from which most domestic intelligence information is derived.

The FBI has embraced the NIPF as a guide for prioritizing US intelligence analysis and collection for its National Security Branch (NSB).[23] It is not clear whether the NIPF priorities extend to law enforcement operations outside of the NSB. DHS's I&A has its own requirements framework to guide homeland security intelligence analysis. Homeland Security Standing Information Needs (HSEC SINs) "form the foundation for information collection activities within the Department and provide other Intelligence Community (IC) and Homeland Security Enterprise members the ability to focus their collection, analytic, and reporting assets in support of the homeland security mission. The HSEC SINs document the enduring all-threats and all-hazards information needs of the Homeland Security Enterprise."[24] Neither the *National Criminal Intelligence Sharing Plan* nor the *Fusion Center Guidelines*—the intelligence bibles that guide domestic intelligence analysis efforts at the state, local, and tribal levels—make mention of an intelligence requirements framework, but both stress the need for sharing information that bears on "all crimes and all hazards."[25]

Information Technology

Information technology to support domestic intelligence analysis both within and across cases is woefully inadequate. When I arrived at the FBI in 2003, my overwhelming feeling was one of information deprivation. While foreign intelligence has since been made available to domestic practitioners, systems to do the same for domestic intelligence— let alone merge the foreign and domestic intelligence to facilitate issue-based strategic intelligence analysis—remain unavailable, as do secure communications and facilities. What systems have been developed within domestic intelligence organizations, such as the FBI's Sentinel, are designed to support case management and provide little support to intelligence analysis across cases. The notable exception to this is the DNI's NCTC, where considerable investment has been made in creating a unified information environment for terrorism analysis from all sources of information. The NCTC performs intelligence analysis on national intelligence information as defined by IRTPA and should be considered a model for integrated intelligence analysis operations for threats other than terrorism.

Role of the ODNI

Since its creation in 2005, the Office of the Director of National Intelligence has been slow to embrace its role in domestic intelligence analysis. While the impetus for IRTPA and the creation of the ODNI was the need to better integrate domestic and foreign intelligence analysis, the Iraq WMD failure occurred as the bill was being drafted. As a result the focus of intelligence reform rightly broadened to address the weakness exposed by the WMD Commission.[26] The broader focus pushed the issue of domestic intelligence into the background but at the same time placed new emphasis on the need to improve intelligence analysis, including analytic methods, analytic standards and training, and even the creation of an ombudsman to whom analysts could appeal when they felt their alternative analytic views were either being ignored or deliberately silenced.

In theory this emphasis on the importance of improving intelligence analysis should have benefited domestic intelligence analysts. In reality none of the four DNIs to date has focused attention on domestic intelligence operations, including domestic intelligence analysis. This is likely both a result of preoccupation with two "hot" wars overseas, as well as legitimate DNI confusion over how to manage domestic intelligence analysis when he has no authority over the collection operations on which that analysis is based.

Improving Professionalism of Analysis in Domestic Intelligence: What Needs to Be Done?

Further efforts to improve the professionalism of domestic intelligence analysis should be focused on strengthening the capability to conduct strategic-level domestic intelligence analysis. This daunting but urgent need can be addressed through a comprehensive effort that should include the following elements:

- Embrace the distributed nature of domestic intelligence *operations* and celebrate and preserve the advances in tactical and operational domestic intelligence analysis that have resulted from the colocation of intelligence analysts with law enforcement professionals. Intelligence professionals should be comfortable with this arrangement, which has a powerful analogue in the integration of tactical and operational intelligence analysis within military organizations in support of war-fighting operations. This integration results in improved operations and develops a cadre of intelligence analysts who specialize in support to military operations. That we have developed a similar capability for domestic intelligence analysis by integrating them with our "domestic warfighters" is a positive development and directly contributes to the professionalism of domestic intelligence analysts.

- Anticipate that tactical and operational intelligence analysis will prove insufficient to protect the homeland, just as it proved insufficient to support military operations. Proactively create the equivalent of DIA—that is, a national-level strategic domestic intelligence analysis organization—before the next intelligence failure.
- The DNI, whose authority over national strategic domestic intelligence analysis is unambiguous, should designate the DHS undersecretary for intelligence and analysis the functional manager for strategic domestic intelligence analysis. The placement of this responsibility in DHS is designed to focus strategic domestic intelligence analysis and the Office of Intelligence and Analysis on securing our borders and critical infrastructure (including our cyber infrastructure) with defensive measures rather than on the pursuit of specific adversaries through offensive means. Strategic domestic intelligence analysis should inform the creation of countermeasures to defeat threats to the homeland before they materialize. Tactical and operational domestic intelligence analysis would then focus on the pursuit of adversaries through offensive means when those countermeasures are not successful.
- Based on this new defensive focus, the president's homeland security adviser should lead the creation of a domestic intelligence priorities framework to guide strategic domestic intelligence analysis. This framework should be produced at the unclassified level and be promulgated by the undersecretary for intelligence and analysis to all domestic intelligence collectors, the private sector, and the public as advisory collection tasking.
- The DNI should charge the undersecretary for intelligence and analysis with adopting the tenets and initiatives promulgated in IRTPA for the FBI Intelligence Career Service as it relates to intelligence analysts for the strategic domestic intelligence analysis career service. Analytic standards found in the *Fusion Center Guidelines* and the *National Criminal Intelligence Sharing Plan* should also be included as a component of the career service.

IRTPA wisely expanded the definition of "national intelligence" to ensure that information bearing on threats inside our borders could be made available to all authorities charged with neutralizing those threats at the national, state, local, and tribal levels. IRTPA also acknowledged correctly that creating an intelligence-collection discipline called "domestic" is not in keeping with either the framework of the US constitution or the federal system. Progress to date in integrating domestic intelligence analysis and domestic protection operations at the tactical level has been encouraging. Missing at the national level is a single authority charged with executing the DNI's clear authority to have access to and analyze all information that bears on security within US borders. The DHS Office of Intelligence and Analysis, like the DNI, has authority only to analyze—not to collect—domestic intelligence. It seems logical that the DNI would designate I&A to be the executive agent for this important work. Until some authority is directly charged with this mission, it is difficult to be optimistic about the creation of a resilient and integrated domestic protection network capable of countering and preventing the threats inside our borders represented by networks of terrorists, criminals, cyber activists, proliferators, and spies.

Notes

1. Since 9/11 the terms "domestic intelligence" and "homeland security intelligence" have often been used interchangeably. Both accurately refer to *information* bearing on the internal security of the United States. Neither term is accurate when used to refer to *operations* to collect that information, because neither domestic intelligence nor homeland security intelligence collection *operations* have been authorized under the Intelligence Reform and Terrorism Prevention Act of 2004 (IRTPA) or other intelligence law. When such operations are conducted, they are done under law enforcement (vice intelligence) authorities.

2. Intelligence Reform and Terrorism Prevention Act of 2004, Public Law 108-458, US Statutes at Large, section 1012, www.gpo.gov/fdsys/pkg/PLAW-108publ458/pdf/PLAW-108publ458.pdf.

3. For a more detailed discussion of these programs, see Congressional Research Service report *NSA Surveillance Leaks: Background and Issues for Congress*, http://freedownloadb.org/pdf/nsa-surveillance-leaks-background-and-issues-for-congress-89928166.html.

4. For a comprehensive discussion, see Richard Posner, *Preventing Surprise Attacks: Intelligence Reform in the Wake of 9/11* (Lanham, MD: Rowman & Littlefield, 2005).

5. See the LEIU home page, http://leiu-homepage.org/index.php.

6. See the IALEIA home page, www.ialeia.org/.

7. Department of Justice, "Joint Terrorism Task Force," www.justice.gov/jttf/.

8. The Department of Homeland Security defines fusion centers as serving as primary focal points within the state and local environment for the receipt, analysis, gathering, and sharing of threat-related information among federal, state, local, tribal, and territorial (SLTT) partners. See www.dhs.gov.

9. Federal Bureau of Investigation, "Eric Velez-Villar, Assistant Director, Directorate of Intelligence, Federal Bureau of Investigation, Statement before the House Homeland Security Committee, Subcommittee on Counterterrorism and Intelligence Washington, DC, February 28, 2012," www.fbi.gov/news/testimonyintelligence-sharing-with-federal-state-and-local-law-enforcement-10-years-after-9-11.

10. Ibid.

11. The Commission on the Intelligence Capabilities of the United States regarding Weapons of Mass Destruction, *Report to the President of the United States, March 31, 2005* (Washington, DC: Government Printing Office, 2005), chap. 8. Hereafter cited as *WMD Commission Report*.

12. See chap. 9 for an elaboration of the scientific method.

13. See *The 9/11 Commission Report: Final Report of the National Commission on Terrorist Attacks upon the United States* (New York: Norton, 2004), 344–48.

14. See chap. 10.

15. Both similarly observed by Henry A. Crumpton in *The Art of Intelligence* (New York: Penguin), 112–13.

16. See "A Ticking Time Bomb: Counterterrorism Lessons from the U.S. Government's Failure to Prevent the Fort Hood Attack," by Joseph I. Lieberman, chairman, and Susan M. Collins, ranking member, Committee on Homeland Security and Governmental Affairs, US Senate, www.hsgac.senate.gov/public/_files/Fort_Hood/FortHoodReport.pdf.

17. See Testimony of Boston police commissioner Edward F. Davis III before the Senate Committee on Homeland Security, July 10, 2013, www.hsgac.senate.gov/download/?id=7810b6aa-5ed6-4e71-8b9f.

18. Chris Strohm, "Ex-Federal Officials Question Pace of FBI Reforms," *Government Executive*, June 6, 2005, www.govexec.com/defense/2005/06/ex-federal-officials-question-pace-of-fbi-reforms/19367/.

19. See the FBI IAA's home page, www.fbiiaa.org.

20. Intelligence Reform and Terrorism Prevention Act, section 1012 c6, www.gpo.gov/fdsys/pkg/PLAW-108publ458/pdf/PLAW-108publ458.pdf.

21. Ibid., title II.

22. Office of the Director of National Intelligence, "Intelligence Integration: Who We Are," www.dni.gov/index.php/about/organization/intelligence-integration-who-we-are.

23. The NSB houses the FBI's Counterterrorism and Counterintelligence Divisions, as well as the Weapons of Mass Destruction Directorate and the Directorate of Intelligence. Both the FBI's Criminal and Cyber Divisions reside outside of the NSB, and neither its analysts nor its agents are funded through the DNI's NIP.

24. Department of Homeland Security, "More About the Office of Intelligence and Mission Analysis," www.dhs.gov/more-about-office-intelligence-and-analysis-mission.

25. See it.ojp.gov/docdownloader.aspx?ddid=1153 it.ojp.gov/docdownloader.aspx?ddid=1153 for *National Criminal Intelligence Sharing Plan* and it.ojp.gov/documents/fusion_center_guidelines_law_enforcement.pdf for *Fusion Center Guidelines*.

26. *WMD Commission Report*, chap. 10.

PART VI

Leading Analytic Change

CHAPTER 17

Building a Community of Analysts

THOMAS FINGAR

Core missions and responsibilities of intelligence analysts are little different today than they were in the Truman, Eisenhower, and Kennedy administrations. Like their predecessors, twenty-first-century analysts are expected to support US government policymakers and other intelligence customers by transforming data into insight, interpreting fragmentary information, and providing objective assessments of complex issues.[1] Analysts' primary responsibility, now as then, is to help other US government officials to make better-informed decisions on matters affecting the security of our nation, the safety of our people, and the success of American policy initiatives. These are important continuities. But US interests, intelligence capabilities, and most other dimensions of the national security enterprise have changed dramatically.[2] The intelligence enterprise has also changed but at a slower pace. The resulting gap between what is expected from the intelligence community (IC) and what it is capable of delivering is both wide and widening.

The mismatch between capabilities and expectations has many causes and impedes performance in many ways. Collectors and analysts are expected to cover more places and more potential problems, stretching capabilities and requiring information and expertise beyond what was needed or developed in the past. Many of the issues and developments that the IC is expected to cover are inherently more complex, and analysis adequate to meet the needs of policymakers requires more granular information and more types of analytic expertise than did most of the issues the IC was (and is) organized to cover. Intelligence customers increasingly demand up-to-the-minute information on often fast-moving (and complicated) developments. If they do not receive that information or sophisticated assessments of what it means, they are disappointed by, and often critical of, the performance of the intelligence community. The gap between capabilities and expectations is made even wider and more dangerous by the increasing demand for "operational" intelligence needed to disrupt terrorist attacks, to interdict illicit shipments of arms, nuclear materials, or other contraband, or to minimize collateral damage and US casualties during military or law enforcement operations. In sum, the demand is for more precise information and more sophisticated analysis on more complex developments in

more places in ever-shorter amounts of time. As a consummate "can do" support organization, the IC must try to meet the escalating requirements.[3]

Most of the time, intelligence professionals find ways to bridge the gap with improvised solutions and hard work. But not always. Sometimes best efforts are not adequate.
Officials who count on intelligence support are disappointed and lose confidence in the
intelligence enterprise. Such "intelligence failures" seldom have the impact or visibility of a Pearl Harbor or a 9/11, but they have a corrosive effect on analyst morale and
relations between intelligence professionals and the people they support. In aggregate
they are more damaging to the national security enterprise than are the mercifully rare
instances of disastrous failure. This is doubly tragic because many of the causal problems
can be alleviated, if not fixed, by enabling intelligence analysts to operate as twenty-first-
century professionals. Requisites of professionalism, as I interpret that term when
applied to intelligence analysts, include subject-matter expertise, disciplinary training,
understanding and rigorous application of analytic methods and standards, recognition
of the value of collaboration, and ascribing higher priority to "getting it right" and providing the best possible intelligence support to US government customers than to the
protection of bureaucratic turf or loyalty to a particular agency. The remainder of this
chapter examines impediments to achieving greater professionalism and steps that have
enhanced the professionalism and performance of the IC analytic community.

Restoring Confidence by Improving Performance

As deputy director of national intelligence for analysis in 2005, my number-one priority was to restore confidence in IC analysis and the people who produce it. Thousands
of dedicated professionals had been discredited by the sins of the few dozen—including me—who produced the now infamous estimate on Iraq's weapons of mass destruction. Those we served, the public, and many analysts lost confidence in our abilities, our
tradecraft, and our products. The best way to do this was to improve the quality—and
the tradecraft—of National Intelligence Council products and the *President's Daily
Brief*. Demonstrating improvement in these flagship products garnered praise from
oversight bodies and provided a model for other analytic vehicles. The strategy worked,
and we built support and momentum for more difficult reforms.[4] The next phase was to
shift from "fixing" what was perceived to be broken to "transforming" analysis to meet
twenty-first-century challenges.

"Analytic transformation" was—and still is—a vision with many components, the
most important of which is to enable IC analysts to work smarter.[5] One part of working
smarter is to adopt and enforce performance standards and teach analysts to apply them.
Another is to overcome structural, cultural, connectivity, security, and other impediments to collaboration. To meet the complex challenges of today and tomorrow, we had
to be able to tap expertise across the IC because no agency alone would have the critical
mass of skills and expertise needed to address more than a handful of issues. To do this
we had to build a community of analysts willing and eager to collaborate.

IC Structure: Pros and Cons

The basic structure of the IC has changed relatively little since it was (re)created in 1947.[6] A few agencies have been added, but the underlying logic has remained the same. According to that logic, the best way to ensure that officials with national security responsibilities (for example, defense, diplomacy, and homeland security) receive the tailored intelligence support they require is to create specialized and subordinate intelligence units (such as the State Department's Bureau of Intelligence and Research, or INR). Intelligence support to other missions and agencies, including the White House, is to be provided primarily by the Central Intelligence Agency, which has the additional responsibility of providing "second opinion" analytic support to agencies with in-house intelligence units.[7]

This structural arrangement's strong points—including development of expertise germane to organizations' key missions and facilitation of analysts' understanding of customer missions, needs, and timelines—also manifest common organizational pathologies. Among them are bureaucratic competition and a tendency to disparage the abilities of persons outside the organization, both of which impede integration and collaboration among analysts.[8] These positive and negative attributes are well understood and are at the heart of proposals to improve IC performance, the latest of which is the Intelligence Reform and Terrorism Prevention Act of 2004 (IRTPA), which created the position of director of national intelligence (DNI).[9]

Integration of the intelligence enterprise has been a top priority of every DNI, but the basic structure has remained unchanged.[10] Progress toward an integrated enterprise has been uneven and insufficient to remove critical barriers to collaboration. Nearly a decade after the establishment of the Office of the Director of National Intelligence (ODNI), analysis in the IC often more resembles cooperation among feudal baronies than collaboration among members of a professional community. Merging all components of the IC into a single Department of Intelligence is not feasible and may not be desirable. Rather than pursue an unattainable goal, the community has reduced structural impediments to collaboration as members of the same team. More needs to be done, but the measures summarized below are effective first steps.

Rules as Impediments and Facilitators

Rules and procedures, like organizational structures and cultures, affect the conduct and quality of analysis in both positive and negative ways. Some of the negative influences that impede collaboration and professionalism today are the product of conditions and concerns salient at the time of the IC's creation in 1947 and during its Cold War decades. Then, as now, it was important to protect sources and methods, and to prevent hostile intelligence services from discovering or disrupting activities we wish to keep secret. But some of the rules to achieve these desirable ends are interpreted and implemented in ways that degrade analytic performance and impede formation of a community of analysts. Examples include legacy—and still operative—restrictions on sharing intelligence reports with analysts in certain agencies or specialties, even when they have the requisite clearances, and injunctions not to reveal policymaker interests.[11]

Such Cold War legacy rules are counterproductive when used to scoop or cut out analysts with relevant expertise who happen to work in a different IC component. The community has made progress in repealing, relaxing, or replacing such counterproductive rules and regulations, but there are limits to what can be done in a top-down fashion, even with the authorities granted the DNI. The IC components and employees remain accountable primarily to their home agency and only secondarily to the DNI. Moreover, every agency has seemed, at least some of the time or on some issues, to be more interested in preserving turf or privileged access than in IC integration.[12]

Rules can also have positive effects. For example, the adoption in 2007 of uniform standards for the production and evaluation of intelligence analysis facilitated the creation of a community of analysts and the professionalization of intelligence analysis.[13] One hallmark of any profession is that members adhere to common rules governing the conduct of professional duties.[14] Until common standards of analytic tradecraft were mandated by IRTPA and implemented by the ODNI (in 2007), each agency inculcated and enforced its own requirements for analytic products.[15] There was overlap, but the absence of common standards exacerbated organizational biases and reluctance to acknowledge the quality of work done by analysts in other IC components. Indeed, there were more common rules governing protection of sources and methods and constraining collaboration than clear guidelines for identifying assumptions, expressing levels of confidence, or other attributes of good analytic tradecraft (see box 17.1). Rules alone do not create a profession or professionalize behavior, but they are a necessary condition.

Organizational charts and rules create the context and conditions within which intelligence analysts work, and in that respect they influence the conduct and quality of analysis. Getting the structure and the rules right, or at least making them more conducive to collaboration and professionalism, is a necessary but not sufficient condition for the production of good analysis.[16] Changing rules is easier than changing structures; both are less important than changing the way analysts think about and do their jobs. Indeed analysts—the people who function within the constraints of IC and US government organizational structures and are constrained or empowered by bureaucratic rules—are the most important determinant of how well the IC performs.

Training and Tradecraft

IC analysts run the gamut from high school graduates with on-the-job training to PhDs who have worked in industry or DOE laboratories. They also have vastly different experience and responsibilities. Other significant differences include place and type of work, proximity to primary customers, and disciplinary or subject-matter focus. The differences are so numerous and so extensive that it is appropriate to ask whether they have enough in common to be considered part of the same profession. I believe that they do.[17]

BOX 17.1   ICD 203 Analytic Standards

The most important requirements mandated by Intelligence Community Directive Number 203 are summarized on a card provided to all analysts for ready reference:

A. Objectivity

B. Independent of Political Considerations

C. Timeliness

D. Based on All Available Sources of Intelligence

E. Exhibit Proper Standards of Analytic Tradecraft

Standards of Analytic Tradecraft:

1. Properly describes quality, reliability of sources
2. Properly caveats and expresses uncertainties or confidence in analytic judgments
3. Properly distinguishes between underlying Intel and analysts' assumptions, judgments.
4. Incorporates alternative analysis where appropriate
5. Relevance to US national security
6. Logical argumentation
7. Consistency, or highlights change
8. Accurate judgments, assessments

Other professions (such as medicine, engineering, law, and education) subsume people with very different specialties and skill levels. What they have in common is commitment to common purposes and standards of conduct. In my experience that is true of intelligence analysts as well.[18]

Although new entrants to the IC evince the diversity of educational achievement noted above, the proportion with advanced degrees is high and apparently still growing.[19] The upsurge in applications from outstanding graduates of top-ranked colleges and graduate programs that began shortly after 9/11 has continued. The IC has people with excellent academic credentials and, presumably, rigorous training in disciplines germane to their work as intelligence professionals.

Advanced degrees bring with them a familiarity, if not full competence, in the wide array of academic disciplines represented in the IC's analytic workforce. The fact that many IC analysts have a firm grounding in disciplines at the core of other professional fields has important implications. First, the majority of IC analysts—most of whom joined after 9/11—are familiar with the latest theories, tools, and analytic methods in their chosen fields and eager to apply them to their new responsibilities in the IC.[20]

The IC could benefit more than it does from the skills and approaches of its newer entrants. Too often agencies treat them more like apprentices who must be retrained for life in an esoteric guild than as young professionals eager to apply what they have already learned.[21] This risks alienating once-eager recruits and increasing the likelihood that they will leave the IC just at the point when they could become significant contributors.

Second, the majority of analysts, now and for the foreseeable future, will think of themselves as members of more than one profession. They expect to become and be treated as intelligence professionals, but they also think of themselves as disciplinary, area studies, or issue specialists eligible for professional groups that transcend the IC. This makes them a potentially important bridge between the IC and academic specialists, corporate analysts, and others working on problems similar to those studied by the IC. In agencies employing large numbers of analysts, this potential benefit cannot be realized because of hoary regulations that discourage, and effectively prevent, contact and collaboration with persons outside the IC.[22] These rules and practices have a detrimental effect on intelligence analysis and the ability of the IC to meet the needs of its US government customers. Security regulations also compel younger analysts to eschew contacts and collaborative practices they have been taught to regard as an essential attribute of professionalism. Instead of effectively compelling analysts to make either-or choices between being an intelligence professional and a professional in one or more other specialties, we should adopt policies that enable them to be both intelligence professionals and members of other professions.

What new entrants bring with them is valuable to themselves and to the IC, but additional training is needed to become an intelligence professional. Even more specialized instruction and mentoring are required to become a professional intelligence analyst. As used here, "intelligence professional" refers to all members of the IC—analysts, collectors, technical wizards, covert action specialists, administrators, and many others. Where they work, what they do, and the materials they utilize differentiate them from others with similar skills who work outside the IC. At its core this means that they have an obligation to protect sources and methods and, as officials of the US government, to respect and protect deliberative processes, negotiating strategies, and other information to which they become privy by virtue of their jobs. The IC adequately instills the need to protect sensitive information and other requirements of intelligence work. But in doing so, it overstates the uniqueness of the IC and, in the process, erects and maintains barriers to the ability of intelligence analysts to function as analytic professionals.[23] For example, IC indoctrination instills the idea that classified information is more reliable than information from unclassified sources and effectively dissuades analysts from looking for unclassified answers and insights. This, in turn, sometimes—or often—causes analysts to judge that because "everything" they know about a subject is from classified sources, they cannot risk disclosure of sources and methods by seeking information or sharing insights with experts who do not have security clearances. In extreme cases, it even limits dialogue between IC analysts and the policymakers they support.

Intelligence tradecraft subsumes a wide range of subjects, but I will focus on those directly related to the conduct of analysis. Though this is admittedly an oversimplification, I think it useful to distinguish among four aspects of tradecraft:

- Expertise and disciplinary training—what analysts bring with them and acquire over the years
- Requirements and procedures that reflect the unique role that intelligence analysis is supposed to play in the national security enterprise
- Protecting sources and methods and providing guidance to collectors
- Use of tools and techniques available to IC analysts

All four categories can be taught, ideally through a combination of classroom instruction, mentoring, and on-the-job training. How they were taught across the IC differed greatly until changes were introduced by the ODNI.[24] Differences were rationalized as necessary reflections of the different missions, customers, and subject expertise of each component, and/or inevitable consequences of differences in size and budgets. This was not entirely bad, but it had negative as well as positive consequences. Two of the most important are that it impeded collaboration among analysts and agencies, and made it difficult to forge a community of analysts able to think and act as members of a common profession.

Tradecraft

The IC has long relied on academic institutions to provide basic and advanced training in disciplinary theories and methods. That is unlikely to change, even though it would be desirable to create more opportunities for IC analysts to obtain advanced training and advanced degrees funded in whole or in part by the community.[25] The National Intelligence University provides advanced training (at the level of a master's degree in intelligence) in a limited number of subjects, but relying primarily on conventional universities works quite well and is likely to remain a viable strategy for the acquisition and upgrading of basic skills.

Training in tradecraft geared to the roles and responsibilities of intelligence analysts may have done more to foster a sense of common purpose, collegiality, and collaboration than any other innovation mandated or facilitated by IRTPA. In that sense it has also fostered professionalization. Key elements in the system introduced in 2006 and steadily refined thereafter include adoption of uniform standards for all agencies and joint training of new officers from all agencies.[26]

Joint training in which new entrants from across the IC receive the same instruction in the same class from the same instructors is important for several reasons. First, the adoption of common standards ensures that analysts in all components are taught the same methods and learn that analytic work across the IC will be evaluated using the standards taught in the joint course. These are not lowest common denominator standards; they are based on requirements mandated in the 2004 reform legislation and designed to elevate the performance of all agencies to a level higher than any had achieved consistently before the program was introduced. In other words, the course—dubbed "Analysis 101"—raised the bar *and* trained new analysts to meet the higher standards.[27] This message was reinforced by the adoption of uniform analytic standards and the requirement that the DNI report to Congress annually on the performance of IC analysts, as measured by the application of those standards. Together with other steps mandated or facilitated by the ODNI and individual agencies, this has helped to improve the overall quality of analytic products.[28]

Second, common standards and joint training can counter some of the pernicious effects of organizational culture, enhance analytic collaboration, and reduce duplication of effort. With joint training, analysts (and their managers) know that counterparts in other agencies have received the same instruction and are held to the same standards. This helps to overcome the effects of bureaucratic parochialism discussed above and thereby creates better conditions for collaboration and integration of effort. This, in turn, enhances the sense of belonging to the same profession. It also helps create the basis for divisions of labor and willingness to utilize products from other agencies.

A third benefit of joint training is that it helps foster a common culture of analytic professionalism. This starts with building trust among individuals and networking across agency boundaries. A few weeks in class together demonstrates to participants that classmates from other agencies are just as smart and just as dedicated as they are. Long-standing behaviors that seek to build élan in one agency by disparaging others impede professionalism and collaboration, and thereby diminish the quality of IC support to the customers who require timely and objective analysis incorporating information and insights from all available sources. Enhanced respect for counterparts transforms them into colleagues.

Knowledge of Customer Requirements

The second aspect of tradecraft involves relationships between the IC and its customers, and between analysts and collectors. These could be treated as separate topics, but I find it useful to think of them as different dimensions of the same phenomenon. The most important characteristics of the relationship between the IC and its customers are dedication, unique information, and objectivity. Dedication subsumes a number of attributes unique to IC professionals in general and IC analysts in particular. One is availability. The IC is part of the US government, and it exists to support the information and analytic needs of US government decision makers. The top priority of IC agencies and individuals is to anticipate information needs, answer questions, and provide insight and warning to specific customers and the government as a whole.[29] For those in the US government, support from the IC is a free good. They can ask for (almost) anything and do not have to pay for any part of the institutions or people that do their best to respond.[30]

IC personnel are dedicated public servants whose highest priority is to ensure that decision makers understand the issues for which they are responsible.

IC analysts constitute the largest analytic component of the US government and the only one exclusively dedicated to support of the national security enterprise. In addition, they have access to sources of information that are not available to others inside or outside the government. There are many talented analysts in universities, think tanks, corporate offices, and elsewhere, but their access to information and ability to pursue answers to very specific questions is not at all comparable to that of the IC. In theory, and often in practice, assessments prepared by IC analysts are informed by information available to any group or individual outside of the IC, as well as by classified information available only to the IC. Much of the money appropriated for the IC is for collection. The IC has impressive human and technical collection capabilities and an unparalleled ability to obtain and process information. These capabilities are dedicated to the support of US government requirements. The assessments prepared by IC analysts are not always better than those prepared elsewhere, but they should be better informed and/or better tailored to the needs of decision makers than are assessments from other providers. Finally, the fact that the IC analytic community is large, skilled, and increasingly able to collaborate means that the assessments provided to government officials could and should incorporate information and insights of multiple agencies and individuals.

Objectivity is an essential attribute of IC analysis that makes IC analytic support different from, and in important respects more useful than, that from the many other inputs available to decision makers. With few exceptions, other sources of information and analysis are intended to influence policymakers to act in a particular way. Bureaucratic components of the US government have favored positions; so do foreign governments, influential members of Congress, lobbyists, and even the media. The IC is supposed to have no agenda of its own and to be as objective as possible in presenting what it knows, what it does not know, and what it thinks about a given subject.[31]

Protecting Sources and Guiding Collectors

As noted above, analysts, like other members of the intelligence community, have both incentives and an obligation to protect sources and methods. Many methods of collection entail high risks, are expensive, and provide information that cannot be obtained in other ways. Revealing information about collection methods can jeopardize lives, create opportunities for those targeted to provide false or misleading information, or terminate access at a crucial time. IC training has long emphasized the importance of protecting sources, and most analysts understand full well that they will lose valuable intelligence if sources or methods are compromised. However, many extant rules and procedures put so much emphasis on protecting sources and methods that they impede utilization of the information collected. We need better balance between protection and utilization. Significant steps toward that goal include the adoption of Intelligence Community Directive 208: Write for Maximum Utility.[32]

Training and rules are necessary, but all such measures must be reinforced by professional norms that make every analyst a steward of the information needed to do his or her job. The development of a professional ethos to protect sources used by others in the community is part of building a professional community of intelligence analysts.

An important part of the IC analysts' ability to provide better-informed judgments to policymakers is their ability to anticipate and translate the information needs of their customers into clear and focused guidance to collectors. Analytic tradecraft includes using access to customers to discern their needs for information and insight, when they need that information, what they already know (or think they know), and what might cause them to change their own assessments of a situation, and using this information to provide guidance to collectors. Analyst understanding of the capabilities of different collection systems is useful but not essential. Being able to tell collectors where to look and what to look for is more important than being able to tell them what methods or systems to use.

Tools and Techniques

The fourth element of tradecraft involves the use of tools and techniques. For many analysts, "tools" is a dirty word because vendors and/or enthusiasts have oversold "magic bullet" technologies that promise to sift data, discover patterns, and integrate multiple streams of information to reveal critical relationships and otherwise hard-to-discover causes and consequences. This problem has been compounded by premature adoption of unproven analytic techniques.[33] As a result, too many analysts shun available tools and prefer to rely on more familiar methods of analysis. This has sometimes been reinforced by knowledge or supposition that customers will not understand quantitative or certain other techniques.

No analyst can be expected to know how to apply all available tools and techniques, but they should know how to determine which might be appropriate in specific circumstances and where to turn for help. They should also know how to evaluate the relative strengths and weaknesses of specific tools and methods of analysis. Moreover, it should no longer be assumed that policy customers will not understand or do not want to receive quantitative analysis, game-theoretic projections, or other types of analysis. Policymakers, like younger analysts, come to their positions with different skill sets and expectations than did their predecessors. If IC analysts are to provide them with the kinds of analysis they desire, the community must update its methodologies and the way it provides analytic products.

Sources of Change: Looking Forward

Intelligence community analysts evince more characteristics of a professional group today than when the first edition of this book was written in 2008.[34] That has not happened by chance or "normal" bureaucratic evolution. It is the result of changing demographics and expectations, widespread recognition among senior managers of analysis that old approaches were inadequate to meet new challenges, and the vision and initiatives promoted by the Office of the Director of National Intelligence. All three were necessary, but individually and collectively they were inadequate to ensure success or lock in needed changes that occurred despite the persistence of bureaucratic and cultural impediments, and resistance from individuals and groups that attached higher priority to preserving status and tradition than to providing quality analytic support to national security decision makers.

Change from Below

In addition to bringing disciplinary skills and up-to-date fields of specialization, new IC analysts bring with them a number of talents and expectations affecting their approach to analysis. While the "Facebook generation" may occasionally err in sharing information that should remain classified, it is essential to capitalize on its attitudes toward collaboration and information sharing.[35] For those who have joined the IC since 9/11—a cohort approaching, if not surpassing, two-thirds of all analysts—"sharing" and collaboration are as natural as multitasking and discomfort with rigid hierarchies and ways of doing things.

These analysts judge the value of information—and their colleagues—more by utility and responsiveness than by source or position. They are comfortable with interactions in cyberspace and team approaches to problem solving. They see a disconnect between what they know works well in other arenas and what they are allowed to do in the IC. Of course, there are differences between professional and personal lives, but "standard" ways of working in the IC often make no sense to them. Giving precedence to classified information, especially if from their home agencies, seems counterproductive when comparable unclassified information is available and easier to share. Likewise, restricting their ability to contact former academic mentors or classmates knowledgeable in their fields seems self-defeating if the goal is expertise-building. This generation's natural instinct is to collaborate to the extent allowed by existing rules and procedures, and fortunately they want to push the envelope in order to achieve results.

Change from the Top

A second important impetus for change has come from senior analytic managers—my counterparts and age cohort. Having made it to the top of the analytic community, this group was in a position to see "big picture" issues and opportunities for change. Happily for the IC and our nation, most were inclined to use their perspective and positions to address problems identified by the 9/11 Commission and the WMD Commission, among others.[36] As important, they recognized the need to transform the way the IC "does" analysis if it is to cope with new responsibilities, meet new challenges, and retain the extraordinary talent that was filling new positions and replacing retiring baby boomers. This leadership group also recognized that events, and to some extent IRTPA had created a once-in-a-generation opportunity for change. We were determined not to squander that opportunity. As one member of the group put it, "they have offered the inmates a chance to transform the asylum. We actually may have an opportunity to change some of the things we complained about when we lacked the stature and authority to do anything. Let's not blow it."

Change from Outside

The third contributing factor was the opportunity and imperative created by IRTPA and the content and success of changes that I was privileged to lead as deputy DNI for analysis. As noted above, persuading analysts to think and act as members of a single enterprise or team—as a community of analysts—was an important part of the vision we called "analytic transformation."[37] As mentioned earlier, attempting to change the structure of the IC was too difficult and would meet too much resistance. That dictated a strategy to overcome existing organizational pathologies and negative stereotypes of "other" agencies and the analysts who worked in them.

One part of that strategy involved the training and tradecraft reforms noted above. With both the reality and recognition that analysts in all components of the IC were trained and held to the same standards and had direct personal experience working with counterparts across the community, collaboration and divisions of labor were easier to achieve. Another part of the strategy required breaking down impediments to information sharing and collaboration in cyberspace.[38] This was more difficult than the introduction of tradecraft standards because it bumped up against hoary regulations governing access to information. A key enabler was DNI Mike McConnell's decision to replace the old criterion of "need to know," which had led collectors and other "information stewards" to withhold intelligence from individuals and agencies with only a very imperfect understanding of who was working on what topic and how issues were interconnected, with "responsibility to provide." The latter formulation obligated information stewards to ensure that those who needed the information received it.[39]

What has been achieved remains uneven, fragile, and vulnerable to disruption or derailment, but current trends will continue to evolve in ways that establish and empower a community of analysts. A key reason for optimism is that enabling intelligence analysts to function more like a profession has enhanced individual and collective performance. It is arguable that doing so has also increased job satisfaction and contributed to the retention of analysts likely to have become frustrated by "old" ways of doing things. Collaboration, functioning as a community of analysts, and new definitions of professionalism are displacing bureaucratic rivalry and monastic scholarship because they produce better results. In other words, we are witnessing a bureaucratic form of "survival of the fittest," in which old attitudes, structures, and types of leadership are gradually being displaced by more successful mutations.

Notes

1. See, for example, Jack Davis, "Sherman Kent and the Profession of Intelligence Analysis," Sherman Kent Center for Intelligence Analysis, Occasional Papers, vol. 1, no. 5 (November 2002), www.cia.gov/library/kent-center-occasional-papers/vol1no5.htm.

2. Roger Z. George and Harvey Rishikof, eds., *The National Security Enterprise: Navigating the Labyrinth* (Washington, DC: Georgetown University Press, 2011).

3. Thomas Fingar, *Reducing Uncertainty: Intelligence Analysis and National Security* (Stanford, CA: Stanford University Press, 2011), chap. 2.

4. Ibid., especially chap. 6.

5. See Mark M. Lowenthal, "Intelligence Analysis: Management and Transformation Issues," in *Transforming U.S. Intelligence*, eds. Jennifer E. Sims and Burton Gerber (Washington, DC: Georgetown University Press, 2005), chap. 13, and ibid., 128–38.

6. See C. Thomas Thorne Jr. and David S. Patterson, eds., *Foreign Relations of the United States 1945–1950: Emergence of the Intelligence Establishment* (Washington, DC: Government Printing Office, 1996), http://history.state.gov/historicaldocuments/frus1945-50Intel, and Amy Zegart, *Flawed by Design: The Evolution of the CIA, JCS, and NSC* (Stanford, CA: Stanford University Press, 1999), chaps. 2 and 3.

7. See Mark M. Lowenthal, *Intelligence: From Secrets to Policy, Fifth Edition* (Los Angeles: CQ Press, 2012), chap. 3, and Thomas Fingar, "Analysis in the U.S. Intelligence Community: Missions, Masters, and Methods," in *Intelligence Analysis: Behavioral and Social Scientific Foundations*, National Research Council (Washington, DC: National Academies Press, 2011), chap. 1.

8. See Rob Johnston, *Analytic Culture in the U.S. Intelligence Community: An Ethnographic Study* (Washington, DC: Center for the Study of Intelligence, 2005), chap. 8, and Catherine H. Tinsley, "Social Categorization and Intergroup Dynamics," in National Research Council, *Intelligence Analysis*, chap. 9.

9. See Michael Warner and J. Kenneth McDonald, *U.S. Intelligence Community Reform Studies since 1947* (Washington, DC: Center for the Study of Intelligence, 2005), and "Intelligence Reform and Terrorism Prevention Act of 2004," Public Law 108-458, December 17, 2004 (hereafter IRTPA), www.gpo.gov:80/fdsys/pkg/PLAW-108publ458/pdf/PLAW-108publ458.pdf.

10. See *The National Intelligence Strategy* (August 2009), www.dni.gov/reports/2009_NIS.pdf.

11. See Jennifer E. Sims, "Understanding Ourselves," in *Transforming U.S. Intelligence*, eds. Jennifer E. Sims and Burton Gerber (Washington, DC: Georgetown University Press, 2005), 32–59.

12. If the IC were an integrated enterprise, then analysts in one component who had learned that policymakers were interested in a subject would immediately alert counterparts in other agencies working on the problem and thereby ensure that they could provide information and insight on that subject to their own primary customers. That does not happen as often as it should. Rivalry between INR and CIA analysts during my tenure in INR resulted in one or the other group failing to inform counterparts until after it had provided its own assessment to particular customers. This happens all too frequently.

13. See Intelligence Community Directive (ICD) Number 203: Analytic Standards (June 21, 2007), www.fas.org/irp/dni/icd/icd-203.pdf.

14. See chap. 4 in this volume.

15. See IRTPA, sec. 1019. Other relevant directives include ICD Number 206: Sourcing Requirements for Disseminated Analytic Products (October 17, 2007), www.dni.gov/files/documents/ICD/ICD_206.pdf, and ICD Number 208: Write for Maximum Utility (December 17, 2008), www.dni.gov/files/documents/ICD/icd_208.pdf.

16. In addition to meeting the quality standards specified in ICD 203, ICD 206, and ICD 208, "good" analysis must be useful to primary recipients. In order to be useful it must be timely, targeted to address customer concerns, and alert policymakers to relevant factors that they might not have considered. See also Lowenthal, *Intelligence*, chap. 6.

17. See Thomas Fingar, "All-Source Analysis," *Intelligencer: Journal of U.S. Intelligence Studies* (Winter–Spring 2012): 63–66, www.afio.com/publications/Fingar_All_Source_Analysis_in_AFIO_INTEL_WinterSprg2012.pdf.

18. See chap. 4 in this volume.

19. This observation is impressionistic, based on what I learned during my tenure as deputy director of national intelligence for analysis (DDNI/A).

20. Judgment based on conversations with analysts and managers in all analytic components of the IC during my tenure as DDNI/A.

21. See Johnston, *Analytic Culture*, chap. 8. One underutilized and often disparaged skill is the ability to collaborate in cyberspace and to tackle complex but transient problems by forming virtual teams based on ability to contribute, not on organizational affiliation.

22. In order to promote collaboration with experts outside the IC, I pressed hard for adoption of an intelligence community directive that would mandate—not just encourage—such collaboration. It is indicative of the strength of opposition that it took three years to secure approval of the relevant directive and that this was achieved only by allowing agencies to craft their own implementing guidance. In one particularly egregious case, the agency guidance effectively vitiated the directive. See *Intelligence Community Directive 205: Analytic Outreach* (July 16, 2008), www.dni.gov/files/documents/ICD/ICD_205.pdf.

23. For an argument that the IC is less unique than it sometimes claims and can learn from the experience of other complex organizations, see National Research Council, *Intelligence Analysis*, especially chap. 1.

24. See Lowenthal, *Intelligence*, chap. 6, and Nancy Bernkopf Tucker, "The Cultural Revolution in Intelligence: Interim Report," *Washington Quarterly* 31, no. 2 (Spring 2008): 47–61.

25. The Intelligence Reform Act (Subtitle D: Improvement of Education for the Intelligence Community) acknowledges the importance of training within the IC and at institutions of higher learning. However, unlike the military, the IC is not staffed to enable more than a small percentage of analysts to undertake full-time training at any one time. As noted by Lowenthal, it does not have analysts "sitting on the bench." Lowenthal, "Intelligence Analysis," 224. This severely restricts the amount of training that analysts can receive.

26. Tucker, "Cultural Revolution in Intelligence."

27. Ibid. and Richard H. Immerman, "Transforming Analysis: The Intelligence Community's Best Kept Secret," *Intelligence and National Security* 26, nos. 2 and 3 (April–June 2011): 159–81.

28. The improvement in the quality of analytic products is both an objective finding reported to Congress in the annual performance evaluations (classified) in accordance with requirements of IRTPA and a subjective judgment relayed to me by numerous senior customers and members of the President's Intelligence Advisory Board.

29. See Fingar, "Analysis in the U.S. Intelligence Community," 9–19.

30. Fingar, *Reducing Uncertainty*, chap. 2, and Lowenthal, *Intelligence*, chap. 6.

31. See Fingar, *Reducing Uncertainty*, 36.

32. See ICD 208, and Intelligence Community Policy Memorandum Number 2007-200-2: Preparing Intelligence to Meet the Intelligence Community's "Responsibility to Provide" (December 11, 2007), www.dni.gov/files/documents/IC%20Policy%20Memos/ICPM%202007-200-2%20Responsibility%20to%20Provide.pdf.

33. On the number of tools and techniques, see Richards J. Heuer Jr. and Randolph H. Pherson, *Structured Analytic Techniques for Intelligence Analysis* (Washington, DC: CQ Press, 2011), and chap. 14 in this volume. See also National Research Council, *Intelligence Analysis*, chap. 2.

34. James B. Bruce and Roger Z. George, "Introduction: Intelligence Analysis—The Emergence of a Discipline," in *Analyzing Intelligence: Origins, Obstacles, and Innovations*, eds. Roger Z. George and James B. Bruce (Washington, DC: Georgetown University Press, 2004), 1–15.

35. Gary Hamel, "The Facebook Generation vs. the Fortune 500," *Freshmix*, September 17, 2010, www.managementexchange.com/blog/facebook-generation-vs-fortune-500.

36. See National Commission on Terrorist Attacks upon the United States, *The 9/11 Commission Report* (Washington, DC: Government Printing Office, 2004); US Senate, Report of the Select Committee on Intelligence on the U.S. Intelligence Community's Prewar Intelligence Assessments on Iraq together with Additional Views, 108th Congress, 2nd sess., S. Report 108-301, July 9, 2004, www.intelligence.senate.gov/108301pdf, and Report of the Commission on the Intelligence Capabilities of the United States regarding Weapons of Mass Destruction, March 31, 2005, http://fas.org/irp/offdocs/wmd_report.pdf.

37. See Immerman, "Transforming Analysis," and Thomas Fingar, *Analytic Transformation: Unleashing the Potential of a Community of Analysts*, September 1, 2008, http://semanti-community.info/@api/deki/files/17689/AT_Digital_20080923.pdf.

38. Key innovations were Intellipedia and A-Space. Additional information can be found in Fingar, *Analytic Transformation*.

39. See Intelligence Community Policy Memorandum Number 2007-200-2.

CHAPTER 18

The Education and Training of Intelligence Analysts

MARK M. LOWENTHAL

This volume takes the position that intelligence analysis has the potential to be and is already becoming recognized as a profession. If one looks at the most basic attributes of a profession, intelligence analysis qualifies on most grounds,

- it is a full-time occupation,
- it requires specialized knowledge,
- it has a degree of exclusivity,
- it has a sense of esprit and internal solidarity, and
- it has implicit codes of behavior.[1]

But as mentioned elsewhere in this volume, some types of professions are also disciplines, and they have additional requirements that are more exacting. Specifically, such disciplines try to ensure the highest possible professional standards of their members, typically through formal or informal governing bodies. More important, they also seek to build and manage knowledge. Disciplines such as law and medicine are professions that retain the collective wisdom of their practitioners and establish standards for archiving and accessing that knowledge. To accomplish this they require licensing and credentialing practices, ethical standards, and continuing education requirements.[2]

The degree to which intelligence analysis meets each of these characteristics can be debated, but most would agree it falls well short. Perhaps the most notable professional weakness of intelligence analysis—but where significant improvements may be achievable—is training and education. Sixty-five years after the creation of the modern US intelligence community in 1947, education and training remains uneven, episodic, and stovepiped. A successful education program must know, at the outset, what its goals are. In intelligence analysis we may have too many goals, given the depth and breadth of analysis. That said, there are areas where solid education and training can advance the profession of intelligence analysis.

This chapter explores the current state of analyst training and education in US intelligence, critiques it against criteria more appropriate to a profession aiming to become a discipline, and suggests some training and education remedies and innovations that could bring the practice of analysis closer to higher professional standards.

One of the oddest aspects of intelligence analysis as a profession or a career is the serendipity by which most analysts (and other intelligence officers) arrive at their jobs. Intelligence is an accidental profession. If one desires to be a doctor, lawyer, or engineer, one essentially has to commit by junior year in college at the latest in order to take the required courses and to prepare for exams that will allow admission to graduate school. No such *cursus honorum* exists for intelligence. Although some aspire to an intelligence career long before they get their first jobs, most of the individuals of my generation who became intelligence officers did so largely because an opportunity presented itself and they took it, without giving it very much thought.[3] Indeed, we pride ourselves on the heterogeneous nature of our analyst population, which argues against a prescribed set of undergraduate courses to prepare one to be an intelligence analyst. This heterogeneity, which is a strength of the analytic community, also presents some challenges when we think about how we can use education and training to create some common practices, norms, and a professional ethos. There may be a change in the offing with the development of intelligence studies programs at private universities and growing interest in homeland security studies at both the undergraduate and graduate levels, but this is fairly recent and in no way compares yet to pre-law or pre-med course curricula.[4]

Background: Education and Training in US Intelligence

Not much thought was given in 1947 to creating professional intelligence analysts. This should not be surprising. At that time the main analytic components of the nascent intelligence community were military intelligence units, which had decades of experience, and the State Department, which could draw on its expertise in writing analytic cables. CIA was created in 1947 to correlate and evaluate intelligence, not initially to be another source of intelligence analysis. Therefore there was no need to educate or professionalize the intelligence analysts—they either had the necessary experience and expertise via the military or the State Department, or did not need it. People who joined the intelligence community drew on their undergraduate education in history, economics, or political science, which was deemed sufficient for many jobs. More significantly, there was almost no discussion or even a literature on the "profession" of intelligence analysis, a glaring gap that Sherman Kent—the father of modern intelligence analysis—pointed out as a major requirement for the discipline of intelligence analysis to become a true profession.[5]

By January 1948, the shortcomings of this system quickly became evident, as evidenced by the Dulles-Jackson-Correa Report.[6] When the Korean War broke out in 1950, the Truman administration moved to revamp the intelligence structure. CIA became an intelligence producer in its own right, with offices for estimates, economic intelligence, and current intelligence within its own analytic directorate.[7] Since then most—but not all—of the major intelligence agencies have created programs to train at least incoming analysts to some degree. CIA has the CIA University, with separate schools for clandestine officers and analysts. DIA has operated a joint military intelligence institution for decades and has now become the home of the National Intelligence University (NIU). The National Security Agency and the National Geospatial-Intelligence Agency (NGA) operate their own agency-specific programs, as well as send analysts to programs offered at the NIU, formerly the National Defense Intelligence College (NDIC) (see box 18.1). The exception has been the small State Department Bureau of Intelligence and Research (INR), which does not have the resources or sufficient turnover year-to-year to justify such a new analyst program. However, INR also has not taken full advantage of other programs within the intelligence community for its new analysts.

BOX 18.1   Intelligence Community Schoolhouses

The education landscape across the intelligence community is varied and largely agency-centric.

A **National Intelligence University** (NIU) has existed since the first DNI in 2005, but it remains very much a work in progress, buffeted by too many leaders in too few years. Currently the NIU is managed by DIA, which is grafting the new structure onto the old National Defense Intelligence College, which had been DIA-centric.

CIA analysts go to the **Sherman Kent School for Intelligence Analysis** (SKS), which is the analytic component of CIA University and offers basic as well as advanced analyst training. The program's centerpiece is the seventeen-week Career Analyst Program (CAP) course. CAP covers basic training in analytic techniques, writing, and briefing skills. In addition, the SKS offers a variety of advanced tradecraft and language courses and has a Mission Academy and a Leadership Academy.

DIA established the **Defense Intelligence College** in 1962 by merging existing military service intelligence analysis programs and developing a graduate-level program in strategic intelligence. It was first accredited as a degree-granting program (unlike other agencies) in 1981 and was renamed the Defense Intelligence College when it added additional courses and a research mission. It was renamed the National Defense Intelligence College in 1993, reflecting its growing graduate-level programs, academic publications, and outreach to students from other national intelligence agencies. It has now been designated the home of the National Intelligence University, which plans to locate its main campus to Bethesda, Maryland, by 2014. DIA currently requires its new analysts to take a ten-week basic analysis course offered by the NIU.

The **National Cryptologic School** (NCS) is a staff component of the National Security Agency (NSA) and is located at the complex of NSA headquarters, north of Washington. The NCS is part of a network of schools in the Department of Defense that make up the Cryptologic Training System, which provides education and skills training in foreign-language analysis and research, computer science, advanced mathematics, physics, engineering, and electronics to military and civilian employees.

The **FBI Academy**, located in Quantico, Virginia, offers new analysts a sixteen-week Intelligence Basic Course (IBC), which introduces them to the intelligence and law enforcement communities, the intelligence cycle, and the role of analysts in the FBI's post-9/11 mission. The IBC core also provides basic instruction on research and critical thinking, written and oral communication, and compliance with constitutional and other applicable laws. The academy also teaches a wide variety of advanced and specialized courses, including those sponsored by the DNI and other IC partners.

NGA's Geospatial-Intelligence College (NGC) delivers learning programs in geospatial intelligence (GEOINT), leadership, and professional development to more than fifteen thousand students from across NGA, DOD, and the intelligence community. It has core training in GEOINT specialties, including analysis, sensors, and military programs. A key strategic objective is to establish and implement standards in training across all parts of the US national system for geospatial intelligence.

What Do Analysts Need?

If we are to arrive at a better method for educating and training intelligence analysts, we need to agree on the purposes and scope of such programs. First, there should be a common agreement on what professional characteristics we look for in an intelligence analyst. Unfortunately, not much has been done within the intelligence community, nor has there been common agreement among agencies on this issue. In the introduction to this volume, James Bruce and Roger George lay out a set of professional analyst attributes that encompass both subject-matter expertise and intelligence-related skills acquired through experience and training.[8] Subject-matter expertise comprises the skills and knowledge that a new analyst should have already acquired before entering on duty; the second set comes with time, experience, and training. In brief, even entry-level subject-matter experts (SMEs) hired as university-educated applicants at either the baccalaureate or graduate-degree levels are expected to already be knowledgeable about some substantive areas (for example, China, Iran, cyberwarfare, counterinsurgency). This is an important point, as analysts are hired for a body of knowledge, not for a skill set. In addition, they are expected to understand basic research methods, have some skill at written expression, and also have enough research imagination and rigor that they are capable of generating and testing hypotheses through qualitative methods. But these basics are not enough.

This second area—skill development—should be the focus of formal education programs and also gained through on-the-job experience. Academic expertise needs to be enhanced with an array of capabilities that can only be acquired through practical experience in the IC and through the special training it offers. These on-the-job attributes include an understanding of unique (and classified) intelligence collection techniques, how the national security policy functions, self-awareness about the influence of cognitive biases on their analysis, openness to contrarian views, the capacity to admit and learn from error, and the ability to work in a collaborative but still competitive environment. Thus, to be fully professional, an analyst must combine both subject-matter expertise *and* additional expertise in the discipline of intelligence. The analyst comes in with the first set—the subject-matter expertise acquired in higher education. The second set, however, is more often left to chance rather than to a coherent curriculum that expands and deepens as the analyst advances in his or her career. This also makes sense in terms of community educational capabilities. The IC does not have the wherewithal to create SMEs out of entering analysts but they can shape the new analyst into a more fully functional analyst.

The question is, how and why does someone get hired for an analytic position? David Moore and Liza Krizan, two National Security Agency (NSA) analysts, have described four sets of core competencies for intelligence analysis: abilities, characteristics, knowledge, and skills.[9] Of these, characteristics is extremely hard to teach. You either have intellectual curiosity, a sense of wonder, a passion for reading, and so on—or you do not. You may be able to learn to do some of these things but unless they are innate, the effort is likely to be perfunctory. The other competencies are more easily taught and align well with the Bruce-George list.

The Moore-Krizan and Bruce-George lists offer a good starting place for creating a core curriculum for incoming analysts, regardless of the subject matter they will be working on or the agency for whom they will be working. Most academic programs devoted to intelligence analysis tend to focus on abilities and skills, to use the Moore-Krizan categories. In part, this is driven by the expectation, noted by Bruce and George, that analysts enter with some substantive knowledge set akin to SMEs. It is also likely driven, in part, by the fact that it is much easier to create coherent intelligence training programs out of abilities and skills, whereas the knowledge sets that intelligence may require are too numerous. Some agencies, such as CIA, do offer young analysts postgraduate opportunities in areas of economics, area studies, and science by covering their tuition. NSA likewise supports various foreign-language programs to produce a potential cadre of skilled linguists. The DNI also established in 2005 the Centers of Academic Excellence (CAE), designed to build knowledge of intelligence-related subjects. The CAE has fostered academic programs as a pool of future intelligence analysts but also to enhance ethnic and cultural diversity in the analytic cadre of the IC, which has always been somewhat problematic.[10] The stated requirements for academic programs to be designated for the CAE emphasize knowledge, abilities and skills, but many of the programs themselves still tend to focus more on the abilities and skills than on knowledge.

A training and education curriculum that builds a new analyst's basic knowledge and skill set is just a starting point. The ODNI has offered an introductory course aptly named "Analysis 101"—though it is presently only two weeks in length. This is the first community-wide course that attempts to begin an analyst's formal training. It introduces analysts to critical thinking, hypothesis testing, and some analytic techniques. Although it has reached only a portion of the new analysts hired in the IC since 2001, over five thousand students, mainly from the DOD intelligence agencies, the FBI, and DHS, had completed the course by the end of 2012.

While this is a good start, there is still a need for a more comprehensive view of an analyst's career and the progression of expected skills as the analyst becomes more senior and takes on more responsibilities. Indeed, if intelligence analysis is to become a profession, then we should develop a more concrete view of the expected skill levels over the course of a career, including a sense of how long it takes to acquire these skills. When he became CIA director, Gen. Michael Hayden posed a rhetorical question to his deputy for analysis: How long does it take to develop a twenty-year professional analyst? The point is that skills and knowledge building require time as well as resources but must also change to fit the needs of advancing analysts. From this should flow the courses that would be necessary to inculcate or refine these skills as the analyst moves along. Each agency has some kind of analytic hierarchy that largely conforms to a junior/mid-level/senior schema (with variations of precise titles). From these we should be able to create Analysis 201, 301, and the senior seminar, 401. Here, regrettably, we have not been overly successful. Although some agency schoolhouses offer some additional training opportunities and some professional certification, this is not consistent across the IC. It suggests that there are areas where the DNI can provide a useful service to all agencies by establishing courses community analysts might enroll in, both to improve their expertise but also to share and gain perspectives they might not get in their narrower agency-specific training programs.

The third issue—the amount of training and education required to be a full professional—gets to the heart of the problem, which is the nature of analysis today. The drive in almost every agency is to keep up "production." Once new analysts have been initially trained and assigned, managers are too often loath to let them go for prolonged periods of further education and training. In that same discussion mentioned earlier, General Hayden remarked that, as a professional military officer, he had spent several years in full-time professional military education, so he found it shocking that a professional analyst would spend a only few weeks or at most a couple of months in full-time training. To be sure, there is a fair amount of on-the-job training in intelligence, just as there is in all professions, but this becomes the main training ground once we are past the more comprehensive "101" phase. Intelligence could profitably copy those professions that require a specific number of courses, conferences, or hours of seminars each year as part of their continuing education.

There is a further implication if we are to think of intelligence analysis as a profession: the necessity of envisioning the overall analytic population as a single cadre, not a series of agency-based entities. Again, one can concede the differences among analysis as conducted in NGA, NSA, the FBI, CIA, and so on, and still educate and train analysts together on an interagency basis for that part of their skill set that has common challenges and requirements across the IC, no matter which agency employs the analysts. This should be self-evident, given how much emphasis we have seen in recent years on creating a more integrated intelligence community. In fact "intelligence integration" is the main goal of DNI James Clapper.[11] There would be two benefits to such an approach. The first is that it would create and instill a common set of analytic skills and, perhaps even more important, professional values across the IC. The second is that such an approach would help promote integration by having analysts from various agencies meet each other at the outset of their careers and at various stages during their careers as they took classes together. It is difficult to integrate intelligence unless the analysts are socialized to integration as a norm, similar to the US military's emphasis on "training the way you fight."

What Should We Be Teaching?

Again, the twin goals of clearer standards and better cross-agency integration noted above offer very good starting points for a more comprehensive professional training program for analysts. ODNI might build on the current Analysis 101 by broadening and lengthening this program to address a range of professional, organizational, and ethical issues that all analysts will likely face, in addition to developing their tradecraft skills. This expanded Analysis 101 should become mandatory for all new analysts, regardless of their agency. One can offer some refinements, including the importance of addressing ethics and values, and the dilemmas that analysts are likely to face as analysts and in dealing with policymakers. Intelligence analysis is at once both a solitary endeavor and a group activity.[12] An individual analyst has to be the initial drafter; however, from that point on, there will be contributors, peer reviewers, senior reviewers, perhaps interagency meetings to coordinate the draft, and so on. A good analyst therefore has to know more than subject-area expertise and the ability to communicate. The analyst must also know how to negotiate ("when to hold 'em and when to fold 'em") and work in a collaborative environment, as well as understand the issues, equities, and behaviors that drive other participants from other offices or agencies.

It would also be useful for analysts to have some appreciation of the history of their profession. As DNI Clapper has said, "The history of rock and roll did not begin the day you turned on the radio."[13] Most of the analysts who have been hired since 2001 have some impression (probably imperfect at best) of the analytic issues behind the 2001 attack and the Iraq WMD estimate. But they are much less likely to understand how much of their profession was shaped by the fifty-year Cold War with the Soviet Union or to know the professional lessons to be derived from the Cuban Missile Crisis, the Tet Offensive, or Pearl Harbor. This leads to the issue of "lessons learned," an important facet of any profession but one where the intelligence community, again, lags behind the US military. The ODNI has created a very bare-bones lessons-learned capability. Not only is the ODNI lessons-learned staff's small size an impediment, but also it is not clear that the lessons, even if they are learned, are then fed back into agencies' training, given the fact that the ODNI has little role in the actual shaping of IC training.

All of this suggests there is room for more IC-wide training—conducted by the ODNI on behalf of the intelligence community—that does not undermine or necessarily duplicate agency-based training. Some fruitful areas might include those where different agencies or their components bring special expertise to educating other analysts outside their organization. Others might be issues on which there should be an IC-wide standard or at least appreciation for the differences among agencies, which cannot be gleaned from agency-specific training programs. Some examples of these courses might include:

- Collection Disciplines for Analysts: Leading experts from the HUMINT, SIGINT, GEOINT, and other collection disciplines provide good understanding of the strengths/weaknesses of their collection systems and methods for analysts using their sources.
- The Role of Warning for Analysts: Courses that examine the "lessons learned" from past warning failures and successes and that cover both the collection and analysis aspects of these cases.
- Dealing with Foreign Intelligence Sources: HUMINT and counterintelligence experts might provide analysts a good grounding in how to use foreign intelligence sources, describing some of the challenges they pose and explaining some of the techniques for working with foreign intelligence counterparts.
- Exploiting Academic Outreach: DNI outreach specialists might offer opportunities for analysts to learn how to develop—safely—networks of professional contacts outside the intelligence community and build up their understanding of open-source knowledge.
- Capstone/Senior Analyst Program: The DNI might sponsor a several-week program for newly promoted senior analysts (GS-15/SIS level) across the community to explore issues of common concern and provide opportunities to meet with senior customers to hear their views on intelligence.

These are just a few ideas that might be explored. Such courses should be designed to broaden analysts' exposure to important issues they will face as they progress through their careers and prepare them for when they will be spending more time working with senior intelligence and policy officials outside their organizations.

Finally, attention should be devoted to the issue of knowledge creation, preservation, and dissemination. Analysts should not simply be transmitters of information to policymakers. One of the holy grails of intelligence analysis is the "value added"—the desired ability of analysts to bring something more to the policymaker than just their sources. One can define this term in many different ways: context, background, insight, or the ability to posit plausible outcomes from an indeterminate situation. The value added, in other words, is the ability to go beyond the available intelligence, regardless of how much or how little there is. In brief, the key expectations for analysts can generally be boiled down to three: producing judgments, forecasts, and insights.[14] These are significant elements in knowledge building and knowledge management. Thus intelligence analysts are, in the words of Peter Drucker, "knowledge workers"[15]—people whose work is primarily with knowledge or who develop and use knowledge. It would advance the profession, and the analysts being trained, to understand what it means to be a knowledge worker, what knowledge is, how it is created and managed, and how well or how poorly intelligence analysis meets the standards of knowledge.[16]

It is difficult to overstate the importance of this facet of intelligence analysis. There has been much discussion in the intelligence analysis profession over the last several years about the significance of data and "big data." Data are important and for some issues essential, but as is discussed below, data are rarely what the policymakers want. No amount of data will get to the core questions uppermost on a policymaker's mind: What will North Korea do next? Are there viable alternatives to a given regime? Will China rise peacefully? Here again we are in that less substantial but very important area of knowledge where the analyst goes beyond his or her data and offers some level of judgment or forecast, or at least frames more and less likely outcomes. There also is the danger—if stringent sourcing standards are taken too far or used narrowly—that analysts will be unable or unwilling to make judgments or forecasts that are not fully backed up by numerous sources. Such caution can undermine the analysts' responsibility to warn of possible dangerous trends long before there is irrefutable proof of such a development. So, reliable knowledge is what we want analysts to create that actually transcends their available sources. Professional-level training in the IC should address these important knowledge-related issues.

Key Training and Educational Hurdles

At least four persistent criticisms have been raised about analytic education and training within the IC. First, these efforts are still largely agency-based, defined and limited by the strong organizational cultures found in each agency. Each analytic component trains its analysts as it sees fit. There is some logic to this, as an NSA analyst's ultimate required skills will be different from an analyst at NGA or CIA. However, some of the basic skills sets will still be the same. Thus this approach also has two shortcomings: It reinforces the agency-centric "stovepipes" that exist in all facets of US intelligence, and by implication it denies the utility of cross-community courses where analysts of all sorts (single-source, multisource, all-source) could not only learn basic skills but also begin to meet fellow analysts in other agencies—preferably early in their careers. The compartmentation culture of the IC also leads, ironically, to stovepipes within stovepipes, in that intelligence analysts, for example, are not encouraged and typically not permitted to take courses with their fellow officers who are learning other tradecraft skills. For example, CIA analysts are trained separately from CIA clandestine case officers, at separate facilities, with little crossover of analysts and case officers in their training programs. Few analysts benefit from training in the collection disciplines offered at the major collection agencies, both human and technical, whether they work at those agencies or elsewhere in the IC.

The second critique is that intelligence agencies have been hard put to delineate the steps and progression in an analyst's career, which then makes it exceedingly difficult to create education that will reflect this progression. In 2008, DNI Mike McConnell signed Intelligence Community Directive 610: Competency Directories for the Intelligence Community Workforce.[17] Many of the competencies are written at such a generic level that they could be applied to any number of professions and do not give distinct definition to intelligence analysts.[18] This competency list offers more guidance as to what is expected of analysts in a general sense but still requires translation into a curriculum to ensure that analysts have the requisite skills or knowledge. However, there is a huge difference between prescribing the skills and knowledge desired of all analysts and ensuring that these issues are actually taught, preferably on a community-wide basis. Again, there is a major distinction between how the US military trains, with emphasis on interservice "joint" training early on, versus the agency approach of the intelligence community.

A third area of controversy is analytic standards. There is universal agreement that standards are one of the hallmarks of a profession. The hurdle has been crafting standards that are meaningful and that are agreed upon across the analytic community. What is it we expect from a given analytic paper? Standards can vary by the nature of the question being answered, the audience for whom it is written, and the time allowed to write the analysis. But even if we take these variables into consideration, there are still some bedrock qualities that should be applicable to most—if not all—analysis. I have written elsewhere that there are four bedrock qualities or standards for analysis: timeliness (the cardinal virtue), tailored to meet the needs of the policymaker, written so as to be easily understood, and clear as to what is known and what is unknown.[19]

The ODNI published a set of analytic standards in June 2007.[20] There was nothing inherently wrong about them, but these standards were written at a fairly high level of generality and probably did not do much to improve demonstrably the content of analytic products, especially if there is no effort to integrate them in a formal educational setting.

That said, CIA's Sherman Kent School has made interesting progress in the area of analytic standards in the creation of the "DI Quality Framework."[21] This framework (see table 18.1) gets into the heart of the analytic and writing process and also differentiates between essential and useful aspects of an analytic piece. Again, there is no guarantee that analytic products will achieve greater accuracy because of these standards, but they do give the analysts and their managers a better sense of the characteristics of a successful analytic piece.

The fourth issue is that of leadership training. The decades-long model in US intelligence is to select successful analysts to become analytic managers and leaders, ignoring the fact that the skills for these two roles are entirely different. There is also a certain self-replicating tendency, as managers naturally gravitate to analysts very much like themselves as protégés and successors. A current managerial fad is to select senior managers from those analysts who have successfully briefed a *PDB* reader—typically a cabinet or subcabinet-level policymakers. This is only one mark of a "successful" analyst and says little about his or her managerial skills. CIA's Leadership Academy is one effort to broaden the basis for selecting managers but has not been replicated widely. Moreover,

Table 18.1 DI Quality Framework

	Analytic	Convincing	Effectively Structured	Well-Written
Main point prominent and clearly stated	*Makes judgments; does not just provide facts*	*Provides sufficient and compelling evidence to support judgments*	Each section, paragraph, and sentence advances the story	Uses precise language, employing concrete examples and avoiding vague, ambiguous terms, and jargon
Main point goes beyond what is obvious to a generalist	Provides necessary context, key drivers, appropriate historical context, comparisons that provide perspective, and scale; indicates whether development is new or consistent with ongoing trend	Free of actual or apparent contradictions (e.g., consistent between title, summary, text, scope note, background note)	One main point per paragraph	Is concise
Main point has a "so what" for the United States	Anticipates a critical reader's questions and answers them in the text	Reliability of information is clearly articulated (e.g., corroboration, access)	Tics are consistent with the paragraphs to which they are attached	Free of grammatical errors, typos, and misspellings
If a change from previous analytic line, explains what factors changed that result in amending the previous judgment	*Makes differing views/alternative explanations clear, providing basis and implications of the difference*	Free of bias, value-laden terms, and advocacy	Avoids redundancy: groups like with like	Avoids awkward constructions
Provides opportunities for the United States	*Is forward-looking*	*Identifies gaps, potential impact on the analytic line, and efforts to fill them*	*Contains graphics that effectively complement the written product*	
Provides warning		*Expresses confidence level in judgment*		

KEY:
Plain Text
Bold Text
Italic Text

Single points of failure
Should be present in all DI analysis
Required where appropriate

Source: Sherman Kent School of Intelligence Analysis, CIA.

the leadership focus, if there is one, is limited to senior management within one's parent organization and does not advance an analyst's skills in working across agencies or developing corporate attitudes toward those outside one's own directorate or service. Once again, unlike the military, very little time is spent on training analysts to move into higher leadership roles. Moving into these analytic leadership positions becomes attractive if only for the fact that they are the way to ensure promotion to higher ranks within the organization and greater professional status.

None of these problems—agency-based training and lack of career development, broadly accepted analytic standards, and leadership selection and training—should be insurmountable. By law the DNI has a mandate to "set standards for education, training, and career development of personnel of the intelligence community."[22] As with most of his other authorities, the DNI must do this "in consultation with the heads of other agencies or elements of the intelligence community, and the heads of their respective departments."[23] But the efforts to set standards have thus far been modest: the Office of the Director of National Intelligence (ODNI) has sponsored a few cross-community courses, specifically its current version of Analysis 101 and IC101: Introduction to U.S. Intelligence.[24] The main problem in both courses has been in maintaining both agencies' and ODNI support. Some institutions have been able to define intelligence career paths and the required courses. For example, the US Army Intelligence Center at Fort Huachuca, Arizona, does exactly that. Additionally, CIA has developed an Advanced Analyst Program for senior analysts in conjunction with the eligibility requirements for membership in CIA's Senior Analytic Service. Still, if the IC is serious about functioning like a community, it should be able to work out an agreed-upon and shared core curricula for analytic skills and provide the necessary education and training of analysts at the entry, mid-career, senior, and then leadership levels.

Where Should Professional Education Be Going—and Why?

The key missing ingredient in how the intelligence community approaches education and training is the absence of a vibrant community center for this function. There is the National Intelligence University (NIU), which was created as part of the ODNI structure in 2005. The history of the NIU, which has been extremely uneven, reflects a good deal of the problem inherent in creating community-wide education and training. Early on there was a debate as to whether the NIU should be "bricks and mortar" or virtual. Either view was ascendant at different times. At the core of the debate was more than just an issue of pedagogic technology and its relative utility. Those who favored a virtual university believed they were more likely to get acceptance from intelligence agencies— and from Congress—if they did not require the large-scale shifting of people or the construction of new buildings. Those who favored bricks and mortar argued that the goal of integrating and socializing the analysts could only take place in a real physical space.

In 2011, DNI Clapper made the Defense Intelligence Agency (DIA)—more specifically the National Defense Intelligence College—the executive agent for the NIU.[25]

This made sense, as the NDIC has been up and running since 1962 when it began as the Defense Intelligence School. In subsequent decades it was renamed to reflect its growing mandate for educating increasing numbers of students from a variety of agencies. This institution now presents several advantages as the base for the NIU besides its longevity. It has taught classes to multiagency student bodies, although primarily within the Defense Department; it has the authority to grant bachelor's and master's degrees in intelligence; and it is an accredited educational institution. The main challenge that the new NIU faces is evolving beyond its DOD roots and becoming a true locus for education across all of the intelligence community.

The political and budgetary issues aside, there is a more fundamental educational issue at stake here, one not confined to the intelligence community. Online courses are becoming increasingly popular throughout academia. Many prestigious universities (Harvard, MIT, and Stanford among them) have decided to post some of their courses online.[26] These "massive open online courses" (MOOCs) can include video lesson segments, embedded quizzes, and immediate feedback, but typically they do not convert to course credit at the sponsoring university. The goal of MOOCs is to make course content available to more people. The concern raised about them is the nature of the learning experience: If the goal is simply to get students through a certain body of material, then online courses probably suffice. But if the goal is to have a broader educational experience—that is, to interact with teachers and with fellow students, which is an integral part of the learning process apart from the content of the syllabus—then online courses do not suffice.[27] Thus if one of the goals of IC education is to help build an integrated community, then online courses or a virtual NIU will do little to integrate the IC or to advance the profession.

The second prerequisite is intelligence agencies' commitment to send their analysts to community-wide courses, especially those that are part of an analyst's introduction to the intelligence community. The record to date is uneven at best. The very real limit of the DNI's authority across the intelligence community is an issue. Although, as noted, the DNI can set educational standards, the DNI cannot easily translate this into mandatory participation in a community-wide program. In fact, it is more likely that many agencies would offer to support any DNI standards but only within the context of their individual programs. Also, to be frank, analyst education and training will never be an issue on which a DNI chooses to expend limited political capital with community leaders. Interagency participation improves somewhat in mid-level courses, where 25 percent of seats can be held open for attendees from agencies other than that hosting the course. As laudable as this is, it is far from the optimal approach to the issue of socialization or intelligence integration. Behaviors form early, not at mid-career.

The third prerequisite for improved intelligence education and training is the need for a full-time senior advocate for learning. At the outset of the ODNI there was an assistant DNI for education and training, who also served as the chancellor of the NIU. The ODNI position was abolished and education subsumed under the chief human capital officer (CHCO), for whom education is only one among a number of human resources–related responsibilities. In June 2012, DNI Clapper created the Intelligence Community Training Council (ICTC) to address "matters pertaining to IC education and training." An IC "chief learning officer" will chair the ICTC. These are all positive steps forward, but their success will depend very much on the degree to which the DNI or his representatives have a concrete plan for a way forward and whether they can get buy-in from all of the agencies.

Strategic Direction: A Question of Leadership

The issue of IC training and education cannot be solved once and for all. Rather it must adapt to suit the changing conditions and challenges facing the intelligence community. Thus the IC will need strategic leaders able to envision where international trends are headed and how they will affect US intelligence requirements. Only then can one create a more professional level of training and education. Assessing future trends is hard enough, but it also requires senior leadership prepared to take the IC where it needs to go. The first task, then, is for the IC to build a corporate view of training and education. Currently we promote and educate leaders almost entirely within their own agencies, so it is no surprise that they have difficulty making the transition from an agency-based culture to a more integrated view of what the intelligence analysis profession requires. Overcoming such barriers may require training and education opportunities for first-line middle managers to assist them in transcending their parochialism before they become senior managers. Some models exist, such as the military's "Capstone" courses for newly frocked one-star generals and admirals. A comparable interagency course for new SIS officers might be a starting point.

Second, training and education needs to remain flexible and agile to meet changing requirements. This means a need to reexamine on a fairly continuous basis the skills and methodologies that are required of and taught to analysts. Some will be constant because they are core skills. Others will change as the policymakers' interests change. Third, if we do take the concept of professionalization in the IC seriously, then we also have to think of analytic education and training as a knowledge-building and knowledge-management goal, as well as a community-wide experience. This would be a major advance, and although it has not been achieved to date, it is achievable in principle. This suggests that our agencies—like NIU—must look beyond just courses aimed at "skills" development (such as briefing, writing, and collection tasking) to include those focused on actual new research methods, knowledge development, and expertise building.

Finally, the task should not be made more complex than it needs to be. There are core skills and abilities that should be part of the training and education of all intelligence analysts, with one final goal in mind: creating analysis that helps policymakers deal with the complex issues before them with greater facility and assuredness. This is, at once, both a simple and extremely difficult goal. It can be achieved by taking a more holistic view of intelligence analysis as a profession. There is a sufficient body of knowledge and of experience, as well as a pool of deeply committed individuals who, given the time and the bureaucratic support, could strengthen the analytic profession's self-definition in terms of required knowledge and skills. The first step is always the most difficult.

Notes

1. One of the earliest and still most frequently cited authoritative works defining a profession is Ernest Greenwood, "Attributes of a Profession," *Social Work* 2 (July 1957): 45–55.
2. See chap. 4 of this volume.
3. This view is based on an ongoing, and admittedly anecdotal, survey of IC officers.
4. There are now several dozen private university programs specializing in intelligence studies. Several colleges and universities have developed intelligence analysis curricula at undergraduate and/or graduate levels for students whose clear intent is to become analysts in the national security or law enforcement fields at the federal and state levels.
5. See Jack Davis, "Sherman Kent and the Profession of Intelligence Analysis," *Kent Center Occasional Papers* 1, no. 5 (November 2002): 7.
6. Allen W. Dulles and William H. Jackson, *The Central Intelligence Agency and National Organization for Intelligence* (Washington, DC: CIA, 1949), www.foia.cia.gov.
7. Mark M. Lowenthal, *U.S. Intelligence: Evolution and Anatomy*, 2nd ed. (Westport, CT: Praeger, 1992), 22–23.
8. See chap. 1 in this volume.
9. David Moore and Lisa Krizan, "Core Competencies for Intelligence Analysis at the National Security Agency," in *Bringing Intelligence About: Adding Value to Information in the U.S. Intelligence Community*, ed. Russell Swenson (Washington DC: Joint Military Intelligence College, 2002): 81–113.
10. See P.L. 108-177, sec. 319 (FY2004 Intelligence Authorization Act). The CAE's website is www.dni.gov/cae/overview.htm.
11. The current DNI's "vision statement": "A Nation made more secure because of a fully integrated Intelligence Community." His first goal is "Integrate intelligence analysis and collection to inform decisions made from the White House to the foxhole." See www.dni.gov/mission.htm.
12. See chap. 8 in this volume.
13. DNI Clapper has expressed this on several occasions in meetings.
14. See chap. 1 in this volume.
15. This phrase first appears in Peter Drucker, *Landmarks of Tomorrow* (New York, 1957).
16. See discussion in chap. 9 in this volume.
17. Intelligence Community Directive 610: Competency Directories for the Intelligence Community Workforce, September 1, 2008, www.dni.gov/files/documents/ICD/ICD_610.pdf.
18. Annex G: *Competency Directory for Analysis and Production* does go into more detail about tradecraft skills for collectors, analysts, counterintelligence experts, linguists, et al. www.dni.gov/files/documents/ICD/ICD_610.pdf.
19. Mark M. Lowenthal, *Intelligence: From Secrets to Policy*, 5th ed. (Los Angeles: SAGE Publications, 2012), 158.

20. See ICD 203: Analytic Standards, June 21, 2007, www.dni.gov/files/documents/ICD/ICD_203.pdf. See also the discussion by former DNI Thomas Fingar in chap. 17 in this volume.

21. DI Quality Framework, provided by the Sherman Kent School.

22. In the Intelligence Reform and Terrorism Prevention Act (IRTPA, 2004, P.L. 108-45).

23. Ibid., sec. 102a.

24. Full disclosure: I created and currently offer IC101 and am a guest lecturer in Analysis 101.

25. In US government usage, an executive agent takes over day-to-day responsibility for a component or activity on behalf of other groups, but this does not change ownership.

26. See, for example, Tamar Lewin, "Harvard and M.I.T. Team Up to Offer Free Online Courses," *New York Times*, May 2, 2012, www.nytimes.com/2012/05/03/education/harvard-and-mit-team-up-to-offer-free-online-courses.html/, and Tamar Lewin, "Instruction for Masses Knocks Down Campus Walls," *New York Times*, March 4, 2012, www.nytimes.com/2012/03/05/education/moocs-large-courses-open-to-all-topple-campus-walls.html?pagewanted=all.

27. See Mark Edmundson, "The Trouble with Online Courses," *New York Times*, July 19, 2012, www.nytimes.com/2012/07/20/opinion/the-trouble-with-online-education.html/.

CHAPTER 19

Analytic Outreach: Pathway to Expertise Building and Professionalization

SUSAN H. NELSON

Understanding the twenty-first-century international challenges has driven the intelligence community (IC) to reform its approaches to analysis. Among the many steps taken, analytic outreach connects intelligence analysts to experts outside the US IC to inject new thinking into the intelligence analysis process. As other chapters in this volume emphasize, analysis of complex foreign developments has demanded an analytic business model that no longer relies on the brainpower of the individual analyst.

This chapter focuses on the contributions made to analysis from more robust analytic outreach—that is, the ways in which intelligence analysts connect with and collaborate with experts outside the IC and the US government who have different perspectives. Such outreach is not new, as Sovietologists inside and outside the US government—along with comparative economists, historians, scientists, and businessmen—often exchanged views to better understand our main adversary during the Cold War. Nor does outreach come in any one form or reside in the domain of any one agency. That said, outreach is no longer a "nice to have" feature but rather has become a necessary feature of intelligence analysis. This chapter addresses the rationale, the forms, and the benefits, as well as some of the challenges, posed by outreach in the twenty-first century.

As mentioned in other chapters, collaboration is essential. Former senior DNI official Thomas Fingar has noted that the new, twenty-first-century requirements and expectations of policymakers—combined with the compression of time and the reductions in resources that can be expected in this new age of austerity—demand collaboration inside the government as well as outside. He has stated elsewhere that "we need to develop and maintain extensive networks of 'outside experts' knowledgeable on particular subjects, willing to share what they know with the U.S. government, and sufficiently attuned to the pace and other requirements of Washington to provide timely and targeted input in a process that simply cannot wait."[1]

In many ways analytic outreach is simply another dimension of the collaboration skill, which is becoming a fundamental element of sound analytic tradecraft, as well as a key feature of an analyst's ongoing professional development. Over the course of an analyst's career, he or she will need to cultivate networks of experts both inside the US government but also increasingly outside the IC to answer some of the most vexing problems facing US national security. Analysts have to understand traditional as well as nontraditional intelligence challenges, be they the future of China or Russia, or transnational security issues such as the rise of international organized crime; illicit trafficking of weapons, humans, and narcotics; pandemics; or climate change. Clearly no single analyst or IC element can deliver that synthesis alone; even all the components of the IC together cannot. Synthesizing contributions from a variety of sources, specialized knowledge, and disciplines is particularly crucial when the issues become so complex as to cut across analytic offices and areas of even senior analysts' expertise.

Many scholars also have acknowledged the additional pressure that the growing volume of information puts on the analyst today. Every analyst knows that Moore's law—that the processing power of computers doubles about every eighteen months—is very real. The information revolution is the driving force in the IC, as it makes sense of a security environment dramatically different from that of the bipolar Cold War. William M. Nolte notes, for example, that "twenty-first-century analysts will truly need to rely . . . to a greater degree [on] research and communication with open sources and experts for the simple reason 'that's where the information is.'"[2] Outside experts can help analysts sort through and validate that information.

Other earlier intelligence analysis studies emphasize that analysts need to work collaboratively in teams, not individually, to generate insights in order to understand this complex world: "The 'lone expert' model will suffice for fewer analytic problems," and "insight will come from the synthesis, not the dissection of knowledge."[3] Analysts can interact directly with a diverse range of experts outside the IC to share ideas, challenge assumptions, and generate new insights to strengthen their analysis. This outreach encourages analysts to consider alternative perspectives. It opens valuable channels for innovation and new thinking on the most challenging issues of the day and beyond. Indeed, among other recommendations for improving the IC's analytic methods, the National Academy of Sciences encouraged the community to enhance collaboration in order to innovate and develop new analytic research methods.[4]

Recognizing the need to incorporate outside views is not new. To understand what life was like in the USSR, analysts during the Cold War often relied on Sovietologists and other professionals outside the US government to gain insights from those who had participated in official exchanges. Such past interactions, however, were ad hoc. The 2005 WMD Commission Report identified the lack of sufficient outreach to experts willing to challenge the conventional wisdom of IC analysts and put the spotlight on the need for more deliberate analytic outreach. That report became the key driver behind Intelligence Community Directive (ICD) 205 on Analytic Outreach.[5]

Codifying Analytic Outreach

In July 2008, the director of national intelligence (DNI) issued the first Intelligence Community Directive (ICD) 205 on Analytic Outreach.[6] It defined analytic outreach as "the open, overt, and deliberate act of an IC analyst engaging with an individual outside the IC to explore ideas and alternative perspectives, gain new insights, generate new knowledge, or obtain new information." Analytic outreach does not task outside experts to collect intelligence. It is an intellectual exchange of ideas and insights, and to be effective it must be mutually beneficial—a genuine two-way exchange between analysts and outside experts.

Original ICD 205 essentially said that (1) all IC analysts shall engage with outside experts, (2) each IC element shall have a designated analytic outreach coordinator, and (3) the State Department's Bureau of Intelligence and Research (INR) shall be the executive agent for analytic outreach for the IC.[7] The clear intent of ICD 205 was to "support, improve and enrich analysis." It justified analytic outreach on the basis that it is a key factor in an analyst's professional development, calling it an element of "sound intelligence analysis."[8] Outreach is part of an analyst's professional responsibilities, and each IC element should create mechanisms to facilitate that outreach. ICD 205 recommended, for example, that senior, seasoned analysts and managers mentor more junior analysts to teach them how to engage with outside experts safely and effectively. It also called for IC elements to state "their expectations for analytic outreach" in position descriptions, vacancy announcements, rewards, and performance standards. IC elements were to "promote career development opportunities that help establish senior analysts as top experts in their fields" including active participation in conferences, seminars, and workshops and presenting papers. ICD 205 was equally clear that there was no "one size fits all" for outreach policies and procedures. The expectation was that each IC element would continue outreach in the context of its specific mission and consistent with security and counterintelligence policies.

The Benefits of Outreach

Outreach comes in many forms and is much more than an event—it is a mind-set. Engaging with outside experts is a cognitive process that can change how an analyst looks at his or her issue. The value of outreach is not so much about getting detailed answers to intelligence questions but about helping the analyst think broadly and creatively about the problem. As former National Intelligence Council (NIC) vice chairman Greg Treverton notes, "Too often [the IC] wants 'ready-made meals' when it should be asking help in improving its 'cooking'—through training in analysis, different disciplines, fundamental research, understanding where to get answers from academia, language, different cultures, the impact of technology on behavior, ethics, and so on."[9] Likewise, Nolte calls for the IC to "empower analysts to be researchers . . . to commission research, build their own networks of outside experts, and to do so without begging permission from collec-tors and security officers."[10] Analysts are not just processing intelligence; they are creat-ing new knowledge in broad collaboration with other IC colleagues and outside experts. The outreach mind-set requires the analyst to be willing to keep an open mind about the portfolio he or she knows so well and to be willing to adjust as new information and ideas come to light. In the spirit of continuous learning and intellectual curiosity, outreach helps keep analysis fresh and analysts growing.

Coupled with unclassified, open-source literature, outreach strengthens all-source analysis. It is now generally recognized that much of the information an analyst needs can be found in open sources. There is a self-reinforcing relationship among outreach, open-source analysis, and education/professional development. Analysts interact with outside experts and research open-source literature to get smarter and serve policymak-ers better. Through this combination of outreach and open-source analysis, analysts can give the policymaker unclassified insights that he or she can actually use in public. To serve their policy customers best, analysts must know their field and be aware of the principal findings of the major researchers in their accounts. Otherwise they run the risk of not being taken seriously by policymakers who themselves may be consulting outside academics and who expect all-source analysts to be at least on par with their counterparts in the academic and think-tank world.

Generating Insights

Analysts can learn a lot from experts outside the IC, who often have access to people and places where US officials often cannot reach—from elite confidants to the grassroots views of the "street," from remote villages to closed societies. These experts share their impressions and understanding of foreign officials they meet or the intimacies of living in another culture. The off-the-record nature of the IC's analytic exchanges promotes the free exchange of opinions so experts inside and outside government can be comfortable positing bold or controversial ideas to generate new insights.

As one advocate of outreach has noted, "Though much of this knowledge is 'open source' in the sense of not being classified, it is not always to be found in a broadcast, a book or journal, or other media form. In fact, much of that knowledge is 'tacit,' meaning it resides largely in the minds of experts who have collected knowledge through study, experience, or other special skills."[11] Analysts can only benefit from those embedded insights by engag-ing directly with experts, including foreign scholars. The all-source analyst brings together knowledge from all these sources—open ones, diverse perspectives through outreach, and classified information—to make sense of his or her intelligence issue for policymakers.

Networking to Build Relationships

The outreach mission is people based, integrating expertise inside and outside govern-ment to build and connect networks. Analytic exchanges are excellent networking opportunities, especially for new analysts who can meet their counterparts in the IC, their key policy customers, and recognized, as well as newly discovered, experts on their issue. Equally important, the outside experts meet many of their senior IC counterparts and new policymakers in their area of expertise. This networking supports the mutually beneficial intent of outreach. It is not just about knowledge sharing but also about establishing professional relationships. Outreach activities integrate the IC's analytic community and its analysts into broader sets of professional circles, tying together diverse networks even within the IC and US government. These networks help strengthen the IC's global coverage and are especially useful for multidisciplinary and comparative analysis.

The National Intelligence Council has been at the leading edge of building enduring relationships with outside experts since it created the NIC Associates Program in 1997 through the Global Expertise Reserve Program. Since 2008, when INR became the executive agent, the renamed IC Associates Program has included about two hundred recognized scholars who help make sense of fast-moving events and identify and assess longer-range trends. Senior IC officials nominate associates who serve for one year on a planned project to help expand the global coverage capability of the IC. They participate in analytic exchanges, prepare commissioned studies, and review national intelligence estimates to give a "sanity check" from an outside perspective. More recently, IC associates have led multiagency analytic teams on their topic of expertise—for example, connected to the NIC's renowned Global Trends series of reports. This cutting-edge program provides targeted opportunities for IC analysts to build enduring relationships in their portfolios with each other and leading subject-matter experts outside of the IC.

Sharing Diverse Perspectives

A major benefit of outreach is the diverse breadth of experience and expertise that can spark the analyst's imagination to pursue new avenues of research and analysis. Outreach is not static. There is always new private-sector talent to tap. Since enacting ICD 205, the IC overall has devoted more effort through the analytic outreach coordinators to help analysts connect with academics, business people, representatives of nongovernmental and international organizations, scientists, journalists, lawyers, and others, from the United States and abroad. International perspectives are especially important to help analysts see beyond the "Western" framework to understand better how others perceive the world, especially the United States.

The NIC sets the gold standard for international engagement through its *Global Trends 2025* and *Global Trends 2030* reports, in terms of drawing upon a diverse set of nongovernment experts. For each report the NIC held over a dozen major conferences in Europe, Asia, and Latin America to collect foreign views of the major trends facing the United States and the world. These events drew in not only intelligence and foreign policy officials but also historians, journalists, business leaders, and other professionals, who were prepared to challenge American perspectives and assumptions, as well as identify issues and trends not considered important in Washington.[12] In the process the NIC also benefited from how such experts view American policies' impact on those trends—an insight that is hard to generate when viewed only through our own eyes.

Thinking Strategically through Outreach— It's Not about Prediction

Diverse perspectives are especially important for strategic analysis or foresight—that is, to looking ahead to anticipate future threats and opportunities. The purpose of strategic analysis is to avoid surprise and help policymakers better shape the future by taking action sooner in ways that are conducive to US security and prosperity. The IC has had a conflicted relationship with strategic analysis as its approach to warning has shifted over time—from the dedicated warning units of the past to today, when every analyst is supposed to be a warning analyst. Nolte notes that the IC has a "tendency for current or short-term analysis to drive out strategic or long-term analysis."[13] The National Intelligence Strategy's mission objective number 3, however, calls for the IC to provide strategic intelligence and warning "so that policymakers, military officials, and civil authorities can effectively deter, prevent or respond to threats and take advantage of opportunities."[14]

As mentioned elsewhere in this volume, too often the IC has been criticized for not "predicting" unexpected events—from the fall of the Soviet Union to the eruption of the Arab Spring. Intelligence analysts cannot, and should not, be expected to "predict" the future. No one has a crystal ball, but there are tools to help anticipate future trends. By working through plausible future scenarios, enhanced through interaction with diverse outside experts, analysts can explore deliberately and systematically how the future could look very different from today.

One of the most useful ways to prepare for the unexpected is to conduct what intelligence analysts know as "scenario analysis." Discussed more in detail elsewhere in this volume by Randolph H. Pherson and Richards J. Heuer Jr., scenarios explore key drivers of the future and help analysts think creatively about "wild cards"—events that are unlikely but that would have a high impact if they occurred. Another leading expert on scenario development, Peter Schwartz, and his colleague Doug Randall explain: "Everyone, from analysts to decision-makers, can see the forces as they are taking shape and not be blindsided when those changes inevitably reshape the global environment. . . . Anticipating strategic surprise gives decision-makers the ability to look in the right place for game-changing events and to track them systematically."[15]

Scenario exercises depend heavily on leveraging outside expertise because they are best done with a diverse set of participants. Schwartz and Randall see this diversity as different "filters" through which to measure and analyze data. They say "a multiplicity of frameworks, perspectives, and experiences is needed, each surfacing different kinds and categories of insight into the baseline information." This is where outreach to outside experts makes a difference; it broadens an analyst's exposure to information and ideas. "We urge organizations to reach out to individuals from multiple disciplines who think differently and use a variety of filters to make sense of information."[16]

NIC Global Trends Series

The NIC's Global Trends series seeks to stimulate strategic thinking by identifying key trends, the factors that drive them, where they seem to be headed, and how they might interact.[17] It uses scenarios to illustrate some of the many ways in which the drivers examined in the study (such as globalization, demography, the rise of new powers, the decay of international institutions, climate change, and the geopolitics of energy) may interact to generate challenges and opportunities for future decision makers. The studies as a whole are more a description of the factors likely to shape events than a prediction of what will actually happen.

Global Trends 2030—released in December 2012—is the fifth installment in the NIC-led effort to identify key "megatrends" likely to shape world events a decade or more in the future. Both the product and the process used to produce it benefited from lessons learned in previous iterations. *Global Trends 2030* is the most collaborative such volume yet produced, as it includes more extensively the work of scientists and technologists in order to address the increasing pace of technology. One novel outreach feature has been its use of a blog post feature, which registered "hits" from experts in 167 countries.[18] Judging from the reception that *Global Trends 2025* received by the Obama administration in 2009, this new document is likely to help shape a second term's development of a national security strategy. As in the past, the newest volume, *Global Trends 2030*, will probably be translated into several foreign languages, as interested researchers in Paris as well as China have found them a useful way to understand how Washington views the future.

The process and spinoff benefits of preparing the Global Trends works are as important as the final product. The ideas generated and insights gained during the preparation of the reports have enriched the work of countless analysts and been incorporated into numerous analytic products published by the NIC and other IC agencies. Anecdotal evidence indicates they have also influenced the thinking and work of many participants in the process who do not work for the US government. This is another example of the mutual benefit of analytic outreach.

Inspired by the NIC's Global Trends series, INR's Office of Outreach (OTR) designed the Actionable Foresight Project in 2010 and 2011 with the National Defense University and the Department of Homeland Security to look for ways to strengthen the linkage between longer-term analysis and national security decision making.[19] For the project OTR defined foresight as the disciplined analysis of alternative futures that provides decision makers with the understanding needed to better influence the future environment. Foresight helps bound uncertainty, illuminate blind spots, build confidence to act in the face of uncertainty, and lengthen response time by identifying emerging or potential crises earlier. As a result the decision maker has more time and therefore more options for action.

The Actionable Foresight Project helped build a multinational community of interest involving about two hundred foresight experts, policymakers from around the US government, and analysts across the IC. The key findings most relevant for analysts were that the IC should (1) engage policymakers directly in strategic conversations about the future and (2) tie the foresight directly to the top priorities and challenges of policymakers today. Analysts need to make the linkages of how various actions taken today plausibly could play out in the future.

Drawing on private-sector expertise, the Actionable Foresight Project also produced a comparative study on global foresight capabilities, showing the governments of Singapore and Finland clearly in the lead. Singapore's Risk Assessment and Horizon Scanning (RAHS) analytic effort, attached to the Office of the Prime Minister, constantly monitors a wide range of indicators looking for discontinuities that signal change. Finland's parliamentary Committee for the Future provides long-term analysis for its lawmakers on such topics as climate change, energy policy, demographics, and technological developments.

Global Futures Forum

The Global Futures Forum (GFF) has been the IC's vehicle for international engagement on transnational security issues of strategic importance. GFF is a multinational network of national security professionals from some twenty-five like-minded member countries focused on transnational security issues of common concern (see box 19.1). Its work is completely unclassified. Canada has been a leading contributor and cosponsor of major events, and more recently Singapore and Finland have led many new activities. Member countries host interactive workshops that draw on regional talent. For example, GFF's Conflict, Violence, and Extremism community of interest (COI) explored on-site the topic of "identity politics" in the Americas, Europe, Asia, and the Middle East, respectively. Each of these regionally focused exchanges featured leading local experts on violent extremism. As a result, the COI is building a comparative assessment of violent extremism across regions.

Many of GFF's strategic issues cross government agency "stovepipes." As a result, the network is particularly useful for examining how change in one regional or functional area impacts other areas, which often can be better understood if multiple nationalities, regional organizations, and disciplines are engaged in the projects. For example, the Scottish government leads the COI on Human and Natural Resource Security, which explores the connections among food, water, energy, environment, and health. The United States leads the COI on Emerging and Disruptive Technologies, which in 2012 sponsored a series of workshops examining technologies that are likely to have the most dramatic impact on human security in the next twenty years, such as robotics and nanotechnology, human augmentation, biotechnology, energy, and computing/communications technology. The underlying assumption is that technological change itself will have a significant impact on human behavior. As the pace of technological change accelerates, exploring potential change in the global operating environment for governments, businesses, organizations, and individuals becomes crucial. GFF facilitates dialogue that brings policymakers, analysts, and planners together with scientists, technologists, and long-term trend

---

BOX 19.1   Global Futures Forum

The GFF is a multinational community of government national security professionals and private-sector experts collaborating to understand emerging and future global security challenges. Its goal is to stimulate cross-cultural and interdisciplinary thinking and to challenge prevailing assumptions.

- Twenty-three member countries
- Twenty-five affiliate member countries
- Fifteen hundred individuals
- Seven communities of interest:
  - Emerging and Disruptive Technologies
  - Human and Natural Resource Security
  - Conflict, Violence, and Extremism
  - Transnational Organized Crime
  - Strategic Foresight and Warning
  - Proliferation
  - Practice and Organization of Intelligence

---

analysts from around the world to debate how these trends may develop and what that might mean for policy decisions today.[20] IC analysts are invited to participate in these GFF workshops, with opportunities to meet experts overseas whom they likely would not meet in Washington and to explore new areas of expertise outside their usual portfolio.

Organizing Outreach: The State Department's Role

Until the DNI was created, outreach was left largely in the hands of individual agencies and analysts, with no overall direction or coordination. Lacking any overarching philosophy or guidance, each agency was free to pursue outreach in its own fashion or to ignore or restrict it if the agency's security regulations prohibited contact with foreign experts. To this day there are still marked differences in the degree of openness to analytic outreach, shaped in part by some agencies' security consciousness and a preoccupation with more traditional intelligence requirements where protection of sensitive sources and methods remains a vital necessity. However, as part of the DNI's overall effort to integrate the activities of the intelligence community better, it determined that analytic outreach could benefit from greater cross-agency collaboration and coordination. Thus, as mentioned earlier, it fell to the State Department—despite being one of the smallest intelligence organizations—to help guide the intelligence community's approach to collaboration with outside experts. That the first ICD 205 named INR as the executive agent for analytic outreach was not surprising, given its experience and comfort with engaging outside experts to enhance its analysis for State Department policymakers.[21]

INR is both a bureau in the State Department, reporting directly to the secretary of state, as well as one of the sixteen members of the IC, reporting to the director of national intelligence. As INR is a direct descendant of the research arm of the Office of Strategic Services (OSS), its analysts have had a close connection to academia. The first analysts were academics who had worked for the Research and Analysis Branch of the OSS during World War II. An academic connection remains, as many INR analysts are still hired in the middle of teaching careers. Today some analysts in INR—along with others in the IC—also serve as adjunct professors at local universities on their own time. In many ways outreach is in INR's DNA.[22]

As the smallest all-source analytic element of the IC, INR must be resourceful in providing continuous education and professional development for its analysts. Outreach has been a critical part of this commitment. Thus the bureau has invested in well-developed analytic outreach mechanisms and has encouraged its analysts to be proactive in regularly engaging with outside academics. They attend seminars at local think tanks and stay in touch with their former academic colleagues and mentors to broaden their knowledge of open-source material. They build new relationships with relevant experts on their own, in compliance with their performance plans. Perhaps more than some other agencies, INR analysts are active and feel very comfortable participating in professional academic associations. For example, its Eurasia analysts regularly present papers or chair panels at the annual meeting of the Association for Slavic, East European, and Eurasian Studies. Its other regional specialists are likewise engaged with comparable regional studies organizations in order to engage with such experts and use them as consultants.

In addition to the bureau's familiarity with outreach, it also has in place administrative mechanisms to support outreach programs. The Office of Outreach connects analysts to outside experts through many channels. INR and other IC analysts regularly work with OTR to design and execute outreach projects on a range of regional and functional topics.[23] INR takes an inclusive approach to outreach, designing its projects in collaboration with and extending invitations to analysts across the IC. In this way analysts from other IC elements that may not have robust outreach programs can attend these exchanges and benefit from the discussion without taking a more prominent role, which may be uncomfortable for them.

INR's approach to outreach has evolved over time from predominantly lengthy commissioned research studies in the early years to today's robust and interactive analytic exchange programs (see box 19.2). For example, OTR organizes approximately 170 outreach projects annually, bringing in several hundred outside experts to participate in exchanges that may feature one or two scholars for a couple of hours or full-day events with eight to ten experts. Over the course of a year, these experts speak candidly with thousands of analysts and policymakers in an unclassified setting under the Chatham House Rule—off the record and not for attribution.[24] Each one is custom designed to strengthen IC-wide analysis on a specific topic in support of policymaking. Topics include looking for new approaches to frozen conflicts, assessing upcoming elections, understanding developments in countries in transition, and exploring transnational

---

BOX 19.2   INR Outreach Design: An Analytic Exercise

Analysts are at the heart of each custom-designed outreach project. INR/OTR takes the lead to do the following:

1. Convene key stakeholders—IC analysts and policymakers with equities in the subject.
2. Define success. How will we know we have succeeded at the end of the project?
3. Construct the key analytic questions to get to success.
4. Identify the "best" outside experts to address those questions by
   • identifying new talent,
   • minimizing the "usual suspects," and
   • ensuring diversity and balanced presentation of alternative views.

Source: Office of Outreach, Bureau of Intelligence and Research, State Department.

---

challenges such as the global financial crisis. Outreach is especially beneficial for science and technology topics, where advances are rapid and constant, and expertise inside departments such as State is limited. As a result, the science and technology adviser to the secretary of state has been a reliable customer for INR outreach programs.

With the creation of the DNI and the mandate for integrating activities across the community, it was almost natural for INR to take the lead in shaping the early strategic vision for outreach in the IC. It chairs the National Intelligence Analysis and Production Board's Subcommittee on Analytic Outreach, in which the designated analytic outreach coordinators from each element collaborate on upcoming plans to reduce redundancies and share best practices for efficiency.[25] Agencies' outreach coordinators bring their comparative advantage to the subcommittee, for example, by extending invitations to their mission-specific outreach events to analysts across the IC.

To be sure, INR is not the only model for analytic outreach. Each IC element has developed its own approach and policies. Some coordinators—for example, the National Geospatial-Intelligence Agency (NGA) and the Defense Intelligence Agency (DIA)—have designed mission-specific speaker series. DIA also updates biweekly a comprehensive list of upcoming outreach events in the IC, in Washington, elsewhere in the United States, and abroad, grouped by topic for easy reference. This is one of the key outreach assets for analysts as a whole. The Institute for Analysis (IFA) is an innovative resource at the National Security Agency (NSA) for analysts and managers who wish to expand analytic thinking and broaden perspectives to improve mission effectiveness. IFA is designed to help analysts seek out and engage recognized industry and academic experts to leverage previously untapped intellectual capital in developing new processes, methodologies, and tradecraft for the analytic community to use when and where appropriate. The institute fosters relationships throughout the IC and works to increase the cognitive capacity of every analyst. It sponsors projects called Challenge Problems, Network Events (a speaker series), and Action Learning Teams that help to integrate their findings with the analysts. Key to IFA's success is its unique collaboration relationship with Monitor 360, a private firm that specializes in solving complex, ambiguous problems and is internationally recognized for having a list of diverse, creative thinkers (in its Remarkable People program) who can be brought into projects of interest to government analysts.

CIA has had an active if less centralized system of outreach, prior to the DNI's creation. Individual analytic offices have maintained contacts with a number of centers of excellence outside government such as the RAND Corporation, where classified and unclassified research had been conducted for years on the Soviet target. Similarly, the office responsible for Middle East analysis has conducted an annual unclassified conference on the region, drawing in academics from all over the country and overseas. Likewise, the counterterrorism specialists at CIA have maintained consultancies with a wide range of outside experts and research centers working on terrorism analysis. More generally, CIA established a "scholars-in-residence" program, which allowed nongovernment experts to spend one to two years working alongside analysts, acting as reviewers and mentors to younger CIA officers. In the 1990s, CIA's Directorate of Intelligence also had established its Strategic Analysis Group (SAG), a unit with a mandate to take a longer-range perspective on a number of crosscutting issues and to engage experts outside the government in developing more speculative analysis of these issues. One such example was the lively give-and-take that SAG analysts had with nongovernment energy specialists on the petroleum markets; another was the SAG's early experimentation with large-scale modeling and scenario development, which benefited from working with outside academics, think-tank experts, and business consultants. Also CIA was the early developer of the Global Futures Forum, as it sponsored it for a number of years before it migrated first to INR then to the NIC as part of the DNI's outreach responsibilities.

Challenges to Outreach

Outreach is not without its challenges, especially given the classified nature of the intelligence community's work and the restrictions imposed on government analysts in dealing with outside experts who do not hold clearances. In the early days of ICD 205, INR worked with the Office of the Director of National Intelligence and an independent consulting firm to assess the state of outreach across the community on behalf of the National Intelligence Analysis and Production Board Subcommittee on Analytic Outreach. Extensive interviews with each IC element surfaced tensions and competing values in the IC surrounding outreach. Many of those tensions remain today.[26] They include

- the security risks of talking to noncleared experts versus the analytic risk of not seeking diverse perspectives,
- the value of classified information versus the value of insights gained regardless of source,

- fact-oriented analysis based on collection versus context-oriented analysis based on insights,
- outreach embedded in analysis versus outreach as a function separate from analysis,
- one-time transactional relationships with outside experts versus enduring relationships,
- outreach designed and conducted in-house versus outsourced, and
- measuring the value of outreach quantitatively versus qualitatively.

These tensions, however, should not be seen as mutually exclusive, and the IC needs to find balance between these dichotomies. There clearly are legitimate security concerns associated with outreach, as there are also costs to staying inside the "classified bubble." Many of these tensions can be eased through education and training. For example, analysts can minimize the risk of talking to noncleared experts by being well grounded in the open-source literature of their portfolio, which gives them a common language for a mutually beneficial and unclassified exchange. In addition, a subset of instructors on the Subcommittee on Analytic Outreach designed a two-day curriculum for analysts on how to do outreach safely and effectively. Outreach coordinators have used the curriculum to develop their own agency-specific training on outreach. Recent well-publicized security breaches have in some cases dampened official enthusiasm for robust analytic outreach. In some agencies the analytic cultures are still far from being entirely comfortable with some forms tried elsewhere; onerous preapproval processes for meeting with academics or foreign experts can often discourage the newer analysts from trying to enlarge their circle of professional contacts. The bottom line is that the IC has to help analysts learn to engage safely with outside experts and then trust those analysts to exercise good judgment in doing so.

One of the biggest challenges to analytic outreach in the IC is the lack of dedicated funding. As good stewards of the taxpayer dollar, outreach coordinators collaborate to share costs and stretch scarce outreach funds as far as possible. Conference and travel funds are often the first items to suffer budget cutbacks, without full appreciation of the impact of those cuts on outreach. As we enter what appears to be a prolonged period of government austerity, there are likely to be even fewer funds available for outreach activities unless senior managers, in the spirit of training and education, advocate for protecting these funds from across-the-board cuts.

Closely related to funding is the challenge of measuring the impact or value of outreach to justify the cost. How do we know what difference outreach really makes to the quality of analysis? How do we measure the insight an analyst gains from interacting with an outside expert? How do we measure the analytic cost of *not* engaging with outside experts? INR's OTR has made a concerted effort to gather and analyze statistics on its analytic exchanges that serve the whole IC.

The OTR conducted a snapshot overview of its outreach activities over a six-month period, drawing on standard survey questions and focus group discussions to illustrate the application of outreach and assess its impact and value added. Results represent the views of 759 exit surveys from analytic exchanges and a focus group with five INR analysts. These respondents obviously represent a select portion of analysts—those who chose to participate in an analytic exchange. A brief summary of findings:

- About 90 percent of respondents said engaging with outside experts is "important" or "very important" for doing their job.
- About 75 percent "agreed" or "strongly agreed" that the exchange provided networking opportunities.
- About 88 percent "agreed" or "strongly agreed" that the exchange increased their knowledge of the topic.
- About 80 percent "agreed" or "strongly agreed" that the exchange explored alternative perspectives.
- About 76 percent "agreed" or "strongly agreed" that they would use the experts from the exchange as a resource in the future.
- About 85 percent "agreed" or "strongly agreed" they could incorporate the exchange in their work.

In the focus group, analysts explained that the value of outreach for them was in the networking and hearing alternate viewpoints. With such feedback, outreach coordinators can refine project design to make the exchanges more meaningful for analysts. The next phase of evaluation will seek to capture the longer-term impact of outreach and to connect with analysts who choose not to participate in analytic exchanges to explore why they don't.

The Way Ahead

The intelligence profession has come a long way from where it began on developing outreach programs and leveraging outside knowledge for the benefit of analysts and policymakers. From an episodic and uncoordinated set of activities, we now have a more integrated and coordinated approach. The first ICD 205 helped to provide the framework to advance analytic outreach in the IC, but it remains a work in progress. Without doubt the IC is better coordinated and integrated internally on outreach activities than it was when the DNI signed ICD 205 in 2008.

However, more progress is still needed. Still, many in the IC are not entirely comfortable interacting directly with outside expects. Both the security-conscious cultures and rules continue to impede the interaction of analysts and outside experts, and in the process impede further professionalization of analysis. It would be hard to identify another profession that has rules inhibiting or preventing its members from interacting with others in the same field of inquiry; however, this is a hurdle that the intelligence profession currently faces. Moreover, such engagement is still too often seen as a "nice to have," not as a "must do," for meeting the IC's goal of delivering the very best analysis possible to policymakers and senior officials. To this day information collected through classified channels is often assumed to have more clout, clarity, and insight than anything an academic or businessman may freely share with the US government.

Finally, the analytic cultures must realize that outreach is by necessity a two-way street; that is, analysts must be prepared to share their views—not sources and methods—with outside experts to give them any benefit from participating in outreach activities. Merely attending an academic conference but never voicing an opinion, exchanging views, or even business cards will not bring analysts credibility with those from whom they wish to extract some valuable insights.

There are steps the IC could take to invest in outreach that would help strengthen analysis. As the intelligence community develops new strategies for understanding emerging intelligence challenges, analytic outreach should become part of the standard set of tools for researching them.[27] Second, more incentives for conducting analytic outreach could be built into analysts' performance evaluations, professional development goals, and training and education plans. In addition to understanding how collection works, analysts need to develop a good understanding of their professional fields outside of the US government. Third, senior intelligence managers should take the lead in rebalancing intelligence priorities from predominantly current analysis to more long-term strategic topics, which can benefit from interactions with leading scholars and researchers in a variety of nongovernment institutions and centers. One of the most important contributions outreach can make to intelligence analysis is to create space for strategic analysis—bringing together the best and brightest inside and outside government to anticipate and be better prepared for future challenges. We need to devise ways to better embed foresight in analysis. As Nolte suggests, the IC should consider "fencing off" a portion of the analytic workforce to focus on longer-term work, along the lines that the military has done with its research centers at war and staff colleges.[28]

The IC has capabilities on which to build, including the NIC's Strategic Futures Group, the Global Futures Forum, and the Actionable Foresight community of interest. Outreach coordinators are well placed to support scenarios and other such exercises that would give analysts the opportunity to think about the future and better prepare for the intelligence demands that are sure to come their way. If analysis is only as good as our ability to comprehend the world as it really is and as others see it, we must be prepared to engage with others who bring different perspectives to our attention.

Notes

As this volume goes to press, the DNI has updated the 2008 ICD 205 but it is not currently available.

1. Thomas Fingar, *Reducing Uncertainty: Intelligence Analysis and National Security* (Stanford CA: Stanford University Press, 2012), 30.
2. William M. Nolte, "Intelligence Analysis in an Uncertain Environment," in *The Oxford Handbook of National Security Intelligence*, ed. Loch K. Johnson (New York: Oxford University Press, 2010), 411.

3. Carmen A. Medina, "The New Analysis," in *Analyzing Intelligence: Origins, Obstacles, and Innovations*, eds. Roger Z. George and James B. Bruce (Washington, DC: Georgetown University Press, 2008), 242, 247.

4. National Research Council, National Academy of Sciences, *Intelligence Analysis for Tomorrow: Advances from the Behavioral and Social Sciences* (Washington DC: National Academies Press, 2011).

5. A number of reports called on the IC to enhance analysis through outreach. The Commission on *the Intelligence Capabilities of the United States regarding Weapons of Mass Destruction: Report to the President of the United States* urged the IC to "think more creatively and . . . more strategically" about how to tap into "external sources of knowledge . . . to challenge conventional wisdom"; March 31, 2005. The president's *National Security Strategy* of May 2010 said to "tap the ingenuity outside government through strategic partnerships"; www.whitehouse.gov/sites.../national_security_strategy.pdf.

6. On July 16, 2008, the then director of national intelligence, Mike McConnell, codified the call for analysts to engage with experts outside the community in Intelligence Community Directive 205 on Analytic Outreach. See ICD 205, www.dni.gov/files/documents/ICD/ICD_205.pdf. All comments in this chapter regarding ICD 205 refer to the 2008 issuance. The ICD has been updated but is not yet available.

7. INR's primary mission is to harness intelligence to serve US diplomacy. Drawing on all-source intelligence, INR provides value-added independent analysis of events to State Department policymakers, ensures that intelligence activities support foreign policy and national security purposes, and serves as the focal point in the State Department for ensuring policy review of sensitive counterintelligence and law enforcement activities. See www.state.gov/s/inr/ and www.intelligence.gov/about-the-intelligence-community/member-agencies/.

8. ICD 205 stated, "Sound intelligence analysis requires that analysts who are dealing with issues of concern network in the U.S. and internationally to develop trusted relationships . . . [including with] experts in academia; think tanks; industry; non-governmental organizations; the scientific world; state, local and tribal governments; other non-Intelligence Community U.S. government agencies; and elsewhere" (section B, Purpose: Number 4). See ICD 205, http://www.dni.gov/files/documents/ICD/ICD_205.pdf.

9. Gregory Treverton, *Bridging the Divide between Scientific and Intelligence Analysis* (Vallingby: Swedish National Defence College, 2009), 26.

10. Nolte, "Intelligence Analysis in an Uncertain Environment," 412.

11. Roger Z. George, "Meeting 21st Century Transnational Challenges: Building a Global Intelligence Paradigm," Studies in Intelligence, Center for Study of Intelligence, www.cia.gov/library/center-for-the-study-of-intelligence/csi-publications/csi-studies.

12. See the introduction to the NIC's *Global Trends 2025*, www.dni.gov/files/documents/Global%20Trends_2025%20Report.pdf.

13. Nolte, "Intelligence Analysis in an Uncertain Environment," 416.

14. National Intelligence Strategy mission objective number 3 states: "The issues and trends that will shape the future security environment—economic instability, state failure, the ebb and flow of democratization, emergence of regional powers, changing demographics and social forces, climate change, access to space, pandemic diseases, and the spread of disruptive technologies, to name just a few—will test the Intelligence Community's ability to provide strategic warning and avoid surprise. Most of the IC's analytic cadre focuses on assessing

ongoing and near-term events of significance. The IC must improve its ability to anticipate and identify emerging challenges and opportunities." See www.dni.gov/files/documents/ Newsroom/Reports%20and%20Pubs/2009_NIS.pdf, 7–8.

15. Peter Schwartz and Doug Randall, "Ahead of the Curve: Anticipating Strategic Surprise," in *Blindside: How to Anticipate Forcing Events and Wild Cards in Global Politics*, ed. Francis Fukuyama (Washington, DC: Brookings Institution Press, 2007), 97.

16. Ibid., 100.

17. The NIC's first Global Trends effort, which looked out to 2010, relied primarily on expertise within the US intelligence community. But subsequent reports relied increasingly on gathering outsiders' views of key trends, and each successive project developed even more elaborate processes to engage foreign experts in the Global Trends reviews. See a description at www .dni.gov/nic/NIC_2025_project.html.

18. National Intelligence Council, *Global Trends 2030: Alternative Worlds*, "Introduction by NIC Chairman Christopher Kojm," www.dni.gov/index.php/about/organization/ national-intelligence-council-global-trends.

19. Credit goes to two intelligence community analysts: Carol Dumaine, who founded the Global Futures Partnership/Forum, for the term "actionable," and Warren H. Fishbein, who served in INR/OTR from 2008 to 2011, for design of the project. He has written extensively on strategic foresight. For example, see *Toward High Reliability Intelligence Sense-Making: Realistic "Foresight for Prevention" in an Age of Complex Threats* at www.kcl.ac.uk/ sspp/departments/warstudies/research/groups/foresight/Programme.pdf and "Emerging Threats in the 21st Century," GFF Strategic Foresight and Warning Seminar Series, www.css .ethz.ch/publications/pdfs/Emerging-Threats-final.pdf.

20. Focusing on five baskets of technologies, GFF brought in a range of experts from technologists to a science fiction writer to explore the possibilities of changes in the technology landscape with intelligence and national security analysts, most of whom were not technologists. During breakout sessions, analysts applied their newly acquired knowledge to analyze the possibilities for convergence of various technologies to form new capabilities and processes. Analytic teams then assessed the security implications (threats and opportunities) of the economic, social, political, and other changes that could emerge from these new capabilities and processes over the next five to fifteen years. For example, in a world of increasingly ubiquitous sensors, there is less privacy—and there are fewer secrets—which poses new challenges for intelligence analysts.

21. INR is organized to reflect the State Department, covering all countries and functional issues. It has a blended workforce of Foreign Service officers with extensive in-country experience and Civil Service specialists with in-depth expertise. Beginning in 1970, INR commissioned studies and conferences under the Office of Long-Range Assessments and Research (LAR). Its role has evolved along with its names. In 2008, it became the Office of Outreach (OTR) to reflect the enactment of ICD 205 on analytic outreach. For more on INR's early outreach activities, see Kenneth E. Roberts, "Bridging the World of Policy and Ideas: How Academic Expertise Can Improve Government's Performance," presented to International Studies Association Meeting in March 2005, www.allacademic.com/meta/p70845_index.html.

22. INR is quite unlike other IC elements. It sits in close proximity to policymakers, does not have any collection component, and because it is part of the State Department, INR analysts meet regularly with foreign diplomats and scholars.

23. There are many ways for analysts to do outreach—either passively by attending IC analytic exchanges, think tank seminars, or professional association meetings, or actively by requesting or designing and organizing an outreach project with their analytic outreach coordinator.

24. The term "analytic exchange" describes all outreach formats—conferences, seminars, workshops, symposia, etc. A typical country-focused exchange will address domestic politics, history, economics and energy, social pressures, security issues, and foreign policy, including relations with the United States. For executive analytic exchanges, the experts provide their perspective on what they think is most important for newly appointed ambassadors to know the day they step off the plane. INR invites analysts from across the IC to these exchanges to contribute to the discussion and to hear from a range of outside experts and a key policy customer.

25. The role of the outreach coordinator is to create opportunities in his or her IC element that will entice analysts away from their desks and get them outside the IC "classified bubble." Coordinators share invitations to upcoming events to disseminate throughout the IC analytic workforce. Coordinators routinely disseminate information about upcoming outreach opportunities to their analysts.

26. The Center for Strategic and International Studies cited many of these same obstacles to outreach in the IC in its study *The Power of Outreach: Leveraging Expertise on Threats in Southeast Asia—A Report of the CSIS Transnational Threats Project*, April 2009.

27. In the effort to integrate analysis and collection, the DNI established in 2011 "country-and issue-specific National Intelligence Managers (NIM)." They are responsible for developing and executing "Unifying Intelligence Strategies (UIS) on key geographic and topic areas." See chap. 13 for more on NIMs. Ideally, each of the UISs—as a living document to guide analysis and collection by intelligence topic—would contain an analytic outreach section with modest funding. UIS lays out the broad priority topics for the IC. http://www.dni.gov/index.php/about/organization/intelligence-integration-who-we-are?

28. Nolte, "Intelligence Analysis in an Uncertain Environment," 416.

CHAPTER 20

Conclusion: Professionalizing Intelligence Analysis in the Twenty-First Century

ROGER Z. GEORGE AND JAMES B. BRUCE

Gentlemen, we have run out of money so now we have to think.

—Sir Winston Churchill

Churchill's timeless inspiration applies directly to intelligence analysis: There is now a deeper appreciation for the necessity of using our brains to develop better approaches to problem solving than merely increasing resources. An era of budget austerity suggests that intelligence must be taken even more seriously. Intelligence is often spoken of as a "force multiplier" and as an "enabler" of American power. Certainly better intelligence analysis can do both. When resources are tighter, then analysis can help provide one essential way to mitigate the dangers the United States faces in an increasingly unpredictable world.

Professionalization of analysis—toward which many practitioners have spent the past decade working—has become a major contributor to both the quality and utility of analysis. As explained in earlier chapters, this analysis is now being provided to an ever-widening set of national security decision makers, especially in the domain of homeland security. Since publishing the first edition of this volume in 2008, we have seen major strides made in many aspects of professionalization. We see signs of progress in virtually all the major characteristics of what constitutes a true discipline—namely, a common body of knowledge, professional standards, codes of conduct, and rigorous training and analytic methods development. The foregoing chapters highlight gains made in intelligence training and education, analytic tradecraft, community-wide knowledge management, and standards. These recent developments document that professionalization is continuing and perhaps even accelerating in some areas. Notably this progress remains uneven across the US intelligence community; however, as is often the case, there must be early adopters who set the pace for the others. To name but a few milestones:

- The National Intelligence University—once only a virtual one—is now a bricks-and-mortar institution operated by the Defense Intelligence Agency, having incorporated a variety of accredited degree programs previously offered by the National Defense Intelligence College.
- The ODNI has offered introductory intelligence analysis training to analysts across the community, which has been particularly important to those agencies not able to provide their own training.
- The creation of the I-Space collaboration tools and the National Library of Intelligence analysis products has begun the cataloging, sharing, and retrieval of intelligence-based information.
- Some agencies have begun advanced intelligence tradecraft training, which in some cases may include a step toward "certifying" analysts as being eligible to enter a more selective group of "senior analysts."

One could cite other examples as well drawn from the chapters of this volume.[1] The point is that professionalization is under way and has become recognized not only as a desirable goal but also an achievable one. We believe this can advance further, even in an era of scarcer resources.

Developed appropriately and used wisely, analysis can provide decision advantage to national leaders, and those operators in the field executing our diplomatic and military strategies. Decision advantage—that is, the ability to give the United States an information advantage or enable the use of national power more quickly than others—has become even more important in today's globalized world of 24/7 communications and interdependency.[2] As intelligence analysts become more proficient in providing informed analysis and reliable forecasts, they become more indispensable in directing the smart use of US national power. As John Kringen notes in this volume, senior commanders have come to rely on intelligence analysis as being an integral part of their understanding the physical as well as virtual battlefields.[3] Likewise, Thomas Fingar underlines that national-level leaders need analysis to comprehend not only the "facts" as we know them but also the "uncertainties" of complex international developments so they can carefully weigh the risks of taking or rejecting specific actions.[4] Increasingly, as US decision makers have to make resource choices on what military strategies and programs to develop, which diplomatic crises to engage in, or what contingency plans to prepare, intelligence can help to assess—or help decision makers assess—the urgency, significance, and consequences or risks those decisions might entail.

A Challenging Twenty-First-Century Environment

As is evident in recent American fiscal and budgetary crises, we are in an era when resources will be more constrained than in the previous decade of rapid budget growth. This is not unusual. In the post–Cold War period, the United States has seen its national security budgets balloon and burst with a series of international conflicts. The Korean and Vietnam conflicts saw rapid and large increases in defense spending and intelligence activities, followed by contraction. Similarly, the collapse of the Soviet Union saw a prolonged leveling-off in US defense spending, accompanied by what some characterize as a nearly 25 percent cut in intelligence spending. This changed dramatically with the 9/11 attacks and the subsequent Afghan and Iraq campaigns. Defense and intelligence spending grew rapidly and continued for nearly a decade. At its height the Department of Defense was spending well over $600 billion annually, and the official national intelligence budget was approaching $80 billion annually.[5]

This era of rapid growth is over. Plans are under way to reduce spending for the coming years. Already the total intelligence budget has decreased two years in a row, falling to $75 billion in 2012.[6] One can surmise that additional cuts might well occur, should the fiscal crisis continue.

The implications of this austerity era are that the US intelligence community also must do better with less. Priorities must be established for what is critical and what is not. Traditionally training is often considered an expendable item, unlike "mission essential" operations. However, as this volume suggests, improved analysis based on more professional training and education can be a key force multiplier of reduced US military and foreign affairs budgets. So it would be counterproductive to slash training programs designed to improve analysis, especially when analysis—as compared with technical collection programs and overseas operations—amounts to such a relatively small percentage of overall intelligence costs. In other words, in our view, better analysis provides a big bang for the buck.

The other major challenge is the dynamic international environment in which the United States will be operating. Looking ahead one can see the beginnings of a new multipolar world, with the rise of China, India, Brazil, and other states. With this diffusion of power, the number of issues and challenges facing the United States will undoubtedly grow. This means more challenging relationships among the rising states and the United States, more potential conflicts, and perhaps more complex events that the US intelligence community must be prepared to follow and help policymakers understand. Joint Chiefs chairman Martin Dempsey has described the future as an "increasingly competitive environment" marked by persistent conflict.[7] DNI James Clapper's annual worldwide threat brief to the congressional oversight committees also stressed the unpredictability of the current environment.[8] Reinforcing this, the NIC's *Global Trends 2030* describes our future world this way:

> The diffusion of power among countries will have a dramatic impact by 2030. Asia will have surpassed North America and Europe combined in terms of global power, based upon GDP, population size, military spending, and technological investment. China alone will probably have the largest economy, surpassing that of the United States a few years before 2030. . . . The shift in national power may be overshadowed by an even more fundamental shift in the *nature* of power. Enabled by communications technologies, power will shift

toward multifaceted and amorphous networks that will form to influence state and global actions. Those countries with some of the strongest fundamentals—GDP, population size, etc.—will not be able to punch their weight unless they also learn to operate in networks and coalitions in a multipolar world.[9]

Such trends will have profound implications for US national security policies and American intelligence priorities. Both the topics and types of analysis will have to shift. Accordingly, the skill sets of analysts will have to go well beyond the traditional analysis conducted by regional, country, or weapons specialists. Multidisciplinary teams of analysts may find themselves focused on the use of social media by transnational groups whose agendas and activities are not entirely clear, or perhaps they will be tracking the climate change–driven mass migration of ethnic groups and assessing their impact on regional stability and conflict. Equally important, if *Global Trend 2030*'s more positive scenarios regarding global governance were to come about, US intelligence analysts would be called on to exchange information on worldwide climate, agricultural, water, and energy trends and challenges, with a wider range of international partners and organizations. This would amount to a paradigm shift away from a narrow "need to know" to what the ODNI has termed a "need to share" philosophy. In such a scenario, far greater analytic outreach can be expected than currently exists today.

Further Professionalization Needed

The twin challenges of a more constrained budgetary era and a more complex international environment suggests that analysis will have to step up its game even more than it already has. Policymakers are likely to become even more reliant on intelligence as their decisions become more complex, with more second- and third-order consequences. Addressing so-called wicked problems—namely, those problems that seem intractable and whose dimensions are poorly defined and that have interdependencies with other critical issues—will demand multifaceted intelligence analysis.[10] Satisfying increasing intelligence demands cannot be accomplished without more professionalization and expertise building over the coming decade. Fortunately the US intelligence community is in a better position to respond to these demands than it was in 2008 when the first edition of this book appeared. The foundation for a true intelligence analysis profession exists, as its pillars are evident in the creation of a real NIU, training programs in structured analytic methodologies, common knowledge libraries, and requirements-based entry to senior analyst status. In each area more can and should be done.

Creating a Joint Professional Analysis Education

Maximizing the contribution of intelligence analysis to informed national security policies will demand a higher priority be placed on professionalization than presently exists across the IC. Not only must current professionalization measures—such as traditional training and education—be protected from draconian budget cuts but also new measures will be needed. We believe that something akin to the Joint Professional Military Education (JPME) system of training and certification should be considered as a model for fully professionalizing the cadre of intelligence analysts (see box 20.1). Many of the current programs—and indeed the expansion of the National Intelligence University programs and establishment of a new campus in northwest Washington, DC—support such a long-term objective. Unlike the profession of arms, the profession of analysis has no progressive set of training requirements through which all future senior analysts must move. It would be worth considering how the ODNI could develop such a career-long program of training and education that would both develop individual analysts' skills and expertise but also create more of a joint analytic culture. By stressing "jointness," we aim to instill a common understanding of the analytic profession, its attributes, and its standards appropriate to an IC-wide approach to analysis, as opposed to agency-specific approaches—not force a homogenization of all analysts that removes the unique skills and work practices required for different agencies.

Such a Joint Professional Analysis Education (JPAE) system need not slavishly copy all aspects of the joint professional military education system, but it would strive to integrate the various training programs directed by individual agencies and establish some common standards for the training each agency gives its analysts. The ODNI might establish something like JPME's OPMET (Officers Professional Military Education Training) standards.[11] Those standards are used throughout the different service command and staff schools and senior service colleges to set common training and education objectives, levels, and achievements. Accordingly, as analysts progress through their careers, different training and education goals could be set. At various points in their careers, they would be assigned to complete those programs in order to advance further in their chosen analytic track.

For example, an analyst entering on duty might be expected to take a basic analysis course offered by an individual agency or by the ODNI. Having completed this entry-level basic training, the analyst might then work on an account for a period of time, before next being expected to take additional full-time training. We believe there are several areas where additional training might be considered, which we will touch on briefly.

Basic Understanding of Epistemology

As mentioned in chapter 9, few analysts are aware of the epistemological basis of their analytic judgments, forecasts, or insights. Knowledge building requires that they understand the basis for what constitutes knowledge since some knowledge is more reliable than others. James Bruce highlights the dangers that analysts often rely too heavily on unsubstantiated information merely because it came from what had been thought to be an authoritative source or because it fit a current mind-set ("habit of thought"). Others rest their arguments too heavily on logic without fully examining the factual basis for the premises used in the logic. Still others tend to accept some data uncritically when different data might tell a very different story. In chapter 8, Jack Davis has warned that analysts' judgments can be swayed by what they believe to be the authority of their more

BOX 20.1   Joint Professional Military Education: Possible Model?

The elaborate system of Joint Professional Military Education (JPME) is built around the "profession of arms," which began in the United States in the 1800s with the establishment of the Military Academy at West Point (1802), the Naval Academy at Annapolis (1845), and later the Naval War College (1884) and the Army War College (1901). In the twentieth century it blossomed to include other senior service colleges, along with many specialized command and staff colleges.

As a result of studying the lessons from World Wars I and II, and after considerable interservice consideration, the concept of *joint* education rather than single-service education took hold. After World War II, Gen. Dwight D. Eisenhower and other wartime flag officers determined that there was a need for advancing senior officers from all the services to be educated together and that more interagency cooperation should be developed. Thus the National War College was founded in Washington in 1946. Since then the JPME programs have expanded well beyond military officers to include senior civilians in the national security enterprise, as well as senior officers from foreign militaries. Many have become fully accredited, degree-granting institutions.

The military leadership has recognized the need to develop professional military skills throughout an officer's career, from basic training courses to specialized disciplines (artillery, air, naval, and other operational specialties) and ultimately to senior-level education that prepares officers for national-level responsibilities. At the earlier stages of an officer's career, "skills" training is emphasized; however, as the officer is promoted, the JPME objectives shift to "educating" the officer in national security strategy development, interagency cooperation, and multinational operations. Such steps in the JPME ladder are considered prerequisites for promotion to higher command and ultimately to national-level decision making. Indeed, the Goldwater-Nichols Department of Defense Reorganization Act of 1986 makes joint professional military education a statutory requirement for promotion to flag-officer rank.

In the course of a twenty-year career, officers can assume undertaking two to three years' equivalent of training and education. At particular points in their careers and ranks, they undergo specified types of training and education. This is presumed to be required for further advancement. To be considered for promotion to general or admiral, officers must move out of the field to gain an understanding of the broader national security context in which their missions have to be performed, as well as to comprehend the roles and missions of other civilian departments and agencies with whom they will have to work. The stress on "jointness"—especially since the Goldwater-Nichols reforms—is accepted practice now, with other civilian agencies recognizing the importance of their senior officers also gaining joint duty experiences on the way to higher positions of responsibility.

Source: Cynthia Watson, *Military Education: A Reference Handbook* (Westport, CT: Praeger, 2007).

senior managers or the organization's past or current assessment of a problem (the "analytic line"), without considering whether such judgments are based on something more empirically or scientifically based. Too few analysts have been schooled in the nature of knowledge or think critically about the basis on which they are reaching conclusions. Thus some attention to basic epistemology that underpins the analytic profession should be a foundational element of every analyst's training.

As part of this training, analysts should be exposed to the power of a more science-based production of knowledge. Science, as chapter 9 underlines, offers the only proven method of identifying and correcting errors in judgment, as it relies on hypothesis testing, objective methods, validation of information, transparency, a degree of replicability, and a constant willingness to revisit conclusions and how they were formed. The trend toward using structured analytic techniques can accelerate the analytic profession's advancement to becoming a true discipline. This is because SATs *structure* the inquiry in a way that emphasizes the more reliable science-based ways of knowing. Hand in hand with a basic understanding of epistemology is knowledge management—namely, the development of an accessible repository of organized, searchable, and retrievable information. This will facilitate a more complete and reliable knowledge base from which lessons can be learned by future generations of analysts.[12] Knowledge management will help ensure organizational learning, a key attribute of more mature disciplines.

Analysis and Collection Disciplines

A necessary area for analyst training will be a deeper understanding of the collection sources on which intelligence judgments rest. As suggested above, too few analysts truly understand "how they know what they know." A key part of this vital knowing process is understanding the capabilities and limitations of collection. Yet too many analysts have only a superficial understanding of where HUMINT, SIGINT, and IMINT come from and how to assess the validity and reliability of the collected information. Only a few analysts invest the time needed to grasp the complexities of how these collection disciplines operate or appreciate the strengths, weaknesses, or biases that such information sources bring to the analytic process. Short of demanding that analysts spend time working with each major collection agency, the next best solution is to develop in-depth training for analysts on how collection systems work, how analysts can best use them, and how to determine confidence levels to have in the wide variety of the raw intelligence reporting that each collection method produces.

Designing a series of advanced training courses for analysts to understand HUMINT, SIGINT, IMINT, MASINT, and open-source collection is not insurmountable and should become an integral part of an analyst's skill set. Collection agencies should offer courses explicitly for analysts or cross-train analysts with their own collection officers. Based on personal experience, we found in our own careers scant opportunities for us to learn about collection operations other than to be assigned full-time to a collection agency or operation, which is not possible for all analysts. Such training opportunities need expansion, along with other such specialized training.

Basic Warning Training

Numerous chapters in this volume have highlighted the classic intelligence warning failures that analysts have encountered. Kerr and Warner detail the mixed record that the IC had on monitoring the Soviet Union along with other global intelligence targets, citing specific cases where warning was lacking or ineffective. James Bruce also notes that the blame for many intelligence failures should be shared by both collectors and analysts, owing to missing information, faulty assumptions, limited mind-sets, and denial and deception by adversaries. Analyst dependency on collection is far greater than is commonly appreciated. Likewise, George and Wirtz lament the persistence of warning challenges in the post-9/11 world where the scope has broadened to include both state and nonstate actors, while the attention placed on warning has shifted from a designated senior warning officer to all analysts having a responsibility to warn. The irony is that training and education on warning have not kept pace with the expanding scope of warning problems, despite the greater expectations on analysts to warn. Yet too few analysts regard warning as a principal responsibility or understand the warning process and perils detailed in the previous chapters. At a minimum, basic analytic training should include a focus on the warning function, greater understanding of how adversaries might employ denial and deception to thwart collectors and analysts, and best practices for communicating warning issues to the broader intelligence community and policymakers.

Another step in an analyst's career-long training might be expertise building. Once an analyst has mastered the basics of analysis and collection operations, developing a deeper substantive grounding in his or her "account" should entail further academic education. Few analysts today are hired at the PhD level; most have had a few courses on their regional, country, or functional accounts as part of undergraduate or master's-level education. Thus there could be real value in refreshing, if not deepening, an incoming analyst's understanding of his or her own field. Not unlike what some agencies currently offer in the way of time off or tuition reimbursement for graduate studies, JPAE would include subject-matter expertise building. Currently, very little of this exists within the IC. It is expected that analysts will show up with basic expertise when they come on board, then will learn in greater depth about their account on the job, and bring language skills with them or pick them up largely on their own time.[13] This is haphazard and does not build expertise in a rigorous way or support the level of professional expertise appropriate to a discipline. A more regulated educational program of subject-matter expertise would expose analysts to new analytic methods and leading experts in their fields outside the IC. In so doing, analysts would expand their own analytic outreach networks and give themselves new appreciation for open sources and their professional field outside the closeted classified world.

A final step in JPAE might then be attendance at a senior service college, much like a few intelligence analysts are able to do now at the military service war colleges and the National War College in Washington. These programs are joint by their very nature, as they bring together senior officers from the services, civilian national security agencies, and the IC. A year-long exposure to the "whole-of-government" system would give intelligence analysts a much broadened perspective on how they can best serve policymakers, warriors, diplomats, and law enforcement officials. Alongside these service college experiences, the National Intelligence University could establish a capstone-style program for senior intelligence officers across the community—to include analysts—as a way of broadening even further those likely future IC leaders into the wide-ranging issues faced by all intelligence agencies, not just their own.[14] This capstone-style course would be offered to those analysts who are about to be promoted into the executive ranks, or to the Senior Analytic Service, making them eligible for senior-level responsibilities.[15]

Standardizing and Testing Analytic Methods

Were a JPAE to be established, it would need to first establish a more uniform and recognized set of training objectives for all analysts. One of the key attributes of the analytic profession is "how we do our work." Analytic methods, techniques, and skills are what set analysts apart from subject-matter experts outside the intelligence community and from nonanalysts within the IC. As Pherson and Heuer have argued persuasively, many structured analytic techniques exist, and they should become more utilized across the intelligence community. This is happening—slowly and unevenly—but it would be further encouraged if the ODNI were to develop community-wide standards, curriculum materials, and courses especially for those agencies not able to support their own analysis training. Workshops in using specific techniques should be ongoing, with the development of case studies on specific examples of how a structured analytic technique (SAT) was used, with what success—or failure—and why. Building up a body of SAT case studies would not only be a good training tool, it would also permit more evaluation of the techniques themselves. Indeed, one of the current weaknesses of using SATs is that beyond face validity, there is almost no research on whether these techniques result in more accurate judgments and forecasts or even more useful analysis.

It should, therefore, be the goal of the ODNI to support more research into effective analytic methods, more documentation of their utility and limitations, and consideration of how to further expand the most proven and most promising analytic methods used by analysts. There is currently a modest "lessons learned" capability that the DNI and CIA have developed at the Center for the Study of Intelligence and at DIA's Knowledge Laboratory. It is the authors' impression that these programs are largely underutilized by the analytic side of the intelligence community, as this work has primarily focused on studies of operational activities.

Thus there would seem to be ample opportunities for a lessons-learned library of analytic cases. Case study writers could be assigned to an analytic team focused on a particular analytic challenge. They would observe the analytic process from beginning to end, noting how the analysts collaborated, what analytic methods they employed, how they reached judgments, and finally how they delivered their findings to policymakers. They could also record the analytic effort's impact and collect whatever feedback policymakers might be willing to provide. The case study should be left open-ended to permit a subsequent evaluation of whether the judgments and forecasts stood up over time. The results would help validate the methods. This would be far superior to the past attempts to evaluate the quality of a product's analytic tradecraft after the fact or to collect policymakers' impressionistic satisfaction levels with analytic support that is typically done long after the policymaker has forgotten a specific analytic product.[16]

Building More Knowledge-Based Learning

The ODNI has made great strides in developing more community-wide databases of analysis and enabling greater collaboration among analysts across the community. The technology available today makes this much easier, in terms of sharing as well as retrieving analytic products remotely across both time and distance. I-Space and the National Library of Intelligence are two such examples of what is now possible. No doubt there can be additional such initiatives that further exploit technology to improve these databases and make them more user-friendly to a larger number of analysts.

Where the intelligence community might devote more attention, however, is in the development of a true peer-reviewed journal of analytic practices. Sherman Kent spoke of this more than fifty years ago. The closest that CIA and the intelligence community have come to this is *Studies in Intelligence* from the Center for the Study of Intelligence. This quarterly journal, published in both classified and unclassified issues, has been the principal journal of record of what CIA and other agencies have learned from their operations and analysis. *Defense Intelligence Journal* is a less well-known or cited publication focusing on military issues. Outside the IC there are at least two academic journals of note that publish articles on a full range of intelligence topics, including historical cases of operations, current analytic issues, and intelligence-policy challenges: *Intelligence and National Security* and the *International Journal of Intelligence and Counterintelligence*.

While these publications are important, there is no journal devoted exclusively to the study of analysis that can become a vehicle for exchanging views on the utility of different forms of analysis, on new analytic challenges or techniques, and on important analytic findings and their implications for the IC. Such a *"Journal of Intelligence Analysis"* could fill a gap that presently exists, becoming the discussion board for analysts who, for example, might take different positions on the utility of certain SATs or have minority views regarding analytic judgments reached by most intelligence analysts or agencies. Most logically, it could become part of the newly expanding National Intelligence University. (Like the National Defense University, which produces a variety of publications including *Joint Force's Quarterly*, the new National Intelligence Press could consider expanding its mission to support a journal on analysis and possibly other fields of intelligence specialization.) We believe there would be value in producing both classified and unclassified versions of an analysis journal (in the manner of the current *Studies in Intelligence*) in order to be able to draw on classified materials in the first instance and also to expose analysts' views to outside examination and commentary in the second. One continuing problem for analysis is its insularity because of classification. Having more contact—another form of analytic outreach—with outside experts in both methodology as well as substantive expertise would be a desirable objective of such a journal in unclassified versions. It would also support a number of university programs in intelligence studies that are eager to improve their curricula and make their courses more relevant to students eager to become intelligence analysts.

Entry and Certification Processes

As mentioned by Mark Lowenthal, intelligence analysis is an odd profession as it has historically not been one of those "callings" for which students in college take preprofessional training. This "accidental" profession could benefit if it became more purposeful earlier in an analyst's career development, in the entry-level requirements as well as the standards one must maintain later in one's career. Given the broad scope of occupational disciplines within professional analysis—military, political, economic, science and technology, leadership, and now targeting, to speak of the broader categories—the notion of a single set of preprofessional educational requirements for an incoming analyst is perhaps too narrow. A successful WMD analyst might have entered with a degree in chemistry, biology, or even political science, depending on which aspects of WMDs he or she might be following.

However, one would expect that any analyst planning to focus on the foreign policy aspects of even a functional issue such as WMDs would be able to demonstrate an interest, if not a specialization, in world affairs, foreign countries, and languages. So, developing a profile of applicants who might mature into successful analysts could include their proficiency not only in their own academic discipline but also in their general knowledge of the world and their analytic skills. To get the right blend of general world affairs knowledge on top of an area specialization, agencies might consider a general entrance exam along the lines of the type long used by the Foreign Service. Individual agencies now only require online applications, possibly writing samples, and documentation of their experience or skills that would be applicable to the analytic profession.

As mentioned above, few entry-level analysts are true "experts" in their fields when they are hired, since they are by their very nature new to the field and still learning. Thus agencies need to know if such applicants have the capacity to deepen their expertise and have an intellectual curiosity that will guarantee their success in the future. Some ways of measuring such characteristics would be useful. Like would-be Foreign Service officers, prospective analysts might be asked to take a standardized test to see what they know about the world; this could be used in conjunction with any specific academic discipline that they would bring to intelligence analysis. Furthermore, the entrance exam could include questions regarding their research, work styles, native curiosity, and capacity for growth, to give recruiters a better understanding of the applicants' abilities to conduct research, collaborate in analytic teams, and become leading experts in their fields as they gain experience.

Moreover, testing analysts, once hired, has never really been part of the analytic culture. On-the-job training (through "doing analysis" while being observed and evaluated by peers and supervisors) and developing a production portfolio have been the sole measures of whether an analyst is progressing in his or her development. This "trial" or probationary period is used to determine if an analyst has what it takes, but it can often be fairly subjective. Many training courses offered by intelligence agencies are still "non-graded." In these courses, only attendance is required. There is little effort to determine whether the analysts have learned anything. A more empirical basis for evaluating analysts' proficiency in conducting analysis is now in order.

A first step is to adopt, as military service colleges and military intelligence courses have, training programs that include evaluation standards. Some have letter grades, while others adopt the philosophy that a student has "met" the standards expected or was "above" or "below" them. Constructing course-evaluation standards, which would be included in an analyst's annual performance appraisal or fitness report, would incentivize more engagement in training and education opportunities, and give supervisors a stronger basis for promoting analysts or holding them back. In skills-based training there should be a way to measure whether an analyst can actually employ an analytic technique or not. Similarly, in more seminar-style courses or simulations, instructors should be able to evaluate how well or poorly an analyst contributes, collaborates, and leads in a group setting.

Whatever system of standards is adopted, it should be tied directly to the kinds of tasks analysts are likely to face, and those standards should then drive curricular development. Some intelligence analysis schools believe they achieve this by sending "seasoned" analysts to become instructors in their basic analyst courses. However, such analysts may not necessarily be the best teachers, even if they have come from the analytic front lines. Instead intelligence schools and the NIU should be looking for instructors who have had practical analytic experience but also who are both interested and talented in instructing.

Once a set of standards in both training and analytic performance are well established, a certification program will become more achievable and acceptable. Without micromanaging every agency, the ODNI should be able to articulate *basic, journeyman,* and *senior* analyst skill levels, which are also tied to the completion of a comparable set of training and education courses, as well as to a production history that reflects progressively more sophisticated understanding of intelligence analysis in the analyst's occupational discipline.

Analysis and Policy

The foregoing chapters have all suggested that professionalizing analysis will advance proficiency, expertise, and ultimately the quality of the analysis we provide to policymakers and other intelligence customers. As suggested earlier in this volume, analysts must have a "prepared mind" to deal with not only their own cognitive biases but also the shroud of secrecy and deception that adversaries use to obscure their intentions and capabilities. Preparing analysts and their organizations to overcome these hurdles to good analysis is the best way to avert new strategic surprises and intelligence failures. We have been blessed over the past decade to have avoided another attack on a scale of 9/11 and an intelligence blunder like the 2002 Iraq WMD NIE. But there is no guarantee that another such event could not occur tomorrow. While most policymakers and Congress take little interest in how the IC prepares itself today, they will most certainly hold analysts and agencies accountable for tomorrow's surprise.

In the end, the measure of the analytic profession's performance is assessed by how its products are received and used. We would take it a step further to suggest that without further professionalization, the IC is more at the mercy of partisan and bureaucratic politics, which sometimes misuse and misrepresent intelligence analysis. The intelligence controversies swirling around the 9/11 attacks and the Iraq WMD estimate painfully remind us how blame for policy failures can be left at the doorstep of intelligence analysts when their professional skills and perhaps ethics have been found wanting. Thankfully, since that time there have been no national scandals involving analysis, although there have been significant debates over other nonanalytic intelligence activities, such as the use of drones, harsh interrogation methods, and domestic surveillance policies. Moreover, as we mentioned at the beginning of this book, the takedown of bin Laden generated a greater appreciation for the combined efforts of analysts, collectors, and special operations units in closing a painful chapter in America's fight against terrorism.

While intelligence failures are sure to happen, the development of more professional skills and the standards of conduct that go with them will mitigate the chances that faulty analytic tradecraft or poor analytic integrity will be at the center of those future controversies. As one scholar has put it, politicization of intelligence is most likely to occur when intelligence is important to national security policies.[17] It is a safe bet that US intelligence analysis on Iran's nuclear program, along with that of North Korea, will remain important and sometimes controversial, as those judgments will be based on limited information, shrouded in the secrecy and complicated by the deception used by such states. Often they must rest on important assumptions analysts are required to make about those foreign decision makers and their intentions and activities. The more transparent, rigorous, and open-minded that analysts can be with policymakers about the limitations of their knowledge and insight, the better informed will be US decisions and associated risks regarding those programs.

Similarly, the rise of China—America's next peer economic, if not military, rival—will bedevil US strategists, making them frustrated at times with the limits of what we can know about Beijing's intentions and capabilities. In the past, CIA analysts have been accused by some conservative critics as being apologists because they did not dramatize enough the Chinese military threat or its potential to harm American interests or allies. Most likely, the debate over China is going to heat up, placing intelligence at the center of those debates over the proper US response (containment, engagement, or something in between). Thus adopting the highest professional standards for analysis, maintaining rigorous analytic integrity, and being as self-critical of ourselves and our performance as our critics can sometimes be will safeguard the IC's credibility with the American public and future administrations. The future is too uncertain and too important to expect anything less from our intelligence community.

Notes

1. Chaps. 4 and 17 detail many such efforts by CIA and the DNI in this regard.
2. See Jennifer Sims, "Decision Advantage and the Nature of Intelligence Analysis," in *Oxford Handbook on National Security Intelligence*, ed. Loch Johnson (New York: Oxford University Press, 2010).
3. Unless otherwise stated, references to authors here are to authors of earlier chapters in this volume.
4. Thomas Fingar, *Reducing Uncertainty: Intelligence Analysis and National Security* (Stanford, CA: Stanford University Press, 2011).
5. ODNI, News Release No. 21-10, "DNI Releases Budget Figure for 2010 National Intelligence Program," October 28, 2010.
6. Mark Hosenball, "Intelligence Spending Fell in 2012 for Second Year in a Row," Reuters, October 2012.
7. Martin Dempsey, *Chairman's Strategic Direction to the Joint Force*, February 6, 2012, 6; available on the CJCS website, www.jcs.mil.
8. ODNI, James Clapper Testimony before the Senate Select Intelligence Committee, March 12, 2013; available on the ODNI website, www.odni.gov/index.php/newsroom/testimonies.
9. National Intelligence Council, *Global Trends 2030: Alternative Worlds* (Washington, DC: Director of National Intelligence, 2012), executive summary, iii.
10. Typical examples cited are global climate change, health care, pandemics, nuclear weapons, drug trafficking, and social injustice. Scholars believe these are so complex as to challenge public policy experts looking for solutions, as they involve so many interdependencies and require a change in attitudes by so many people.
11. For an excellent treatment of Joint Professional Military Education, see Cynthia Watson, *Military Education: A Reference Handbook* (Westport, CT: Praeger, 2007).
12. This progress will, however, be slowed by the lack of a developed taxonomy of intelligence topics and the multiple layers of classification and clearance requirements that are part of a "need to know" intelligence culture. More efforts on these fronts will also be needed.
13. With few exceptions, full-time language training is offered only to those analysts assigned overseas; otherwise, in-house, part-time language training is principally focused on maintenance of existing language skills, for which analysts do receive annual bonuses.
14. In the military system a capstone course is offered to newly selected or promoted flag-rank officers who will need to understand higher-level strategy and will be operating at the national level. The course is of shorter duration (roughly six weeks) than the year-long, full-time service college programs (which some capstone students have already attended), is led by serving and former three-star officers, and each class is much smaller, facilitating more

of a seminar-style of learning. The State Department once had a similar program called the Senior Seminar, which drew in promising senior Foreign Service officers, as well as selected officers from the intelligence community and the military.

15. Within the executive branch, senior-level executives are given the designation of Senior Executive Service (SES), while in the IC a comparable classification is Senior Intelligence Service (SIS). Promotion into these services traditionally signifies that such officers' experience and professionalism have singled them out to be future executive-level leaders of their departments or agencies.

16. The one exception to this "after-the-fact" feedback is the way *PDB* briefers, after presenting intelligence analysis to the president and cabinet-rank officials, immediately hear comments about those *PDB* items and receive new tasks. This instant feedback is of course valuable but seldom can put the contribution of such analysis into a broader context of ongoing support on a particular issue or evaluate the longer-term effectiveness of the analytic methods used, which is what a case study can do more systematically.

17. Joshua Rovner, *Fixing the Facts: National Security and the Politics of Intelligence* (Ithaca, NY: Cornell University Press, 2011).

GLOSSARY OF ANALYSIS TERMS

all-source analysis. The best reporting available from all sources, including HUMINT (human intelligence), IMINT (imagery intelligence), SIGINT (signals intelligence), MASINT (measurement and signatures intelligence), and open sources. All-source analysts are those experts able to access both classified and unclassified sources, and who are not working principally or solely with a single source of information as do imagery or SIGINT analysts.

alternative analysis. Term often used in the 1990s to apply to a range of structured analytic techniques used to challenge conventional thinking on an analytic problem. The word "alternative" is used to underline the importance of using various techniques—such as Devil's Advocacy, Team A/Team B, or Analysis of Competing Hypotheses—to surface alternative interpretations of available information.

analysis. Cognitive and empirical activity combining reasoning and evidence in order to produce judgments, forecasts, and insights intended to enhance understanding and reduce uncertainty for national security policymakers. Analysts prepare "finished" assessments spanning current intelligence or more strategic research issues, addressing the information requirements of government officials. Analysis includes understanding and tasking collection, assessing and using open-source and classified information, generating and evaluating hypotheses about events or developments, and identifying their implications for US security policies.

Analysis of Competing Hypotheses (ACH). Technique for identifying alternative explanations (hypotheses) for a development and evaluating all available evidence to evaluate and help disconfirm, rather than confirm, these explanations. The process arrays all the data against multiple hypotheses and determines which pieces of evidence are consistent or inconsistent with each hypothesis. Analysts can quickly see that much or most data often support multiple hypotheses and only a few will stand out as the ones that disprove a specific explanation.

analytic assumptions. Any hypothesis that analysts have accepted to be true and that forms the basis of their assessments. The use of assumptions is part of the analytic process, but it is often difficult for analysts to identify these hypotheses in advance. Implicit assumptions can drive an analytic argument without ever being articulated or examined. Good tradecraft identifies and evaluates them.

analytic tradecraft. The principles and tools used by analysts to instill rigor in their thinking and prevent cognitive biases from skewing their analytic judgments. Through the use of structured analytic techniques, analysts make their evidence, argumentation, and logic more transparent and subject to further investigation.

anchoring bias. A form of cognitive bias, this occurs when a previous analysis of a subject acts to prevent analysts from reassessing their judgments and allows for only incremental change in their forecasts. In essence the initial judgment acts as an anchor, making the final estimate closer to the original one than should be the case, given the new information available to analysts.

basic intelligence. The fundamental and factual reference material on a country or issue that forms the foundation on which analysts can base current and estimative analysis. Examples include economic statistics, topographic and geographic information, and documentary information on a country's form of government, rules of law, and electoral procedures and patterns. The CIA's *World Factbook* is a product containing basic information on major countries of the world.

353

caveat. Suggests analysts are qualifying their judgments because of a problem in sourcing or in interpreting available information regarding an intelligence topic. Caveats include the use of qualifying statements such as "we believe" or "we estimate," which indicate that analysts are reaching judgments, not stating facts.

classified intelligence. Information that requires special, expensive, or risky methods to collect, either by technical systems or by humans, which must be protected. The risk of compromising these sources and methods is given a security classification level (confidential, secret, or top secret). Classified intelligence is then shared only with those individuals who have clearances and a "need to know" this information. Analysts use this information in written assessments, and they carefully mark these reports with the classification level according to the information used in order to restrict the use of these materials to only those who are cleared to receive them.

cognitive bias. Mental errors caused by unconscious and simplified information-processing strategies. The human mind's natural tendency to develop patterns of thinking or "mind-sets" often distorts, exaggerates, or dismisses new information in ways that produce errors in judgment or thinking. Forms of cognitive bias can include mirror imaging, anchoring bias, confirmation bias, and hindsight bias, to name a few.

collection gap. Analysts identify gaps in their knowledge on a subject, and these collection shortfalls become "requirements" for future collection efforts. Identifying important collection gaps aids not only collectors but also sensitizes analysts to the need to qualify or "caveat" their judgments or set more modest levels of "confidence" in reaching their analytic conclusions.

collector. A person who collects intelligence or an organization that operates a variety of technical systems or espionage units. Such organizations are part of the US intelligence community and are tasked by analysts through the development of complex sets of "collection requirements." For example, the National Security Agency is the principal SIGINT collector, while CIA's National Clandestine Service is the principal HUMINT collector.

combat support agencies (CSAs). The secretary of defense, in consultation with the director of national intelligence, can develop policies and missions for certain national intelligence agencies in support of military combat operations. These presently include the Defense Information Systems Agency, the Defense Intelligence Agency, the Defense Logistics Agency, the National Geospatial-Intelligence Agency, and any other Defense Department agency he so designates.

competitive analysis. Refers to the explicit use of competing sets of analysts or analytic units to reach judgments on the same intelligence subject. The goal is to determine whether competitive analysis will uncover different sets of assumptions, use of evidence, or contrasting perspectives that would enhance analysts' understanding of an important topic. Historically the "Team B" challenge to the official ("Team A") estimate of Soviet strategic forces in 1976 provides the best-known example, and analyses produced by CIA and DIA often provided competing analyses of Soviet military developments, typically based on different assumptions about Soviet behavior.

confirmation bias. The human tendency to search for or interpret information in a way that confirms a preconception. Analysts will often seek out or give more weight to evidence that confirms their favored hypothesis or the "conventional wisdom" while dismissing or devaluing disconfirming information.

coordination process. Many analysts or units often review an assessment because it may discuss aspects covered by more than one expert. Analogous to scholarly peer review, the lead analyst or unit will "coordinate" its product with other experts across the agency or even with experts in other analytic agencies. This coordination process produces a "corporate" product that reflects the collective views of an agency or the entire intelligence community rather than the individual view of the principal drafter. Coordination is sometimes blamed for watering down judgments to a lowest common denominator. Conversely, coordination ensures analytic accountability because many analysts and managers have checked sourcing, language precision, and the quality of a product.

counterintelligence (CI). Information gathered and activities conducted to identify, deceive, exploit, disrupt, or protect against espionage, other intelligence activities, sabotage, or assassinations conducted for or on behalf of foreign powers, organizations, or persons, or their agents, or international terrorist organizations or activities.

critical thinking. That mode of thinking about any subject, content, or problem in which the individual improves the quality of his or her thinking by skillfully analyzing, assessing, and reconstructing it. Critical thinking is largely self-directed, self-disciplined, self-monitored, and self-corrective thinking. It presupposes rigorous standards of excellence and mindful command of their use.

current analysis. Reporting on developments of immediate interest that are disseminated daily or even more frequently, allowing for little time for evaluation or further research. Driven by timeliness, current analysis appears in daily publications such as the *President's Daily Brief* (*PDB*) or the *Worldwide Intelligence Report* (*WIRe*), as well as other departmental intelligence publications.

deception. The manipulation of intelligence by introducing false, misleading, or even true but tailored information into intelligence collection channels with the intent of influencing analytic judgments and those who use them in decision making. Deception is used in conjunction with denial (together referred to as D&D) by both state and nonstate actors to gain advantage by reducing collection effectiveness, manipulating information, or otherwise attempting to manage perceptions by targeting intelligence producers and, through them, their consumers (for example, policymakers and war fighters). Classic intelligence failures such as Pearl Harbor (US), the invasion of Normandy (German), and the Yom Kippur War (Israeli and US) involved deception.

denial. Activities and programs by an intelligence target intended to eliminate, impair, degrade, or neutralize the effectiveness of intelligence collection against them, within and across human and technical collection disciplines. Examples of denial include communications encryption for SIGINT, camouflage and concealment for imagery, and operational security for HUMINT and all collection disciplines. Successful denial causes intelligence gaps, and the resulting missing information often degrades analysis.

departmental intelligence. Intelligence distinguished from national intelligence in that it is produced within a single department and is largely for the use of that department's senior officials. For example, the State Department's Bureau of Intelligence and Research produces departmental intelligence principally for the use of the secretary of state and other senior State Department officials, as does the Defense Intelligence Agency for the Defense Department.

Devil's Advocacy. An analytic technique designed to challenge a consensus view held on an intelligence topic by developing a contrary case. Such "contrarian" analysis focuses on questioning the key assumptions, evidence, or interpretations used by analysts holding to the conventional wisdom. Designed more as a test of current thinking than a true alternative to it,

Devil's Advocacy has been used by some intelligence agencies on those issues said to be "life or death" matters.

diagnosticity of evidence. Refers to the value of evidence in evaluating, testing, confirming, or disconfirming multiple hypotheses regarding an intelligence topic. If a piece of data is consistent with only one hypothesis instead of many, then it would be judged to have high "diagnosticity" for determining the strength of a hypothesis. If, on the other hand, the data can support multiple hypotheses, it is relatively unimportant and thus of little diagnostic value.

director of national intelligence (DNI). The head of the US intelligence community. The DNI also acts as the principal intelligence adviser to the president, the National Security Council, and the Homeland Security Council. He (or she, if appointed) also oversees and directs the implementation of the National Intelligence Program.

Directorate of Intelligence (DI). The major branch of CIA in which all-source analysis is conducted on both regional and functional topics. Within the DI there are offices responsible for Europe/Russia, Asia, Africa and Latin America, the Near East, and South Asia, as well as offices responsible for analyzing transnational issues, weapon developments, proliferation, and arms control subjects.

domestic intelligence. Information or activities involving threats that bear on security conditions at or within US borders. Domestic intelligence has a homeland security focus inside the United States both as to target and source and is distinguished from, but may sometimes overlap with, foreign intelligence that focuses on security threats that emanate from abroad.

epistemology. A branch of philosophy that deals with the theory, origins, and nature of knowledge. It also deals with the methods of producing knowledge and issues concerning how one knows something, including evaluating claims that something is true or false. Common epistemologies in intelligence analysis often rely on authority (the use of sources or other authoritative references), habit of thought (which is akin to anchoring bias), rationalism (that is, the different forms of reasoning), and empiricism (the use of collected sensory data). By combining rationalism and empiricism, the epistemology of science improves analytic reliability through internal self-corrective mechanisms that are lacking in other ways of knowing.

estimative intelligence. Finished intelligence assessments that are focused on longer-term and inherently unknowable events or outcomes are termed "estimative" to convey that analytic judgments rest on incomplete or sometimes even nonexistent evidence. Assessing the future actions, behavior, or military potential of known adversaries is by definition estimative. The best-known form of estimative intelligence is the national intelligence estimate, which is produced by the National Intelligence Council.

fact. Verified information about something that is known to exist or to have occurred, demonstrated through observation or evidence.

finished intelligence analysis. The written assessments produced by all-source analysts who evaluate raw intelligence reporting and prepare reports that are then disseminated to other US government agencies. Examples of finished intelligence include the *President's Daily Brief*, the *National Intelligence Daily* (now called the *WIRe*), and the Defense Intelligence Agency's *Military Intelligence Digest*—all of which are produced daily. Finished analysis also includes longer-term assessments such as NIEs.

forecast. An intelligence judgment concerning the future. In analysis such estimative or predictive statements aim to reduce or bound uncertainty about a developing or uncertain situation and highlight the implications for policymakers. Forecasts are typically accompanied by probability statements ranging, for example, from highly likely to very unlikely, or by specifying numerical "odds" that an event outcome will or will not happen.

foreign intelligence (FI). Activities, operations, or information pertaining to intelligence collection and analysis addressing the capabilities, plans, and intentions of foreign powers, persons, organizations, networks, or their agents. In the United States, FI focuses on threats to US security emanating from abroad, including to its people, property, and interests.

GEOINT. See IMINT.

groupthink. A concept that refers to faulty group decision making that prevents consideration of all alternatives in the pursuit of unanimity. Groupthink occurs when small groups are highly cohesive and must reach decisions under severe time pressures. The psychologist Irving Janis developed this notion in studying US decision making during the Vietnam War. It is often misapplied to analytic failures where there might have been cognitive errors.

hindsight bias. The inclination to see past events as being more predictable and reasonable than they appeared at the time. Analysts tend to remember their own past predictions as being more accurate than they were after the fact. Analysts become biased, in effect, by knowing what has actually happened when evaluating an earlier forecast of what might occur.

HUMINT (human intelligence). Collection activities conducted by humans (vice technical sensors alone) to gain access to people (agents or liaison services), locations (for example, "denied areas"), or things (such as information systems) to obtain sensitive information that has implications for security interests. Examples would be information collected clandestinely by foreign agents who have penetrated targeted organizations, obtained from intelligence services of foreign governments ("liaison"), or more openly acquired by diplomats, military attachés, or other government officials posted abroad. HUMINT is particularly valuable for analysts when assessing the plans and intentions of governments or nonstate actors.

hypothesis. Usually a testable idea or theory about an intelligence topic or target that the analyst attempts to confirm or disconfirm by examining all available evidence. It can be a general proposition about how an adversary might be expected to behave or an explanation for why some event has occurred, which can be tested by evaluating all available information to see if that data is consistent with the hypothesis.

IMINT (imagery intelligence). Sometimes referred to as GEOINT (geospatial intelligence) or PHOTINT (photo intelligence), IMINT is derived from imagery collected from a variety of platforms, ranging from handheld cameras to space-based and other overhead technical imaging systems controlled by a government. Imagery analysts study specific intelligence targets through the use of imaging systems and issue reports based principally on those collected images. The National Geospatial-Intelligence Agency processes and analyzes IMINT and geospatial data for use by all-source analysts and other US government agencies.

indications and warning (I&W). A generic term used to describe intelligence activities needed to detect and report time-sensitive information on foreign activities that constitute a national security threat.

indicator. A generalized, theoretical statement of a course of action or decision that analysts expect to be taken in preparation for a hostile action against a US interest. An indicators list compiles the observable military, political, diplomatic, and internal factors a foreign adversary might be expected to take if it intended to initiate hostilities.

insight. A new way of perceiving an issue that the policymaker finds useful and/or thought provoking in fashioning policy initiatives or in rethinking current policies. An insight is characterized by a clear or deep understanding of a complex situation.

intelligence community (IC). As of 2013, the US intelligence community includes the following sixteen agencies or key elements of them: Air Force Intelligence, Surveillance, and Reconnaissance Agency (AFISRA); Army Intelligence; Central Intelligence Agency (CIA); Coast Guard Intelligence; Defense Intelligence Agency (DIA); the Department of Energy's Office of Intelligence and Counterintelligence (OICI); the Department of Homeland Security's Office of Intelligence (I&A); the State Department's Bureau of Intelligence and Research (INR); the Department of the Treasury's Office of Intelligence and Analysis (OIA); the Drug Enforcement Administration (DEA); the Federal Bureau of Investigation (FBI); the Marine Corps Intelligence Activity (MCIA); the National Geospatial-Intelligence Agency (NGA); the National Reconnaissance Office (NRO); the National Security Agency (NSA); and the Office of Naval Intelligence (ONI). The director of national intelligence (DNI) heads the IC.

intelligence failure. While there is no commonly accepted definition, intelligence failure occurs when there is a systemic or organizational inability to collect correct and accurate information in a timely fashion or to interpret this information properly and analyze it in a timely way in order to alert policymakers to a major new development. Typically, an intelligence failure is characterized by collection and analysis problems, insufficient priority, as well as insufficient attention to bringing a warning to policymakers so they can respond appropriately.

Intelligence Reform and Terrorism Prevention Act (IRPTA) of 2004. Legislation that created the position of director of national intelligence and implemented many of the recommendations of the 9/11 Commission, as well as other studies and commissions that focused on intelligence reform. Among the recommendations that this legislation implemented was the creation of a director of national intelligence (DNI), a National Counterterrorism Center, and a National Counterproliferation Center. Establishment of the DNI expanded the intelligence community (IC) responsibilities formerly held by the director of central intelligence (DCI), who formerly headed both CIA and the IC. The DCI position was abolished, and the new title for the head of CIA is director, Central Intelligence Agency (DCIA).

interagency process. Analysts participate in many interagency meetings where they present their intelligence assessments for use in policy discussions between the National Security Council, State Department, and Defense Department. Working-level interagency meetings are often held prior to more senior-level meetings where decisions will be made. Typically analysts support discussions at the working level and participate in those meetings. For deputies committee (deputy secretary–level) or principals committee (secretary-level) meetings, analysts will provide briefing papers or prepare senior IC leaders who will represent the IC at those discussions. Interagency coordination refers to review of analytic products such as national intelligence estimates among multiple agencies in the intelligence community.

judgment. A conclusion or inference based on analysis of incomplete and uncertain information, with some generally bounded probability and possibly including qualifiers in terms of confidence levels. A judgment is not a fact but an interpretation of facts or evidence that can prove to be correct or wrong. Estimates largely depend on such judgments about the future as they go beyond the facts.

knowledge. Justified true belief. It comprises facts, ideas, and an understanding or cognition of what is known or is the fact or condition of knowing something.

lessons learned. An approach to knowledge management whereby an organization's tacit and explicit intellectual capital is captured, validated, stored, and disseminated in order to provide all members access to the wisdom gained from the experiences of others. The primary goals of any lessons-learned initiative are to learn from past failures and develop best practices, improve training, locate expertise, and refine and improve policies and procedures. Noteworthy lessons-learned programs include NASA's Lessons Learned Information System and the US Army's Center for Army Lessons Learned.

level of confidence. Analysts must determine how confident they are in reaching analytic judgments based on the quality of the information available and the complexity of the issue. Assigning a "low" level of confidence to a judgment may result from collection gaps, contradictory information, or accounting for denial and deception. "High" confidence may result from having very sensitive HUMINT or extremely precise technical intelligence on a military plan or a weapon system that is corroborated from multiple independent sources.

MASINT (measurement and signatures intelligence). Technically derived intelligence data other than standard imagery and SIGINT. It employs a broad group of disciplines, including nuclear, optical, radio frequency, acoustics, seismic, and materials sciences. Examples of MASINT are the detection of low-yield nuclear tests by seismic sensors or by collecting and analyzing the composition of air and water samples.

military analysis. Encompasses basic as well as current and estimative assessments of a foreign government's or nonstate actor's combat capabilities and intentions, including order of battle, training, tactics, doctrine, strategy, and weapon systems. It also examines the entire battle space (that is, land, sea, air, space, and cyber), as well as transportation and logistics capabilities. Other broad areas are the military production and support industries; underground facilities; military and civilian command, control, and communications systems (C^3); camouflage; concealment and deception; foreign military intelligence; and counterintelligence.

mind-set. A type of cognitive filter or lens through which information is evaluated and weighted by the analyst. Beliefs, assumptions, concepts, and information retrieved from memory form a mind-set or mental model that guides perception and processing of new information. Typically a mind-set rests on a series of assumptions about the way the target of the analyst's investigation behaves. Closely related to mind-set is a "mental model," which connotes a more highly developed set of ideas about a specific subject. Mind-sets and mental models form quickly and become hard to change, particularly when they prove useful in forecasting future trends; once they are proven successful, analysts may accept them uncritically despite changes in the environment that would suggest they have become outdated or inaccurate.

mirror imaging. A cognitive error that occurs when analysts presume that a foreign actor will behave much as they would in the same situation. In this sense the analysts see their image when they observe the foreign actor. Often analysts have developed a strong expertise on a subject and believe there is a logical way to develop a weapon system, conduct a coup, or reach a decision. They will, then, presume that a foreign actor would go about these tasks as they would. Classic examples include analytic views that assumed risk-adverse Soviet behavior in the Cuban Missile Crisis and similar Arab reluctance to start a war with Israel in 1973.

National Clandestine Service (NCS). Formerly known as the Directorate of Operations (DO), the NCS, a component of CIA, is responsible for directing all HUMINT operations across the US government, including the FBI and Department of Defense, for conducting foreign intelligence collection, and for covert action abroad. The NCS is the collection manager for HUMINT like the National Security Agency is for SIGINT.

National Counterproliferation Center (NCPC). Established in 2005 within the Office of the Director of National Intelligence, the NCPC coordinates intelligence support to stem the proliferation of weapons of mass destruction (WMDs) and related delivery systems. It also develops long-term strategies for better collection and analysis on future WMD threats.

National Counterterrorism Center (NCTC). The part of the Office of the Director of National Intelligence that integrates all intelligence—both foreign and domestic—within the US government pertaining to terrorist threats and counterterrorism policies. Established by the Intelligence Reform and Terrorism Prevention Act of 2004, the NCTC conducts strategic operational planning and also produces intelligence analysis on terrorism for key policy agencies.

national intelligence. As defined in the 2004 IRPTA legislation, it encompasses all intelligence related to national security threats to the United States, regardless of the source from which it is derived and includes information gathered within or outside the United States.

National Intelligence Council (NIC). A group of roughly a dozen senior intelligence officers (known as national intelligence officers) responsible for producing national intelligence estimates (NIEs) for the US government and for managing community-wide production of intelligence by the intelligence community.

National Intelligence Daily (NID). A compilation of significant current intelligence items published six days a week by CIA's Directorate of Intelligence in consultation with the Defense Intelligence Agency, the State Department's Bureau of Intelligence and Research, and the National Security Agency. It was provided to senior officials throughout the US national security agencies and to overseas commands and diplomatic posts. In its new form (including electronic versions), the *NID* has been redesigned and named the *Worldwide Intelligence Report (WIRe)*.

national intelligence estimate (NIE). Usually a strategic assessment of the capabilities, vulnerabilities, and probable courses of action of foreign nations or nonstate actors produced at the national level as a composite of the views of analysts throughout the US intelligence community (IC). It is prepared under the auspices of the National Intelligence Council, with one or more national intelligence officers guiding its drafting. Analysts throughout the IC participate in preparing and approving the text. The NIE is then presented to the heads of the US intelligence community and officially released by the director of national intelligence as the IC's most authoritative statement on an intelligence subject.

national intelligence manager (NIM). Constituted under the auspices of the ODNI Office of the Deputy Director for Intelligence Integration (DDII), national intelligence managers oversee and integrate all aspects of the intelligence community's collection and analytic efforts against a particular region or function. Each NIM serves as single focal point within the ODNI for the integration of all activities related to the particular region or function.

national intelligence officer (NIO). A senior expert on either a region (for example, Europe, Asia, Africa, Middle East) or a functional area (for example, weapons of mass destruction, transnational threats, conventional military forces) who directs the production of NIEs on those topics. They guide and evaluate the quality of analysis in their substantive areas. NIOs represent intelligence community analysts at interagency meetings and interact regularly with senior policy officials to ensure intelligence production is directed at policy issues of importance.

need to know. A principle used by senior intelligence managers to determine whether intelligence will be shared with other intelligence professionals, policy officials at federal, state, and local levels, or foreign governments. According to executive order, the knowledge or possession of such information shall be permitted only to persons whose official duties require such access in the interest of promoting national defense.

opportunity analysis. Sometimes referred to as action analysis, it directly supports implementation of US security policies by assessing the factors that could help policy planners and other decision makers to seize opportunities presented to them. While not endorsing any policy options, opportunity analysis assesses the costs and benefits of different policy actions that policymakers might consider.

order of battle (OOB). In military analysis, OOB identifies military units, their command structure, and the strength and disposition of personnel, equipment, and units of an organized military force on the battlefield.

OSINT (open-source intelligence). Involves collecting information from unclassified, publicly available sources and analyzing its significance to the US government. Open sources include newspapers, magazines, radio and television broadcasts, and computer-based information in many foreign languages; public data found in government reports, press releases, and speeches; and professional and academic journals and conference proceedings. Increasingly open-source intelligence gathering has focused on exploiting the internet world of websites, bloggers, and even social media. The Open Source Center is the intelligence community's primary organization responsible for the collection and analysis of open-source information.

paradox of expertise. Scholars of analytic organizational cultures believe that the more expert analysts become, the more prone experts are to making errors because of overconfidence in, or overreliance on, developed mental models or mind-sets. The paradox is that their substantive knowledge of a subject has led them to discount unlikely scenarios or "weak signals" of a major discontinuity, and favor interpretations of continuity.

politicization. There is no generally accepted definition of politicization, but it commonly refers to the intentional biasing of intelligence analysis to suit a particular set of policy or political goals or agendas. Analysts can be prone to politicization if they allow their personal views to influence their analytic judgments or if they become too receptive to policymakers' views that may compromise their own objectivity. Policymakers can also "politicize" intelligence by trying to persuade analysts to tailor their judgments to suit a policy agenda or by misrepresenting analysis as supporting their preferred policies.

***President's Daily Brief* (PDB).** A compilation of current intelligence items of high significance to national policy concerns, provided daily by the Central Intelligence Agency, the Defense Intelligence Agency, and the State Department's Bureau of Intelligence and Research. A briefer delivers it to the president, and other briefers provide it to a select group of very senior officials designated by the president as recipients, typically at the cabinet level. The *PDB* is refined after every election to suit the individual preferences of each president for format, presentation style, and length.

Red Team Analysis. A structured analytic technique aimed at countering cultural bias and the mirror-imaging problem by constructing a team of analysts who will consciously try to "think like the enemy" rather than like American intelligence analysts. Red Team analysts study and then role-play the key decision makers in a foreign government or perhaps a terrorist cell. They adopt the same decision-making styles, goals, or methods that an adversary might use in accomplishing their objectives. The Red Team assessments provide US policymakers with an unconventional look at how their opponents might perceive a situation. Some use the term "red hat" to describe this kind of analysis and apply the term "red team" to contrarian analysis designed to challenge conventional wisdom along the lines of CIA's "Red Cell," which has an official "outside-the-box" mandate.

satisficing. Cognitive theorists have determined that the human brain searches for the quickest way to explain observed phenomena. Accordingly the brain stops seeking out better explanations for some phenomena once it finds a good-enough, or "satisficing," hypothesis. In decision-making situations, cognitive psychologists also have observed that groups often settle on the first satisfactory explanation for a problem and then rely upon it, despite subsequent information that might undermine the credibility of this initial hypothesis.

Scenarios Analysis (or Scenarios Development). A structured analytic technique designed to generate multiple hypotheses about a future trend or development through the use of group-designed exercises that create alternative futures. Scenario exercises bring together experts from diverse fields and invite them to brainstorm on key factors that will shape future trends. After determining the key factors (often called "drivers"), the exercise designs three or more different futures by combining these drivers in different ways. The technique has been used extensively in business consulting firms and is now regularly employed by intelligence and other national security agencies.

SIGINT (signals intelligence). Interception and analysis of a target's transmitted technical signals and communication systems. It encompasses COMINT (communications intelligence), ELINT (electronic intelligence such as collection against radars), and FISINT (foreign instrumentation or telemetry). The National Security Agency is the principal SIGINT collector in the US government.

signature. Analysts rely on understanding unique "signatures" or perceived patterns in the way a target operates, equips, or deploys military forces or weapon systems. For example, patterns of military communications can also indicate how military forces are likely to operate in the field; these signatures might indicate levels of readiness or whether operations were under way. Changes in signatures are closely monitored.

situation reporting. Commonly called "sit-reps," this is analysis that is rapidly disseminated as soon as analysts receive it, to give policymakers the most up-to-date information for a quickly developing story. Sit-reps typically focus on what the facts are and any immediate implications of the event. Reporting on coups, deaths of world leaders, military clashes, and sudden breakdowns in order or negotiations would be the most likely topics of such reporting.

sources and methods. Those human and technical means of gathering information clandestinely on intelligence topics. A source can be a satellite imaging system operating high above a foreign country, a diplomat's reporting from an embassy, or a foreign agent's reporting from clandestine meetings with a case officer on high-level discussions inside his government. Analysts must "source" their reports and assessments by demonstrating they have a variety of reporting, preferably from diverse sources and collection disciplines, and assess the validity and credibility of the reporting. Such scrutiny reduces the chances of deception or fabrication of reporting if it came from a single source.

strategic analysis. Unlike situational reporting or current analysis, strategic analysis focuses less on events than on long-term trends. It is usually performed only on subjects of enduring interest to the United States. For example, strategic analysis of foreign ballistic missile developments or of the Chinese military would be of enduring interest to policymakers, regardless of their immediate policy agendas. Strategic analysis is inherently "estimative," as there is little detailed information on trends beyond a year or more.

structured analytic techniques (SATs). Techniques used to provide more rigor to analytic judgments and to make them more transparent and testable. Often referred to as analytic tradecraft, various structured analytic techniques—such as Structured Brainstorming, Key Assumptions Check, Devil's Advocacy, Analysis of Competing Hypotheses, or Scenarios Analysis—attempt to guide and record the logic, methods, and use of evidence employed by analysts in reaching judgments. By structuring the analysis according to a set of principles (for example, listing key assumptions, evaluating the quality of information, examining multiple hypotheses, identifying collection gaps, and detecting possible denial and deception), analysts can establish more systematically their levels of confidence in judgments reached. Moreover, they can also track changes in their judgments over time and revisit conclusions that new evidence might appear to challenge.

Team A/Team B Analysis. A structured analytic technique that uses separate analytic teams to contrast two or more strongly held views or alternative hypotheses about an intelligence topic. Each team develops its assessments using the available evidence after laying out its key assumptions about the topic. The value comes in arraying the competing views side by side, which highlights how different premises cause analysts to reach different conclusions.

tradecraft. Originally the term applied to operational methods, techniques, and equipment used to maintain the secrecy of a clandestine relationship between a foreign agent and case officer in order to protect the operation from discovery by hostile counterintelligence. Adopted in analysis, the term refers to the cognitive and methodological tools and techniques used by analysts to gather and organize data, interpret their meaning, and produce judgments, insights, and forecasts for policymakers and other users of finished intelligence products. Examples of tradecraft include SATs such as the Analysis of Competing Hypotheses.

warning analysis (strategic and tactical). Analysis that anticipates potentially threatening or hostile activities and alerts policymakers to the possible implications should the activity occur. "Strategic" warning refers to relatively long-term developments, which provide sufficient time during which a policymaker can develop policies or countermeasures to the forecasted event or trend. "Tactical" warning refers to alerting policymakers to near-term events, for which there is little time to prepare.

Worldwide Intelligence Report (WIRe). CIA's current publication circulated throughout the US government to senior policy officials. Having replaced the *National Intelligence Daily (NID)*, *WIRe* is a more Web-based publication with an electronic dissemination within Washington and overseas. It can be updated frequently throughout the day, rather than operate as a once-a-day publication like the *NID*.

worst-case analysis. Analysis that results when analysts "assume the worst" in reaching judgments about a future event. It can happen when analysts base their analysis on assumptions that an adversary will always select a course of action aimed to create the worst problem for the United States or that the adversary's intentions are uniformly hostile toward the United States. Analysts are often accused of using such assumptions in an effort to ensure that they never fail to warn a policymaker of a possible surprise. Worst-case analysis, then, becomes a rationale for policymakers to ignore warnings that were actually far more balanced than assumed.

CONTRIBUTORS

Maureen Baginski is a private consultant. Following a twenty-five-year career at NSA as an educator, linguist, analyst, and executive, she joined the FBI as executive assistant director for intelligence, where she established the first FBI intelligence analysis program. She now serves as the chairperson of the National Intelligence University's Board of Visitors.

Michael Bennett is a subject-matter expert on denial and deception and coauthor of *Counterdeception Principles and Applications for National Security* (Artech House). He has over twenty-five years of experience in a variety of intelligence-related disciplines in both the government and private sectors.

James B. Bruce is a senior political scientist at the RAND Corporation and an adjunct professor at Georgetown University in the Security Studies Program. A retired career intelligence analyst after twenty-four years, he served with CIA's Directorates of Intelligence and Operations and with the National Intelligence Council as deputy national intelligence officer for science and technology. He has taught previously at the National War College and at Columbia and American Universities, and has written on intelligence and deception.

Peter Clement has served as the CIA deputy director of analysis since 2005, after holding a variety of senior positions in the Directorate of Intelligence, including issue manager for Russia/Eurasia and *PDB* briefer. A career CIA analyst for the past thirty-five years, he has worked extensively on Russian affairs, analytic tradecraft issues, and policy support.

Drew Cukor is a US Marine Corps lieutenant colonel with twenty years of tactical intelligence experience. He has served as an intelligence officer at various levels, from the infantry battalion to the marine expeditionary units.

Jack Davis is a retired career CIA analyst who has written numerous articles and monographs dealing with the development and improvement of analytic methods. He is a former national intelligence officer for Latin America and served for many years as a senior instructor in CIA's analytic training program. He continues to consult with CIA on analytic methods.

Thomas Fingar is the Oksenberg-Rohlen Distinguished Fellow in the Freeman Spogli Institute for International Studies at Stanford University. His intelligence career spanned almost four decades, including at the State Department's Bureau of Intelligence and

Research, where he served as assistant secretary and deputy assistant secretary for analysis. He also served as chairman of the National Intelligence Council and deputy director of national intelligence for analysis. His most recent book is *Reducing Uncertainty: Intelligence Analysis and National Security*, published by Stanford University Press.

Rebecca Fisher is a writer, researcher, and librarian whose career before joining the intelligence community was spent in medical libraries, including Georgetown University School of Medicine's Dahlgren Memorial Library, where she taught evidence-based medicine research techniques to medical students, faculty, and researchers. She has a particular interest in how users select and evaluate information products and how information-seeking behaviors and access to information affect life choices.

Roger Z. George is professor of national security strategy at the National War College and an adjunct professor at Georgetown University in the Security Studies Program. He was a career CIA intelligence analyst who served at the State and Defense Departments and has been the national intelligence officer for Europe. He is coeditor of several volumes on intelligence and national security studies, most recently (with Harvey Rishikof) *The National Security Enterprise: Navigating the Labyrinth*, published by Georgetown University Press in 2011.

John H. Hedley is a former editor of the *President's Daily Brief* and served as chairman of CIA's Publications Review Board. He has been the CIA officer in residence and an adjunct professor teaching intelligence at Georgetown University. In retirement he is a part-time consultant for the National Intelligence Council and serves on the editorial board of the *International Journal of Intelligence and Counterintelligence*. He has written widely on intelligence issues.

Richards J. Heuer Jr. is a retired career CIA officer who served in the Directorates of Operations and Intelligence. He has written extensively on analysis, deception, counterintelligence, and personnel security. His book *Psychology of Intelligence Analysis* discusses the cognitive issues associated with analysis and is widely used in training analysts throughout the intelligence community. He is the coauthor, with Randolph Pherson, of *Structured Analytic Techniques for Intelligence Analysis*.

Rob Johnston is an ethnographer who specializes in national security and the anthropology of work. He is the manager of the Lessons Learned Program at CIA's Center for the Study of Intelligence. He has been an associate of the National Intelligence Council and a visiting scholar at the Sherman Kent Center, and he is the author of *Analytic Culture in the U.S. Intelligence Community: An Ethnographic Study*.

Richard J. Kerr is a former acting director and deputy director of Central Intelligence at CIA. He spent more than thirty years as a career intelligence analyst, beginning in

1960, when he started analyzing Soviet military developments. He has held senior analytic positions at CIA, including deputy director for intelligence and office director for East Asian analysis. Since his retirement in 1992, he has served on numerous high-level boards to review the quality of intelligence analysis. He also spent seven years as the US member of the UK–Irish Commission monitoring the Good Friday Agreement.

John Kringen served as a senior intelligence adviser to the US European Command from 2008 to 2011. Previously, he held senior analytic and managerial positions in CIA, including as deputy director for intelligence and director of the Crime and Narcotics Center. He also served as director of the Office of Imagery Analysis in what is now the National Geospatial-Intelligence Agency. He presently is a senior researcher with the Institute for Defense Analyses.

Joseph Larson III is a US Marine Corps Reserve major, an intelligence officer, and a lawyer. He has served multiple combat intelligence roles in Iraq, Southeast Asia, and Afghanistan.

Mark M. Lowenthal is president and chief executive officer of the Intelligence & Security Academy and an adjunct professor at Johns Hopkins University. He has worked on intelligence analysis at the Congressional Research Service and Department of State, as well as served as staff director of the House Permanent Select Committee on Intelligence. His last government post was assistant director of Central Intelligence for Analysis and Production at CIA. He is the author of *Intelligence: From Secrets to Policy*.

John McLaughlin is a former acting director and deputy director of CIA. He is currently Distinguished Practitioner in Residence at the Paul H. Nitze School of Advanced International Studies, Johns Hopkins University. During his thirty-two-year career at CIA, he held numerous senior official positions, including deputy director of intelligence, acting chairman of the National Intelligence Council, and director of offices covering the former Soviet Union and Europe. In addition to his agency career, he worked on Capitol Hill and in the US State Department, and served as a US Army officer, with a tour in Vietnam. He is a member of the Council on Foreign Relations and the American Academy of Diplomacy.

Susan H. Nelson is director of the Office of Outreach in the Bureau of Intelligence and Research (INR) at the US Department of State, where she has worked for over thirty years. In this capacity she has managed INR's outreach mission, bringing together multidisciplinary expertise within government and from the private sector. She chairs the ODNI Subcommittee on Analytic Outreach of the National Intelligence Analysis and Production Board. She also is executive director of the Program for Research and Training on Eastern Europe and the Independent States of the Former Soviet Union.

Randolph H. Pherson is chief executive officer of Globalytica, LLC, president of Pherson Associates, LLC, and founding director of the Forum Foundation for Analytic Excellence. He was a career CIA intelligence analyst, last serving as the national intelligence officer for Latin America. He teaches advanced analytic techniques and critical thinking skills to analysts in the government and private sector. He is coauthor with Richards J. Heuer Jr. of *Structured Analytic Techniques for Intelligence Analysis* and has published numerous other books that present intelligence analysis case studies, structured analytic techniques, and critical thinking skills.

Matthew Pottinger served as a marine corps intelligence officer in Iraq, Afghanistan, and Japan. He completed active duty in 2010 and is now chief executive officer of China Six LLC, a consulting firm focused on East Asia.

James B. Steinberg served as deputy secretary of state for President Barack Obama from 2009 to 2011 and as deputy national security adviser to President Bill Clinton from 1996 to 2000. He is also a former director of the State Department's Policy Planning Staff and a former deputy assistant secretary of state for Intelligence and Research. After leaving government, he was the director of Foreign Policy Studies at the Brookings Institution, as well as dean of the Lyndon B. Johnson School of Public Affairs. He is now the dean of the Maxwell School of Syracuse University.

Vincent Stewart, a US Marine Corps major general, is a senior intelligence officer with over thirty years of tactical intelligence experience. He has served at both company- and battalion-level commands, and his principal intelligence officer assignments include one deployment in support of Operation Desert Shield and Operation Desert Storm and two deployments in support of Operation Iraqi Freedom.

Michael Warner serves as a command historian in the US Department of Defense and has written and lectured widely on intelligence history, theory, and reform. He has taught at American University, Columbia University, and Johns Hopkins University. His book *The Rise and Fall of Intelligence: An International Security History* was recently published by Georgetown University Press.

James J. Wirtz is the dean of the School of International Graduate Studies at the Naval Postgraduate School, Monterey, California. He has served as the chair and program chair of the Intelligence Studies Section of the International Studies Association. He has written and lectured widely on the theory of surprise, and his coedited anthology *Intelligence: The Secret World of Spies* was published recently by Oxford University Press.

INDEX

Boxes, figures, notes, and tables are indicated by b, f, n, and t following page numbers.

outside experts, 319–20. *See also* outreach efforts
overconfidence, 210

Pahlavi, Mohammad Reza. *See* Iranian Revolution
Pakistan, monitoring of, 225
Pan Am flight 103 bombing (1988), 48
Panetta, Leon, 220
paradox of expertise, 124, 125
PATRIOT Act, 268
PDB. See President's Daily Brief
Pearl Harbor as example of intelligence failure, 138,
 158–59, 170t, 173n6, 198, 199b, 203
peer review, 143
Peirce, Charles, 141
Penkovskiy, Oleg, 11, 12, 18n34
peripheral vision, 97
Persian Gulf War. *See* Gulf War
Pesechnik, Vladimir, 164–65, 175–76n29
Petraeus, David, 108
Pherson, Randolph H., 7, 231, 247n23, 324, 345
Pillar, Paul, 7
policy bias, 130–31, 217b
policymaker-analyst relationship: and accuracy,
 89; and alternative views, 90; bridging the
 divide, 84–85, 97–99, 130; and clarity, 89;
 communication with policymakers, 10, 188;
 on domestic level, 278; drivers of closer
 collaboration, 104–6; informing policy,
 9–10, 85–90; literature on, 7; members of
 policymaker community, 91–92n2; military-
 analyst relationship, 103–17; minimizing
 risks of politicization, 100; policy culture vs.
 intelligence culture, 81–84; policymaker's
 perspective, 93–101, 185; problems in,
 94–95; and revising judgments, 90; solutions
 to problems in, 95–97; structural fixes to,
 99–100; and timeliness of analysis, 13–14,
 89–90; unrealistic expectations in, 94
policy neutrality, 12, 95
politicization: of analysts, 131; CIA history of, 50;
 literature on, 7; minimizing risks of, 98, 100
Pollack, Kenneth, 162
Popper, Karl, 155n44
Pottinger, Matthew, 249
Premortem Analysis and Structured Self-Critique,
 240–41, 242
Presidential Decision Directive 35 (PDD-35), 98,
 101n8
President's Commission on the Intelligence
 Capabilities of the United States, 197
President's Daily Brief (PDB), 10, 31–32, 34, 107,
 110, 113, 187, 187b, 288, 351n16
priorities of intelligence analysis, 87

privacy issues, 195n10
problems of analysts. *See* denial and deception;
 diagnosis and prescription
professional analysts, 28–29; building community
 of, 287–301; collector relationship, 157–77;
 core competencies, 306–7, 312; defined, 83;
 domestic intelligence role, 278–79, 281–83;
 evolution to professionalization, 33, 293,
 304; expertise in intelligence-collection
 disciplines, 67; further professionalization
 needed, 294, 340–48; "good analysts," 122;
 improving performance to restore confidence,
 288; skill set of, 5–6, 306–7; SMAT experts,
 258; standardizing and testing analytic
 methods, 345–46; subject-matter experts
 (SMEs), 5–6, 306, 319; in twenty-first
 century, 337–51. *See also* collector-analyst
 relationship; diagnosis and prescription;
 intelligence community; military support;
 training of intelligence analysts
propaganda of enemy, 261
provisional results, 143–44
psychological problems, 123–27
Psychology of Intelligence Analysis (Heuer), 6, 121,
 149, 232

Qaddafi, Moammar, 49
Quadrant Crunching, 240, 241, 244
quasi-quantitative analysis, 236, 236t

Randall, Doug, 324
RAND Corporation, 232
rationalism, 137, 139–41, 146–47, 150
rationality bias, 123, 126
raw intelligence, 18n27, 275
Reagan administration, 45, 47, 83
Red Cell, 70
Red Team Analysis, 18n22, 46, 115, 165
Reducing Uncertainty (Fingar), 7
Reichenbach, Hans, 142, 152n10
reliability of intelligence judgments, 136, 137b. *See
 also* epistemology
replicability, 143
Research and Analysis Branch (R&A), 24–25
review and coordination problems, 127–29
Rice, Condoleezza, 100–101n3
Roosevelt, Franklin D., 23–24
Rovner, Joshua, 7
Rumsfeld Commission, 46
Russia, monitoring of, 225
Russo-Georgian tensions, 222

SACs (special agents in charge), 270